D1555236

Mitokh Ha-Ohel

MAGGID

Mitokh Ha-Ohel

מתוך האוהל

**Essays on the Weekly Parashah from the
Rabbis and Professors of Yeshiva University**

Rabbi Daniel Z. Feldman
and Stuart W. Halpern, Editors

The Michael Scharf Publication Trust
of Yeshiva University Press
New York, N Y

Maggid Books

Mitokh Ha-Ohel
Essays on the Weekly Parashah from the Rabbis
and Professors of Yeshiva University

First edition, 2010

The Michael Scharf Publication Trust
of Yeshiva University Press

Maggid Books
An imprint of Koren Publishers Jerusalem Ltd.

POB 8531, New Milford, CT 06776-8531, USA
& POB 4044, Jerusalem 91040, Israel

www.yutorah.org/yeshivapress.
www.korenpub.com

ISBN 978 159264 324 0, *hardcover*

A CIP catalogue record for this title is
available from the British Library

Printed in the United States

*To President Richard M. Joel and
Chancellor Rabbi Dr. Norman Lamm,
in recognition of their devotion to the
maintaining, enhancing, and
strengthening of our tent*

Contents

ספר שמות

ספר ויקרא

ספר במדבר

ספר דברים

Editors' Preface

I t is considered an extraordinary privilege to be able to live within the tent; to be, in the words of the *hadran* recited at every *siyyum*, "from those who sit in the *Beit Hamidrash*." The tents of Yaakov, which we reference every morning at the beginning of our day, are understood by our tradition to be tents of study. It is the dwelling within these tents that has preserved the tradition and the wisdom of the Jewish people to this day.

We are uniquely privileged here at Yeshiva University to live in a profoundly special tent. It is a tent that faithfully maintains the spirit of Yaakov's tent, and it is at the same time a "big tent," a tent of diversity, complexity, and the integration of interdisciplinary wisdom.

This volume endeavors to display the breadth and depth of the "tent" of Yeshiva University, by bringing together its multi-faceted voices, as represented by our rabbis and professors, in a collection of essays that address all of the *parashiyyot* of the *Chamishah Chumshei Torah*. These essays constitute contributions from the faculty and administration of the Rabbi Isaac Elchanan Theological Seminary, Yeshiva College, Stern College for Women, the Mazer Yeshiva Program, the Irving I. Stone Beit Midrash Program, the Isaac Breuer College of Hebraic Studies, the James Striar School of General Jewish Studies, the Marsha Stern

Talmudical Academy, the Graduate Program for Women in Advanced Talmudic Studies, the Bernard Revel Graduate School of Jewish Studies, the Azrieli Graduate School of Jewish Education and Administration, the Benjamin N. Cardozo School of Law, the Albert Einstein College of Medicine, The Ferkauf Graduate School of Psychology, the Center for the Jewish Future, and the Caroline and Joseph S. Gruss Institute of RIETS in Jerusalem. These articles range from textual analysis to homiletic exposition to halakhic analysis to academic exploration and to all points in-between. What they share in common is the goal of bringing a wide range of approaches towards the honoring, elucidating, and exploring of our Holy Torah. Almost all of the essays in this book are appearing for the first time in print (although a handful of articles have been adapted from other media).

We are profoundly grateful to our teachers and administrators for the time and effort they have invested towards this project. Just as the great leader of the Jewish people, Yehoshua ben Nun, was praised for "not leaving the tent" (*Shemot* 33:11), so too our leaders have devoted so much of their lives to remaining within our tent, to preserving its character and expanding its reach. Their schedules are full and their hours are long, and yet they made the time to produce new contributions to the world of scholarship for this endeavor.

We are also grateful to Lauren Eskreis-Winkler for aiding in editing, proofreading, and other tasks essential to the production of the book, as well as to Rabbi Dovid Feinberg for his hard work in ensuring that every aspect of the book is *mehudar*. We are grateful for the enthusiastic support of President Richard M. Joel and of Rabbi Yona Reiss, the Max and Marion Grill Dean of RIETS, and for their counsel and insight. This publication is made possible by the support of the Michael Scharf Publication Trust of Yeshiva University Press, which for many decades has played a vital role in the production of Torah scholarship under the auspices of Yeshiva University. We thank Matthew Miller and the staff at Koren for their wonderful efforts in bringing this work to the reading public.

Most importantly, we express our profound gratitude to the *Ribbono Shel Olam*, for allowing us to dwell within the tent and to express its character through this publication.

We write these words in the middle of the period of *Bein Ha-Mitzarim*, a time when we cry over the destruction of our Holy Temple, our ultimate Tent. May it be His will that through the words of Torah in this book, we accomplish some small measure towards hastening the Redemption and the rebuilding of that Tent.

Rabbi Daniel Z. Feldman
Stuart W. Halpern

A Note on Transliteration and Spelling: We have tried to strike a balance in this work between consistency of spelling and language and maintaining the distinct voice of the individual authors. As that entails much subjectivity and compromise, we hope the readers will indulge the results of that effort.

President Richard M. Joel

Foreword

After thousands of years, the tent of Avraham and Sarah still serves as a model worthy of emulation. When commenting on the tent of our patriarch and matriarch, Rashi writes, שכל זמן ששרה קיימת היה נר דלוק מערב שבת לערב שבת, וברכה מצויה בעיסה, וענן קשור על האהל – "For as long as Sarah was alive, her candles burned from Friday to Friday, the dough was blessed, and a cloud hovered over the tent" (*Bereishit* 24:67). Many have noted that these three miracles represent the three basic components of a fulfilling Jewish life. The lights stand for illumination, the bread represents nourishment, and the cloud symbolizes transcendence. Every Jewish home endeavors to represent these ideals.

The image of a tent offers many opportunities for metaphor. Though open and accessible, a tent also retains fixed dimensions. Avraham and Sarah professed their dedication to a Godly existence while creating a warm and nurturing environment within their four walls. Similarly, for us, their children, the boundaries of the big tent enable all Jews to enjoy the boundlessness of Jewish expression and celebration within the boundaries provided by the Torah.

Of course, the other crucial tent in the history of Israel similarly stresses this point. The *Mishkan* – Tabernacle – also known as the *Ohel Moʿed* – the Tent of Assembly – served as the dwelling place of the Almighty on earth. Though it was conceived by God, the Israelites earned the responsibility to construct this portable Sanctuary and to dwell around it when He commanded ועשו לי מקדש ושכנתי בתוכם – "Build for Me a Sanctuary that I may dwell among them." The *Ohel Moʿed*, in its finite proportions built by man, housed the infinite and eternal as a symbol of the centrality of God in the lives of Israel, representing the partnership we all can aspire to have with the *Ribbono shel Olam*.

As the exemplars par excellence for Jewish living, the deeds of our forefathers still influence the lives of Jews today. At Yeshiva University, we aspire to mimic the domicile of our progenitors by creating our own big tent through our ideology of *Torah u-Madda*. We welcome ideas while living within the boundaries of our Torah tradition.

This volume, *Mitokh Ha-Ohel*, "from within the tent," deliciously features the unbelievable variety found within the Rabbi Isaac Elchanan Theological Seminary and all of the divisions of Yeshiva University. Through the words of our Torah luminaries and erudite scholars, *Mitokh Ha-Ohel* serves as a physical embodiment of Yeshiva University's passion for seeking nuanced wisdom through Torah from multiple sources.

Mitokh Ha-Ohel has particular relevance to the philosophic core of Yeshiva University. For well over a century, this institution has radiated the light of Torah around the world. By offering a volume that encompasses perspectives on each week of the year by an eclectic array of scholars and rabbinic thinkers, we manifest our ongoing commitment to sharing our *ohel*. I am proud that we continue this pursuit with passion. In the past decade, the yeshiva has grown and thrived, Yeshiva University has expanded its Bible and Jewish history departments, hundreds of people attend our semi-annual *Tanakh Yimei Iyun*, and the popular YUTorah.org contains over 30,000 *shiurim* accessible to all.

The wicked Bil'am, though trying to curse the children of Israel, beheld their camping ground and uttered the famous line מה טבו אהליך יעקב – "How goodly are your tents, Jacob." This work will continue the legacy of this verse; it truly represents a goodly tent where knowledge-seekers can enjoy the nourishment, illumination and transcendence of the Torah through the gathering of the words of many of Yeshiva University's fine minds.

ספר בראשית

Rabbi Dr. Norman Lamm

Introductory Essay: How to Read the Torah[1]

I

These comments on "How to Read the Torah," are not meant to be a demonstration of cantillations or a means of training formal Torah readers. Rather, they are an attempt to set some guidelines as we begin again the cycle of portions of the Torah.

At one point in this *sidrah*, we read "*zeh sefer toledot adam*," which translates as "this is the book of the generations of Man" (*Bereishit* 5:1). Most commentators take that to mean not "book" in the formal sense of a volume, but as a listing of the generations that derived from Adam. Ramban, however, takes the word *sefer* literally, and tells us that "*kol ha-Torah kulah sefer toledot adam*," it refers to the entire Torah, which is the "book of the generations of Man" (Ramban, *Bereishit* 5:1–2, s.v. *zeh sefer toledot adam*). Torah is the story of mankind. The Book is apposite to Man.

The *Kabbalah* affirmed this idea in many ways. For instance, the Holy Ari maintained that by mystical permutations, the number of souls

---

1. Adapted from a sermon delivered on October 16, 1971.

of Israel present at *Har Sinai* is equal to the number of letters in the Torah. Again, we find the equivalence between Book and Man.

Hence, the approach to know the Book is akin to that of knowing Man. You learn how to understand the *sefer* from how you understand *Adam*. Books may teach us much about people; but people can tell us more about books. And this is so especially concerning the Book of Books, the Torah. *"Zeh sefer toledot adam."*

II

The first thing that we must learn is: respect. In order to genuinely know a man, you must consider him worthy of your study and friendship and concern. If he is not worthy, then your knowledge of him is superficial and unimportant. And what is true of man, is true of text, of Torah. At the very least, respect means not to ignore it. To sit in the presence of Torah and not consider it, is like staying in the presence of another human being and acting as if he does not exist – few insults are more humiliating than that. To read Torah, you must be serious, and that means high-minded – truly religious. A real student of Torah may never be flippant. You may be puzzled by a *pasuk*, or be put off by a *parashah*, but you must always approach Torah with humility.

The founder of the *Chabad* movement, in his *Shulchan Arukh*, gives us an interesting derivation of the Jewish custom to walk with one's head covered. The reason is *tzeni'ut*, modesty. Clothing is worn for one of two reasons: warmth or modesty. The head covering is too small to serve for purposes of warmth; it is there for reasons of *tzeni'ut*. It is our way of expressing before God the limitations of our intellectual self-sufficiency. We cover our heads to indicate that we have a degree of bashfulness about our intellectual inadequacy in the face of God. This is how we approach the study of Torah – with respect and humility. This does not mean that what is demanded of us is intellectual capitulation and submission, only modesty and reverence.

Respect for Torah also means that we must not assume too much about Torah in advance. Do not approach the sacred text with ready-made conclusions. I know people who read a portion of the Torah with a "nothing but" attitude: the Torah is "nothing but" a collection of Mid-Eastern myths; "nothing but" a record of early religious superstitions;

"nothing but" primitive science; "nothing but" the fear of the unknown expressed magically. With such presumptuous attitudes you emerge from your encounter with Torah knowing nothing more than the smug prejudices with which you began.

In a sense, I would say that respect means not to get too close to Torah. Despite the fact that Torah is closer to us than anything else – *"ki karov elekha ha-davar me'od"* (*Devarim* 30:14) – you must not get too close to it, you must avoid excessive intimacy, the familiarity which breeds contempt – a fact true both of men and of books. When we are too much "at home" with Torah, when we are "pals" with the text, and we lose the distance which makes both for reverence and perspective, we allow ourselves the liberty of making snap judgments which are unworthy. That is why when we read the Torah we use the silver pointer. The *Halakhah* forbids us to touch the inner part of the Torah scroll. Should we contact the parchment, our hands become unclean – *tum'at yadayim* – and the reason is, primarily, to keep us respectful by forbidding us to handle the sacred scroll directly. We must not lay hands on the Torah; thus we learn to respect it.

III

The second guideline in how to read the Torah is – the awareness of its depth. *"Zeh sefer toledot adam."* Just as you do not "read" a man, because he is too complex and deep and requires studying and investigation, analysis and pondering, so it is with Torah. When you say of a man, "I can read him like a book," you diminish his humanity, you reduce him to a manageable and controllable automaton, one whose Pavlovian reactions are all predictable, and hence one who has been de-personalized into a mere mechanism. So if we ask, how do you read the Torah? The answer is: don't *read* it! Go much deeper than reading. Reading of the Torah in the synagogue, in its formal sense, with all its carefully prepared melodies and exact text, is only the challenge to what we ought to do, each of us, privately: go deep, ever deeper. It is not enough to read, one must study; it is not to *lein* the Torah, one must learn; it is inadequate to have *keri'ah*, one must have *limmud* of the Torah. For both Man and Torah are living things, organic beings, and merely reading the Torah is like describing a man's physical qualities: in neither case have I captured the soul, the essence.

That is why our tradition recommends at least four methods of interpretation, the famous *Pardes*. It is because we know that there is depth upon depth and layer upon layer, and that various forms of interpretation are valid.

Several years ago, someone wrote a book in which he tried to trace the origins of Freud's seminal idea of depth-psychology, that the human consciousness consists of layer upon layer of awareness, and that we can dig ever deeper until we come to the root of a man's psychic life. This writer (Bakan) maintained that Freud derived his notions, despite the paucity of his formal Jewish education, from the Jewish ideas which were vaguely, but pervasively, present in his environment. One of these great ideas was that of the *Kabbalah* and its teaching that the Torah must never be understood only on one level, but that it is a mine or reservoir of infinite layers of meaning, and that when you have plumbed one, you must still plumb the next, and when you have done the next, you must prepare to dig even deeper to a newer and more profound level of meaning. I do not know if that writer is right or not; I believe he exaggerates. But certainly today *we* must reverse the direction of the equation. Today we know a great deal about depth psychology, about the layers of meaning in a man's life. We must now conclude the same about Torah – for this is "the book of the generations of Man." What is true of Man is true of Torah: each contains depth upon depth, layer upon layer and level beneath level.

IV

The third thing that we must learn in approaching Torah is that, despite all our scholarly techniques and modes of analysis to probe depth, learning must yet remain an existential encounter. When you truly know another human being, you know more than the sum of his various parts, his physical description, his psychic condition, his clothing and the state of his liver and bile and cardiogram. There is more to man than merely that. There is a sense of mystery. The encounter with him is a genuine experience. Meeting him is what Buber calls an "I-Thou" relationship. You see him as an equal *gestalt*, not as a mere "it." And so it is with the text of Torah. You must look upon it not as merely an ancient document, not merely as a problem in legal philosophy, not merely as a record of ancient history, but as something living, something dynamic, as an encounter with a "thou" that preserves and realizes the eternal Thou.

In Hebrew, *Da'at* means more than intellectual cognition. "Knowledge" in the Biblical scheme means total knowledge, which includes the physical and the spiritual, the material and the psychological and the intellectual. When Adam "knew" his wife Eve, the knowledge covered all areas of human existence, from the sexual to the spiritual. The same word *Da'at*, or knowledge, is used for the knowledge of God: it means more than merely a profound grasp of theology or a listing of the philosophical interpretations of the negative attributes of God. It comprehends the totality of existence. So too, we learn from Man to Book: *Da'at Torah*, the knowledge of Torah, is more than analysis; it is a profoundly existential meeting with Torah itself. In a word, it is a learning of love.

This encounter of love, both in the case of Man and in the case of the Book, involves a recognition that the one we encounter has absolute individuality, a uniqueness that is irreplaceable. If I know (love) another human being, then I know that person as one who cannot be duplicated, who is utterly different. The same holds true when I know a passage of Torah.

Furthermore, to know in the sense of love means – to want to know more! Maimonides, in the beginning of his great Code, teaches us, concerning the love of God, that when you contemplate the marvels of nature, you begin to love God and then "*miyad hu … mit'avveh ta'avah gedolah leida Ha-Shem Ha-Gadol*" (Rambam, *Mishneh Torah*, *Hilkhot Yesodei Torah* 2:2) – immediately you are seized with an uncontrollable passion to know the great Name. So it is with Man too. When you love someone, your desire for knowledge, your appetite for knowing him or her more, is insatiable. The more you know, the more you want to know. And that is precisely the condition that one must obtain in Torah study. If you study Torah with an attitude to love, you will never be satisfied with what you know, you will always strive for more.

Reading or studying Torah with love also sensitizes you to the novelties and surprises that are latent within Torah. It sensitizes you to the unpredictably delightful ideas waiting to be conjured up by love and intelligence.

A year or two ago, there appeared a book edited by Marshall and Hample, which was a collection of children's letters to God. One of them, most appropriate to this *parashah*, read as follows:

> Dear God:
>> Maybe you can write some more stories because we've already read everything you have written more than once. Thanks in advance.

Some people take that childish attitude with regard to the study of the Torah as we commence *Bereishit* once again: the same stories, the same laws, not a single change. Indeed, should the Torah reader decide to make a single change, we pounce upon him and correct him. The conclusion – it is repetitive and boring. But that is a childish attitude. If our attitude is mature, if we approach Torah with respect, with awareness of its depth, and with love, then the new cycle of *sidrot* means for us the anticipation of new discoveries, novel insights, great ideas we have not yet been introduced to.

V

Fourth, and finally, the right attitude for the study of Torah means that we must read it critically and persistently, using every tool of intelligence and research. To approach Torah with respect and with love does not mean that we can get away with *frumkeit*, with piety, alone. A student of Torah must be pious, but piety itself is no guarantee or substitute for scholarship. If you acknowledge that Torah has depth, and you approach Torah with respect and love, you will also want to be deserving of Torah's love and respect in return. As with a human being, if you relate to him or her uncritically, without discrimination and taste, gullibly and simply – you may not find your affections reciprocated. Torah, too, is not satisfied with unsophisticated naiveté. It demands far more from us – a critical attitude, a willingness to meet Torah's problems head on, acumen, and discriminating intelligence.

The *Zohar*, in a remarkable passage that sounds as if it were taken out of the courtly tradition of love, compares the Torah to a damsel locked in a castle. The student of Torah, enamored of the princess, marches to and fro waiting for a glimpse of his beloved. No one recognizes what he is doing there or what goes on in his heart. The damsel occasionally comes to the balcony, shows herself, and quickly returns. He is tempted to look for her and come to the castle. The princess then hides behind the curtain, only letting him occasionally hear her voice. As he pursues his search, she rewards him with an occasional glimpse of her face, challenging her lover to seek her, to discover her. But if the lover (or student of Torah) is discouraged too quickly, if he is impatient, if he ceases his search because he is frustrated, she is annoyed at him and calls out, "*Peti*" ("fool")! "*Peti ya'amin le-khol davar*" ("a fool believes anything")! (*Mishlei* 14:15). He is uncritical, he can be bluffed! The Torah does not want fools. It does not even want innocent and pious fools. It demands persistence, criticism, determination and intelligence. It wants the brightness that God gave us to be applied to it and its problems, to searching it out and to finding it out.

What real student of Torah does not know of the delight of this flirtatious game played by Torah as part of the romance of the study of the Torah? If you are impatient, if you have no verve, no ambition – then you do not even know that there is a princess in the palace! If you do know it, then by all means follow the lead, search her out, never stop in your persistent search for Torah and for truth, using every ounce, every fiber of criticism and intelligence. You must follow through the tantalizing leads, the ideas waiting to be exposed, the insights teasingly concealed but anxious to be found out. Torah hides only because she wants you to find her.

VI

These are the four elements in how to read the Torah. "*Zeh sefer toledot adam*," they are equivalent to the knowledge of Man. In both, genuine knowledge requires respect, awareness of depth, love, and a persistent and critical attitude. These must be employed as we proceed upon another year of the study of Torah, both in the synagogue during services and especially in the various classes in which all of us are called upon to attend.

VII

The rewards are beyond description. At the very least they will give us a pride, a sense of identity, a sense of sufficiency of the spirit. A learning Jew is not a frightened Jew. Only an *am ha-aretz*, an ignoramus, is always afraid and apprehensive. A learning Jew can take any anti-Semitism in stride; an *am ha-aretz* is always seized with panic and hysteria, usually out of proportion to the threat.

Some time ago I discussed with an uncle the problem of anti-Semitism. I know how American Jews react to it, but I was curious as to the psychology of the Jew who lived all his life in the *shtetl*. This uncle, who has shared in both cultures and both worlds, told me of how when he was a child he was walking with his grandfather, my great-grandfather – the man after whom I am named, and who was known reverently and affectionately in our family by the name of the town where he served as Rav, the Kretzinsker *Zeide* – they were accosted by a young Polish peasant who hurled at them every foul-mouthed anti-Semitic insult, which has become a venerable tradition among both Polish peasants and intellectuals. My uncle, having been exposed to the modern world, was shaken. Yet he noticed that my great-grandfather simply continued, as if nothing at all had ever happened: impassive, unruffled, unconcerned. Said my uncle to my great grandfather: "How come? How can you just continue? Aren't you bothered by all this?" The Kretzinsker *Zeide* replied: "What are you talking about? How can I possibly be concerned by the likes of him? Don't you understand? – '*Ich hob dach a Toirah*' – I am a man who has a Torah! A man who has Torah is never concerned by the rantings and the ravings of some semi-ignorant lunatic. The slings and arrows of that kind of fortune can never hurt him."

So let us begin this year with the pride of having the Torah. Let us be people of Torah. Let us never be satisfied with merely hearing the Torah being read on *Shabbat*. Let us proceed to study it during the week as well. If we are Orthodox Jews, if we are proud Jews, we must be studying Jews. "*Ki hem chayeinu ve-orekh yameinu*" (Rav Amram Ga'on, *Siddur*) – because that is what life, certainly Jewish life, is all about.

Rabbi David Fohrman

בראשית: The Mystery of *Shabbat*

For most of us, the weekly *Shabbat* experience eventually becomes part of our regular routine. We refrain from performing labor on *Shabbat* almost instinctively. The light switch, the telephone, the car – it seems as natural to avoid these things on *Shabbat* as it does to use them during the week.

So it can seem surprising to us when someone from outside the system questions the meaning of our day of rest. But every once in a while, that happens. In an office, on a plane trip – we'll get questions from strangers about *Shabbat*. One of the most common questions concerns what seems like a quirk in the way Orthodox Jews observe *Shabbat*: switching on a light on *Shabbat* is for some reason considered "work," and is off-limits during this day of rest. But dragging a heavy table from one end of a room to another somehow escapes classification as work, and is a permitted activity. This sounds bizarre and nonsensical. We are often asked: Is there any rhyme or reason to be found here?

But other questions abound, too. In this essay, we will explore the *pesukim* in the Torah that introduce *Shabbat*, and we shall do so through the prism of various questions – various conundrums we face when we try and define the Jewish concept of *Shabbat* to strangers. By so doing, we will gain a greater ability to explain *Shabbat* to both the strangers in our lives, and to ourselves.

TWO THEOLOGICAL QUESTION MARKS

Let's begin with an almost childlike, philosophical question: "Why, exactly, would God feel it necessary to rest after creating the Universe? Was He tired?"

The question isn't as facetious as it sounds. We conceive of the Almighty as an All-Powerful being. That, indeed, is why we call Him "the Almighty." So if God is really All-Powerful, how difficult would it have been for Him to create a Universe? Presumably, this didn't require a lot of exertion on His behalf. Well, then, why did He need to rest afterwards?

And here's another conundrum: Most of us assume that our observance of *Shabbat* is reflective of our faith that God is the Creator of the Universe. After all, the Torah explains the observance of *Shabbat* by telling us that God created the world in six days and rested on the seventh. But there is something odd about this. For why do we commemorate God's creation of the Universe through a day of rest? Wouldn't it have been more appropriate to set aside, instead, a day of creation?

In case this question doesn't strike you as all that troubling, let's make it more concrete. Let's leave the realm of theology behind, and couch the problem in more mundane terms.

Imagine that the Federal government decided it would be a good idea to create an annual "Rosa Parks Day" on the calendar. The idea would be to set aside a day on the yearly calendar when all Americans would commemorate the civil rights triumph of Rosa, the black woman who refused to give up her seat to a white man on a segregated bus in Montgomery, Alabama. And imagine that a committee was casting about for some sort of symbolic activity that citizens could perform on this day to honor Rosa Parks' great act. Some members of the committee suggested that concerned citizens could ride local city buses, and crowd to the front of the bus. For a symbolic trip around town, no one would sit in the back. But then, somebody in the back of the room had a different idea. On Rosa Parks Day, everyone should go home, and take a nap in bed. Why? Because, you see, after Rosa Parks took her historic ride on the bus, she was tired and she went home to rest in bed. So let's all do the same: we too shall take a nap, just like Rosa did.

Few people would consider this a spectacular idea. Yet somehow, on *Shabbat*, it seems like precisely this is happening. We commemorate *Hashem's* historic act of creating the world – yet we do so by *resting*. But shouldn't we instead remember Creation by creating? The point isn't that God rested – it's that He made the world, right? Isn't "rest" just incidental?

BACK TO THE TEXT

Let's turn to the text of the Torah and see what it has to say to us about all this. In *Bereishit*, the Torah chronicles the coming into being of the very first *Shabbat*. Read the following *pesukim* carefully and pay attention to this question: According to the text, what exactly is *Shabbat* designed to commemorate?

> God finished on the seventh day the work that He had made, and He rested on the seventh day from all the work that He had made. And God blessed the seventh day and made it holy, because on it He rested from all the work that God had created to make. (*Bereishit* 2:1–3)

These *pesukim* tell us why *Hashem* deemed the Seventh Day special: *because on this day He rested*. As strange as it may seem, the Torah is telling us that *Shabbat* is not, actually, a celebration of God's creation of the Universe. Rather, it is a celebration of *His rest*.

This idea, when you reflect on it, is downright astounding. How could anyone think that God's rest is more important than His work – than the very act of creating the world? It sounds roughly like saying that the purpose of work is vacation. Vacation might be nice, but is vacation really what the work is all about? Yet, strangely, what the Torah is saying is clear: *Shabbat* is not a celebration of creation; it is a celebration of rest.

In case you missed the point, the Torah emphasizes the same idea again, later on, in *Sefer Shemot*. In the verses we recite as *kiddush* on *Shabbat* morning, the Torah tells us that *Shabbat*, "Is a sign between

Me and the Jewish People that: six days, God created the Heavens and the Earth…and on the seventh day He rested" (*Shemot* 31:17).

According to the *pasuk*, what is the essential fact that the "sign" of *Shabbat* testifies to? That God created the world in six days? No. Were that true, the Torah should have ended the *pasuk* halfway through. The emphasis of the text is on the final clause, *"and on the Seventh Day He rested."* *Shabbat* commemorates that *after Hashem* got through creating the world in six days, He decided to rest on the seventh.

But what's the big deal about that rest? It just sounds anti-climactic.

PURPOSEFUL REST

Evidently, the verses are telling us we need to reassess our ideas about work and rest. God's rest, apparently, had very little in common with the idea of vacation. It was not something that merely happened after God created the world; it was not that God took some time off for a breather. The Creator's rest was a deliberate act. It was a kind of rest that was, somehow, an end in and of itself – "You made the seventh day holy for Your Name, it being the very purpose of the making of Heaven and Earth."

These words come from the Friday night *shemoneh esrei* that we recite every week. But listen to what we are saying. *Shabbat*, and its rest, is portrayed as the very purpose of Creation, the end for which the entire Heavens and Earth were created.

What does it mean to see rest in this way, not as something you do to help you work, but rather as something which is the very point of all your labor? Why would God consider His rest more worthy of commemoration than His successful Creation of a Universe?

The question becomes even more insistent when we remember that God deemed *Shabbat* to be special long before there was any nation around to celebrate it. According to the *pesukim* in *Bereishit*, Ch. 2, God blessed and made *Shabbat* holy immediately after creating the Universe. He shared that day with us only centuries later, when He gave us the Torah, letting us in on His special secret. Thus, *Shabbat* was not crafted by God for the benefit of people – that only happened later. Rather, this island in time was designed by the Creator for Himself, as it were.

Why would the Creator be so personally committed to His own day of rest?

EXACTLY WHAT *WAS* GOD DOING ON THAT SEVENTH DAY?

A clue comes from the *pasuk* in the Torah that first introduces us to the idea of *Shabbat*. One of these *pesukim* seems to contradict itself: "And God finished on the seventh day the work that He had made, and He rested on the seventh day from all the work that He had made (*Bereishit* 2:2)."

Perhaps you spotted the difficulty: What, exactly, did *Hashem* do on the seventh day? Did He rest or did He work? The answer seems to depend on which part of the verse you focus upon.

The first part tells us that God finished on the seventh day the work that He had made. This seems to suggest that *Hashem* did *some* work on the seventh day. He completed His efforts on that day.

But then the verse goes on to say that *Hashem* rested on the seventh day from *all* the work that He had made. This second phrase seems to tell us that God was *not* working on the seventh day. To the contrary, He rested from *all his work* on this day.

So which is it? Did God rest from all His work on the seventh day, or did He create something on this day?

RASHI'S ANSWER

As it turns out, we are not the first to come upon this question. Rashi addresses it and gives two possible answers to the problem.

One answer Rashi suggests is that perhaps God finished creating the world at the very instant that the sixth day ended and the seventh day began. In that way, He would have finished creating on the seventh day, i.e. on the instant the day began, but would still have rested for the entirety of that day.

That's Rashi's first answer. But he gives a second answer as well, a solution that doesn't require us to split hairs in time between the sixth and seventh day.

Rashi's second answer suggests that the contradiction is just an illusion. Rashi argues that God indeed created something on the seventh day – and simultaneously, He was completely at rest on that day. The thing that the Almighty created on the seventh day, Rashi says, was rest itself. God brought rest into existence on the *Shabbat*.

Now, this answer certainly seems ingenious; it allows us to see how God could both rest and create at the same time. But, the answer smacks a bit of wordplay. What does it mean that God "created" rest? Is rest something that needed to be created? Rest is just the absence of work. If God wanted rest, all He would have to do is stop working. Right?

Wrong.

Rashi is suggesting to us that there is such a thing as rest that needs to be created. It is a kind of rest that is different from the rest we usually experience, which is the mere absence of labor. It is a rest which is not just a negative phenomenon, but a positive one. It is not an absence, but a presence.

UNDERSTANDING REST BY UNDERSTANDING "WORK"

To get a better handle on this elusive notion of God's rest, we might do well to ponder for a moment the nature of God's "work." If we can understand more clearly what God was up to those first six days, we may be better able to understand what it means to say that He "rested" from this activity on the seventh.

The term that *Halakhah* assigns to labor on *Shabbat* is *melakhah*. The word is borrowed from *Bereishit* Ch. 2, which describes the "labor" that God was involved in when creating the world. The labor which we desist from on *Shabbat* corresponds in some fundamental way to the labor God desisted from on the original *Shabbat*.

The truth is, "labor" is probably the wrong word to be using here. The English term "labor" conjures up images of sweat and hardship – images which obviously have little to do with Divine creation of the Universe (how *hard* is it for an All-Powerful God to create a world?).

Melakhah is a more specialized word, and is different than the other, more common word for work, *avodah*, which indicates a mundane, run-of-the-mill kind of labor. It suggests the kind of work that requires exertion and makes you tired. *Melakhah*, on the other hand, calls to mind something else entirely.

The Torah classifies thirty-nine basic acts as *melakhah*. With the possible exception of carrying, the common denominator of all thirty-nine is the idea of transformation, of taking a certain substance present in the world, and transforming it into a higher, more developed state of being, through an intelligent agent's conscious intervention. When I bake something, I take mere raw ingredients and make them into a cake. When I weave something, I take mere threads and create a cloak. I am developing the world around me, molding it to suit my will.

It was this kind of work that the Almighty engaged in for most of the six days of Creation.

Think about it. In the first moment of *Bereishit*, God made something from nothing. First there was Nothing; then, all of a sudden, there was Something.

From then on, though, He was pretty much doing something else. He was generally taking that which was, and molding it into something more complex and sophisticated. He was taking electrons and protons and molding them into hydrogen atoms. He was taking water, and causing species of marine life to arise from it (*Bereishit* 1:20). He was taking earth, and fashioning out of it the body of a human being (ibid., 2:7). God was performing *melakhah*, the kind of thing you do when you want to create a world.

GOD'S *MELAKHAH*; MAN'S *MELAKHAH*

We are now, incidentally, ready to respond to that co-worker, acquaintance or seatmate on a plane who asks about the funny way we seem to observe *Shabbat*.

The answer lies in an understanding of the nature of *melakhah*.

When God created the world, His activity had very little in common with dragging a heavy table around the house. But it had everything to do with igniting the filament inside a light bulb.

Dragging a table just moves things around. It isn't "transformative" in any way. Igniting the filament, though, – as routine as it seems – is an act of *melakhah*, one in which man purposefully transforms his surroundings to suit his needs. Every time man kindles fire, plows, weaves – no matter how easily and routinely he does it – he masters the world around him and molds it to suit his liking in a way that animals could never do. In fact, one might even argue that the more routinely man engages in these actions, the more his mastery is evident. When man takes the raw material of the world around him and molds it – brings it into higher states of being in accordance with his will – he imitates his Heavenly Creator.

בראשית

Hashem refrained from *melakhah* on the seventh day. And He deemed the rest which replaced that *melakhah* to be the ultimate meaning of His Creation.

THE REST OF AN ALL-POWERFUL BEING

So why would an All-Powerful God need to rest after creating the world? Was He tired?

I think we are now in a position to answer that question, too.

If God's activity for six days had consisted of mere *avodah*, then the rest that would be demanded would be conventional rest – and yes, it would seem strange that the All-Powerful God needed to rest and "recoup His energy" on the seventh day. But God was not performing *avodah*. He was performing *melakhah*. His activity in those six days was not defined by exertion but by creativity. And creativity demands a different kind of rest entirely.

Rest, in other words, always provides a complement to work. But different types of work call for different kinds of rest. Exertion calls for a kind of rest we call relaxation; lack of exertion helps us become refreshed. But the complement to creativity is not a similar kind of absence. The complement to creativity is, perhaps, the mysterious phenomenon we talked about earlier, the thing we called positive rest.

Creativity is a powerful word. Creation seems so self-sufficient. What else, indeed, does a creator need but to create? But creativity *does* need something else to be complete. It needs *Shabbat*. For in reality, creativity is only a means to an end. Creativity is about bringing something into being. But that's not a final goal. The final goal of creativity is "being" itself.

Positive rest is not something we are all that used to. It seems foreign to us. And perhaps that is only natural, for we live, as it were, in a world of change, a world of becoming. In our world, *melakhah* – changing things, building them, making the world more sophisticated – that's what it is all about. To understand positive rest in all its brilliance, we need to transcend that world, and try and perceive what life might be like in a world not of "becoming," but of being.

We have a word for a world of being. It's called: *Olam Ha-Ba*, the World to Come. Let's take a break, for a moment, from talking about *Shabbat* – and let's talk briefly about that realm that lies beyond.

IS WORK REALLY WORTH IT?

In the world down here, we all work for a fair part of our lives. But there's something unsettling about this activity we call work.

This fact was made clear to me years ago by a teacher who took particular delight in tormenting us eager students with what might be charitably called healthy servings of philosophical cynicism. He once assigned a particularly difficult paper to my classmates and myself and then, before we started working on it, he posed the following challenge to us. He said, "it's going to take you many hours of work if you want to achieve an A on this paper." And then he said that "if you put in those hours of work, and you hand in a really top-notch draft, and then I decide to give you that A, what would happen next?"

We shrugged. It was an important class, and most of us really wanted that A.

"You'd be ecstatic," he said. "You might jump up and down and run down the hall to call your mother. You'd tell your friends."

"But then what will happen? For how long will you remain excited? An hour? Three hours? A day?"

"Soon, it's going to wear off. You'll get restless. You'll be ready for something new…"

"So ask yourself," he concluded, "maybe it's just not worth it. Why are you bothering to do this?"

In effect, our professor was asking us to make a simple profit-loss analysis: If you spend sixty hours working on a paper and you get only two or three hours of satisfaction from your grade afterwards, well, why bother? It doesn't seem to add up.

Now, don't get me wrong. The professor was not trying to convince us that we should get lazy on our papers. What he was really trying to do was help us clarify our goals.

CLARIFYING GOALS

If we told ourselves that the goal of our work was *the satisfaction we would receive in the end*, well then, he would argue, we were just fooling ourselves. That kind of satisfaction is very fleeting. It evaporates after a couple of hours or a couple of days.

Rather, he was suggesting, the work was only worth it, if we saw it as satisfying in and of itself. The *process* of writing that paper, of struggling to meet the challenge, had to be seen as its own reward. If we couldn't take pride in that process, if we couldn't see the process itself as valuable, then we might as well just forget it.

A TROUBLING CONCLUSION

But the professor's point, while it might ring true, is unsettling. It's not so bad, maybe, when the only thing at stake is your college paper. But when you apply his logic outside the classroom, to life in the real world, things start to look a little depressing. For just about anything worthwhile we do in life requires work, and if we make a similar profit-loss analysis about the meaning of *any* work, we will reach similar conclusions.

In other words, say you're toiling away on a five-month project your boss assigns you, or that you are spending years writing a book. You invest seemingly countless hours in your labors. How much satisfaction will you possibly get at the end?

Enough to justify your weeks or months of toil? Not likely.

A friend I know worked tirelessly writing a book for the better part of three years. When it was finally published, his wife threw him a surprise party and invited the neighborhood. He was thrilled with the feeling of completion. But his thrill faded after a matter of days. He was restless, and his recent success was no comfort. He related to me that in the years since finishing the work, he almost never went back to crack open the binding of the book he wrote. That chapter in his life was filed away. It was time to move on.

There's something depressing about this. All of life's successes seem to fade so quickly. No feeling of satisfaction or well-being ever lasts very long. Yes, you can take pride in the process. You can see the act of writing as its own reward. That's all very nice. But if what we did was truly worthwhile, why can't we hold onto the pleasure of actually achieving our goal, as well? Why must the satisfaction of success be so fleeting?

The more successful one gets, the more one is troubled by this problem. One of the most successful men in Jewish history was terribly troubled by this problem; he wrote an entire book recounting how he was haunted by it. That book, canonized as part of the *Tanakh*, is known as *Kohelet*. In *Kohelet*, *Shelomo Ha-Melekh* pours out his frustration at a world that won't let any mark of success stand for very long at all. The world is constantly in motion, constantly changing. Nothing – not the fact of success, nor our pleasure in the face of it – endures long enough to be ultimately satisfying.

I think the phenomenon that the Torah calls the *Shabbat* is meant, in part, to address this problem. *Shabbat*, in a way, is designed to provide an antidote to the boredom of success. And this, perhaps, may provide a key to our puzzle. The *Midrash* tells us that *Shabbat* is *"me'ein Olam Ha-Ba"* – "a taste of the World to Come." The phrase rolls off our lips easily; it's something most of us have been taught since childhood. But what does it really mean? What fundamental similarity does *Olam Ha-Ba* have with the phenomenon we know as *Shabbat*?

WHAT IS LIFE LIKE IN HEAVEN?

The answer is the world's best-kept secret. Billions of people before us have died, but no one has yet come back with an eyewitness report of what things look like from the other side. Be that as it may, our *mesorah* assures us that it's all worth it and that the reward of the righteous in the hereafter is something we ought to be looking forward to. *Tzaddikim*, we are told, live onwards in a state of eternal bliss.

But here's the problem: Eternity is a pretty long time. For just how long do you think eternal bliss remains satisfying? Wouldn't bliss get kind of boring after a while?

Imagine you really enjoyed cruises, and someone offered you a free cruise to Alaska with five-star dining, a deck-side luxury cabin, the works. For how long do you think you might enjoy such a cruise?

Two weeks? A month. What about six months?

And what if the cruise lasted for eternity? How many times could you see the same icebergs and watch the same penguins? At some point, it would stop seeming like a vacation and it would start seeming laborious. At some point, it would seem like the very opposite of Heaven.

So if Heaven's eternal bliss really lasts for an eternity, why doesn't it get boring? Why in Heaven do we look forward to Heaven?

בראשית

THE PROBLEM WITH REST; THE PROBLEM WITH WORK

This problem is related to the same question we raised about our work in *this* world. Hundreds of hours of work don't seem justified by a fleeting few hours of reward. But, as we've just seen, the idea of "reward" is just as problematic as the idea of "work." The notion of eternal reward seems downright boring. Neither work, nor reward, seem all that satisfying in the long run. What's the way out of this pickle?

The answer, I think, requires us to look more closely at the nature of life, that is, in This World and life in the hereafter, life in the Next World. What, really, is the difference between these two worlds?

Judaism's answer is that This World is a world of *becoming*, and the Next World is a world of *being*. The next world is a *"yom she-kulo Shabbat,"* as it were – a day that is all *Shabbat*. What does this really mean?

In creating the world, *Hashem* split our experience into two realms. The first realm, the world we live in, we might call a "World of Becoming." In this world, the only real lasting satisfaction that we can derive comes from the process of work itself – through building the world around us, indeed, through building ourselves. While we are in this world, we find that constructive engagement is the only "satisfying" reward we can really hope for. Vacations, while nice once in a while, eventually get boring. And the reason is simple: It is because this world was wired for labor, not for the enjoyment of the fruits of that labor. Yes, we can experience fleeting satisfaction when we complete a task, but then it's on to the next thing, or we quickly become bored.

There is, however, another realm. There is the Next World, a World of Being. The World of Being is wired not for work, but for the appreciation of our labors. All that we have accomplished, all the relationships that we worked so hard to cultivate in This World – we experience them for what they truly are in the Next World.

A TASTE OF THE WORLD TO COME

If you think about it, things *had* to be this way. Imagine, for a moment, that the Almighty allowed us to truly experience the fruits of our labors in This World. Imagine that we could truly appreciate, in an enduring way, the satisfaction that comes from a hard-won achievement. Imagine that in this world, we could fully and forever taste the rich, spiritual joy that is the natural consequence of potential fulfilled. What would happen in such a world? You'd work at one thing, you'd achieve it, and then you'd spend the rest of your life reveling in your success. You'd never accomplish anything again. That wasn't what the Almighty had in mind. He was after something more productive than that.

We can now see why the idea of reward, the lasting enjoyment of any accomplishment, is so hard to come by in this world. Indeed, even the thought of an eternity of enjoyment seems boring to us; something we would want to avoid. Why? Because we are looking at it through the wrong lenses – through the lenses of This World, a world wired for becoming, not being. When we actually experience this "reward," though, we will ultimately experience it through different lenses – the lenses of the Next World; a world where working to become more is impossible, a world that is hard-wired just for being. When we experience the fruition of our work in the Next World, we will do so within a world that allows us to truly tap into the timeless essence of this treasure.

So, while it may seem depressing that in This World, we can't really take much lasting pleasure in accomplishment, we *do* have a consolation prize. We have *Shabbat*, a little taste of being, right smack in this World of Becoming.

Shabbat is not your average, run of the mill, day of rest. Remember: *Halakhah* permits you to *shlep* heavy tables up flights of stairs on *Shabbat*, but it forbids you to strike a match or gently plow the earth. The latter violates the sense of rest that *Shabbat* demands, while the former, although tiring, does not. Why? Because the *Shabbat* is not really about the kind of rest which helps you catch your breath. Instead, it is about a kind of rest that even the Master of the Universe would need. The kind of rest that is not a *break* from work, but is the very purpose of work; it is "being," in all its glory. It is the kind of rest we might call, in the words of our Friday night *tefillah*, "*takhlit shamayim va-aretz*" – the very purpose of Creation itself.

Indeed, it is this kind of rest that saves creativity from death at its own hands.

THE DEATH OF CREATIVITY

The act of creating, when you get right down to thinking about it, is seductive. It can perpetuate itself indefinitely. And when it does so, it will, eventually, kill itself.

The examples are everywhere. The artist who always has one more brushstroke to add; the editor who needs to rearrange sentences one last time; the parent who has one last admonition to give a child who is no longer listening anymore. All of these are acts of creation gone bad. When the process of *melakhah*, of improvement, never ends, it destroys itself. At some point, a creator needs to let go. Paradoxically, the final act of creating is ceasing to create.

A creator finds it hard to let go, because that seems like the end. Letting go engenders a natural sense of mourning. But perhaps, like death itself, it is really just the beginning; it is really just a transition from a world of "becoming" into a world of "being." When a creator stops creating, he is finally ready to realize the purpose of his labors. He is finally ready to let the thing be what it is, and to relate to that which he created.

That's what positive rest means. Positive rest doesn't mean stopping to catch your breath. It means stopping to tinker, and beginning to appreciate. It means letting a thing just be, and appreciating it *for what it is in itself*, not for what you can still try and make it into.

This type of rest was inaugurated into the world on the first *Shabbat*, the seventh day of Creation. As the sixth day came to a close, the Almighty made a conscious, fateful decision to stop tinkering with the Universe. He looked at His handiwork and declared: *"hineh tov me'od"* –"indeed, it is very good." This proclamation signaled *Hashem's* willingness to stop making the Universe better, to stop fixing it, and to begin the process of relating to it for what it was.

The Almighty stopped not because the work was over. The work of improvement is never over. But He pulled back and left that work in our hands, in the hands of mankind. It was now up to us to pick up the mantle of *melakhah* – to become earthly creators, to "guard the world and to work it," to leave to the next generation a world better than the world we were given.

Hashem, in His benevolence, decided to share with the earthly creators the gift of *Shabbat*. Through it, man learns to emulate His Creator, and to crown creativity with rest. Living as we do in This World, a world wired for work, it is tempting to overlook the importance of *Shabbat*. It is tempting to let *melakhah* trick us into thinking that there is nothing more to life. But if we fall into that trap, we will never really create anything. In the act of resting from *melakhah*, we rest from the process of trying to shape the world around us to suit our needs. In this letting go, we are finally able to appreciate the world for what it is, not just for what it can do for us. On *Shabbat*, we escape the relentless need to keep on tinkering, and we taste the deliciousness of pure being.

And it's not just the world that we learn to appreciate through rest; it's the people in that world as well. We all have our top five ways we would like to change our spouse to suit our needs. And most of us, in at least subtle ways, try to make these wishes known as gently as possible, of course. But as long as you are in the process of tinkering, trying to improve him or her, you are not in the process of appreciating. To let go is to make a powerful statement: that I love you, that I appreciate you – right now, for the person who you are now – not just for what I might make you into in the future.

Hashem gave us a sliver of time, *Shabbat*, to help us make this stance a regular feature of our lives. If and when we do, we will have truly bought ourselves a piece of Heaven on Earth.

Dr. Yitzchak Schechter

נב: A Leaning Tower of *Bavel*: A Psychological Reading of *Migdal Bavel* and Reflections on Vulnerability in Religious Experience

The epic saga of the *mabbul* wiping out a morally and ethically corrupt society is a central theme of the Biblical story of the unfolding of the new world. A form of this narrative appears throughout the records of Near-Eastern cultures and beyond and has been a powerful symbol defining God's relationship with emerging history. After the great flood, the story falls from view of the narrative and is fully appreciated only through the eyes of later generations studying its symbolic and spiritual value and meaning. In the enigmatic nine *pesukim* (*Bereishit* 11:1–9) of the account of *migdal Bavel*, however, we find a description of the next generation's response and its psychic effect on the culture that emerges after the *mabbul's* immense destruction. As with all Biblical narratives, the text can be read as the account of people and stories, or seen as the natural history, vicissitudes and challenges of the soul/psyche within the individual. The aim of this article is to derive the psychological and spiritual meaning of *migdal Bavel* in relation to vulnerability in religious experience and trace this motif through the emergence of Avraham and aspects of the Torah's ideal of religious experience. The text of *Bereishit* (11:1–4) reads:

> And it was that all the land *was of one language and of unified purpose*. And it was in their sojourning from the east and they found a valley in the land of Shin'ar and they settled there. *And they said man to his fellow* "come let us bake bricks and fire it in the kiln," and they had bricks for stones (i.e. building) and mortar for cementing. And they said "come let us build a city and tower and its pinnacle in the Heavens and we will make a name lest we shall be spread upon the face of all the land."

After the devastation of the *mabbul*, the people of the world had a common language and purpose; there was a sense of common experience that could be shared through joint communication. This shared experience was the product of their common ancestry, as well as of the loss and the awareness of their fragility that resulted from the disruption of the flood only a generation prior. This opening passage sets the tone and central theme for the concepts encoded in the story: that connection with the Other emerges from the acceptance of fragility and vulnerability.

Facing the looming susceptibility to harm that engulfs the generation, the people are now faced with the task of mobilizing a response to the trauma.[1] To this end, the Torah's narrative describes the emergence of new technology – new technological advancements that are

---

1. Rashi, *Bereishit* 11:4, s.v. *pen nafutz* – "*she-lo yavi aleinu shum makah lehafitzenu mikan*" – "because they were afraid of another calamity befalling them therefore they built a tower." (see *Gur Aryeh*, ad loc.)

able to more effectively control the situations of life and shelter the community from the dangers of the world. With the promise of new engineering and construction techniques, a defensive response is now put in place, through which they attempt to control the world around them. By developing a strong "edifice complex," the people attempt to distance themselves from, or – more correctly – deny, the possibility of their weakness and susceptibility to having the force of God or nature again affect their burgeoning civilization. As the *Midrash Rabbah* (as quoted by Rashi, ad loc.) describes their desire, they sought to provide support to the Heavens to prevent the repetition of what they thought to be a natural 1656 year flood cycle (*Midrash Rabbah* 38:1, 6).

Another perspective of the *Midrash* is that indeed by building a tower to the Heavens they were looking to remove God from His seat on high, and replace Him with themselves (*Midrash Rabbah* 38:6; *Sanhedrin* 109a and Rashi, ad loc.). Here the reading of the midrashic sources further highlights the theme, by suggesting that mankind was trying to make war on God. Man becomes a subject of "inflation" – people here attempt to replace God and his centrality in the psychic experience with themselves. The numinous function of the God concept (*mysterium tremendum et fascinans,* "the great awe and power of God") is replaced by the artificial creations of man.[2] Consistent with this theme, the numinous experience has historically been supplanted with many replacements, such as the power of the state, leader, science or idea; but replacing it in any of these fashions is a dangerous state of affairs.[3]

This is also how Seforno, based on *Pirkei de-Rebbi Eli'ezer,* interprets the building of the tower – as an attempt to create a central and supreme power under which everyone will be subjugated (Seforno, *Bereshit* 11:4, s.v. *u-migdal ve-ro'sho va-shmayim ve-na'aseh-lanu shem*). As *Pirkei de-Rebbi Eli'ezer* describes – "*R. Akiva omer hishlikhu me-aleihem malkhut shamayim ve-himlikhu aleihem Nimrod*" – "R. Akiva says 'they removed from themselves the yoke of heaven and [instead] raised Nimrod to be their king'" (*Pirkei de-Rebbi Eli'ezer,* Ch. 24). The *Midrash* continues on to say that Nimrod then suggests to build a tower because, he

---

2. C.G. Jung, *Psychology and Religion* (Yale University Press, 1938).
3. Ibid. In this context Jung discusses the rise of Nazism and Communism.

claims, "God is only powerful on earth and water, but if we ascend He would be powerless against us."[4]

The belief that either the individual or the collective, through the development of defensive technology, can fully protect and make itself impervious to any threat is parallel to pathological narcissism. The psychiatric diagnosis of narcissistic personality disorder in an individual is defined as a pattern of overvaluing one's worth and power, together with the inextricable failure to assess one's weaknesses. The outgrowth of this combination is the hallmark of narcissism – a marked impairment of empathy and connection to others. A group lacking the fundamental awareness of vulnerability leads to a communal narcissistic personality disorder with the ultimate end product being a Tower of *Bavel* scenario – featuring a complete breakdown of language and communication. The psyche that denies its vulnerability and the reality of imminent dangers closes itself off from the possibility of any genuine interaction with the Other. Our inherent imperfection and fragility is what allows us to value and relate to others. Thus, what naturally develops from the denial of weakness is a narcissistic attitude that denies the possibility of something being outside of its control. In this narcissistic state, the one who can no longer live with the possibility of weakness organizes his life around its denial. This is the ultimate tragedy of the narcissistic personality; it causes its victim to become mute and disconnected from the organic reality of the world of others, and remains a stagnant shell of its calcified idealization. It is this disconnect and lack of empathy that enveloped the world "so that they would not hear the language of their fellow" (*Bereishit* 11:7). The loss of language and genuine communication is the natural evolution of the narcissism of the age of *Bavel*. While the people started with a unified purpose (ibid., 1, 3–4) the outcome was a collective narcissism that denied the individuals and their experiences and ultimately marked the end of the cooperation of their project – "and they ceased from building the city" (ibid., 8).

The obsession of this generation with its own power and mission, and subsequent distortion in the interpersonal realm so endemic

---

4. Or, according to the other edition (and consistent with the text of *Sanhedrin* 109a), it would read "go into His domain and attack Him with our weapons."

to the narcissist, is vividly brought to bear in the midrashic account mentioned above (*Pirkei de-Rebbi Eli'ezer*, Ch. 24). "If a person fell [off the tower], and died they wouldn't even pay any attention to him, but if one brick fell they would sit and cry and say 'woe is to us, when will another brick be brought up in its place?'"[5] Individual people, and even their deaths, had no meaning or impact, whereas a minor inconvenience to their pride was a loss to grieve. The height of the tower, i.e. the extent of their collective imperviousness, was inversely correlated with their removal from the experience of loss in human experience. Conversely, God emerges as a character in the story with humility and in a relational context. While God is always *yachid*, alone, here we find God mirroring the rallying cry of the people in the text – "*havah*" – (ibid., 3–4) in his Heavenly court – "*havah nerdah ve-navlah sham sefatam*" – "Come, let Us come down and confound their language" (ibid., 7). As the *Midrash*, quoted by Rashi, says: "He consulted with His Heavenly court due to His abundant humility" (*Bereishit Rabbah* 8:8). Furthermore, God goes down, "*va-yered Hashem lir'ot*" (ibid., 5). As Rashi says, quoting the *Midrash Tanchuma*, "to teach judges that they cannot convict those being judged until they go down and understand" (Rashi, ad loc.). God emerges with humility, descending as He does with His Heavenly court to more fully understand the convicted.

Ultimately God's intervention of the dispersion of language (read: disconnection of experience of other) is clearly "*middah keneged middah*" and is the direct outgrowth of the psychic oeuvre that developed in this era.[6] Perhaps even more tragic than the loss of language is indeed the confusion or mixing of languages; their communications were hollow and meaningless verbalizations that did not carry any substance. As the Maharal in *Gur Aryeh*, ad loc., points out, if it were just a lack of understanding, they would have ceased the building and could still have

---

5. See the comment of R. David Luria, ad loc., in *Pirkei de-Rebbi Eli'ezer* (glosses 39 and 25), who comments that the valuing of bricks over people and the greater mission over the individual was a foreshadowing of Egypt. This is of particular interest given that the midrashic and kabbalistic theme of speech being in exile was present in Egypt as well.

6. See *Gur Aryeh* on Rashi (ibid., 8): it was automatic since their language was mixed up.

stayed together; but instead, it was the discord, fights and aggression that resulted in their dispersion over the face of the earth. It is the loss of meaning and its painful disconnect that affected them, as the *Midrash* quoted by Rashi on this passage attests: "'So that they will not understand the language of their fellow.' This one asks for a brick and the other brings mortar, and then he stands up and smashes his skull" (*Bereishit Rabbah* 38:10). Similarly, in *Pirkei de-Rebbi Eli'ezer,* they wanted to talk with each other but "they did not recognize each person the language of their fellow. What did they do? Each one took his sword and battled everyone against each other to destroy each other and half the world fell by the sword" (*Pirkei de-Rebbi Eli'ezer,* Ch. 24).[7] The communication and desire were expressed, but the needs of the people were unable to be fulfilled; they lacked communication and empathy and had no ability to mediate their unmet needs. This is no different than the narcissist who attempts to have a meaningful relationship and desires warmth and affection but responds with frustration and anger when his needs are not perfectly or correctly met due to his own difficulties, and he thereby ends up destroying the relationship.

This story of the Tower of *Bavel* and the cautionary tale it supplies is a direct rejoinder to Freud and other early psychoanalysts who wrote on the psychogenesis of religion and its psychic evolution. Freud, in his classic work *Future of an Illusion,* sees religion, and the entire concept of God, as an illusion created by primitive man to exorcise the terror of nature and the existential vulnerability that man feels in front of the power of nature. The power of religion and God is that it is a wish fulfillment that allows the person to feel powerful and no longer fearful of their being left up to the whims of nature. The problem, he continues, is that it makes men feel too powerful and makes them lose their sense of vulnerability, and that ultimately it is only modern man and his rationality and adherence to *logos* that will assure civilization's success.

In this way, then, the symbol of *migdal Bavel* is a response to Freud, and belies a message of not building false hopes in technology,

---

7. R. David Luria, ad loc., describes it slightly differently. He says that the fighting was due to the dissolution of their bonds and that they no longer felt connected to each other, and subsequently, everyone was a stranger to everyone else.

science and pure rationality. The new technology of construction and brick will not protect us. Rather, we must always retain an undying sense of exposure in our place in the world. Even the great name we make for ourselves with our culture – *"na'aseh lanu shem"* – cannot protect us from ourselves and the world, and we must accept its basic insecurity. Ironically, Freud's book was written in 1927, only a few short years before the greatest act of directed aggression and violence occurred from the center of "civilized man."

The theme of vulnerability in the story of *migdal Bavel* is the beginning rather than the end. Emerging from the "ruins" of the tower grows the new hero and progenitor of the Jewish people – Avraham. It is his life as the archetypal father of the Jewish people, and his rise, challenges and message, which epitomize this new form of conscious vulnerability and deep-seated *chesed*. Avraham and all he embodies fittingly follow this story.

The life of Avraham is that of tests and challenges that rock the comfort and certitude of life. This is evident in our first introduction to Avraham's relationship with God. It is this encounter that distinguishes him from the long list of virtually unknown generations in the *parashiyyot* of *Bereishit* and *Noach* that precede him. *"Va-yomer Hashem el Avram lekh lekha me-artzekha u-mi-moladtekha u-mi-beit avikha el ha-aretz asher ar'eka" (Bereishit* 12:1). God says to Avraham upon entering his personal and historical religious journey *"lekh lekha"* – leave the emotional, psychological and acquired comforts of your home, family and place and go to the place I will show you – the destination and promised land itself is not even known. Going as a nomad with no known destination, Avraham leaves everything in the name of his conviction and connection with the Divine. As his life continues, the story of Avraham and the *havtachot* (the promises given to him by God) are all tied to the well-known and counted *nisyonot* – the tests that highlight this fundamental insecurity of his religious life. Avraham's faith and conviction in God are firm and unwavering; it is only the confidence in himself and his actions that is insecure. The *nisyonot* are challenges that lead to and demand doubt, whether it be not having children, choosing to send away one of the children he finally has, and of course, the pinnacle of these challenges (when eventually God's promise is fulfilled and he has the child with Sarah, and it is that very child that must be brought as a sacrifice, leaving him bereft of even the security of the fulfillment of God's promise). Even then, he is commanded to serve *Hashem* with a gnawing sense of insecurity.[8] This is the essence of Avraham and his children.

The keen awareness of his own vulnerability and that he is not "in charge" is intimately linked, then, with his characteristic and consistent *middah* of *chesed* – his ability to connect with others and provide loving-kindness to whomever he encounters. One simple example of this is Avraham's encounter with the *palit* (refugee) (*Bereishit* 14:13). An unnamed refugee from the raging war, who has escaped with his life and possibly little more, comes to inform Avraham of his nephew being captured. As Seforno describes, the refugee did not know of the relationship between Lot and Avraham; rather, Avraham was the natural address for such problems. Not surprisingly, then, is it specifically here that the Torah describes Avraham as *Avraham Ha-Ivri*. The *Midrash* (43:8) famously teaches the derivation of this name: "*R. Yehudah omer kol ha-olam kulo me-ever echad ve-hu me-ever acher*" – "The whole world stands on one side and he stands on the other" (*Midrash Rabbah* 43:8).

Consciousness of our uncertainty leads to shedding a false sense of power, control and ownership. Ultimately, it is God who is the one that determines all things. The concepts ensconced in the symbols of these stories are directly related to the essence of Jewish ideals. They speak to the ability to identify with the Other in misfortune, and the capacity for empathy, as the individual or collective society knows what this feels like so they can experience it as well. If one (individual or community) has built up the rigid wall of denial around their experience and has isolated their affect regarding weakness and imperfection, they will likely not allow a genuine experience of the Other. This, of course, is reminiscent of "*ve-ahavta le-rei'akha kamokha*" – "And you shall love

8. It is critical to note here and throughout this chapter that when talking about vulnerability and insecurity in the religious experience this is not to be confused with pathology or low self-esteem. This discussion assumes maintenance of a healthy sense of one's self and one's worth (i.e. essential or 'healthy' narcissism) and not an undervaluing or overvaluing of one's self. This is similar to the definition of *anavah* (humility) being an unbiased and fiercely accurate perception of self and not self-abnegation.

your neighbor as yourself" (*Vayikra* 19:18). It is only through the experience of self that the Other can be understood and felt as real (i.e that the love of the fellow is *"kamokha"*). In fact this is a well-known dictum of Rabbi Akiva: *"zeh kelal gadol ba-Torah"* – "[Loving one's fellow as oneself] is a primary rule in the Torah."

This is, of course, correlated with the essential story of Hillel (*Shabbat* 31a). When a non-Jew came before Hillel to convert on the condition that he could learn the whole Torah while standing on one foot (i.e. in its simplest encapsulated form), Hillel calmly responded, "What is hated by you do not do to others – the rest is a commentary, go and learn." To describe this fundamental precept as the *raison d'être* of the Torah is not to embrace an absolution from the particulars of law but to embrace new meaning in practice and spiritual experience. It places at its center the dyad of self and Other.[9] The Other may be defined in variable contexts and as different recipients, but it is a fundamental component of the religious experience.

This message of the Tower of *Bavel* and Avraham continues in *Chumash* to be the collective lesson and challenge for *Benei Yisrael* as they move from being lowly slaves to (seemingly) controlling their destiny and maturing into a powerful and conquering nation in *Eretz Yisrael*. The constant admonition of Moshe is to remember that we were once slaves, *"gerim"* (foreigners) and outsiders. The national experience of slavery was not just a historical reality; it was a collective phenomenology, with the purpose of first imbuing a sense of humility and then developing a sense of empathy and appreciation with those less fortunate. This fact is consistently highlighted by the many frequent reminders, including: (i) "And do not oppress a stranger, for you know the heart of a stranger, as you were strangers in the land of Egypt" (*Shemot* 23:9); (ii) "The stranger that sojourns with you shall be as the home-born among you, and you shall love him as yourself, for you were strangers in the land of Egypt" (*Vayikra* 19:34); (iii) being at the core of many *mitzvot* throughout *Devarim* such as *ha'anakat avadim* (giving parting gifts to freed slaves) (see *Devarim* 15:15); and (iv) the commandment of

---

9. Consistent with Hillel's approach we find the dialectic of self and other in his pithy maxim (*Pirkei Avot* 1:14): *"Im ein ani li mi li, u-ke-she-ani le-atzmi mah ani?"*

remembrance in its own right, "And you shall remember that you were slaves in Egypt" (*Devarim* 16:12).[10]

The rejection of this ideal, and the taking of an arrogant and complacent stand with regards to the nation's success, has the potential to be the cause of its ensuing destruction – as Moshe so dramatically exhorts the Jewish people in the last moments of his life at the end of *Devarim*: "*va-yishman Yeshurun va-yiv'at shamanta, avita, kasita vayitosh Eloka asahu*" – "Yeshurun becomes corpulent and scoffs ... and he forsakes the the God Who made him" (*Devarim* 32:15), and, as is repeated in warning for when the Jewish nation says in their narcissistic omnipotence: "*My power and the strength of my hand have gotten me this wealth*" (*Devarim* 8:17). They will shortly learn the falsehood of that belief, and that it was God alone giving that ability and strength (ibid., 18). Thus, even at what should be *Benei Yisrael's* most victorious moment, as they are about to pass through the Jordan river to finally take possession of the Promised Land, Moshe warns them not to think that it is their greatness that has led them here; rather it is God and the promise to the forefathers.

With this in mind, the detesting of the idolatry of narcissistic defensiveness is palpable throughout the reading of *Tanakh*. One of the great dangers of idolatry, which all the prophets warn against, is that of impenetrable complacency – the idolatrous soothsayers prophesying peace and tranquility and that no harm shall befall the people – "your prophets have seen visions for you of vanity and delusion, and they have not uncovered your iniquity ... but have prophesied for your burdens of vanity and seduction" (*Eikhah* 2:14). They therefore say, "What bad can befall us?" When society exists in a state of narcissistic impunity, it cannot introspect or expect the negative, but rather revels in its defensiveness. But of course, that defensiveness cannot withstand the test of reality, and ultimately the Jewish people return to God after the experience of vulnerability – "and in the time of trouble, they will arise and say to God 'arise and save us!'" (*Yirmiyahu* 2:27).

This theme has many expressions throughout the words and symbols of *Chazal*, but perhaps finds it fullest expression and greatest hope in the image and interpretation of the passage of "Behold your

10. See Shoshana Schechter's article on *Parashat Re'eh* in this volume.

king comes to you; he is triumphant and victorious, lowly and riding upon a donkey, and upon a colt the foal of a donkey" (*Zekharyah* 9:9; see also *Sanhedrin* 99a). The vision of *Mashiach* himself who will serve as the leader and a guide for a new epoch of history appears simply as a humble (literally poor) man riding a lowly donkey. Even in the greatest glory and redemptive vision of the Jewish people, simplicity and vulnerability remain essential features.

Rabbi Assaf Bednarsh

לך לך: From Sodom to Jerusalem

> *And Malki-Tzedek king of Shalem brought forth bread and wine. He was a priest to God, the Most High.* (Bereishit 14:18)

The *Or Ha-Chayyim Ha-Kadosh* wonders what lesson the Torah intends us to derive from Avraham's encounter with Malki-Tzedek, interposed here in the midst of Avraham's interactions with the king of Sodom. The *Or Ha-Chayyim* explains that this interpolation is meant to contrast the behavior of the righteous and the wicked. While the king of Sodom, who should have offered some token of gratitude to Avraham for rescuing his entire nation, proffers nothing, the stranger Malki-Tzedek ("King of Righteousness"), who owes Avraham nothing, brings food and drink for the weary soldiers returning from the battlefield.

This observation dovetails with the well-known midrashic theme attributing the ultimate destruction of Sodom to their ethical corruption,

לך לך

and specifically to their deficiency in the practice of charity and their insensitivity to the plight of the stranger and the poor and downtrodden. In the words of the prophet (*Yechezkel* 16:49):

> Behold this was the iniquity of thy sister Sodom, she and her daughters had pride, plenty of bread and untroubled tranquility, and yet she did not strengthen the hand of the poor and the needy.

The wealth and luxurious lifestyle which the Sodomites took for granted led them to an insensitivity and inability to empathize with the plight of the less fortunate among them. This stands in contrast to the keen ethical sensitivity of Malki-Tzedek and his people.

This contrast is made more poignant by the realization that Shalem, in *Tanakh*, is synonymous with the city of Jerusalem. (See, e.g., *Tehillim* 76:3, "*va-yehi be-Shalem suko u-meonato be-Tzion*," – "In Shalem also in His Tabernacle, and His dwelling place is in Zion.") This distinction, then, symbolizes not only the difference between two Canaanite potentates four millennia ago, but the essential divergence between the ideals of the Jewish people, whose world centers around Jerusalem, and the Sodomites who represent all that we hope not to become. We are left to wonder, though, what circumstances led the Sodomites to this state of moral depravity, while the ancient Jerusalemites, who may well have enjoyed equal prosperity and success, remained uncorrupted.

A clue to the answer may be found in the first substantive mention of Sodom in the Torah, earlier in *Parashat Lekh Lekha* (*Bereishit* 13:10–13):

> Lot looked up and saw that the entire Jordan Plain, all the way to Tzo'ar had plenty of water. (This was before God destroyed Sodom and Gomorrah.) It was like God's own garden, like the land of Egypt. Lot chose for himself the entire Jordan Plain. He headed eastward, and the two separated. Avraham lived in *Eretz Kena'an*, while Lot dwelt in the cities of the Plain, having migrated as far as Sodom. But the people of Sodom were very wicked, and they sinned against God.

Lot chose to dwell in Sodom because he saw that its fertility was comparable to that of the land of Egypt, with which he was personally familiar from his sojourn there with Avram. What was unique about the land of Egypt? In *Sefer Devarim* (11:10–13), the Torah describes the essential difference between the lands of Egypt and Israel:

> The land which you are about to possess is not like Egypt, the place you left, where you could plant your seed and irrigate it by yourself, just like a vegetable garden. But the land which you are crossing to occupy is a land of mountains and valleys, which can be irrigated only by the rain. It is therefore a land constantly under God your Lord's scrutiny; the eyes of God your Lord are on it at all times, from the beginning of the year until the end of the year.

The Rashbam (ad loc.) explains the spiritual message of this passage as follows: Egypt is watered by the Nile. It requires hard work to transport the water up to the fields, but the farmer is assured that if he puts in the effort, he will see the fruit of his labors, as his source of water is always available. The Land of Israel, however, has no such mighty rivers, and even if it did, it would be impossible to carry the water up the steep hillsides that define the Judean geography. Instead, the Israeli farmer relies on the rainfall, which has the advantage of requiring no effort on his part, but the disadvantage of being completely outside of his control. No matter how hard he works, he can grow nothing without rain, and he can do little more than hope and pray that the rain will fall.

The Rashbam explains that the greatness of the Land of Israel lies exactly in this disadvantage. The Egyptian farmer can easily fool himself into believing that he is the master of his own fate, but the Israeli farmer can never forget that he is dependent on the largess of the Creator for his very sustenance. He literally lifts his eyes to heaven each day, looking for the clouds that will water his thirsty fields, and reminds himself that he is not the master of his fate, and that it therefore behooves him to seek out his true Master. The Land of Israel is not only subject to constant Divine providence, but trains its inhabitants to see the hand of *Hashem* acting in their lives (see also *Devarim* 8:7–18, 11:13–21).

Returning to the story of Avraham, we can now achieve a deeper insight into Lot's tragic decision. He saw that Sodom and its environs were not only lush and fertile, but resembled the land of Egypt. Unlike Avraham's homestead, they were so sufficiently watered by streams and rivers that their inhabitants could forget their dependence on their Maker, and pride themselves alone on their success and accomplishment. Perhaps Lot, after living with Avraham and his message of faith and trust in *Hashem* for so many years, yearned for the existentially complacent lifestyle he witnessed in Egypt, free of the challenging relationship with the Divine which the Land of Canaan demanded. He was therefore attracted to the land of Sodom. (See also Rashi, *Bereishit* 13:7 for a midrashic elucidation of this approach.) Avraham, of course, never intended to suggest that Lot take up residence in Sodom. He offered Lot the option of *"im ha-sem'ol ve-eiminah, ve-im ha-yamin ve-asme'ilah"* – "If you go to the left, I will go to the right; if you go to the right, I will go to the left" (*Bereishit* 13:9). In Biblical Hebrew, 'left' and 'right' mean respectively North and South (so translates Onkelos here). Avraham offered Lot the choice of the northern or southern Judean hills, both within the topographical boundaries of the Land of Canaan, but Lot chose for himself a third option, leaving only Avraham living in *Eretz Kena'an*, and migrating to the spiritual wasteland of Sodom.

Perhaps this understanding of the spiritual bankruptcy of the people of Sodom can provide a deeper insight into their ethical failings. The Sodomites were not congenitally coldhearted and cruel. Rather, their lack of ethical sensitivity flowed from their spiritual insensitivity. One who realizes that he is dependent on the Other for his very sustenance, who recognizes that he does not provide for himself but is rather the recipient of Divine charity, will be more inclined to be charitable to the others who depend on his largess. On the other hand, one who views himself as self-sufficient and ascribes all of his worldly success to his own talent and hard work will have no reason to empathize with the indigent. In the Torah, *"bein adam la-chavero"* (between man and his fellow) is a correlate of *"bein adam la-Makom"* (between man and God). The descendants of Avraham place their faith in *Hashem* rather than themselves, and therefore see their possessions as entrusted to them by their Creator in order to share with all His creatures (see *Avot* 3:7). They are characteristically benevolent, *"gomlei chasadim"* (*Yevamot* 79a), and were chosen by *Hashem* specifically because of their commitment to charity and justice, which the Torah deems the "path of *Hashem*" (*Bereishit* 18:19). This attitude is epitomized by Malki-Tzedek, priest of righteousness.

This contrast between Jerusalem and Sodom reverberates throughout the history of Avraham and his family. Lot, raised in Avraham's household, manages to retain his values even in the midst of Sodom, as evidenced by his hospitality to the plainclothes angels in *Parashat Vayera* (*Bereishit* 19:1–9). His children, however, educated in the cultural milieu of Sodom, were permanently influenced by its theology and ethics, which are antithetical to the Abrahamic value system. Hundreds of years later, Lot's descendants were ultimately excluded from the Jewish people, by language reminiscent of our *parashah*:

> An Ammonite or Moabite may not enter God's congregation. They may never enter God's congregation, even after the tenth generation. This is because they did not greet you with bread and water when you were on the way out of Egypt (*Devarim* 23:4–5).

Unlike Malki-Tzedek, who welcomed Avraham with bread and drink, they demonstrated their allegiance to the heritage of Sodom by refusing to provide sustenance to Avraham's weary descendants in their time of need. Unfortunately, Lot's sojourn in Sodom impressed upon his descendants a way of life that is irreconcilable with the values of the descendants of Avraham, the heirs to Malki-Tzedek's priesthood in Jerusalem.

In later Jewish history, the prophet Yeshayahu would remind the children of Avraham, residents of Jerusalem, of this contrast. In the very beginning of his book (*Yeshayahu* 1:10), Yeshayahu castigates the Jewish people, guilty of perverting justice and oppressing the weak and vulnerable, by comparing them to the ancient Sodomites – "*Hear the words of the Lord, oh chieftains of Sodom.*" Much of *Yeshayahu*, including this opening chapter, juxtaposes criticism of the ethical failings of the Jews of his time with a negation of the value of their sacrifices and Temple worship. This has led to a longstanding misinterpretation that Yeshayahu preached the centrality of social justice at the expense of religious worship.

Based upon the insights we have developed, however, it seems that the opposite is true. Yeshayahu preached the message of true spirituality and worship of *Hashem*. However, he understood that a 'religious' person whose religion does not lead him to charity and social justice does not really acknowledge his dependence upon his Master, but rather considers himself the master of his own universe. A sacrifice brought without a feeling of utter dependence on *Hashem* is not an act of worship, but a mere payoff and a perversion of the spiritual aims of the *Beit Ha-Mikdash*. It is this pretense of spirituality, intolerable to a soul attuned to the beauty of true religious worship, which Yeshayahu railed against. He preached to his compatriots that the true worship of *Hashem* is the spirituality which erases pride and hubris, which generates humility and generosity, and which inspires its adherents to recognize that they were placed in this world not to promote themselves, but to share the Divine grace and charity that they have been fortunate enough to receive.

May we merit seeing the return of the Jewish people to the heights of faith and spirituality personified by our forefather Avraham, and may our concomitant heightened practice of justice and charity bring about the ultimate redemption, speedily and in our days. *"Tzion be-mishpat tipadeh ve-shaveha be-tzedakah"* – "Zion shall be redeemed with judgment, and those that return to her with righteousness" (*Yeshayahu* 1:27).

Dr. Michelle J. Levine

ויירא: The Potency of Prayer[1]

R. Chama bar R. Chanina observes in *Bereishit Rabbah* (52:13) that the term for "prayer," *"tefillah"* [in its verbal form *"va-yitpallel"*], is mentioned for the first time in *Bereishit* Ch. 20, a chapter which relates Avraham's and Sarah's ill-fated experiences during their temporary sojourn in Gerar.[2] Having reproved Avimelech, king of Gerar, for kidnapping Sarah, God insists, "But now, you must return the wife of this man, for he is a prophet and he will *pray* on your behalf so that you may live" – *"ki navi hu va-yitpallel ba-adkha ve-cheyeh"* (*Bereishit* 20:7). God declares that Avraham's intercession through prayer will bring about healing and recovery from all of the afflictions that were causing distress to the king and his household "because of the matter involving Sarah, wife of Avraham" (ibid. 17–18). Questioning why this incident

---

1. Translations of Biblical verses and commentaries are my own. All midrashic citations derive from *Midrash Bereishit Rabbah*, ed. J. Theodor and Ch. Albeck (Jerusalem: Shalem Books, 1996), unless noted otherwise. All citations from medieval Biblical commentaries derive from *Mikra'ot Gedolot "Haketer,"* ed. Menachem Cohen, 2nd. edn., Vols. 1, 2 on *Bereishit* (Ramat Gan: Bar-Ilan University Press, 2001, 2004), unless noted otherwise.
2. See Theodor-Albeck, *Midrash Bereishit Rabbah*, 2:553.

warrants the codification of this means of spiritual communication with the Divine, R. Chama answers rather cryptically, "Once Avraham our forefather prayed, this knot was untied" – "*hutar oto ha-kesher.*"[3] A narrow contextual reading of this statement relates to the recovery process, for, as the Biblical text indicates, the afflictions had consisted of a type of "stoppage" and obstruction (*"atzar"*) of the reproductive capacities of the king and his women (ibid. 17–18).[4] Nevertheless, it appears that R. Chama intends to convey a broader thematic insight with regard to the ramifications of Avraham's intercession on behalf of Avimelech, an insight with wide-ranging implications for the significance of prayer.

While the episode of *Bereishit* Ch. 20 appears on the surface to read as a replay of Sarah's abduction to the palace of Pharaoh in *Bereishit* 12, there are significant differences which explain why prayer serves a crucial role only in the incident with Avimelech. As opposed to Pharaoh, Avimelech merits a night dream in which God warns him of the severe consequences of his actions, allows the king to defend himself, and ultimately provides the king with a prescription for redeeming himself and his household (*Bereishit* 20:3–7). Apparently, as noted by Ramban, Avimelech "was honest and upright and his people were decent," and Sarah was only brought to the palace once her status as the "sister" of Avraham had been discerned. This stands in contrast to Pharaoh, who took her to the palace against her will, without consideration of her status, after hearing his officers' praise of her beauty (*Bereishit* 12:14–15).[5]

---

3. The Vilna edition of *Bereishit Rabbah* (Jerusalem: n.p., rpt. 1975) has a slightly different version of this phrase: *"hutar ha-kesher ha-zeh."* Moshe Aryeh Mirkin, ed., *Bereishit Rabbah* (Tel Aviv: Yavneh Pub., 1985), 2:235, notes on *Bereishit Rabbah* 52:13, posits that the midrashic sage derives the meaning of *tefillah* by reversing its letters to read *"petil,"* "a thread," thereby interpreting that through prayer, knots of a thread are untied, and harsh decrees are nullified.

4. Compare Ramban, *Bereishit* 20:17–18, who observes that Avimelech had been afflicted with impotence, while the women of his household had been restrained from being able to give birth at the end of their terms of pregnancy. Compare Radak, *Bereishit* 20:4, 6, 17, who maintains with regard to Avimelech that his sexual desire had been taken away after Sarah was brought to the palace.

5. See Ramban, *Bereishit* 20:2, in relation to his commentary on *Bereishit* 12:11–13, 15 [*Ha-Keter*, 1:127]. However, Joseph Bekhor Shor, *Bereishit* 20:5, 16, in relation to his commentary on *Bereishit* 12:14–15, maintains that while Pharaoh relies on his officers'

While Ramban infers that Avimelech was afflicted for "days," neither repenting from his wrongdoings, nor attempting to clarify the source of his distress,[6] and Avraham maintains that "there is no fear of God in this place" (*Bereishit* 20:11), it is noteworthy that God allows for a measure of justification and innocence on Avimelech's part. As God declares, "I also know that you did this with the innocence of your heart (*ve-tam levavekha*)" (*Bereishit* 20:6). God reveals further that He had prevented Avimelech "from sinning against Me" by restraining the king from "touching" Sarah (ibid.). Avimelech's concern for the "sins" which he had perpetrated are reflected in the great "fear" that his people express after hearing about their king's vision (ibid. 8) and in his subsequent confrontation with Avraham, in which the king proclaims, "What have you done to us, and how have I sinned against you (*u-meh chata'ti lakh*) that you have brought on me and on my kingdom this great crime (*chata'ah gedolah*)" (*Bereishit* 20:9)?[7]

While Avimelech is not completely innocent, having taken Sarah against her will,[8] these indications of spiritual insight – and despite

word that Avraham is claiming Sarah as his sister, Avimelech insists in *Bereishit* 20:5 that he did not rely on Avraham's initial declaration, but asked Sarah herself about her relationship to Avraham. Only when Sarah admits that he is her brother, does Avimelech take her to his palace.

6. Ramban, *Bereishit* 20:17. Radak, *Bereishit* 20:17, specifies that Avimelech and his household were stricken with sexual and reproductive afflictions for a day, a night, and the following day until Avraham prayed for them. This analysis, therefore, assumes that the later revelation of Avimelech's afflictions and that of his household at the end of *Bereishit* Ch. 20 is out of chronological order. On this atemporal organization of the episode, compare Meir Sternberg, *The Poetics of Biblical Narrative: Ideological Literature and the Drama of Reading* (Bloomington: Indiana Univ. Press, 1987), pp. 315–16. Sternberg maintains that this final disclosure reveals ultimately that "Avimelech is after all just another Pharaoh (ibid., p. 316)."

7. For a literary comparison between the episodes in *Bereishit* Ch.'s 12 and 20, see David Petersen, "A Thrice-Told Tale: Genre, Theme, and Motif," *Biblical Research* 18 (1973), pp. 35–41. Compare Yoel Bin-Nun, *Pirkei Ha-Avot: Iyyunim Be-Parshiyot Ha-Avot Be-Sefer Bereishit*, 2nd printing (Alon Shevut: Tevunot Pub., 2004), pp. 107–8.

8. See Radak, *Bereishit* 20:7, who observes that even if Sarah was unmarried, it was an "evil thing (*davar ra*)," to forcefully take her to the palace, even more so since she is the "sister" of a "righteous man," against whose will she is taken as well.

Avraham's assumptions, the acceptance of God's authority and powers –[9] impart a different tone to the narrative of *Bereishit* Ch. 20. Avimelech's understanding of God's role in his fate is evidenced by his beseeching of Avraham, who subsequently prays for the king and brings a recovery for him and his household (ibid., 17). As the commentary of Maharzu on *Bereishit Rabbah* maintains, petitionary prayer (*tefillah*) has the power to "straighten the perverse and untie the twisted [knots]" – "*le-yasher ha-ikesh u-le-hatir ha-petaltal*," obstacles and crooked paths created by sin that must now be cleared and rectified through importuning God.[10]

In this episode, Avraham is enjoined to entreat God to reverse a Divine decree, which will bring about healing and recovery, transformation and metamorphosis of another person's life situation. This is not the first time, however, that Avraham prays to God to attempt to influence, *kaviyakhol*, the Divine intent and change the course of events. In *Bereishit* Ch. 18, Avraham "approaches" God in prayer (*Bereishit* 18:22–23), challenging the Divine decree against the people of Sodom.[11] Noting that God chooses to reveal to Avraham His plan to destroy Sodom because

9. Note how Ramban, *Bereishit* 20:1, maintains that Avraham was the one who "suspected them" of being an immoral people, even though he did not necessarily have clear evidence of such, even though Ramban, *Bereishit* 20:17–18, acknowledges that Avimelech did not repent from his ways on his own, despite his afflictions.

10. See the Vilna edition of *Midrash Rabbah*, Vol. 1, on *Bereishit* 52:13, p. 214, in the commentary of Maharzu, in which he explains *tefillah* as a derivation of *petaltal*, adapting from the commentaries of Onkelos and Rashi on *Bereishit* 30:8, in which Rachel declares, "*naftulei Elokim niftalti*." In that context, Onkelos maintains that Rachel prayed and her prayer was accepted, while Rashi explains, based on *Devarim* 32:5 ("*ikesh u-petaltul*") that Rachel declares how she "wrestled with God" and was persistent in her requests to be like her sister, beseeching God to be fertile ("*nit'akashti ve-hiftzarti petzirot ve-naftulim la-Makom*").

11. See Rashi, *Bereishit* 18:23, who maintains that Avraham "approached" God with the multiple objectives: to challenge His intent ("*hagashah le-milchamah*"), to persuade by appeasement and humility ("*hagashah le-piyus*"), and to pray for mercy ("*hagashah le-tefillah*"). Compare Maharal's commentary on Rashi, *Gur Aryeh*, on *Bereishit* 18:23, in *Chumash Gur Aryeh Ha-Shalem*, ed. Yehoshua David Hartmann, Vol. 1 on *Bereishit* (Jerusalem: Makhon Yerushalayim, 1989), pp. 315–16, in which he observes that these objectives encompass "prayer" in all of its different nuances. Avraham challenges through prayer God's apparent plan to destroy the innocent along with the wicked (*Bereishit* 18:23); he appeases God through humbly declar-

this patriarch understands the "way of God to do justice and righteous-ness" (*Bereishit* 18:19), the Biblical text reveals that Avraham enters into a protracted dialogue with God, which ultimately proves the validity of the judgment. While Ramban maintains that God had not finalized the decree of destruction against Sodom until Avraham had exhausted all possibility of recourse to Divine mercy,[12] the end result of Avraham's beseeching on this national plane was the confirmation that the people of Sodom deserved punishment. Avraham's prayer does not achieve a reversal of decree, but it serves another important function, revealing an additional dimension of the purpose of prayer. As the commentary of *Be'er Yitzchak* on Rashi's exegesis explains, the Biblical text emphasizes that Avraham continued to "stand before God" (*Bereishit* 18:22; see as well *Bereishit* 19:27) – an unusual reference to a prophetic experience – in order to teach that God "wanted him to pray about them so that He may respond immediately to his [Avraham's] arguments in order to elucidate for Avraham (*lema'an yitbarer le-Avraham*) the absolute integrity of His verdict (*kol yosher dinav*) and that they [the Sodomites] have no chance of escape."[13] Perhaps deriving the concept of *tefillah* from the root, *pll*, judgment and argument,[14] this exposition highlights the fact that prayer also serves as an opportunity to achieve clarity and clarification, to gain a better understanding of how God relates to the world. It is this prayer that establishes, according to *Chazal*, the institution of *tefillat shacharit*.[15]

Avraham's inability to avert catastrophe for the people of Sodom makes a deep impression on Avimelech. Echoing the words of Avraham's argument before God in *Bereishit* 18:23–25, Avimelech exclaims, "My

ing himself unworthy of asking for a change of decree (*Bereishit* 18:27, 32); and he beseeches God for mercy for the wicked in the merit of the innocent who dwell in the city (*Bereishit* 18:24).

12. See Ramban, *Bereishit* 18:20–21, 23.
13. Isaac Horovitz, *Sefer Be'er Yitzchak Ve-Hu Perush al Perush Rashi zt"l Al Ha-Torah*, Vol. 1 (Israel: Books Export Enterprises, n.d.), p. 46, on Rashi, *Bereishit* 18:22, *Ve-Avraham odennnu omed lifnei Hashem*.
14. Compare *Tehillim* 106:30, and the parallel analysis of this context in *Sanhedrin* 44a.
15. See *Berakhot* 26b.

Lord, will you kill a nation, even if it is innocent" – "*ha-goi gam tzaddik taharog*" (*Bereishit* 20:4)?[16] The *midrash* elaborates and observes,

> "'Avimelech rose early in the morning and called all of his servants…and the men became very afraid' (*Bereishit* 20:8). R. Chanan said: Since they were assessing [the situation of Sodom],[17] the smoke of Sodom rising up like that of a fiery furnace, they said, 'Perhaps the angels that were sent to Sodom have come here?' Because of this, they were exceedingly afraid."[18]

Just as Avraham had arisen early in the morning and looked out over the land of Sodom and Gomorrah, only to witness a rising column of smoke "like that of a furnace" (*Bereishit* 19:27–28), Avimelech begins to wonder if his corrupt manner of "hosting guests" in his land would lead to a similar fate of destruction. Acknowledging that Avimelech has some integrity (as opposed to the people of Sodom),[19] God deems it fitting to nullify His decree against the people of Gerar and restore their health.

In this context, Avraham succeeds through prayer to transform another's destiny. His prayer "loosens the knots" of the Divine decree and brings about renewal and rejuvenation. Concerning this remarkable achievement, R. David Luria, commenting on this midrashic metaphor, conjectures that perhaps this is why the term "*ve-yitpallel*" is used for the first time in the Torah in this episode. Avraham was able to achieve what had not been accomplished previously; through prayer, a Divine decree was reversed. In doing so, Avraham "opened the door" and dem-

---

16. Compare Robert Alter's analysis of this phrase, *The Five Books of Moses: A Translation with Commentary* (New York/London: W.W. Norton and Co., 2004), pp. 98–99, notes on *Bereishit* 20:4.

17. This translation follows the insights of the commentary of *Yefeh To'ar* on *Bereishit Rabbah* 52:9, in the Vilna edition of *Midrash Rabbah*, Vol. 1, p. 107, which observes that Sodom was quite a distance from Gerar, and it would have been impossible to actually see the smoke rising from the ruins of Sodom. Therefore, one should interpret their "seeing (*lefi she-ro'im ashan Sedom*)" as an interior perception and subjective assessment of the circumstances.

18. *Bereishit Rabbah* 52:9, in Theodor-Albeck, *Bereishit Rabbah*, 2:549.

19. Note as well that as opposed to Pharaoh who expels Avraham and his family, Avimelech eventually invites Avraham to remain in his land (*Bereishit* 20:15).

onstrated the power of prayer to reach up to God and "influence" Him in how He relates to the world.[20] It is significant, however, that the prayer in this narrative scene is not articulated by the one who is afflicted, but by another, who, while he has a vested interest in the matter, is an outsider, untainted directly by the distress that is the impetus for the prayer itself. What is God's intent in sending Avraham, who is identified as a "prophet," to beseech Him on Avimelech's behalf? Aware that the characterization of an individual as a *"navi"* appears for the first time in the Torah within this narrative scene, Rashbam explicates that a *navi* is "one who is habitually in My [God's] company, who relates My words, and I love his words, and listen to his prayer."[21] In this context, Rashbam maintains that a prophet functions not only to relate God's word to others, but he acts as a mediator to God, communicating man's situation to Him, and God, in turn, willingly takes note and pays attention.[22] In order to impress upon the protagonists of this episode the potency of prayer as a means of influencing the Divine in His relation with man, God determines that Avraham, the prophet, should intercede on behalf of Avimelech. Nevertheless, while one might infer that such an act would certainly highlight Avraham's spiritual position and elevated relationship with God before a foreign king, fulfilling the promise, "And all the peoples of the earth will be blessed through

---

20. See the commentary of R. David Luria on *Bereishit Rabbah* 52:13 in the Vilna edition of *Midrash Rabbah*, Vol. I, p. 214. Compare *Mo'ed Katan* 16b: "I [God] rule over man. And who rules over me? A righteous person, for I decree a decree and he nullifies it."

21. Rashbam, *Bereishit* 20:7, derives the meaning of the noun *"navi"* from the related adjectival phrase in *Yeshayahu* 57:19, *"niv sefatayim,"* which has been understood in an applied sense as "speech of the lips;" compare its meaning in *Devarim* 32:13, *"tenuvot sadai"* – *"the* fruits of the field." See as well the commentary of *Metzudat David* on *Yeshayahu* 57:19, which points out that speech is the fruits of one's lips. On this derivation of the meaning of *"navi,"* compare Rashi, *Shemot* 7:1.

22. See Martin I. Lockshin, *Rabbi Samuel Ben Meir's Commentary On Genesis: An Annotated Translation* (Lewiston: Edwin Mellen Press, 1989), pp. 81–82, n. 1, who observes that Rashi's qualification of a prophet in *Shemot* 7:1, as one who communicates God's rebuke to the people, does not apply contextually to the episode in *Bereishit* Ch. 20. Therefore, Rashbam broadens the role of a prophet to relate to his role as one who prays on behalf of others.

you" (*Bereishit* 12:3), this analysis does not fully explain why Avraham must be the intercessor in this particular context.

In this episode, all of the protagonists are involved in bringing about the final resolution of the circumstances. According to Radak, Avimelech is enjoined by God not only to return Sarah to her husband, but also to ask Avraham for forgiveness in order to ensure the efficacy of the subsequent prayer.[23] On the other hand, the *Midrash* presumes that the overtly silent victim, Sarah, also plays an active role in changing the course of events. As the *Midrash* relates,

> The entire night, Sarah lay down on her face and cried out: Master of the Worlds, Avraham set forth because of promise, and I went out because of faith (*Avraham yatza be-havtachah va-ani yatzati be-emunah*). Avraham is outside of the prison, while I am in prison. God responded to her: Everything that I will do, I will do because of you; and everyone will say, "It is because of the matter of Sarah, wife of Avraham." (*Bereishit* 20:18)[24]

According to the *midrash*, Sarah makes God aware of the injustice of her plight through prayer, and she seeks guidance and assistance regarding her circumstance. Sarah asserts that she left her homeland on the coattails of her husband, to whom God exclusively revealed His promises of blessing and prosperity. On faith alone has she continuously operated, trusting in God's word, albeit having learned of it through indirect channels. Presuming that faith trumps overt guarantees, Sarah wonders aloud at the travesty of her fate. In the face of apparent powerlessness, Sarah has found the power of prayer and communication with God. God responds in kind, assuring her that He will bring about her redemption

---

23. See Radak, *Bereishit* 20:7. Nevertheless, note that Ramban, *Bereishit* 20:16, maintains that Sarah continued to argue with Avimelech, refusing to accept his forgiveness and appeasement.
24. *Bereishit Rabbah* 52:13 in Theodor-Albeck, *Bereishit Rabbah*, 2:553–54; compare similarly, *Bereishit Rabbah* 41:2, which maintains that this same prayer was expressed by Sarah while in Pharaoh's palace as well.

through miraculous Divine intervention.[25] God, however, wants Avraham to pray as well. Sarah's prayer may suffice to redeem her from her predicament, but to "loosen the knots" of punishment, there needs to be an act of mediation, whereby Avraham creates a new bridge between Avimelech the perpetrator and God the judge. The purpose of this bridge is to melt away their original relationship which resulted in punishment, and effect a new destiny of recovery. What message is God sending to Avraham and all those who are affected by these circumstances?

God deems it necessary that Avraham extend himself beyond his own ego to concentrate on the suffering of another, in order to teach an essential lesson about one's own reality. Sometimes in order to transform oneself, one must first transform the situation of someone else. By "loosening the knots" between yourself and another, by erasing the boundaries that stand between ego and other, prayer succeeds in revealing the unity of the universe and the bridges that must be constructed between all entities in order to metamorphose reality, change a decree, upend one's destiny. By extending beyond one's own condition, getting past your own reality to look outside of yourself, prayer of this mode reveals the essence of man's existence. In order to fulfill the purpose for which the world was created, no man can be an island. "Knots" must be loosened, and then, carrying the metaphor further, new ties must be bound, ties that unite and create a bond of partnership and sharing. Prayer in this fashion not only establishes an intimacy between man and God, but between man and man as well, and this ultimately develops an integral unity between all entities, creating a harmony which God desires within the world.

One may clarify the objective of this type of prayer by Avraham by recalling Rashi's analysis, based on a midrashic insight, concerning Sarah's accusation of Avraham when things go very wrong after Hagar marries her husband.[26] When Hagar chides Sarah after she becomes pregnant, Sarah lashes out at Avraham in outrage: "*Chamasi alekha!*"

---

25. Compare Avivah Gottlieb Zornberg's analysis of this midrashic passage, *Genesis: The Beginning of Desire* (Philadelphia: Jewish Publication Society, 1995), p. 113.

26. See Rashi, *Bereishit* 16:5, based on *Bereishit Rabbah* 45:5 [*Bereishit Rabbah*, Theodor-Albeck, 1:451–52].

(*Bereishit* 16:5). Rendering this declaration to mean, "The wrong done to me incurs a punishment on you," Rashi explains that when Sarah realizes Hagar and her progeny will not be the answer to the patriarchal future, she criticizes Avraham for not pre-empting the crisis in the first place. As she asserts to Avraham,

> When you prayed before God, 'What will you give *me* for *I* am barren?' (*Bereishit* 15:2), you prayed *only for yourself*, and you should have prayed *for both of us*. Had you done so, I would have been remembered [by God] together with you [and the child would have been both of ours, not that of this foreign woman].[27]

Sarah teaches Avraham that prayer not only has the power to change one's own reality but, perhaps more importantly, the reality of another. When one is not thinking about oneself but focuses on another, leaving behind selfish interests and egotistical desires, it is then that God especially listens.[28] In *Bereishit* Ch.'s 12 and 20, Avraham does not appear from a *peshat* perspective to pray in order to resolve his predicaments in contrast to Sarah's prayer-filled voice, at least according to midrashic interpretation. When Sarah is taken against her will to the palaces of Pharaoh and of Avimelech, one does not hear Avraham's cries of prayer on her behalf.[29] Once Avraham is given the opportunity to entreat God on behalf of others in a national setting in the Sodom episode,[30] God

27. Compare the commentary of the Maharsha on *Yevamot* 64a, regarding the efficacy of prayer on behalf of another as compared to prayer for oneself. In that context, the Maharsha also cites the midrashic comment on *Bereishit* 16:5.

28. Without evaluation, Radak, *Bereishit* 16:2, observes from a *peshat* perspective that Avraham may not have prayed for Sarah regarding children as compared to Yitzchak who prayed on behalf of Rivkah.

29. Ramban, *Bereishit* 12:10, in fact, chastises Avraham for leaving *Eretz Kena'an* for Egypt and for establishing the wife/sister ruse which endangered his wife, claiming that Avraham should have trusted in God to save him and his family.

30. According to Ibn Ezra, *Bereishit* 18:26, Avraham demonstrated insight concerning the need for the righteous to actively intervene on behalf of others. In his view, Avraham asked God to save the city of Sodom only if there were enough "*tzaddikim be-tokh ha-'ir*" (*Bereishit* 18:24), those who demonstrated their fear of God in public. As

deems it appropriate to provide Avraham this same opportunity on a more personal level in his prayer for Avimelech and his household. But, whereas the decree against Sodom was not reversed despite Avraham's entreaties, and its main goal was to clarify God's ways of justice, in this context, healing is effected as a result of prayer. Avraham is taught an acute lesson of the value of prayer; he learns the power of a *navi*, one who has an intimate bond with God and to whom God listens, to bring about change not only in himself but in others as well.

What does prayer on behalf of another accomplish within the wider framework of the purpose for which the world was created? Perhaps one may gain insight through the Maharal's explanation of Rashi's commentary on the creation of the human being in *Bereishit* Ch. 1–2. Analyzing the symmetry between the creations on the successive days of creation, Rashi observes that on the first day, "heaven and earth" were created, while on each of the following days, either a creation in the heavens was brought forth (as on the second and fourth days) or a creation was brought forth on earth (as on the third and fifth days). In order to maintain symmetry and avoid *"kin'ah,"* disproportion among the created beings, God needed to create a being on the sixth day that was comprised of both heavenly and earthly components. The human being was therefore created from the dust of the earth and was bestowed with a Divine *"nishmat chayyim."*[31] Expounding on the ramifications of this *"kin'ah,"* Maharal explains that God wanted the entire world to be integrally connected (*"mekushar"*) such that the upper world (*"elyonim"*) would be linked to the lower world (*"tachtonim"*). In order to bring about this state of harmony, God created the human being, a supreme creature

Nehama Leibowitz, *Iyyunim Be-Sefer Bereishit Be-Ikvot Parshaneinu Ha-Rishonim Ve-Ha-Acharonim* (Jerusalem: Ha-Histadrut Ha-Ziyyonit Ha-Olamit, 1969), pp. 131–32, explains, only those righteous individuals who circulate within the city, influencing the masses, can truly bring the merit of salvation to the city at large.

31. See Rashi, *Bereishit* 2:7, based on *Bereishit Rabbah* 12:8; compare Rashi, *Bereishit* 1:26, based on *Bereishit Rabbah* 8:11.

who would unite all living things,[32] and through his unique composition, this being would also create a bridge between all parts of the universe.[33]

This conception of harmony within the world at large also explains, in Maharal's opinion, the midrashic approach that the human was initially created "two-faced (*du partzufim*)," the male-female components fused together.[34] The human being cannot remain a single unit, as this would lead to the misconception that there are two deities in the universe, a god in the upper realm and a god in the lower one.[35] Nevertheless, God determined that the human's preliminary creation would be in the form of a unified body in order to be able to serve its unique purpose in the created world. As the supreme, single creature in the lower world, it would have the capacity to unite all of the other living beings, as a king unites all of his subjects under his rule. Creating this uniformity in the lower world enables the human being to serve as a conduit to connect to the higher, Divine realm as well.[36]

Accordingly, God established the capacity of prayer so that the human being would have the potential to develop a link between himself and the Divine, a connection between the *Olam Elyonim* and the *Olam Tachtonim*. When an individual prays on behalf of another, creating a bridge between the living beings on earth and uniting with others, this facilitates the realization of a universal harmony which draws down God's Divine blessing on earth.

The healing of Avimelech and his household's reproductive capacities is linked within the narratives of *Bereishit* to God's remembrance of Sarah and the reversal of her state of barrenness, as reported in the first two verses of Ch. 21. While the promise of progeny through Sarah was already stipulated in Ch.'s 17–18, it is not implemented until this juncture. With successful prayer on behalf of another, for the sake of healing

---

32. As Rashi, *Bereishit* 6:7, notes, "Everything was created for the human being." Compare *Sanhedrin* 108a.
33. See Maharal's explanation of Rashi, *Bereishit* 2:7, in relation to Rashi, *Bereishit* 1:26, in Hartmann, ed., *Chumash Gur Aryeh Ha-Shalem*, 1:43, 63, respectively.
34. See Rashi, *Bereishit* 1:27, based on *Berakhot* 61a; compare *Bereishit Rabbah* 8:1.
35. See Rashi's comments on *Bereishit* 2:18.
36. See Maharal's explanation of Rashi, *Bereishit* 1:27, in Hartmann, ed., *Chumash Gur Aryeh Ha-Shalem*, 1:46–47, and see especially nn. 294, 295.

another, the realities of both Sarah and Avraham can be changed now as well.[37] Maintaining that Sarah's barrenness is reversed even prior to Avimelech and his household's recovery, Rashi explains,

> Whoever prays for mercy for the sake of another, when he himself is in need of that very same thing [for which he prays for the other person], he will be answered first. As it is stated, "Avraham prayed … and God remembered." God had already remembered her before He healed Avimelech.[38]

Prayer for another is emulated by Avraham's son, Yitzchak, when his wife, Rivkah, is in a state of barrenness. As *Bereishit* 25:21 relates, "Yitzchak entreated God (*va-ye'etar Yitzchak la-Hashem*) on behalf of his wife[39] for she was barren, and God listened to his entreaty, and Rivkah his wife conceived." Presuming that the unusual verb for the act of prayer, "*va-ye'etar*," derives from *atar*, a pitchfork, the talmudic sage, R. Yitzchak, explains: Just as a pitchfork overturns the wheat in a granary from one place to another, the prayers of the righteous serve to overturn God's attribute of anger to that of mercy.[40] Commenting on this context, R. Bechaye elaborates that "through prayer, especially on behalf of another, the

---

37. As Zornberg observes concerning Avraham's prayer for Avimelech, *Genesis: The Beginning of Desire*, p. 113, "The definitions that separate self from other are swept away, a law of nature dissolves, widening possibility. As a result, not Avimelech alone but Abraham himself finally becomes fertile." Compare Alter, *The Five Books of Moses*, 101, notes on *Bereishit* 20:18, who observes the theme of procreation that is reflected in the episodes before and after *Bereishit* 20, beginning with Lot's daughters' cohabitation with their father for the sake of reproduction and ending with Sarah's fertility.

38. Rashi, *Bereishit* 21:1, based on *Bava Kamma* 72a; see Rashi's analysis of that talmudic passage, where he explains that this exposition is based on the usage of the perfect *pakad*, as opposed to the imperfect verb with a *vav* conversive, *va-yifkod*, thereby acquiring the meaning of a pluperfect.

39. This translation of "*le-nokhach ishto*" follows the interpretations of Rashbam, Radak, and Bekhor Shor, *Bereishit* 25:21; Radak also posits that one may render, "in his wife's presence." Rashi, *Bereishit* 25:21 (based on *Bereishit Rabbah* 63:5), interprets that Isaac prayed in one corner, and Rivkah also prayed on her own behalf in another corner.

40. See *Yevamot* 64a.

righteous individual rises up from his mundane, earthly reality, elevates himself to reach out to the Divine, and draws down God's presence in the world, revealing His Divine providence (*ha-tzaddik bi-tefilato, mach-shavto meshotetet ve-olah mi-matah le-ma'alah ve-achar kakh mamshikh u-morid ha-shefa mi-ma'alah le-matah*)."[41]

Within the same talmudic passage, R. Yitzchak comments that our ancestors suffered from barrenness because "God desires the prayers of the righteous." This desire for prayer is especially connected to the bringing forth of new life, the creation of a child. Why is prayer so necessary for our ancestors with regard to the establishment of their legacy through progeny? The potency of prayer from this perspective is particularly illuminated by recalling that the first instance of "blessing" (*berakhah*) relates to God's directive to "be fruitful and multiply" and fill the earth with offspring, as related in *Bereishit* 1:22, 28. Blessing involves God establishing a connection between Himself and other living things. God blesses the world by bestowing upon the world certain powers and capacities to be able to fulfill the ultimate purpose for which it was created. These powers, however, involve a type of emulative act of godliness, because through propagation of offspring, one is in essence performing an act of creation.

This power is also evident in God's expectation that man should pray in order to bring forth the rain from which the grasses will sprout and the trees will flourish. Commenting on *Bereishit* 2:5, "*ve-khol siach ha-sadeh*[42] *terem yihyeh ba-aretz ve-khol esev ha-sadeh terem yitzmach ki lo himtir Hashem Elokim al ha-aretz ve-adam ayin la-avod et ha-adamah*" – "no shrub of the field was yet in the earth, and no herb of the field had yet sprung up, for the Lord God had not caused it to rain upon the earth, and there was not a man to till the ground," Rashi relates that only when man, who could pray for rain and recognize it as a necessity in the world, was created, did God release these rains for growth and propagation.[43] In Rashi's talmudic source, the statement is reiterated in that context con-

---

41. R. Bechaye, on *Bereishit* 25:21, in Chaim Dov Chavel, ed., *Rabbenu Bechaye: Bi'ur al Ha-Torah*, Vol. 1 (Jerusalem: Mosad Harav Kook, 1966), pp. 220–21.

42. Note as well the possible play on words between *siach* and *sichah*, conversation.

43. Rashi, *Bereishit* 2:5.

cerning God's desire for the prayers of the righteous.[44] To bring forth new life, to serve in the role as "creator," man requires blessing from above, and he must pray from below so that God may open the "spigot" and let flow His will on earth. As Maharal explicates, "[T]here did not exist here a *connection between the upper and lower* [*worlds*] (*she-lo hayah kan chibbur elyonim ve-tachtonim*), that the upper world should bestow rains downward, until man, who is between the upper and lower worlds (*she-hu bein elyonim ve-tachtonim*), brought forth the rain from the upper to the lower worlds through the prayer that man prayed."[45] Through prayer and blessing, God wants a connection to be established between Himself and the world below, and He wants man to raise himself up to establish this connection as well. Through prayer, man acknowledges that God is actively involved in the world, so much so that even nature is a kind of continuous providential act.[46] This is especially necessary in order to bring about fruition and fertility within the world. The union between man and God is what brings about procreation, growth, and development. Such a union is also apparent in prayer on behalf of another, which creates a harmony between two separate beings together with the quest for an intimate connection with God.

Ramban describes prayer as a miracle and as an expression of "*chesed*" from God who, though transcendental and distant, makes Himself accessible through the gift of prayer.[47] R. Yehudah Ha-Levi describes prayer as "food for the soul."[48] By serving as a medium for "loosening knots" and tying new bonds, prayer, as taught by the actions of our patriarchs and matriarchs, creates a forum for establishing a dialogue

44. *Chullin* 60b.
45. Maharal, *Sefer Chiddushei Aggadot Maharal Mi-Prague* (London: L. Honig and Sons, 1960), Vol. 4, p. 98, on *Chullin* 60b; this source is also cited in Hartmann, ed., *Chumash Gur Aryeh Ha-Shalem*, Vol. 1 on *Bereishit*, p. 56, n. 29.
46. As we say in the blessings before Shema, "*ha-mechadesh be-tuvo be-khol yom tamid Ma'aseh Bereishit.*" Compare R. Meir Leibush Malbim's definition of nature as a continuous miracle in his commentary on *Tehillim* 93:1.
47. Ramban, *Bereishit* 46:15. See as well Ramban's comments on the fifth positive commandment in Chaim Dov Chavel, *Sefer Ha-Mitzvot Le-Ha-Rambam im Hasagot Ha-Ramban* (Jerusalem: Mosad Harav Kook, 1981), p. 156.
48. See Judah ha-Levi, *Sefer Ha-Kuzari*, translated, annotated, and introduced by Yehuda Even Shmuel (Tel Aviv: Dvir Pub., 1972), p. 101, in *Ma'amar* 3:5.

between man and God. This ongoing conversation cultivates an individual's awareness of his own reality and the reality of others, and the ultimate dependence on God for one's very existence and state of being.[49]

---

49. Compare Ramban, *Shemot* 13:16, on this latter point, in Chaim Dov Chavel, ed., *Rabbenu Moshe ben Nachman: Perush Ha-Torah* (Jerusalem: Mosad Harav Kook, 1959), Vol. 1, p. 346.

I would like to thank Dr. Ephraim Kanarfogel and Dr. David Shatz who read a draft of this essay and provided helpful suggestions, many of which I have incorporated into the final version.

Rabbi Daniel Z. Feldman

חיי שרה: Living the Double Standard

I

The test that Eliezer[1] devised to discover a proper match for Yitzchak must be considered one of the most successful creative strategies of all history. Charged by the first founding father of the Jewish people, Avraham, with finding a match for the second, Yitzchak, Eliezer prays to God for a "*chesed*" that his mission will be successful based on the following plan: having travelled to the area of Avraham's family, Eliezer will wait by the wells that provide water to the locals; when the women come out to draw water, he will approach one and ask to be given water; one who not only provides water for him, but also offers to give water to his camels, will show herself to be the appropriate match. Apparently granted the Divine assistance he requested, Eliezer is introduced by his plan to Rivkah, an exquisitely qualified candidate who becomes one of

---

1. Although the text itself does not name the "*eved*," it is traditionally understood, and explicit in rabbinic literature, that the reference is to Eliezer.

the matriarchs of the Jewish people and thus a key builder of the moral and spiritual foundation of the *am hanivchar*.[2]

It is therefore perhaps surprising to note that *Chazal* seem to maintain a somewhat critical attitude towards Eliezer's methods, as expressed in at least two talmudic statements.[3] In one,[4] Eliezer is described as one who asked "improperly" (*bikesh she-lo ke-hogen*), and was nonetheless answered "properly." He neglected to ensure that his test would exclude any candidate who would be for some reason undesirable; despite this negligence, his stratagem brought about a worthy result.[5]

More striking is a second passage[6] which appears to allege a halakhic violation. In discussing the prohibition of *nichush*,[7] which might loosely be translated as "superstitious behavior," the Talmud asserts, in the name of Rav, the following standard: "Any *'nachash'* that is not as Eliezer the servant of Avraham or as Yonatan ben Shaul[8] is not *nachash*." In other words, it seems that Eliezer's behavior serves as the baseline to determine when one is in violation of the Biblical prohibition of *nichush*.

This assertion is shocking on at least two levels. On one level, it is difficult to believe that Eliezer would act inappropriately. Yes, Eliezer was not Jewish or bound to the *mitzvot* of the Torah; but whether it is assumed that Eliezer adhered to the standards of his distinguished master,[9] or it is taken to be the case that superstitious practice is forbidden to non-Jews as well,[10] there is ample reason to expect Eliezer to avoid transgressing in this way.[11]

---

2. *Bereishit* Ch. 24.
3. It should be noted, however, that some statements in rabbinic literature are more positively inclined toward Eliezer's plan; see, for example, *Kallah Rabati*, end of Ch. 3.
4. *Ta'anit* 4a. See also *Bereishit Rabbah* 60:3.
5. A creative interpretation to this passage can be found in R. David Shlomo Eibeshutz, *Arvei Nachal, Chayyei Sarah, derush* 3.
6. *Chullin* 95b.
7. *Vayikra* 19:26.
8. The reference is to *Shemuel* I (14:6–12).
9. See Rashi, *Bereishit* 15:2 and 24:42.
10. See *Sanhedrin* 56b.
11. The assumption that Eliezer was observant of *Halakhah* is presumably also included in the literature that exists deriving rules of *shelichut* (agency) for marriage from

But there is a more fundamental problem. The nature of the objection to superstition is that it is irrational, and involves living one's life based on meaningless signs. No one would maintain that one cannot make decisions based on rational, relevant factors; that is the essence of intelligent living. In the case of Eliezer, he was seeking, most appropriately, a paragon of *chesed*. Accordingly, he devised a rational test to identify one who would act in a manner displaying *chesed*. How could that plan be considered in any way connected to the transgression of *nichush*?[12]

This issue underlies a debate among the *Rishonim*. The Rambam,[13] in delineating the prohibition of *lo tenachashu*, gives several examples of proscribed practice, and closes with the words, "...like Eliezer the servant of Avraham – and so too all things like this are prohibited, and one who commits one of these acts is subject to lashes." Apparently, the Rambam is accusing Eliezer of the transgression of *nichush*, or at least what would be a transgression for a Jew.[14] The Ra'avad takes sharp issue

Eliezer's behavior (see, for example, R. Asher Weiss, *Minchat Asher, Bereishit* #27). Tangentially, it is interesting to note that R. Levi Yitzchak of Berditchev, in his *Kedushat Levi*, even assumes that Eliezer was observant of custom, in that he declined an offer of food (*Bereishit* 24:23), apparently because he was an agent (*shaliach*) for *kiddushin* on behalf of the groom, and thus fasted in keeping with the custom that the groom fasts on his wedding day (see Rama, *Even Ha-Ezer* 61:1). While some question this assumption based on the fact that in the process of testing Rivkah, Eliezer drank water (see *Minchat Asher*, ibid., fn 1), it is possible to defend R. Levi Yitzchak (who, after all, was the great defender of the Jewish people) by noting that the premise that a *shaliach* fasts is based on the theory that the fast is to prevent drunkenness (see the glosses of *Ikvei Sofer* to *Responsa Hit'orerut Teshuvah, Even Ha-Ezer* 25), and some *posekim* maintain that such reasoning indicates that the groom is permitted to drink water during his wedding day fast if necessary (see *Arukh HaShulchan, Even Ha-Ezer* 61:21).

12. In fact, R. Yonatan Eibeshutz (*Tiferet Yehonatan* to *Chayyei Sarah*, s.v. *vi-hayah;* see also s.v. *vatimaher*) asserts that no *nichush* could have been involved, because the sign Eliezer was requesting was a "*siman muvhak*," or an unusually compelling indication. This is so for reasons that combine personal qualities with Divine guidance: providing water to all of the camels would be an extraordinarily demanding task, and the willingness to do so would be an irrefutable statement of Rivkah's character, while the miraculous nature of her being physically capable of doing so (see Rashi 24:17) would be an equally irrefutable endorsement from Above.

13. *Hilkhot Avodat Kokhavim* 11:4.

14. The *Kesef Mishneh*, ibid., suggests that the Rambam is doing so consistent with his

with the Rambam's formulation, maintaining that Eliezer's behavior was permissible, that questioning it is unthinkable, and that the Rambam was confused by the Talmud's choice of language.[15]

Indeed, other *Rishonim* maintain that Eliezer was innocent of any sin in this case.[16] These *Rishonim*, represented by the Ran,[17] assert that the Talmud invokes Eliezer (and Yonatan) not to allege any impropriety, but to focus on one isolated detail: Eliezer's absolute commitment to his test. Indeed, Eliezer's test was a rational one, not at all subject to the prohibition of *nichush*. However, if one is utilizing an irrational indicator, he would violate *nichush* if he relied on this sign with a commitment equal to that of Eliezer to his permissible test.[18]

Thus, it emerges from the Talmud that in order to violate *nichush*,

apparent view (*Hilkhot Melakhim* 9:1) that non-Jews are not barred from *nichush*, while the Ra'avad can be understood as disagreeing.

15. In applying the Eliezer model to practical *Halakhah*, the Rama (*Yoreh Deah* 179:4) quotes two opinions on the matter, and appears to recommend stringency, while the Vilna Gaon adopts the view of the Ra'avad.

16. Included among these *Rishonim* is *Tosafot* (s.v *ke-Eli'ezer*). However, their suggestion, that Eliezer actually reserved judgment until later, is difficult in that it not only exculpates Eliezer, but in doing so apparently removes any relevance whatsoever to *nichush*, thus leaving the talmudic passage unexplained; accordingly, the Maharsha notes that this explanation is only given in accordance with the assumption that a non-Jew is prohibited in *nichush*, while Rav, the author of the talmudic statement, was assuming that Eliezer was permitted to engage in *nichush*. See also Chizkuni (*Bereishit* 24:23) and Radak (*Shemuel* I 14:9).

See also R. Yaakov Ariel's *Mei-Ohalei Torah*, pp. 49–51, where he offers an innovative explanation based on the theory that the Rambam's criticism was addressed not at what Eliezer actually did, but at the slightly different sequence of events he related to Lavan.

17. *Chiddushim* to *Chullin*, and *Derashot*, #12. See also *Sefer Yereim*, 335; *Kesef Mishneh*; Abarbanel, *Devarim*, 18:9; and *Bach, Yoreh Deah* 179.

18. An alternate version of this interpretation defends Eliezer not because of his rationality, but because his faith was not really placed in his sign but rather in God, as per his prayer, and thus his dependence was not only defensible but actually laudable as an expression of *bitachon*. Note also Ritva to *Chullin* who invokes the merit of Avraham in this context. See *Seforno; Bach, Yoreh Deah* 179; *To'afot Re'em* to *Sefer Yereim*, ibid., #6; *Torah Temimah, Bereishit* Ch. 24, # 17; and R. Yaakov Etlinger, *Chiddushei Binyan Tziyon* to *Chullin*. See also R. Aharon Miasnik, *Minchat Aharon, Bereishit*, pp. 215–223, and the lengthy excursus on this in R. David Kviat, *Sukkat David* to *Chayyei Sarah*, pp. 262–268, and that of R. David Yitzchak Mann in his

two conditions must be present: a) the basis for the decision must be irrational, and not actually relevant to the issues involved; b) the decision must be made as a result of complete commitment to the irrational sign, and not be the result of a combination of factors. Apparently, according to the second view in the *Rishonim*, the relevance of Eliezer is only to condition (b); as his condition was rational, it is instructive only in its level of commitment. It remains somewhat startling then, that Eliezer, acting rationally and innocently, should be held up as a negative role model.

While this second view of the *Rishonim* exonerates Eliezer of any guilt, perhaps it might nonetheless be suggested that the tinge of disapproval exhibited by *Chazal* is rooted in this very approach.

True, it was rational and appropriate for Eliezer to devise a test to ascertain if Rivkah was a person of *chesed*. Where the test merited criticism, however, was in its absolute quality – the assumption that if Rivkah passed, she was a person of *chesed*, and if she didn't, she wasn't. In other words, the test assumed a perfect correlation between an attribute and an action.[19] While clearly a relationship between the two must exist, it is

Dei Ba'er to *Chayyei Sarah*, pp. 218–222. This approach is also implicit in Rashi; see *Da'at Zekeinim Mi-Ba'alei Ha-Tosafot* who questions him based on the talmudic statement that he asked "improperly."

The *Levush* has a different formulation: the *nichush* that is prohibited is when one wishes to divine the future based on his sign. However, if one is attempting to ascertain a fact already in existence, such signs are permitted. As such, Eliezer can be defended in that he was searching for personal attributes already inherent in the candidate; while at the same time, his commitment can be used as a model for the prohibited version of *nichush*.

19. There are two assumptions being made here: a) that indeed, Eliezer was testing for *chesed* solely through this single challenge; and b) that Eliezer tested only for *chesed*, and no other attributes or factors. Admittedly, both assumptions can be questioned. The first assumption is consistent with the Biblical text (although not exclusively so) and particularly the talmudic text, and is expressed by the Maharsha to *Chullin* (within the view of Rav, who connects Eliezer with *nichush*).

The second assumption is stated by Rashi, but is challenged by the Ramban, who argues that Eliezer must have checked for other attributes as well. (R. Simcha M.Z. Broide, in his *Sam Derekh* to *Bereishit*, pp. 134–135, suggests that the debate between Rashi and the Ramban is paralleled in the debate between the Rambam and the Ra'avad.) According to the *Beit Ha-Levi*, Eliezer's test actually tested for not the case that an action always accurately displays the attribute from which it is assumed to emanate. The observer might misjudge the source of a discrete action or inaction; or it may simply not be representative, colored by some other factor of which the observer is unaware. A kind person may not help out a person in need because of preoccupation or justifiable distraction, while an unkind person may help because of an ulterior, selfish motive.

The automatic linking of attribute and action is the source of much of human conflict: "if he was a really nice guy, he would do what I need;" "if she really loved me, she wouldn't do such and such." All too often, the interpretation is artificial or incomplete, and the other party forms a completely inaccurate impression. This is related to what is now identified by psychologists as the "fundamental attribution error," a reference to the human tendency to see the actions of others as wholly representative of their character, while the one evaluating readily minimizes such interpretations when applied to his own actions. If he, the "other," fails to do the "kind" thing, he is unkind; if I fail to do that same thing, I am generally kind but at the moment attending to other priorities.

It might be suggested that this tendency is one reason for the prohibition of *lashon ha-ra*, which forbids the relating of derogatory information, even when it is true. Unfortunately, human nature is such that it is very difficult not to form a character judgment after hearing of an incident that, while factually true, may be isolated or otherwise unrepresentative. As such, we are required to refrain from relating such facts, as their technical accuracy does not prevent the violation of "do not bear [or transmit] a false report."[20]

---

three attributes (see also R. Eliezer Perlow, *Imrei Eli'ezer* to *Bereishit*, who innovatively suggests that Eliezer himself was tested). R. Yosef Shalom Elyashiv asserts that Rivkah was also tested (afterwards) for *yirat Shamayim*; see *Divrei Aggadah*, pp. 59–66. By contrast, see *Sukkat David*, ibid., who explains the assumption that the *chesed* test was sufficient for all purposes.

20. *Shemot* 23:2; see *Pesachim* 118a.

II

The question then becomes, if Eliezer indeed acted improperly in his request, why was he so gloriously successful? Why did God reward an unseemly request with a perfect response?[21]

It would seem that this was one instance where the test specifically asked for an absolute correlation, for a quality that expressed itself constantly, without exception. As Rav Joseph B. Soloveitchik noted:[22]

> What key virtue did the members of this household possess that made them fit for and worthy of joining the covenant? The answer is *hesed*, kindness expressed through *hakhnasat orechim*, hospitality… *hakhnasat orechim* may have its source in one of two human qualities: either genuine kindness or civility and courtesy. A polite person quite often conveys the impression of being charitable and good, but inwardly he is completely indifferent and detached. The act of the polite person is related to an etiquette, the act of the kind person to an ethic.
>
> The criterion that enables us to distinguish between politeness and kindness is quite obvious. The element of perseverance and patience is to be found in the kind person but not in the merely polite person. The kind person has unlimited patience. The needy may call on a kind person for help over a long period of time, for years and years. The appeal will always be heard and acted upon. The polite person's patience is limited. If repeatedly approached, he will stop extending help. Any illogical plea for help, any exaggeration or crossing the borderline of decency, will be harshly rejected and condemned if the helper is merely acting in accordance with etiquette. But in the case of kindness, there is no limit to the benefactor's perseverance and tolerance. He helps

---

21. This question is also addressed, from the perspective of those *Rishonim* who believed that a transgression was committed, by R. Aharon Yehudah Grossman in his *Ve-Darashta Ve-Chakarta Al Ha-Torah*, III, pp. 44–47.
22. "Abraham's Journey: Reflections on the Life of the Founding Patriarch" (eds. David Shatz, Joel B. Wolowelsky, and Reuven Ziegler, Toras HoRav Foundation/KTAV Publishing House, inc, New York, NY 2008) pp. 195–196.

even people who are vulgar and coarse. He takes abuse. Nothing can alienate him from the person in need.

Eliezer wanted to find out what motivated Rebecca's actions. Was it spiritual nobility and kindness, or good manners and civility? He asked her to do things that were outrageous. He said, "Let me sip a little water from your pitcher" (Gen. 24:17), as opposed to asking her to hand him the pitcher. In other words, he told her that he would do nothing; she was to draw water from the well and pour it into his mouth. Isn't this distasteful and tasteless? Had she just been polite, she would have splashed the water in his face. Why did he ask a young girl to water the camels, something women did not do in antiquity? Couldn't one of his servants have taken the pitcher down to the well, brought up the water, and taken care of the animals?

The answer is that Eliezer was testing her patience. She passed the test with flying colors. She did not feel hurt; she was not repulsed by the newcomer's primitive bluntness and lack of good manners. She practiced hospitality even though the traveler was coarse and rude. The quality of *erekh appayim* prevailed, and Rebecca became the mother of the nation.[23]

Rav Soloveitchik's comments appear to be stating that the test was not just for *chesed* in any basic sense, but specifically in an absolute sense; that only one who would express kindness without exception and in all circumstances would qualify. As such, it is understandable that actions could, in this unusual case, be equated absolutely with attributes; the unique demand of the situation called for it. Further, it seems that the very nature of Rivkah's *chesed* was itself one of transcending the "action-based judgment" toward others. Similarly, the *Chatam Sofer*[24] notes that since Yitzchak's dominant attribute was *din*, or strict justice, his comple-

23. Compare also R. Baruch Mordechai Ezrachi, *Birkhat Mordechai, Bereishit* pp. 263–265; R. Chaim Mordechai Katz, *Be'er Mechokeik*; and also R. Avraham Heshel Ryzman, *Iyyunim BaParshah, Bereishit* pp. 153–156. See also R. Avraham Rivlin, *Iyyunei Parashah*, pp. 90–96, who also provides an evocative description of just how difficult Rivkah's actions were.
24. *Torat Moshe, Bereishit* 24:14

mentary match would best be found in one who was representative of complete, nondiscriminatory *chesed*.[25]

Without a doubt, Rivkah's behavior is extraordinary, and can hardly represent the expectation placed upon the average person.[26] Nonetheless, perhaps there is a valuable lesson to be learned from this episode for all human relationships, marriage and otherwise. This lesson is the benefit of living life by a double standard: when evaluating others'

---

25. See also R. Pinchas Friedman, *Shevilei Pinchas, Bereishit* v. 11, # 12 and 14. See as well the lengthy discussion of this in R. Elisha Chaim Horowitz, *Bei Chiya*, pp. 69–75, including his citation of *Kol Mevasser Al Ha-Torah*.

26. It is also striking that some *posekim* feel that Rivkah displayed halakhic nuance as well. The *Sefer Chasidim* (#531), cited by the *Magen Avraham* (*Orach Chayyim* 167:18), cites Rivkah's behavior as proof that the prohibition against eating before one's animals do (*Berakhot* 40a, *Gittin* 62a) only applies to food, and not to drink; accordingly, Rivkah gave water to Eliezer first, and only afterward volunteered to give water to the camels. The *Or Ha-Chayyim*, however, maintains that Rivkah acted as she did because she perceived Eliezer to be in mortal danger from thirst (and thus her behavior should not be assumed to be normative; see also *Meshekh Chokhmah*, and R. Yaakov Moshe Feldman, *Meshivat Nefesh*, *Bereishit* 24:18). See also R. Avraham Meir Goldner's essay in *Ma'ayan Ha-Shabbat* (pp. 18–21) and R. Avraham Stern, *Mesadder Chillukim Ve-Shittot*, 25, for further challenging of the *Sefer Chasidim*.

Assuming the *Sefer Chasidim*'s position to be accurate, R Tzvi Pesach Frank (*Responsa Har Tzvi, Orach Chayyim*, 90) posits two possible explanations: a) thirst is a more urgent and severe crisis than hunger, and thus the priority balance is shifted to humans (see *Torah Temimah, Bereishit* Ch. 24, #18, for a similar approach); or b) the concern in general is that one will become preoccupied with one's meal and thus forget to feed the animals; apparently, if one is only drinking, this concern is not present.

Alternatively, the *Ketav Sofer* (*Responsa, Orach Chayyim* 32) agreed that Rivkah acts here as a halakhic role model, but disputes the specific conclusion of the *Sefer Chasidim*. In his understanding, Rivkah was free to serve the human before the animal because she was giving a gift to another; the prohibition only applies when one is feeding himself. See also R. Meir Yosef Birntsweig, *Otzerot Megadim, Bereishit* (pp. 281–288); R. Avraham Mattatyah HaKohen Kagan, *Mattet Yadi* (*hashmatot*, p. 237–238) and R. Yechiel Michel of Plotzk, *Chashrat Mayim* (*hashmatot* to *Gittin* 61). (The *Ketav Sofer* cites his position in the name of his father, the *Chatam Sofer*, who indeed asserts likewise in his *Torat Moshe* to *Bereishit* (s.v. *ve-amrah*); see there where, based on that position, he attributed even greater halakhic awareness and acumen to Rivkah in interpreting her actions. Similarly, see R. Moshe Yehudah Yakobovitz, *Zikhron Moshe* to *Bereishit*, and *Torah Temimah, Bereishit* Ch. 24, # 19.)

actions, one should recognize the frequent lack of correlation between these actions and their actual attributes; understand that they can be kind people even if not always displaying the actions we would identify with kindness. When one is considering one's own actions, however, one should act with the opposite mentality, recognizing that one's own positive attributes are often only perceived by others through the actions that usually display them; accordingly, one would try to manifest his quality of *chesed* (for example) as unilaterally and absolutely as possible. In other words, harmony is best served by attitudes that are the reverse of the more instinctive "fundamental attribution error."

Indeed, this approach, this "double standard," is far from instinctive. To separate the behavior that we see from the sweeping evaluations that we are inclined to make is profoundly challenging. Likewise, to strive to avoid relying on exceptions in our own actions – to express positive traits as consistently as possible, regardless of the circumstances – requires a discipline and a commitment evocative of a *Rivkah Immenu*. Nonetheless, striving to actualize *Ma'aseh avot siman le-banim* is the proud legacy and challenge of the Jewish people.

Rabbi Dr. Aaron Levine

תולדות: The Sale of the Birthright and the Bilateral Monopoly Model

INTRODUCTION

In the teaching of our Sages, Yaakov personifies the character trait of
emet (truth).[1] One of the challenges in understanding Yaakov's character
is that the Biblical account of a number of episodes of his life appears
to be inconsistent with the attribute of *emet*. One such instance is the
Biblical description of how Yaakov acquired the birthright from Esav:

> Once when Yaakov was making a stew, Esav came in from the
> fields famished. Whereupon Esav said to Yaakov: "Let me swallow
> some of that red pottage, for I am exhausted[2] and famished!"[3] ...
> said Yaakov: "First sell me your birthright." Said Esav: "I am about

---

1. Nachmanides, *Ha-Emunah Ve-Ha-Bittachon* 15; R. Bechaye b. Asher, *Bereishit*
    25:27.
2. Rashi, *Bereishit* 25:29; R. Chizkiyahu b. Manoach, *Chizkuni*, *Bereishit* 25:29.
3. *Chizkuni*, *Bereishit* 25:29; R. Chayyim b. Moshe Attar, *Or Ha-Chayyim*, 25:31.

to die; of what use is a birthright to me?" Said Yaakov: "First give me your oath." So he gave him his oath, and sold his birthright to Yaakov. Yaakov then gave Esav bread and stewed lentils. He ate and drank, then rose and went away. Thus did Esav disdain the birthright. (*Bereishit* 25:29–34)

Should we regard the sale of the birthright as a "fair deal" entailing a *net gain* in well-being for both Yaakov and Esav? No. Mutual net gain can only be presumed when parties enter into a transaction on a *voluntary* basis. In this context, A would not give up something to B unless A felt he was getting from B something more valuable than what he was giving up. Similarly, B would not give up something to A unless he felt that what A was offering was more valuable to him than what he was asked to give up. Mutual net gain cannot, however, be presumed in the case at hand. Given Esav's exhausted and famished state when he sold the birthright, the transaction should be regarded as a *coercive* one from the standpoint of Esav. How can conducting a transaction of coercion be reconciled with the attribute of *emet*?

Consider, however, that the birthright must inhere in either the person of Yaakov or Esav and cannot be transferred to anyone else.[4] Yaakov's negotiation with Esav for the birthright therefore falls into the economic model of bilateral monopoly. The salient feature of this model is that no one other than the buyer participating in the negotiation is offering a bid for the item the seller wants to sell. Likewise, no one else is selling the item the seller is offering for sale. Accordingly, neither buyer nor seller can claim that a better opportunity was available at the time the transaction took place. The outcome of the negotiation will therefore depend on the relative leverage each party perceives he has over his opposite number.

From the perspective of economic theory the birthright case fits into the bilateral monopoly model, with the distinctive feature of the case being that leverage is lopsidedly in the hands of Yaakov.

Notwithstanding the ethically indifferent attitude economic theory would take in regard to the birthright sale, for Jewish law the issue

---

4.   *Or Ha-Chayyim*, *Bereishit* 25:33.

of fairness remains. In a commercial transaction the price terms of an agreement are subject to the law of *ona'ah* (price fraud). Moreover, one may question the propriety for Yaakov to play a waiting game and strategically make his bid for the birthright when Esav was exhausted and famished. Does this not constitute exploitative conduct on Yaakov's part?

THE BILATERAL MONOPOLY CASE IN JEWISH LAW

Our purpose here will be to explore the above two issues. Let's begin with the issue of price fairness within the context of a bilateral monopoly model. The relevant case here is the following Baraitha:

> It has been taught, R. Yehudah b. Batera (mid 1st. cent.) said: The sale of a horse, sword and buckler on (the field of)[5] battle are not subject to *ona'ah* (price fraud), because one's very life is dependent upon them.[6]

To see why the battlefield transaction falls into the ambit of the bilateral monopoly case we need only note that under the life threatening conditions of the battlefield neither buyer nor seller will seek an alternative to the opportunity at hand. What this means is that certainty that the seller's asking price exceeds the ordinary price for the item will not cause the buyer to withdraw. Likewise, certainty that the buyer's bid is below what the item ordinarily trades at will not cause the seller to withdraw. Since there is no alternative for both parties other than the transaction at hand, it will be the relative perceptions of leverage that will determine the outcome.

Whether R. Yehudah's ruling represents mainstream talmudic thought is a matter of dispute among the early decisors. R. Hai ben Sherira of Pumbedita (939–1038 CE)[7] and R. Yitzchak ben Yaakov Alfasi of Algeria (1012–1103 CE)[8] rule that R. Yehudah b. Batera's opinion represents a minority view and should therefore be rejected. R. Chananel

---

5. Rashi, *Bava Metzia* 58b.
6. Baraitha, *Bava Metzia* 58b.
7. R. Hai b. Sherira, cited in Rif, *Bava Metzia* 58b.
8. Rif, *Bava Metzia* 58b.

b. Chushiel, an eleventh-century North African decisor, however, rules in accordance with R. Yehudah b. Batera.[9]

Note that the ethics of the battlefield case turns on whether the law of *ona'ah* applies in the setting of a battlefield.[10] Let's proceed to identify the ethical norm of *ona'ah* and the rationale behind it.

One of the Torah's central tenets for the marketplace is the prohibition against price fraud: "When you make a sale to your fellow or when you buy from the hand of your fellow, do not victimize one another" (*Vayikra* 25:14).

The law of *ona'ah* prohibits an individual from concluding a transaction at a price that is more favorable to himself than some reference price.

Depending on how widely the price of the subject transaction departs from the reference price, the injured party may have recourse to void or adjust the transaction at hand. The Sages identified three degrees of *ona'ah*. Provided the price discrepancy is assessed to be within the margin of error,[11] the plaintiff's right to void the transaction is recognized when the difference between the sale price and the reference price is more than one-sixth.[12] We shall refer to this level of *ona'ah* violation as first-degree *ona'ah*. The plaintiff's right here consists of only a right to cancel the transaction at hand, but does not extend to a right to keep the transaction intact and demand a price reduction on the basis of the *ona'ah* involved.[13]

Second-degree *ona'ah* occurs when the differential is exactly one-

---

9. *Bava Metzia* 58b.
10. In the opinion of R. Moshe Ha-Kohen of Lunel (quoted in *Shiitah Mekubbetzet*, *Bava Metzia* 58b), the disposition of the battlefield case hinges on whether it can be compared to a similar case recorded at *Bava Kamma* 115a. The elements of the *Bava Kamma* case are: an absconding criminal agrees to pay a ferryman an above market price for providing him with conveyance across a river. Given the coercive circumstances, the criminal is entitled to recoup the differential. For an analysis of the two cases see Aaron Levine, *Case Studies in Jewish Business Ethics* (Hoboken, New Jersey; KTAV Publishing Company Inc. Yeshiva University Press, 2000), p. 159.
11. *Bava Batra* 78a and Rashi, ad loc.
12. *Shulchan Arukh, Choshen Mishpat*, 227:4.
13. *Sh. Ar.*, op. cit. 227:4 and *Sema*, ad loc., n. 6. Expressing a minority opinion in this matter is R. Yonah b. Avraham Gerondi.

sixth. In such a case, neither of the parties may subsequently void the transaction on account of the price discrepancy. The plaintiff is, however, entitled to full restitution of the *ona'ah* involved.[14]

Finally, third-degree *ona'ah* occurs when the sale price differs from the reference price by less than one-sixth. Here, the transaction not only remains binding, but, in addition, the complainant has no legal claim to the price differential.[15]

Elsewhere we have demonstrated that the reference price for the *ona'ah* claim is nothing other than the competitive norm. Identifying the reference price as the competitive norm makes the *ona'ah* complaint an opportunity cost claim. We have also demonstrated that the *ona'ah* claim is not just a claim of ignorance of the market norm at the time the transaction took place. Instead, the law of *ona'ah* confers a market participant with the *right* to transact on the basis of the competitive norm. This right is not lost unless the plaintiff signals that he waives his right in this matter.[16]

Once we recognize that *ona'ah* is an opportunity cost claim, the relevant marketplace for adjudicating the *ona'ah* claim should be demarcated by the *mekomo ve-sha'ato* (lit. its place and its time) rule. Pertaining to the liquidation procedure for property dedicated to the Sanctuary, the rule states that the sale of such property for the benefit of the Sanctuary must be conducted both in the locale ("*mekomo*") where the dedication was made and in the time period ("*sha'ato*") when the dedication was made ("*ein le-hekdesh ela mekomo ve-sha'ato*").[17] The *mekomo ve-sha'ato* rule, according to Nachmanides (1194–1270 CE)[18] and R. Yom Tov Ishbili (ca. 1250–1330 CE),[19] applies not only to the Sanctuary but to monetary matters generally. Explicitly positing the *mekomo ve-sha'ato* rule in connection with the law of *ona'ah* is R. Avraham David

---

14. *Sh. Ar.*, op. cit. 227:2.
15. *Sh. Ar.*, op. cit., 227:2.
16. Aaron Levine, "*Ona'ah* and The Operation of The Modern Marketplace," *Jewish Law Annual*, Hebrew University, vol. XIV (2003) pp. 225–258.
17. *Erakhin* 6:5.
18. Nachmanides, *Kiddushin* 12a.
19. Ritva, *Kiddushin* 12a.

Wahrmann (ca. 1771–1840 CE).[20] On a practical level, *mekomo* says that the reference marketplace for adjudicating the *ona'ah* claim is confined to the geographic area where the plaintiff would realistically engage in a market search for alternatives. Similarly, *sha'ato* says that the reference time period is confined to the window of time surrounding the moot transaction when supply and demand conditions are the same as when the moot transaction took place. [21]

Proceeding from the above understanding of the underpinning of the *ona'ah* claim is the following explanation of the view that validates the *ona'ah* claim in the battlefield case: Crucial here is the notion that the *market norm* is always the reference point for judging the "fairness" of the price terms of a transaction. *Mekomo ve-sha'ato* says no more than if there is a market price at the time the transaction took place; we limit the reference price to the relevant time frame and geographic area. However, if there is no organized marketplace at the time the transaction took place, the *ordinary price* that prevails under an *organized marketplace* is used as the reference point.

R. Yehudah, who throws out the *ona'ah* claim in the battlefield case, rejects the notion that the market norm is assigned the exclusive role in determining the "price fairness" of a transaction. To be sure, if a market norm exists at the time the transaction took place, it is the market norm that determines the "fairness" of the moot transaction. However, the principle of *mekomo ve-sha'ato* says that if an organized marketplace does not exist at the time the moot transaction took place, the market norm is no longer the arbiter as to whether the price terms of the moot transaction was fair. Here, the judgment of whether subjective equivalence was achieved by the plaintiff in the transaction at hand takes over as the arbiter of whether the price terms of the moot transaction was fair.

Bolstering the notion that subjective equivalence enters into the

20. R. Avraham David Wahrmann, *Kesef Ha-Kedoshim* at *Sh. Ar.*, op. cit. 227:9.
21. While the *mekomah ve-sha'ato* rule applies for the liquidation procedure for property dedicated to the Sanctuary and to the reference price for the purpose of adjudicating *ona'ah* claims, the *relevant* marketplace for these two issues is not the same. For the development of this theory see, "*Ona'ah* and The Operation of The Modern Marketplace," op. cit. pp. 243–248.

adjudication of *ona'ah* claims can be seen from R. Asher b. Yechiel's (Rosh, 1250–1327 CE) analysis of third-degree *ona'ah*.

Noting the absence of any provision for legal redress in third-degree *ona'ah* cases, R. Asher speculates whether it might be permissible, in the first instance, to contract into third-degree *ona'ah*. Pivotal to the resolution of this question, in R. Asher's view, is the definition of market price. Is market price to be understood as a single value, or is it to be defined as the range of deviations of less than one-sixth from the competitive norm? Rosh defends the range of prices view on the basis of both demand and supply considerations. Consider, if the buyer has a particular liking for the item at hand, he may be willing to pay a little more than what he believes the competitive norm is. Likewise, if a seller is in need of cash, he may deliberately agree to sell his merchandise a little below what he believes the market norm is.[22] Adopting the latter view leads to the conclusion that third-degree *ona'ah* is not fraud at all. Subscription to the single value reference price benchmark leads, however, to the conclusion that knowledge of the market norm prohibits either party from contracting into a price agreement that is even slightly more favorable to himself than the norm. The absence of legal redress for third-degree *ona'ah* would then be explained by the presumption that when the degree of *ona'ah* involved is of such a relatively small amount, the plaintiff waives his claim to restitution. This presumption follows from our inability to fix the value of the article sold.[23] While some experts would insist that *ona'ah* took place, others would just as vehemently deny it. Because the experts are divided as to whether *ona'ah* occurred,

---

22. In defending the range of values approach to third degree *ona'ah*, Rosh anticipates by at least five hundred years the modern economic concepts of consumer surplus and inventory cycle. For a detailed presentation of this contention, see, ibid., pp. 236–238.

23. Implicit in Rosh's analysis is the presumption that the product is differentiated. It is for this reason that experts would likely not be in agreement if price fraud took place when the degree of the *ona'ah* under dispute is third-degree *ona'ah*. If, however, the product market was homogeneous, there would be no dispute among experts. Everyone would agree that price fraud took place. For elaboration and sources for this point, see "*Ona'ah* and The Operation of The Modern Marketplace," op. cit. p. 239.

and, if it did, by how much, we may safely presume that the victim of this possible price fraud waives his rights to restitution.[24]

In throwing out the ona'ah claim in the battlefield case on the basis of the judgment that the plaintiff achieved subjective equivalence, R. Yehudah finds precedent in that third degree ona'ah cases are thrown out, according to one approach in the Rosh, based on this self-same judgment that the plaintiff achieved subjective equivalence.

We should note that Halakhah adopts the view that it is prohibited to deliberately conduct a transaction that one knows entails third-degree ona'ah.[25] What follows from this rule is that the judgment that the plaintiff achieved subjective equivalence plays no role in adjudicating ona'ah cases. This leads to the proposition that mainstream Halakhah rejects R. Yehudah's view.

The above discussion leads to the proposition that the law of ona'ah would not invalidate the birthright sale. Unlike the battlefield case, where a market norm for the items traded under ordinary conditions can be identified, no such norm can be identified for the sale of the birthright. Since there is no norm to refer to under any conditions, the opinion that upholds the ona'ah claim in the battlefield case would agree that an ona'ah claim is thrown out in the birthright case. In addition, given the "exhausted and famished" condition of Esav when he sold the birthright, Esav surely achieved subjective equivalence when he sold the birthright.

THE ETHICS OF ENGAGING IN STRATEGIC BEHAVIOR

The basic issue that Yaakov's strategic conduct presents is the ethics of springing an offer on Esav to buy the birthright when Esav was in an exhausted and famished state. Does not this conduct amount to maneuvering Esav into a situation where he would feel coerced to accept the offer to sell his birthright for a pittance? No. The economic concept of reservation price will clarify this point.

---

24. Rosh, Bava Metzia 4:20.

25. Maimonides on interpretation of Even Ha-Azel; Ramban, Vayikra 25:17; Rosh, Bava Metzia 4:20; Arukh Ha-Shulchan, Choshen Mishpat. For minority view on this mater see Chinukh 337.

The reservation price is the minimum offer that a party to a negotiation would accept. Characterizing Yaakov's conduct as maneuvering Esav into a coercive situation would be valid only if *absent* his famished state Esav would value the birthright above the stew of lentils he ended up getting. But, let's not lose sight of what Esav said just after Yaakov made his offer: "…I am going to die, what need do I have with the birthright?" Rashi understands this to mean that Esav asked what the nature of the sacrificial service is. To this Yaakov answered that several prohibitions and death penalties are associated with it, e.g. performing the Temple service after having drunk wine, etc. To which Esav responds rhetorically "I am going to die through the birthright, if so what is there in it that I would want?"[26]

R. Chizkiyahu b. Manoach (ca. mid-13th century) understands Esav's words "I am going to die…" to convey the sentiment that the main benefit of the birthright was in respect to inheriting the Land of Israel. Since Esav was very familiar with the Divine promise that the descendants of Avraham would not inherit the land until approximately four hundred years later, and Esav did not expect to be alive then, Esav was reconciled to accept a "stew of lentils" for selling the birthright. Alternatively, what Esav conveyed with his words "I am going to die…," was that the birthright has value to him only if he outlives his father. But, given his dangerous preoccupation with hunting, Esav felt he might not outlive his father and therefore was willing to sell his birthright for a pittance.[27]

Proceeding from the various interpretations cited, Esav's declaration "I am going to die…" conveyed that *absent* his exhausted and famished state, the birthright under normal conditions had a zero, and perhaps, even a negative value for him.

Let's note that after the birthright sale was completed, the Torah testifies: "Yaakov gave to Esav bread and lentil stew, and he ate and drank and got up and left and Esav despised the birthright" (*Bereishit* 25:34). The clear message here, points out R. Chayyim b. Moshe Attar (1696–1743 CE), is that the negative value Esav attached to the birthright did not only reflect his attitude toward the birthright when he desperately

---

26. Rashi, *Bereishit* 25:32.
27. *Bereishit* 25:32. In his commentary ad loc, Ramban opines Chizkuni's second rationale.

needed the lentil stew to relieve his exhausted and famished condition, but reflected his attitude toward the birthright even under normal and calm conditions.[28]

Now, if Esav's reservation price for selling the birthright was under normal conditions above the value of a stew of lentils, Yaakov's strategic conduct would be characterized as maneuvering Esav into a coercive situation to sell the birthright below the value Esav usually assigns to the birthright absent his famished condition. But, since Esav's reservation price for selling the birthright under normal conditions was zero, Yaakov's strategic conduct should not be regarded as a maneuver to box Esav into a coercive situation. Instead, Yaakov's conduct should be viewed as only *distracting* Esav from focusing on Yaakov's reservation price as the terms for the sale, and instead to conclude the deal on the basis of his own reservation price.

SPRINGING AN OFFER OR SEIZING AN OPPORTUNITY

Let's take note that Esav's reputation as a wicked person became public knowledge when Esav and his twin brother Yaakov reached the age of thirteen.[29] But Yaakov's offer to buy the birthright from Esav took place in the aftermath of the death of their grandfather, Avraham, which occurs a full two years later. The stew of lentils Yaakov gave Esav as the price he paid for the birthright was the traditional mourner's food Yaakov had originally prepared for his father, Yitzchak.[30] The question then arises: since Yaakov's motive in pursuing the birthright was only because he felt that Esav was unworthy to take on the responsibilities that went along with the privilege of the birthright,[31] why did he not take the initiative and make his offer as soon as Esav's reputation as a wicked person became a public matter?

One possibility is to view Yaakov's inaction as manifesting strategic conduct on his part to secure the birthright at the lowest possible price. To be sure, Yaakov was certain that Esav placed no value on the

---

28. *Or Ha-Chayyim, Bereishit* 25:34.
29. *Bereishit Rabbah* 63:10.
30. *Me'Am Loez, Bereishit* 25:29.
31. *Bereishit Rabbah* 63:13.

birthright, but this circumstance in no way guaranteed that Yaakov could buy the birthright for a pittance. Yaakov's reputation as both a student of Torah and one not adept in deception[32] should have told Esav that he could extract an exorbitant price for transferring the birthright to Yaakov, who would prize its possession and to boot had no guile as a negotiator. Moreover, initiating negotiations for the birthright entailed great risk because it would communicate an *anxiousness* and *urgency* on the part of Yaakov to acquire the birthright, which, of course, would put Yaakov at a disadvantage. Accordingly, Yaakov played a waiting game. The right moment came when Yaakov found Esav in an exhausted and famished state. As soon as that moment arrived, Yaakov sprung his offer on Esav to sell him the birthright for a stew of lentils.[33]

We reject this approach because it does not flow naturally from the character portraits our Sages depict of Yaakov and Esav. Let us see why:

Expounding on the Biblical description of Esav as an *"ish tzayid"* – "a man who knows hunting" (*Bereishit* 25:27), *Midrash Rabbah* explicates that he knew how to ensnare and to deceive his father with his mouth. He would ask him "father, how do we tithe salt and straw?" His father would thus be under the impression that Esav was meticulous about the fulfillment of commandments.[34] Along with being a deceiver, Esav was filled with self-righteousness. In this regard, *Yalkut Shimoni* depicts Esav in the World to Come as wrapping himself up in a prayer shawl and sitting himself down right next to Yaakov. Esav's delusion that he is equal to Yaakov is smashed when God Himself expels Esav from the exalted place he abrogated for himself and thrusts Esav into the pit of destruction.[35]

Yaakov, on the other hand, is depicted by the Sages as the prototype of the person "who has no slander on his tongue" (*Tehillim* 15:3).[36]

---

32. Rashi, *Bereishit* 25:27.
33. *Keli Yakar, Bereishit* 25: 32 apparently takes an approach along these lines.
34. *Bereishit Rabbah* 33:10
35. See full text of *Yalkut Shimoni* based on the verse "If you go up high like an eagle, and if (you) place your nest among the stars (interpreted to mean Yaakov), from there I (God) will bring you down (*Ovadiah* 1:4)."
36. *Makkot* 24a.

What this says is that Yaakov meticulously adhered to the prohibition against *"lashon ha-ra"* (making an evil but true report).

Given the contrasting character traits of Yaakov and Esav, it is understandable why Yaakov did not report to Yitzchak the evil conduct people said Esav was guilty of. The prohibition against *lashon ha-ra* prevented Yaakov from doing this. This is so because one aspect of these laws is the prohibition for A to report B's evil conduct to C, when A has no first-hand knowledge of B's misconduct.[37] Accordingly, since Yaakov's knowledge of Esav's misconduct was only second-hand, it would be prohibited for him to report this misconduct to Yitzchak. Moreover, given Yaakov's second-hand knowledge of Esav's wrongdoing, it would be prohibited for Yaakov to use the information in a manner that would cause harm to Esav.[38]

The practical import for Yaakov to not use second-hand information against Esav is to refrain from making an offer to buy the birthright from Esav. This is so because by virtue of the fact that Esav was born first, the birthright is his entitlement unless he proves himself unworthy to take on the responsibilities it entails.[39] However, on the day Avraham dies and Esav returns from his hunting expedition, Esav's declarations to Yaakov gave Yaakov *first-hand information* that he (Esav) was not worthy of the birthright. The *Midrash* punctuates this point by connecting "And Yaakov boiled a stew…" (*Bereishit* 25:29) with "Yaakov said [to Esav], 'Sell, as this day, your birthright to me'" (ibid., 31). The connection is that Esav expressed curiosity as to why Yaakov was preparing a stew of lentils. In reaction to Yaakov's response that Avraham had died and the stew of lentils was the traditional mourner's food he had prepared for Yitzchak, Esav goes into a tirade and says if the righteous Avraham died, there is no reward and no resurrection.[40] Hearing *directly* from Esav that he was a non-believer, Yaakov set out immediately to make an offer for the birthright.

37. Chafetz Chayyim, *Hilkhot Issurei Lashon Ha-Ra* 10:2.
38. Ibid., 6:11
39. Yaakov's motivation in pursuing the birthright was only to rescue the birthright from unworthy hands; see *Bereishit Rabbah* 63:13.
40. *Bereishit Rabbah* 63:11.

Let's take note that as a proof text to support the notion that Yaakov was the prototype of the person "who has no slander on his tongue," the Talmud sites the verse: "Perhaps, my father will feel me and I shall seem to him as a deceiver" (*Bereishit* 27:12). Consider that this verse relates to the episode where Rivkah instructs Yaakov to masquerade as Esav, and thereby secure for himself the blessings meant for Esav. Commenting on this dictum, R. Shemuel Eliezer b. Yehudah Ha-Levi Edels (Maharsha, 1555–1623 CE), understands that Yaakov's objection to his mother's scheme was based on the fear that if Yitzchak discovered the masquerade, Yaakov would be forced to justify his actions by repeating the evil talk he heard about Esav.[41] We take both the proof text and Maharsha's comments as not saying that Yaakov's only encounter with the temptation to speak *lashon ha-ra* occurred in the masquerade incident. No. Yaakov showed his mettle earlier when he refused to take the initiative to buy the birthright based on the second-hand information he picked up that he (Esav) was unworthy of the birthright. Yaakov's most difficult test in resisting the temptation of *lashon ha-ra* came, however, when he had first-hand information, but did want to use the information as the justification for the masquerade.

We need not venture far to theorize why Yaakov did not want to use even first-hand information to condemn Esav: Yitzchak held Esav to be a righteous person. Accordingly, it stands to reason that Yitzchak would have made no judgment against Esav that the latter was unworthy of the birthright until Yitzchak would hear Esav's reaction. Given Esav's self-righteous nature, can there be any doubt that Esav would have vehemently denied any accusations against him, and even turned the tables by relating that Yaakov actually bought the birthright from him, but played a "waiting game" and timed his offer to buy the birthright for a "stew of lentils" only after he had found Esav in a famished state?

The upshot of the above analysis is that Yaakov's inaction for two years in not pursuing the acquisition of the birthright was not motivated by the hope that the framework for the negotiations with Esav might become more favorable and allow him to strike a better deal. To be sure, Yaakov picked up on the rumors that Esav was a wicked person, but as

---

41. Maharsha, *Makkot* 24a.

an exemplar for avoiding violation of the laws of *lashon ha-ra*, rumors alone were not sufficient for Yaakov to launch an initiative to buy the birthright from Esav. It was not until Esav made direct statements to Yaakov that showed that he was not worthy of the birthright that Yaakov was motivated to pursue the birthright. This moment of truth about Esav happened to coincide with the circumstance that Esav was famished. Yaakov's purchase of the birthright hence did not manifest the execution of a plan to make an offer to Esav for the birthright when the latter was famished. Instead, the timing of the purchase merely reflected Yaakov's desire to buy the birthright as soon as he was certain that Esav was not worthy of holding it.

CONCLUSION

We have analyzed the sale of the birthright from the standpoint of its price terms consisting of a stew of lentils and what appears to be strategic conduct Yaakov adopted to achieve this result. In terms of the price, given that there is no objective market value to serve as a reference price for the transaction, the law of *ona'ah* would not modify or overturn the transaction. Moreover, there should be no ethical objection to Yaakov's strategic conduct. This is so because Esav's reservation price to sell the birthright absent his famished state was either zero or negative. Accordingly, Yaakov's strategic behavior of springing his offer to buy the birthright when he found Esav famished should not be viewed as timing his offer to exploit Esav's famished condition. Instead, Yaakov's conduct can be viewed as *distracting conduct* to induce Esav to focus on the value the birthright meant for himself, rather than on the value the birthright meant for Yaakov.

More fundamentally, given that Yaakov is cited as the prototype of the person who "had no slander on his tongue," it stands to reason that Yaakov *did not engage in strategic conduct* to obtain the birthright at a pittance. Quite to the contrary, Yaakov had no interest in acquiring the birthright until he became aware through Esav's own declarations that he (Esav) was unqualified to carry out the responsibilities of the birthright. Because Esav's famished state spurred him on to make declarations to the effect that he was not worthy of the birthright, the motivational force to acquire the birthright and the opportunity to buy it at a pittance came together for Yaakov at the same moment. Accordingly, Yaakov seized upon the opportunity that was thrust upon him. Yaakov's conduct was therefore not opportunistic, but, instead, was driven by a desire to remove the birthright privilege from unworthy hands as soon as possible.

Prof. Yael Leibowitz

ויצא: Idols, Indignation and Inspiration

In a *sefer* brimming with accounts of seeming deception and counter-deception, *Parashat Vayeitzei* tells a fascinating story. In one of *Bereishit*'s most enigmatic episodes, Rachel, immediately prior to fleeing back to *Eretz Kena'an* with Yaakov and the rest of the family, takes advantage of Lavan's temporary absence to steal his *terafim* (household gods) (*Bereishit* 31:19). When Lavan subsequently pursues and catches up with Yaakov, he accuses his son-in-law of kidnapping both his family and his gods. Unaware that it is Rachel who has taken the *terafim*, Yaakov swears to his innocence on the life of the unidentified thief, and challenges Lavan to find the gods. Lavan accepts the challenge and begins a systematic search of Yaakov's camp. Going from tent to tent, he ultimately finds himself in Rachel's tent, where only his daughter's claim that she is menstruating prevents Lavan from discovering the *terafim* she has secreted in the saddle of her camel (ibid., 33–35).

Conspicuously absent from this account is Rachel's motive for the theft. Traditional attempts to supply that motive range from the altruistic notion that Rachel, herself a monotheist, wanted to rid her father of his pagan idols,[1] to the notion that Rachel believed in the efficacy of the idols as objects of divination and wanted to ensure that Lavan didn't utilize them to track Yaakov down.[2] More recently, scholars with newly available, extra-Biblical evidence at their disposal have suggested that since the idols effectively functioned as the title to Lavan's estate, Rachel was actually attempting to secure Yaakov's familial predominance through her acquisition of them.[3] While each of these explanations is compelling in its own right, none of them pay attention to the obscurity of the text, or make sense of the fact that the story, for all intents and purposes, never progresses to a conclusion. The text jumps directly from Lavan's search to Yaakov's monologue, in which he fulminates against twenty years of deceit and abuse at the hands of his father-in-law. The *terafim*, never discovered, are never mentioned again.[4] This lack of resolution remains unaccounted for.

Taking a look at the account from a slightly different perspective, however, may prove fruitful. By broadening our focus, we notice something interesting: Rachel's actions do not comprise a single narrative unit. Rather, they are interspersed throughout a chapter whose main theme is the confrontation between Yaakov and Lavan. The theft, when viewed through this wider lens, appears as one component of that intra-familial confrontation, and its ramifications seem to be limited to it. Looking carefully at Yaakov's angry response to Lavan, we sense that the latter's false charges[5] have served as a catalyst for what proves to be a defining moment in the former's life. And so we must ask: are we perhaps underestimating Rachel by not entertaining the possibility that she anticipated the outcome? And if she did foresee it, does that insight help us account for both her behavior and the unusual manner in which that behavior is depicted by the text?

---

1. Rashi, ad loc.
2. Ibn Ezra, ad loc.
3. See for example M. Greenberg, "Another Look at Rachel's Theft of the Teraphim", *Journal of Biblical Literature* 81 (1962), pp. 239–48; K. Spanier, "Rachel's Theft of the Teraphim, A Struggle for Family Primacy," *Vetus Testamentum* 42 (1992), pp. 404–12.
4. Whether Yaakov's instructions to his entourage (Ch. 35) to rid themselves of their foreign gods can be understood as an allusion to the *terafim* is open to discussion.
5. In particular verses 36–37.

No chapter in the Torah is to be read in a vacuum, and the chapter we have been discussing is no exception. As we search for stylistic, linguistic and thematic similarities to the story of Rachel and the *terafim*, we find ourselves drawn to a strikingly similar episode that occurs, not coincidentally, in the lives of Rachel's sons. Although it occurs many years after Rachel's death and many miles from Charan, *Bereishit* Ch. 34 similarly depicts a long-brewing intra-familial confrontation sparked by a false charge of theft.

Yosef, the then-viceroy of Egypt, has his royal goblet[6] secretly planted in Binyamin's sack of provisions. Like his mother's act of stealing the *terafim*, Yosef's act of planting the goblet is recorded by the text with no explicit motive attached. Yosef's agents pursue his brothers and accuse them of the stealing of the goblet – just as Lavan pursued Yaakov and accused him of stealing the *terafim*. Like their father before them (*Bereishit* 31:32), Yosef's brothers steadfastly proclaim their innocence, in the process uttering a curse condemning the unidentified thief to death (*Bereishit* 44:9). Like Lavan searching through Yaakov's camp, Yosef's agents conduct a systematic search of the brothers' belongings. This search proceeds in order of the brothers' ages, culminating with the search of the youngest brother's sack (ibid., 12), just as Lavan's search culminated in the tent of his younger daughter (*Bereishit* 31:33). When the goblet is ultimately "found" in Binyamin's sack, the brothers are led back to the city, setting the stage for the climactic confrontation between Yosef and Yehudah, echoing, of course, the confrontation between Yaakov and Lavan.

The state of Yaakov's family prior to this confrontation between Yosef and his brothers certainly seemed to be deteriorating. Fathers appeared to be shirking paternal responsibilities,[7] sons were lying to

---

6. *Bereishit* 44:5. The goblet was used both for drinking as well as for divination. Its function in the chapter makes us that much more acutely aware of the similarities between the two episodes.

7. Yaakov's obvious and inflammatory favoritism of Yosef in Ch. 37, as well as Yehudah's initial failure to offer his son Shelah as a levir for his dead brothers in Ch. 38 are two examples. One might argue that Reuven's offering of his two sons (*Bereishit* 42:37) falls into this category as well.

their fathers,[8] and, most importantly for this discussion, brothers were figuratively, if not literally, at eachother's throats.[9] At the center of this turmoil stands Yosef, arguably the greatest victim of the family's breakdown, who has been struggling throughout his years in exile to understand the dynamics that tore his family apart. Now, twenty years after being sold into slavery, Yosef takes advantage of his position of authority, and of his brothers' failure to recognize him, to put into play a series of ruses orchestrated to test his brothers. Keeping his identity secret from them, he observes their behavior and eavesdrops on their ostensibly private conversations. He deliberately seems to place Binyamin at risk, first by insisting that he be brought to Egypt and then by framing him for the theft of the valuable and symbolically significant goblet. The implications of the ruse then begin to unfold.

The brothers, who had earlier been largely responsible for destabilizing the family, now act in unison to protest and prevent the damage Yosef is threatening to inflict upon it. When Binyamin is accused of the stealing the goblet, his brothers immediately and unequivocally come to his defense. They tear their clothing in anticipation of the pain their father would surely endure if Binyamin were lost (*Bereishit* 44:13), a far cry from the callousness with which they caused Yaakov to tear his clothing years earlier (*Bereishit* 37:34). They offer themselves as slaves in place of their brother (*Bereishit* 44:16), in contrast to their earlier sale of Yosef into slavery. Articulating their understanding of the gravity of the situation, of the irrevocable damage caused by men who don't assume their rightful position as their brother's keeper, the brothers rise to Yosef's challenge. Refusing to stand idly by while the remaining son of Yaakov and Rachel goes missing, the brothers offer themselves in his place. Yosef's subterfuge works. His threat to Binyamin compels the brothers to do something they had not been able to do before. He forces them to reach inside themselves and find the resolve to take a stand, to behave

8. The most obvious example is that of the brothers misleading Yaakov after the sale of Yosef in Ch. 37.
9. The vitriol that escaped the brothers' lips as they callously plotted to kill and then sell Yosef into slavery is disquieting even for those of us who know how the story turns out. Along similar lines, the deceptive means by which Onan prevented siring a son for his brother, undermined the very essence of fraternal fidelity.

responsibly and fraternally. In the process, of course, Yosef uncovers not only his brother's collective regret for their misdeeds, but Yaakov's heartbreaking ignorance of past events.[10] The healing has begun, thanks to the brothers' newfound sense of responsibility.

With this in mind, we return to the account of the *terafim* and notice that the long-awaited confrontation between Yaakov and Lavan, like the confrontation between Yosef and his brothers, is the climax of an escalating family drama.

Early in that drama, as Yaakov and his wives begin a family, we find ourselves simultaneously delighted and disturbed. On the surface, Yaakov is fathering many children, just as God had promised (*Bereishit* 28:14). However the undertow of emotions that the Torah describes in *Bereishit* (Ch.'s 29 and 30) is both troubling and confusing. Leah's sheer presence is a constant reminder to Yaakov of Lavan's deceit, and his resentment of Lavan leads to his ill-concealed contempt of his first wife (*Bereishit* 29:33). That contempt is, the text explicitly tells us, compensated for by a God-given fecundity (*Bereishit* 29:31) – a fecundity that has the unfortunate side-effect of tainting Leah's relationship with the barren Rachel.

Perhaps as a result of the expectations set up by the text's description of Yaakov's love for Rachel at first sight (*Bereishit* 29:18), their marital relationship (as depicted in Ch. 30) proves a disappointing reality. Rachel, distraught over her childlessness, turns to her husband (*Bereishit* 30:1). Yaakov's curt response (ibid., 2) is jarring, especially in light of the *Tanakh*'s presentation of other men in similar situations.[11] Furthermore, while Yaakov sires many children (Ch. 30), he appears relatively passive from the textual perspective. Aside from his one, short, emotionally charged conversation with Rachel, Yaakov doesn't utter a single word throughout the course of the birth stories. Even more telling is the fact that the wives, not Yaakov, perform the important ritual of naming each

---

10. *Bereishit* 44:28 is ostensibly the first time that Yosef finds out that his father assumed him dead. It may also be the first time that Yosef realized that his father was not implicated in the sale.

11. Yaakov's own father for example, prayed on behalf of his barren wife (*Bereishit* 25:21). Elkanah displayed his concern and devotion to his wife Chanah, in an attempt to assuage her pain (*Shemuel* I 1:8).

one of their children.[12] As husband and father, Yaakov seems somewhat detached from both roles.

Conceivably the most heartbreaking ramification of this tangled web of relationships is the tension felt by Yaakov's children. In the touching account of a young Reuven bringing mandrakes to Leah, for example, we recognize the tragedy of a child internalizing the pain of his parent.[13] Interestingly however, Leah doesn't keep the mandrakes. She gives them to Rachel in return for a night with her own husband (*Bereishit* 30:15). We can hardly imagine the shame Leah must have felt as she intercepted Yaakov on his way to Rachel's tent, informing him that she had, in effect, hired him for the night (ibid., 16). Once again, the inference that Yaakov may have overlooked his marital obligations to Leah is hard to ignore, as is his continued passivity vis-à-vis his marriages.

Of particular importance in the episode of the mandrakes is the language Leah uses. When she says, "*sakhor sekhartikha*" – "I have hired you" (*Bereishit* 30:16), to inform Yaakov that she has hired his marital services, she is echoing the words her father used soon after Yaakov's arrival in Charan. Soon after Yaakov arrived, Lavan, feigning magnanimity, says that rather than *work* for free, Yaakov should receive *wages* for his services: "*ha-gidah li mah maskurtekha*" – "tell me, what shall your wages be?" (*Bereishit* 29:15). The words *work* and *wages*, from the roots *'vd* and *skr*, are key words defining the relationship between Yaakov and Lavan.[14] Lavan's seemingly generous offer is, in effect, a rejection of Yaakov as a member of the family. He is not a beloved nephew, but a naïve employee to be exploited. By the same token, Lavan exploits his daughters, substituting Leah for the betrothed Rachel in the hope of extending Yaakov's economic servitude. Lavan, in short, forfeits any

---

12. The only exception is the name of Binyamin (*Bereishit* 35:18), which was revised by Yaakov. That took place at a later date however, and so has little bearing on our discussion.

13. Although it could be argued that Reuven was too young to know what the mandrakes were used for, the counter-argument is that the Torah did not need to include his role in the story at all, and so if it did, it did so for a reason.

14. J.P. Fokkelman, *Narrative Art in Genesis: Specimens of Stylistic and Structural Analysis* (Eugene, Oregon, 1991), p. 126.

right to the title "father" or, for that matter, "uncle."[15] It is Lavan who sees family ties as nothing more than economic opportunities. Thus, despite his absence from Ch.'s 29 and 30, Lavan's presence remains palpable, as evidenced by Leah's use of the word *sakhor* to describe her marital relationship. Lavan's twisted understanding of family seems to have had a hand in shaping intra-familial relationships among Yaakov, his wives, and their children.

One can only speculate, based on facts the Torah discloses about Yaakov, as to why he allowed himself to be browbeaten by his father-in-law. Earlier events in his life, it seems, played a role. When Yaakov was still living with his parents in Canaan, at the bidding of his mother, Yaakov impersonated his older brother Esav in order to obtain his father's blessing (*Bereishit* 27:1–29). The guilt engendered by this duplicity may help account for his inability to stand up to Lavan.[16] Yaakov, stupefied at finding himself married to the wrong sister, demands to know why Lavan has deceived him (*Bereishit* 29:25). The word Yaakov uses to describe Lavan's trickery is the same one Yitzchak used to describe his younger son's usurpation of the blessing that rightfully belonged to his first-born brother (*Bereishit* 27:35).[17] While Yaakov's choice of words may have been made subconsciously, Lavan's words, responding to his new son-in-law, were no doubt chosen with care. Radak suggests that Lavan blunted Yaakov's outrage at being fooled by referencing Yaakov's own, not dissimilar, subterfuge.[18]

In a similar vein, when the Torah introduces Rachel and Leah's relative positions in the family, it uses the words "*gedolah*" and "*ketannah*," "older" and "younger" (*Bereishit* 29:16). By contrast, when Lavan responds to Yaakov, he refers to them as "*tze'irah*" – "the younger," and "*bekhirah*" – "the firstborn," pointedly telling Yaakov that here, in Charan, we most emphatically do not allow younger siblings to co-opt the rights of the firstborn (ibid., 26). Lavan's cunningly placed barb is meant to

---

15. Fokkelman, p. 127.
16. An in depth look at this issue is beyond the scope of this discussion. See S. Klitsner, *Wrestling Jacob: Deception, Identity, and Freudian Slips in Genesis* (Teaneck, NJ, 2009) for an insightful and compelling explanation.
17. *Bereishit* 27:35 בא אחיך במרמה ויקח את ברכתך and 29:25 ולמה רמיתני...מה זאת עשית.
18. Radak, *Bereishit* 29:26.

tell Yaakov that, as a deceiver in his own right, he is in no position to demand fair play from those around him.

And so for twenty years, Yaakov is kept off balance by the manipulative Lavan,[19] and this disequilibrium, these feelings of guilt, resentment and repressed anger, poison every facet of his life.

When Yaakov finally leaves, he packs up his family and flees Lavan's house without notice (*Bereishit* 31:17–21). Rachel, knowing of Yaakov's plans to flee (ibid., 5–16), steals Lavan's *terafim*. Lavan pursues Yaakov, catches up with him, and proceeds to hurl a series of accusations at him, accusing him of "stealing his heart," treating his daughters as "captives of the sword" and denying him an opportunity to bid them a proper farewell (ibid., 26). Given the history between these two men, these accusations are disingenuous and no doubt infuriating. But they are not totally without merit.

Absent Rachel's theft of the *terafim*, it is hard to imagine Yaakov articulating his anger and frustration any more in this instance than when Lavan switched brides on him. After all Yaakov *was* sneaking out, and his wives had *not*, in fact, taken the kids to say goodbye to their grandfather.[20] Cognizant of his own culpability, Yaakov would not have had the wherewithal to defend himself and Lavan's accusations would have remained unanswered. The long chapter of Yaakov in Lavan's househould would have ended much as his last days in Yitzchak's household had, with the accusations of an aggrieved relative ringing in the air.[21] It is Yaakov who would have been remembered as perpetrating the final scam in a long cycle of trickery and deceit. The emotional consequences of their final confrontation might have continued to preclude Yaakov from fully being the husband and father that he should be. In the event, though, Rachel saw to it that the scene played out differently.[22]

There is little doubt that Lavan would have pursued Yaakov

---

19. See for example *Bereishit* 30:25–43. Yaakov practiced an ancient form of genetic engineering after Lavan found loopholes in the terms of their agreement, and took off with all of Yaakov's animals.
20. *Bereishit* 31:15.
21. Ibid., 27:36.
22. It is clear from Rachel and Leah's words in *Bereishit* 31:14–16 that they too recognized and resented Lavan's manipulative behavior.

whether or not he discovered that his *terafim* were gone. But Rachel's theft altered the ensuing confrontation in one crucial respect. It ensured that Yaakov would find at least one of Lavan's accusations to be completely baseless. For the first time since meeting his father-in-law, Yaakov demonstrably holds the moral high ground. He denies the charge of theft and, as Lavan makes his way slowly and deliberately through each tent in Yaakov's camp, we sense Yaakov's rising indignation. In a revealing juxtaposition of verses, Lavan's failure to find the *terafim* (*Bereishit* 31:35) is immediately followed by Yaakov's forceful reiteration of his innocence. Rachel's stratagem has sparked the tinderbox that was Yaakov and Lavan's relationship. The Torah tells us that Yaakov "became incensed," (ibid., 36) lambasting Lavan for his accusations. In a verse dripping with bitter sarcasm, Yaakov taunts Lavan: "You rummaged through all my things; what have you found of all your household objects? Set it here, before my kinsmen and yours, and let them decide between us two" (ibid., 37). Pushed beyond the brink, Yaakov angrily confronts Lavan about the abuses and exploitations he has suffered at his hands (ibid., 38–42). At long last, Yaakov reclaims the side of himself that has for so long been smothered by Lavan's manipulations and by his own guilty conscience.

Like her son Yosef and his goblet, Rachel uses her father's *terafim* to engineer a situation designed to achieve a specific goal. Knowing the significance of the *terafim* and the value her father placed upon them, and painfully aware of Lavan's relationship with Yaakov, Rachel steals the *terafim* in order to manipulate the context of the inevitable and final confrontation between the two men. Rachel's machinations set the tone for that confrontation, and Yaakov's response at that critical juncture sets the trajectory of his future. As Rachel planned, Lavan's "false" accusation becomes the proverbial straw that breaks the camel's back. That Lavan has capitalized on, and taken advantage of, Yaakov's feelings of guilt, is one thing. But his accusation that Yaakov is a thief is unbearable (ibid., 42). As a result, Yaakov's long-suppressed rage and indignation come pouring forth, creating a final break between the two men, a break concretized by the construction of a physical boundary between the two families (*Bereishit* 32:45–51). Lavan's influence is at an end, no longer serving to manipulate Yaakov or destabilize his family life.

Studied in a vacuum, the account of Rachel's theft of the *terafim* raises questions that remain unanswered. By working backwards, however, from the effect the theft ultimately has on the narrative, we can begin to appreciate how Rachel's actions drove that narrative and influenced its climactic moment. The definitive close to the Yaakov-Lavan narrative marks the triumphant conclusion of the *terafim* episode. As such, the very design of the text which was initially puzzling proves illuminating.

The break between the House of Yaakov and the House of Lavan signifies the final stage of a process that began in the days of Avraham. In *Bereshit* Ch. 12, God commands Avraham to uproot himself and relocate to *Eretz Kena'an*. Avraham does so, but for two generations Avraham's offspring continue to migrate eastward to marry,[23] returning to the very family that Avraham has purportedly left. Yaakov's decisive break with Lavan's family heralds in the next stage in the history of Avraham's descendants. The sons of Yaakov would soon transition to the nation of Israel, with endogamy as a cornerstone of their national identity. Thanks to Rachel, the break from Lavan was a "clean one" and the line that had tethered the two families was permanently severed. As the daughter of Lavan, Rachel came by her ability for deception naturally, but rather than tear Yaakov's family apart, her act of deception allowed him to wholly own his role as husband and father. Emboldened, Yaakov is ready to move on to the next chapter in his personal life, and the next phase of the nation's history.

---

23. See Avraham's request of his servant (*Bereishit* 24:1–9) and Yitzchak's words to Yaakov (*Bereishit* 38:2–4).

Rabbi Yitzchok Cohen

וישלח: To Be a *Tzaddik*

One of the themes of *Sefer Bereishit*, "*Ma'aseh avot siman le-banim*," is readily apparent in *Parashat Vayishlach*. By "*Ma'aseh avot siman le-banim*," *Chazal* meant that we should be cognizant of the fact that the various episodes that were endured and experienced by our *Avot*, Avraham, Yitzchak and Yaakov, are real and true examples for us as to how we should act and behave in our lifetimes. Let us explore the encounter that Yaakov had with his brother, Esav, after 22 years of exile:

At the beginning of *Parashat Vayishlach*, *Yaakov Avinu* commands his messengers to relay a message to his brother, Esav, stating the reason why Yaakov delayed in coming home, was because "*im Lavan garti*" (*Bereishit* 32:5) – Yaakov was involved with Lavan, working constantly, and unable to leave his father-in-law. Rashi famously comments (ad loc.) that Yaakov is saying to Esav that while he was in Lavan's house, Yaakov was still able to observe the 613 *mitzvot*. This statement of Yaakov is followed by another, which at first glance is not connected with Yaakov's observance of the 613 *mitzvot*. The second statement in Yaakov's message was: "*va-yehi li shor va-chamor*" – that Yaakov had grown prosperous with his flock. Rashi comments (ad loc.) that Yaakov suspected that Esav would be envious of Yaakov's wealth, therefore Yaakov assured Esav that his prosperity was not a result of his receiving the *berakhot* from *Yitzchak Avinu*. (The *berakhah* that Yaakov received mentioned that Yaakov would receive dew from heaven and the best crop from earth, but didn't mention animals. Thus, Yaakov had gained these animals on his own merit, and not as a result of the *berakhah* he had taken from Esav).

The question that arises is: What message did Yaakov wish to impart to Esav by mentioning first that he observed the *taryag mitzvot* while in the house of Lavan, and second, that he was successful in obtaining abundant amounts of sheep and cattle?

One can answer this question by examining the *halakhah* which the Rambam learns out *halakhah le-ma'aseh* from *Yaakov Avinu*.

The Rambam states in *Hilkhot Sekhirut* (13:7):

כדרך שמוזהר בעה"ב שלא יגזול שכר עני ולא יעכבנו כך העני מוזהר
שלא יגזול מלאכת בעה"ב ויבטל מעט בכאן ומעט בכאן ומוציא כל היום
במרמה אלא חייב לדקדק על עצמו בזמן שהרי הקפידו על ברכה רביעית
של ברכת המזון שלא יברך אותה, וכן חייב לעבוד בכל כחו שהרי יעקב
הצדיק אמר כי בכל כחי עבדתי את אביכן, לפיכך נטל שכר זאת אף בעולם
הזה שנאמר ויפרץ האיש מאד מאד.

Just as the employer is enjoined not to deprive the poor worker of his wages or withhold them from him when they are due, so is the worker enjoined not to deprive the employer of his work by idling away his time, a little here and a little there, thus wasting the day deceitfully. Rather, the worker must be very punctual with his time, as we see that the Sages said the worker shouldn't even say the fourth *berakhah* of *birkat ha-mazon* [while at work]. The worker must work with all his power, as *Yaakov Ha-Tzaddik* said "And you know that I served your father with all of my strength," and therefore Yaakov was able to receive reward even in this world, as is says "and the man increased exceedingly."

Yaakov wished to convey to his brother, Esav, that Yaakov's wealth was only a result of his complete commitment and dedication to his job (as Yaakov had conveyed to his wives), and it was only because of this absolute drive to work with all his physical strength that he was rewarded with material wealth in the form of the sheep and cattle. Thus, the Rambam states that when one works for an employer, the employee must work with all his strength and might and not waste precious time, following the model of behavior that was demonstrated by *Yaakov Avinu*.

As an additional point, it is interesting to note the language which the Rambam uses when describing Yaakov's actions – he refers to *Yaakov Ha-Tzaddik*. The term *tzaddik* is also often applied to Yosef, Yaakov's son. Yosef was involved with a situation with Potiphar's wife, which required utilizing a great deal of *gevurah* (strength), as well as dedication to his principles, in order to overcome his *yetzer ha-ra* (evil inclination), and not indulge in an immoral act. This similarity of dedication and strength might be why the Rambam chose to refer to Yaakov as a *tzaddik* in our context.

We see Yaakov's saintliness and dedication further highlighted in an exchange with Lavan. In *Parashat Vayeitzei*, the Torah tells us that Lavan accused Yaakov of stealing his idols, and of not giving Lavan any clue that Yaakov and his family were leaving. Yaakov responded to these accusations by defending how hard he had worked for Lavan, only to be mistreated by Lavan over and over again. As Yaakov says, "*hayiti va-yom akhalani chorev ve-kerach ba-laylah va-tidad shenati me-einai*" – "Thus I was: in the day the drought consumed me, and the cold by night; and my sleep fled from my eyes" (*Bereishit* 31:40).

And what did Lavan respond to Yaakov's describing how hard he had worked for him? "*Ha-banot benotai ve-ha-banim banai ve-ha-tzon tzo'ni ve-khol asher attah ro'eh li hu*" – "The daughters are my daughters, and the children are my children, and the flocks are my flocks, and all that thou see is mine" (*Bereishit* 31:43).

We see that Lavan disregarded everything Yaakov said, and continued to justify the accusations he had leveled against him!

Thus we see that *Yaakov Ha-Tzaddik* had worked for Lavan for over 20 years, without any recognition or appreciation on the part of his father-in-law at any point! In fact, *Chazal* even tell us that Lavan was poor before Yaakov came and made them both rich, which only compounds the sin of Lavan's ingratitude.

Thus, to answer our original question, by juxtaposing his having kept *taryag mitzvot* to his having flourished materially, Yaakov is telling

Esav that both of these things happened *despite* Lavan's attempts to sty-mie Yaakov's spiritual and material development.

Applying this teaching to us in our day is necessary and impor-tant. It is only natural that a person will work to his potential, both in the spiritual and material realms, if he receives encouragement and rec-ognition. If, however, one is not recognized and praised for his efforts, it is easy to slack off and not put in the effort commensurate with one's abilities and strengths. *"Ma'aseh avot siman le-banim"* teaches us that we have no right to justify our lack of effort and drive and determination to perform our *Avodat Hashem*, whether it be *bein adam la-Makom* or *bein adam la-chavero*, even if we are not recognized for our efforts. That is the mark of a *true tzaddik*. Yeshayahu states, *"ve-ammekh kulam tzaddikim"* (*Yeshayahu* 60:21) – our nation is all *tzaddikim*. We all have within us the power and potential to be determined and steadfast in our perfor-mance of *mitzvot*, as well as in our responsibilities and duties, regard-less of whether or not someone is encouraging us to do so. Hopefully, we can internalize this message of *Yaakov Avinu*, and grow in all facets of our endeavors.

Rabbi Kenneth Brander

יׁשוּב: We Have Met the Enemy... and He Is Us

T he *Talmud Yerushalmi* (*Megillah* 4:1) discusses Moshe's legislation to read from the Torah on *Shabbat*, holidays and *Rosh Chodesh*. It continues discussing the legislation of Ezra to mandate abbreviated reading from the Torah on Monday, Thursday and *Shabbat minchah*.[1] While there is clarity regarding the establishment of the reading of the Torah, it is unclear when the *haftarah*, the reading from the Book of Prophets, was legislated.

R. Hai Gaon indicates that the reading of the *haftarah* in the *Shabbat* prayer service began in the time of the Prophets:

> One asked: "From what time was there a commandment to translate in the synagogue the reading of the Torah as well as to read the *maftir* [*haftarah*] from the Prophets?" This law is inherited from the times of the Prophets. (*Teshuvot Ha-Geonim, Sha'arei Teshuvah:* 84)

---

1. See also *Bava Kamma* 82a.

Shmuel Weingarten writes in his essay *"Reshitan Shel Ha-Haftarot"* that at this early stage[2] in the reading of the *haftarah*, there was no particular codified portion of the Prophets that was to be read every week with the Torah portion. Rather, the *haftarah* was to be chosen based on current community events. He continues that those who propose that the enactment of *haftarot* was established this early in Jewish history, as seen in the responsa of R. Hai Gaon, believe that the reason for the enactment of the *haftarah* is due to the fact that the words of the Prophets offer consolation to the Jewish people, accentuating the ideal that redemption is possible. This is especially reassuring when the Jewish people experience the challenges of a Diaspora existence (p. 106). Joseph Heinemann, in his book *Ha-Tefillah Be-Tekufat Ha-Tana'im Ve-Ha-Amoraim,*[3] calls the *haftarot "pirkei nechamah"* (chapters of comfort), a way of comforting the people during their trying times.[4] Zechariah Frankel elaborates upon this point, suggesting that the words from the Prophets were originally used as introductory remarks to the rabbi's sermons. Since the words of the Prophets were powerful and redemptive, they served as a wonderful introduction to the weekly sermon. Frankel explains that the institution of the *haftarah* evolved, eventually becoming a legislated part of the service to be read prior to the sermon. He suggests that the etymology of the word *"haftarah"* comes from פטר or פתח, meaning "opening" – the beginning of the sermon (*Reshitan Shel Ha-Haftarot*, 108).

This connection between the sermon and words of consolation from the Prophets is consistent with the comments found in *Massekhet Soferim* (14:2):

> When is it required to [minimally] recite twenty two verses for a *haftarah*? When there is no *targum* or sermon. However if there was *targum* (during the Torah reading) and [there is to be] a

---

2. See Isaac Hirsch Weiss in his famous book *Dor Dor Ve-Dorshav: Hu Sefer Divrei Ha-Yamim La-Torah She-Be-Al Peh* (Vilna, 1911), vol. 1, p. 48.; there he articulates this same position.

3. Joseph Heinemann, *Ha-Tefilluh Be-Tekufat Ha-Tana'im Ve-Ha-Amoraim* (Jerusalem, Israel, 1964).

4. Ibid., p. 144.

sermon then the *haftarah* does not need to be more than three or five or six [verses from] the Prophets and that is sufficient.

Others suggest that that the institution of *haftarah* was established at a time in Jewish history in which it was forbidden to read from the Torah. As such, the Rabbis chose specific sections from the Prophets that had a similar message to the weekly *parashah*. Rabbi David Abudraham, a 14th century Spanish Jewish communal leader and expert on liturgy, compiled the laws and customs of the Jewish prayers in his magnum opus, *Sefer Abudraham*. In this book, he writes about the institution of the *haftarah*:

> And after [completing] and wrapping the Torah scroll, we read the *haftarah*; which needs to be connected to the [Torah] portion of the day. And why do we read from the Prophets? Because of the legislation imposed upon the Jewish people forbidding them from reading from the Torah… (*Laws of Shabbat, Shacharit*)

Rabbi Yoel Sirkes, one of the great 17th century talmudic scholars of Poland, in his commentary on the *Shulchan Arukh* known as the *Bach*, (an acronym for *Bayit Chadash*), concurs with the opinion found in the *Sefer Abudraham*:

> And the reason [for the *haftarah* is because] there was a time in which anti-Semitic legislation forbade reading from the Torah and therefore it was established to read from the Prophets on a theme similar to the *parashah*. (*Bach, Shulchan Arukh, Orach Chayyim* 284:1)

Rabbi Yom Tov Lipmann Heller, in his 17th century commentary on the *Mishnah*, the *Tosafot Yom Tov*, further develops this idea, suggesting that the particular persecution causing the introduction of the *haftarah* happened during the period of *Chanukkah*. When the Greek Emperor Antiochus IV Epiphanes prohibited reading from the Torah, the Rabbis instituted that sections from the Prophets be read, focusing on a theme similar to the Torah portion:

> The reason for the *haftarot*…that Antiochus king of Greece leg-
> islated that the Torah should not be read in public. What did the
> Jews do? They chose a section from the Prophets that was the-
> matically similar to the Torah portion of the week. Even though
> this [anti-Semitic] legislation has been annulled the custom [of
> reading from the Prophets] was not discarded. (*Megillah* 3:4)

While not stating the particular anti-Semitic incident that caused the
introduction of the *haftarah,* this reason is also found in the writings of
R. David ben Samuel Ha-Levi, known as the *Taz,* from the initial letters
of his work on the *Shulchan Arukh, Turei Zahav,* (*Taz, Shulchan Arukh,*
ibid., 1) as well as the 19th century commentary of R. Yisrael Meir Ha-
Kohen Kagan (*Chafetz Chayyim*) in his *Mishnah Berurah* (*Shulchan
Arukh,* ibid., 2).

Many scholars[5] challenge this approach, suggesting that if there
was legislation banning reading from the Torah, it seems obvious that
the legislation would also include reading from the Prophets.

In response to this challenge, some suggest that the legislation
was actually enacted after the Hasmoneans succeeded in their battle
against the Greek Syrians. Torah scrolls were scarce, since many were
destroyed; therefore, reading from the Prophets was enacted until additional Torah scrolls could be written and could once again be a part of
the prayer liturgy.

Citing earlier sources, 20th century rabbinic scholar Reuben
Margaliot, in his commentary *Nefesh Chayah* on the *Shulchan Arukh,
Orach Chayyim* (284), as well as Professor H. Graetz in his *History of
the Jews,*[6] suggest that the institution of the *haftarah* was established in
response to the Samaritans. The Samaritans did not accept the holiness
of the Temple or Jerusalem, nor did they embrace the authenticity of the
words of the Prophets. The Rabbis instituted the *haftarah* as a response
to this heretical approach, which not only gave additional credibility to
the Prophets, but also focused on the redemption of the Jewish people
coupled with the restoration of Zion and Jerusalem (vol. 1, p. 400).

5. See the essay *"Reishitan Shel Ha-Haftarot."*
6. Heinrich Graetz, *History of the Jews* (Philadelphia, Penn, 1949).

Whatever historical reason is correct, the common narrative to all these ideas is that the *haftarah* was established as words of solace and redemption during challenging times within the history of our people. Indeed, as R. Soloveitchik once commented regarding the *haftarah*, if one wishes to truly understand the message of the *parashah* one needs to find the common theme between the *parashah* and *haftarah*.[7] He also pointed out that themes of the blessing of the *haftarah* accentuate the purpose of the *haftarah*, representing the national yearning for *geulah* (redemption). The blessings do not particularly focus on *Shabbat* or the holidays, but rather center upon the hope of redemption. Themes include the yearning for the rebuilding of Zion, the coming of Elijah and his heralding the *Mashiach*, the removal of foreign rulers and the re-establishment of Davidic dynasty. It is for this reason that R. Soloveitchik suggested that etched within the institution of the *haftarah* is the requirement that every portion contain words of solace and redemption. Even the *haftarah* recited on the most mournful day of the year, *Tishah Be-Av*,[8] concludes with words of redemption:

> For you shall go out with joy, and be led forth with peace: the mountains and the hills shall break forth before you in singing, and all the trees of the field shall clap their hands…. The Lord God who gathers the outcast of Israel says, 'Yet will I gather others to him, beside those of him that are already gathered…' (*Yeshayahu* Ch. 55:12–56:8; *haftarah* for *Tisha Be-Av* afternoon as well as the afternoon service of all fast days).

Yet, there is one *haftarah* which deviates from this imposed norm, in which words of redemption are not found: the *haftarah* for this week,

7. There are times during the year when the *haftarah* focuses on specific calendar events and is not connected to the *parashah*. Examples include: *Shabbat Shuvah* prior to Yom Kippur, *Shabbat Ha-Gadol* prior to *Pesach*, the three weeks leading up to *Tishah Be-Av* and the seven weeks following.
8. In discussing the *haftarah* of *Tishah Be-Av* morning, R. Soloveitchik contended that since the pre-*chatzot Tishah Be-Av* does not focus on reconciliation but rather focuses on exploring the depth of the Diaspora tragedy, words of reconciliation are reserved for the *haftarah* of *Tishah Be-Av* afternoon.

Parashat Vayeishev. If one scans the *haftarah,* one finds no words of consolation. Why is it that on *Tishah Be-Av,* the day in which we mourn and weep over the destruction of two Temples, the atrocities of the Crusades, the ordeal that befell us during the Black Plague, the Inquisition, the Chmelnitsky massacre, the Holocaust and so much more pain and suffering that was inflicted upon us during the Diaspora existence, we find words of comfort in the *haftarah,* and on this *Shabbat* we do not? R. Soloveitchik explains that *Parashat Vayeishev* relates a story that is even more tragic than a foreign enemy burning our Temple. Our *parashah* relates the first story of *sinat chinam,* baseless hatred between Jews. The fact that a Jew could have such enmity for another, for a brother, such that Yosef was sold into slavery, is the greatest tragedy that can befall us as a people. As the *haftarah* of this week's *parashah* begins:

> Thus says the Lord, for three transgressions of Yisrael I will turn away punishment, but for the fourth I will not turn away punishment; because they sold the righteous for silver and the poor for a pair of shoes. (*Amos* 2:6)

Redemption is guaranteed from events such as foreigners burning our Temple and banishment from our land. However, redemption is not possible when one Jew turns against another. Words of solace can be added to the *haftarah* of *Tishah Be-Av* – for communal salvation from those events is guaranteed. However, deliverance is not possible in the climate of events portrayed in our *parashah.* Complete redemption is only possible when we celebrate the ideals of *ahavat chinam* (unconditional love).

It is interesting to note that the tradition of the *Eidot Ha-Mizrach* community is to begin the *shacharit* prayer service with the following prayer of introduction:

> For the sake of the unification of the Holy One, Blessed be He, and His Divine Presence, in reverence and love…I accept upon myself His all-powerful Kingship and in my fear and love of Him I am prepared to serve the Almighty. [In preparation for prayer] I accept the commandment of Love thy neighbor as thyself and I [accept upon myself] all persons of Israel like my soul…and

[now] I am able to accept upon myself the commandment of
Keriyat Shema, and the morning service ...

The tradition of those who pray in *nusach Sephard* and *Chabad* is to
recite a more truncated version of the above prayer – one sentence: "I
accept upon myself the positive commandment: 'Love thy neighbor as
thyself.'" In his commentary on the *Shulchan Arukh*, the 17th century
scholar, Rabbi Abraham Gombiner, known as the *Magen Avraham*,
suggests (*Shulchan Arukh, Orach Chayyim* 46) to the members of the
Ashkenazic community that they too should recite the above sentence
before beginning the morning service.

This introductory passage highlights that engagement with
another Jew is a necessary prerequisite for creating a rendezvous with
God. It does not matter if that Jew practices differently, looks different,
or has a different outlook on life. Redemption for us as a community
will only be achieved when we realize that often our greatest danger
is from within, and our fatal flaw is a lack of tolerance for a fellow Jew.

Rabbi Dr. Michael Rosensweig

מקץ: Yosef's Complex and Comprehensive Reconciliation with His Brothers

I

Among the most pervasive themes in *Sefer Bereishit* is that of *"Ma'aseh avot siman le-banim."* The conduct and standards of the patriarchs establish ideals to which we should aspire, and dictate the parameters of appropriate interaction and normative behavior for future Jewish generations. Hence, the *Midrash* and later commentaries subject the motivation and behavior of the *Avot* to microscopic scrutiny.

On the surface, the episode of Yosef and his brothers represents a rare opportunity to chronicle the ideal response to adversity and gross mistreatment. Following this line of thinking, one would have anticipated that Yosef, whom *Chazal* characterize with the appellation *"ha-tzaddik,"* the righteous, would react to his victimization by his brothers with selfless graciousness, unqualified forgiveness, and boundless understanding. Yet strikingly, we encounter an exceptionally complex and ambivalent posture, demanding clarification and analysis.

II

In the *parashah*, Yosef appears to toy with and manipulate his brothers. According to the *Midrash Tanchuma* (*Bereishit* 45:3, ad loc.), he puts them through psychological torture before revealing his true identity:

> "Yosef said to them: 'Did you not tell me that this one's brother is dead? I will summon him and he will come to me.' And he called, 'Yosef son of Yaakov, come to me.' And they looked at the four corners of the house. He said to them, 'Where are you looking? I am Yosef your brother.' Immediately, their souls departed, and they could not answer him for fear."

Even when he evidently reaches out to them – "*Geshu na elai, va-yigashu*" (*Bereishit* 45:4) – he uses deliberately enigmatic language, undoubtedly designed to leave them wondering about his true intentions. The term "*geshu*" connotes both appeasement and readiness to do battle. Moreover, his formulation – "I am your brother Yosef whom you sold to Egypt" – was bound to accentuate their guilt. In the next verse (ibid., 5), as he seemingly allays their anxiety – "Now, do not be distressed or reproach yourselves because you sold me hither; it was to save life that God sent me ahead of you" – *Chazal* understood that Yosef intentionally emphasized the contrast between their malicious intent and God's Divine providence. The fact that they were the beneficiaries of their own act of betrayal could not have been lost upon the brothers, nor could it have brought them much comfort. These ambivalent references take place even as Yosef risks his own life to protect the brothers' reputation in the eyes of Egypt (see Rashi and the *Midrash*, ibid., 1–2) and in the eyes of their father (see Ramban, ad loc.).

An analysis of various other verses (ibid. 9–15; 22, 24), including those at the end of *Sefer Bereishit* (*Bereishit* 50:15–21), reinforces the impression that Yosef's ambiguous terminology was intentional, that his agenda was complex, and that his posture was ambivalent. How does all of this fit the picture of *Yosef Ha-Tzaddik*?

Perhaps, Yosef's complicated response reflects his religious obligation as well as his personal need to assimilate and relate to that which he experienced at the hands of his brothers on different levels. Yosef's personal integrity, as well as his historical responsibility, precluded the simplistic, one-dimensional, unqualified forgiveness, although that approach might have been more personally satisfying.

III

On one level, Yosef simply did not have either the right or the capacity to completely absolve his brothers, as their crime transcended their personal confrontation. Yosef was not the only victim of the brothers' treachery. In his tone-setting revelation (*Bereishit* 45:3), Yosef perhaps intends to juxtapose his personal inclination to forgive ("I am Yosef"), with his role as his father's only reliable protector ("Is my father still alive?"). The message he effectively conveys is that only he deserves to be identified as his father's son, as the others have forfeited their role by virtue of the suffering they have inflicted (see Seforno, ad loc.). The Netziv notes that the term *"chai"* (alive), connotes a certain quality of life associated with happiness, something which the brothers undermined, and which Yaakov only experienced again upon receiving the news that Yosef was alive – "And the spirit of their father Yaakov was revived" (ibid., 27). [The final *parashah* in *Bereishit* begins with the word *"Vayechi,"* referring not only to the chronology but quality of Yaakov's life. The *Ba'al Ha-Turim* suggests that this word's numerological value of 34 refers to the most productive years, starting with Yosef's birth until his disappearance, and continuing with the period after their reunion!] According to many of the *Rishonim*, Yosef elected never to inform Yaakov of his sons' betrayal in order to minimize his suffering. In any case, Yosef was not in a position to concede his father's pain.

IV

Moreover, Yosef was undoubtedly sensitive to the fact that *Kelal Yisrael* had suffered an irrevocable loss of spiritual leadership due to Yaakov's personal distress. This loss was compounded by the fact that the nation was in its most formative stages at the time. The term *"Yisrael,"* used to designate Yaakov's destiny and legacy in his role as spiritual mentor to the nation, is largely absent from the Torah's narrative until Yaakov becomes aware that Yosef has, indeed, survived. The one prominent exception (*Bereishit* 43:6–11), in which Yaakov is uncharacteristically forced to take the initiative and set aside personal grief that has paralyzed him in order to insure the future of *Kelal Yisrael*, provides a sharp contrast which reinforces this impression (see, also, Netziv, ibid. 6). *Chazal* convey this theme when they indicate that "And the spirit of their father Yaakov was revived" signifies the return of the *Shekhinah* to Yaakov once he was able to extricate himself from the despair which had dominated his life during Yosef's disappearance. While Yosef might graciously forgive his brothers for their cruelty, the potential of those years of lost spiritual development for the Jewish nation could never be recovered.

V

Furthermore, the brothers' behavior constituted an enormous *chillul Hashem*. *Chazal* declare that even sincere repentance does not fully neutralize desecration of God's name. This harsh ruling reflects not only the severity of the breach, but also the fact that the impact upon others exposed to such conduct cannot easily be retracted.

And Yosef's treatment at the hand of his brothers was hardly an ordinary case of *chillul Hashem* either. Consider the implications for others if the sons of Israel, who were destined to exemplify personal integrity and spiritual leadership, were able to exhibit such intense jealousy and cruelty to one of their own. Thus, *Chazal* perceive that the sale of Yosef was a betrayal of transcendent proportion and significance, which compromised the very standards of Jewish, and even human, interaction. The connection to the execution of the *asarah harugei malkhut* (*Midrash Mishlei* 1 s.v. *Kol Hon Yakar*; see R. Bechaye 37:28), the epitome of viciousness and cruelty, undoubtedly reflects not only punishment, but some measure of cause and effect.

The broader implications of the sale of Yosef could not simply be dismissed or glossed over even by a *Yosef Ha-Tzaddik*. Only by persistently accentuating the impact of their betrayal, even as he extended personal forgiveness, could Yosef hope to ultimately sensitize his brothers to the enormity of their flawed world view, and thereby begin the process of overcoming the effects of their behavior.

VI

Yosef's complex and ambivalent agenda also facilitated the twin processes of *teshuvah* and *mechilah*. *Teshuvah* entails a delicate balance between spotlighting and camouflaging sin. On the one hand, one must be careful not to embarrass the *Ba'al teshuvah* by reminding him of his sins (see Rambam, *Hilkhot Teshuvah* 7:8). At the same time, the need to confront one's errant past is a prerequisite for *teshuvah* – "it must be perpetually before him" (ibid., 2:4–5). Yosef's use of ambiguous language contributed to this process by insuring that while his brothers need not be humiliated, they would also be encouraged to engage in a comprehensive introspection and fully confront the enormity of their actions.

Moreover, he may have intuited that their psychological well-being may have demanded the release of guilt. This need is already evident in their own projection of a link between their troubles in Egypt and their sale of Yosef, before they were even aware of Yosef's identity, as documented in the *midrash*. Perhaps their response to Yaakov's death reflects this theme as well. Some render "*lu yistemenu Yosef*" – "lest Yosef hate us" (*Bereishit* 50:15), as "*halev'ai*" ("would that he would hate us") – a secret desire to be punished or at least admonished for their actions. (The *Tur* interprets the word accordingly, but takes an opposite approach to its significance.) In some circumstances, unwarranted and exaggerated kindness can be a form of cruelty.

VII

The passage of time and the re-integration of Yosef within the *shevatim* did not significantly alter Yosef's complex posture towards his brothers. Possibly, this reinforces the impression that his reaction constitutes a normative, rather than a primarily emotional, response. The ambiguities and ambivalence persist and re-surface in the aftermath of Yaakov's death. Yosef, returning with his brothers from his father's funeral, stops at the pit in which his tribulations began to recite a *birkat ha-nes* (blessing on a miracle). Was his purpose to put the past behind him once and for all and to affirm the role of Divine providence, or to provide a jarring reminder to his brothers? He responds with ambiguous tears – "*va-yevk Yosef be-dabram elav*" (*Bereishit* 50:17), indicating, according to different views, either his continuing sense of anguish over what had befallen him, his sense of loss vis-à-vis his father, or an expression of pain at having been accused – falsely or accurately? – of harboring hostility towards his brothers. Undoubtedly, this range is not mutually exclusive, particularly if our analysis of the underpinnings of Yosef's perspective is correct.

VIII

R. Bechaye (*Bereishit* 50:17) concludes that Yosef came to terms with, but never fully pardoned, his brothers:

> "His brothers asked for his forgiveness, but the Torah does not mention that he granted it. Our Sages have explained that one who sins against his fellow is not forgiven [by God] until he appeases his fellow. And even though the Torah mentions that Yosef 'reassured them, speaking kindly to them,' from which it seems that Yosef was appeased, we still never see the Torah mention that he forgave them, or that he absolved them of their guilt. If so, they died in their sin, unforgiven by Yosef, for they could not obtain atonement unless Yosef were to forgive them. Therefore, the punishment was stored away for a future time, i.e. the *asarah harugei malchut* (ten leading scholars martyred by the Romans)."

The predominant rabbinic view, however, is that Yosef was ultimately able to embrace his brothers and extend his forgiveness, even if he was unable to fully absolve them of their guilt. The fact that he eschewed a simplistic and perfunctory act of *mekhilah*, electing instead to address the full implications of their betrayal, ultimately enhances his stature as *Yosef Ha-Tzaddik*. The *Midrash Tanchuma* concludes: "'He kissed all his brothers, and wept over them' – just as he only reconciled with his brothers through weeping … so does the *yeshu'ah* (salvation) come to Israel only through weeping." May our sensitivity to Yosef's complex perspective hasten the *yeshu'ah*.

Prof. Nechama Price

ויגש: The Significance of the Seemingly Insignificant

The Torah only tells us information that is critical for our understanding of the Jewish people or to impart a fundamental lesson. There are no superfluous words, phrases, or episodes in the Torah. From the earliest years of grade school we are taught this axiom of *Chazal* and the *mefarshim*. Yet, based on this tenet, *Parashat Vayigash* poses a challenge.

This *parashah* includes two critical narratives of Yosef. The first, Yosef's revelation of his true identity to his brothers, and, the second, the descent into Egypt of Yaakov and his progeny. In this context, the Torah appears to go off message, devoting about half a *perek* (thirteen *pesukim*) with barely a fleeting relevance to the Jewish people or the relationship of *Yosef* and his family when, in *Bereishit*, Ch. 47, the Torah describes in exacting detail how Yosef re-sold the food (to the Egyptians) that he previously collected from the Egyptians. In brief summary, here is the progression of these *pesukim*: In exchange for the food, he initially collected the monetary wealth of the Egyptian masses. After the money was used up, they gave him their animals. Upon depletion of animals, they offered Yosef their land. Over time, Yosef acquired all their land, then moved all the people around into different lands and made them pay him a fifth of their harvest.

It would seem this entire story could have been deleted from the Torah, with little repercussion to our understanding of the Jewish people's story. In light of *Chazal's* axiom, we are forced to ask why the Torah even bothers to mention this story and why it allocates thirteen *pesukim* to articulate every last detail.

I. THE STRUCTURE OF *PEREK* 47

(יא) ויושב יוסף את אביו ואת אחיו ויתן להם אחזה בארץ מצרים במיטב הארץ בארץ רעמסס כאשר צוה פרעה: (יב) ויכלכל יוסף את אביו ואת אחיו ואת כל בית אביו לחם לפי הטף: (יג) ולחם אין בכל הארץ כי כבד הרעב מאד ותלה ארץ מצרים וארץ כנען מפני הרעב: (יד) וילקט יוסף את כל הכסף הנמצא בארץ מצרים ובארץ כנען בשבר אשר הם שברים ויבא יוסף את הכסף ביתה פרעה: (טו) ויתם הכסף מארץ מצרים ומארץ כנען ויבאו כל מצרים אל יוסף לאמר הבה לנו לחם ולמה נמות נגדך כי אפס כסף: (טז) ויאמר יוסף הבו מקניכם ואתנה לכם במקניכם אם אפס כסף: (יז) ויביאו את מקניהם אל יוסף ויתן להם יוסף לחם בסוסים ובמקנה הצאן ובמקנה הבקר ובחמרים וינהלם בלחם בכל מקנהם בשנה ההוא: (יח) ותתם השנה ההוא ויבאו אליו בשנה השנית ויאמרו לו לא נכחד מאדני כי אם תם הכסף ומקנה הבהמה אל אדני לא נשאר לפני אדני בלתי אם גויתנו ואדמתנו: (יט) למה נמות לעיניך גם אנחנו גם אדמתנו קנה אתנו ואת אדמתנו בלחם ונהיה אנחנו ואדמתנו עבדים לפרעה ותן זרע ונחיה ולא נמות והאדמה לא תשם: (כ) ויקן יוסף את כל אדמת מצרים לפרעה כי מכרו מצרים איש שדהו כי חזק עלהם הרעב ותהי הארץ לפרעה: (כא) ואת העם העביר אתו לערים כי מקצה גבול מצרים ועד קצהו: (כב) רק אדמת הכהנים לא קנה כי חק לכהנים מאת פרעה ואכלו את חקם אשר נתן להם פרעה על כן לא מכרו את אדמתם: (כג) ויאמר יוסף אל העם הן קניתי אתכם היום ואת אדמתכם לפרעה הא לכם זרע וזרעתם את האדמה: (כד) והיה בתבואת ונתתם חמישית לפרעה וארבע הידת יהיה לכם לזרע השדה ולאכלכם ולאשר בבתיכם ולאכל לטפכם: (כה) ויאמרו החיתנו נמצא חן בעיני אדני והיינו עבדים לפרעה: (כו) וישם אתה יוסף לחק עד היום הזה על

אדמת מצרים לפרעה לחמש רק אדמת הכהנים לבדם לא היתה לפרעה:
(כז) וישב ישראל בארץ מצרים בארץ גשן ויאחזו בה ויפרו וירבו מאד:

In this *perek*, the Torah begins by discussing the Jewish people (*Bereishit* 47:11–12), transitions to the episode of the Egyptians sacrificing everything to purchase food from Yosef (ibid., 15–26), and concludes with the success of the Jewish people (ibid., 27). The details in the middle of this *perek* – of Egypt's situation – are sandwiched between *pesukim* relating to the Jewish people. This contrast could very well be intentional, precisely to lure the reader into comparing the middle section with the information mentioned both before and after it.

As such, this comparison highlights how the Jewish people were in the exact opposite predicament as the Egyptians. Whereas the Egyptians gave up all their money and possessions to buy back the food that they had given Yosef during the years of plenty (*Bereishit* 47:13–15), Yaakov's family (who never even gave any food during the years of plenty) were provided with all the food they need without having to provide recompense (ibid., 12). Moreover, the Egyptians were forced to give up their animals to Yosef (ibid., 16–18), just as the Jewish people moved to Goshen to continue their livelihood as shepherds (ibid., 3–4). Thirdly, the Egyptians had to give up their land and move to unfamiliar parts (ibid., 19–26), while the Jews were *given* land in Egypt.[1]

---

1. In this regard, the *pasuk* provides two important details: (a) the land they are given is specifically part of the "good land" of Egypt and (b) they are given the land as an *achuzah*, land that they own (*Bereishit* 47:11,27). The language of *achuzah* means getting land to own (not just live temporarily). Here are a few examples in *Tanakh* to illustrate this definition:

   Avraham bought *ma'arat ha-makhpelah* for Sarah as an *achuzah*, as there are details of how much money he gave to make his purchase (*Bereishit* 23:20) ויקם השדה
   והמערה אשר בו לאברהם לאחת קבר מאת בני חת.

   The *benot Tzelofchad* requested land in *Eretz Yisrael* from Moshe to be their permanent inheritance, utilizing the language of *achuzah* (*Bemidbar* 27:4) למה יגרע
   שם אבינו מתוך משפחתו כי אין לו בן תנה לנו אחזה בתוך אחי אבינו.

The outcome of this *perek* then, is that the Egyptians have no money and do not own their own land, while, concurrently, the Jews have their wealth and are dwellers of valuable real-estate. Obviously, these lead to opposite results; the Egyptians were weakened, while the Jews are strengthened, so much so that they are able to start growing into a nation, even during the time of a famine (ibid., 27).

Seeing the *perek*'s structure now allows us to answer the original question about the goal of the *perek*. Our *pesukim* are coming to teach us about the status of the Jewish people, in contrast to the Egpytians.[2]

In fact, Abarbanel presupposes that this contrast between the Egyptians and the House of Yaakov serves to highlight how *Hashem* specifically watches over those dearest to Him by allowing them to survive the famine without the onerous burdens that had been imposed on the Egyptians.[3]

II. CLUES IN THE TEXT OF THE *PEREK*

We return to the text of the *perek* to help understand the significance of these verses. When reading it in the earlier citation, the reader likely noticed the exaggerated (and underlined!) reference to Pharaoh. In fact, a cursory glance at these thirteen *pesukim* reveals that this word

---

The tribes of Reuven and Gad requested to have their *nachalah*, permanent inheritance, be outside of *Eretz Yisrael* and used the language of *achuzah* (*Bemidbar* 32:5) ויאמרו אם מצאנו חן בעיניך יתן את הארץ הזאת לעבדיך לאחזה אל תעברנו את הירדן.

    Hashem describes *Eretz Yisrael* to Moshe as the land that will be an *achuzah*, permanent inheritance of the Jewish people (*Devarim* 32:49) עלה אל הר העברים הזה הר נבו אשר בארץ מואב אשר על פני ירחו וראה את ארץ כנען אשר אני נתן לבני ישראל לאחזה.

2. This phenomenon exists elsewhere in *Tanakh*, where a story will include many details regarding other nations as contrast to the Jewish nation. In one example: the battle of the four and five kings (*Bereishit* Ch. 14), where the *perek* is clearly broken into two sections: (i) the battles of the other nations, and then (ii) the story of Avraham saving Lot. One approach to explain all the initial details is to view them purely as background to the relevant story, i.e. Avraham saving Lot. As such, this entire episode would be superfluous if not for the background information it provides the reader about Lot and why Avraham came to save him.

3. Abarbanel writes (ויגש מו, עמ' תבג):

הנה נכתב כל הספור הזה בתורה לסבות האחת להודיע שעיני ה' אל יראיו למיחלים לחסדו לחיותם ברעב כי הנה בהיות בכל הארץ רעב, מופלג יעקב וביתו לשוד ולכפן צחקו. ובהיות המצרים מוכרים כספם ומקניהם גופותיהם ושדותיהם לכל בני ישראל היה לחם במושבותם בלא כסף ובלא מחיר מקנה.

appears twelve times.[4] Taking a closer look, though, reveals something more striking – in many of these instances, the word "Pharaoh" is not focal, rather it is used to contextualize Yosef's actions (e.g., to clarify that Yosef collected the money "for Pharaoh" and took the land "for Pharaoh" and followed the rules "of Pharaoh" to not take the land of the priests). In this way, the verses are stressing that Yosef was acting in every way as Pharaoh's agent and not on his own accord.

Accordingly, this *perek* informs on the relationship between Yosef and his master Pharaoh. However, although these verses do highlight that relationship, we will have to look beyond this brief text to best understand the dynamic between these two men. And for that, there are two models for analyzing the relationship between Yosef and Pharaoh: (A) Yosef was completely controlled by Pharaoh and operated as his "puppet" and (B) Yosef was free to rule as he saw fit and had developed his own basis for authority.

A. Yosef as Pharaoh's "Figurehead"

Throughout the unfolding of Yosef's leadership in Egypt, during numerous episodes, the reader would expect Yosef to act on his own authority and yet he sought out Pharaoh's permission. For instance, Yosef requested Pharaoh's permission to invite his family to Egypt (*Bereishit* 45:17–18). Again, he sought out Pharaoh's permission to send his father wagons to transport him to Egypt (ibid., 19).[5] Similarly, before Yosef could give his family land to settle in Goshen, he requested permission from Pharaoh (*Bereishit* 47:5–6). Yosef could not even bury his father in Israel without Pharaoh's permission (*Bereishit* 50:4–6)!

---

4. There are many times in *Tanakh* where identifying words repeated throughout the section helps to highlight the focus of the text and its message. For example, in *Bereishit* Ch. 11, within the story of the Tower of *Bavel*, the *shoresh* of שם shows up 6 times. Clearly, stressing this root word is conveying a message regarding their search of making a 'name' for themselves.

5. After the actions are done by Yosef, the *pasuk* goes out of its way again to remind the reader that this was only done because Pharaoh allowed it:
בראשית מה:כא: ויעשו כן בני ישראל ויתן להם יוסף עגלות על פי פרעה ויתן להם צדה לדרך: בראשית מז:יא: ויושב יוסף את אביו ואת אחיו ויתן להם אחזה בארץ מצרים במיטב הארץ בארץ רעמסס כאשר צוה פרעה:

With these other *pesukim* and episodes as backdrop, we ought to re-examine our *perek's* stress of the word "Pharaoh." The story in our *perek*, which appears to be about Yosef saving food during the years of plenty and re-selling it during the years of famine, is actually about Pharaoh. Yosef was being the 'front man' for Pharaoh in his scheme to aggregate all the power and wealth in Egypt. Let's look back at how this relationship developed, and why Pharaoh wanted Yosef as his 'cover.'

Pharaoh had a major dilemma after hearing Yosef's interpretation of his dream. If he ignored Yosef's warnings (and claimed that Yosef was mistaken), and the famine occurred, the Egyptians would blame him for not listening to Yosef. This could precipitate a rebellion against his rulership. On the other hand, if he heeded Yosef's dire predictions and hoarded his people's food during the years of plenty, and no famine materialized, the Egyptians would be just as furious for being forced to give him their food for seven years. Again, he would risk a rebellion.

What was Pharaoh's response to this quandary? He created a potential scapegoat in Yosef by leaving him in charge of implementing the plan. By making Yosef the food collector, he was able to sufficiently remove himself from that process. Therefore, if the famine did not occur, the Egyptians would first blame Yosef (who was, after all, who they associated with this policy), not Pharaoh. However, if the famine were to occur, Pharaoh fully intended to take credit for electing Yosef.[6]

---

6. A similar relationship between king and viceroy is found in Yehoshua Bachrach, *Kitvuni Le-Dorot* (Jerusalem, 1989), 64–65 when discussing the relationship of Achashverosh and Haman.

   Achashverosh was paranoid of being overthrown. His initial response was to befriend the constituents of his kingdom by making big parties for the people in his kingdom, in order to win their favor. Unfortunately, soon after his parties, he realized he was unsuccessful, when he was informed of the plan by Bigtan and Teresh to kill him.

   Thereafter, Achashverosh created a second plan to ensure his own safety – but this one took the opposite approach. Whereas the initial approach stressed an 'open kingdom,' where the monarch was available to the masses, for the second approach, he essentially closed himself off in the palace (not allowing anyone to enter without being called). He took this to such an extreme, that even entering his chambers unannounced was considered treasonous and deserving of the death penalty unless the king accepted the entrant.

Fast forwarding to when the famine takes place, Pharaoh realized that he could leverage the situation. Instead of instructing Yosef to *give* his people sufficient food, Pharaoh instructed Yosef to *sell* the food back to the Egyptians. In this way, Pharaoh acquired all their money, possessions and land. However, from the people's perspective, it was Yosef – not Pharaoh – who had taken all this from them. In this way, Pharaoh ensured that any Egyptian hostility or anger would be directed at Yosef and not himself. With this backdrop, we appreciate why our *perek* so frequently asserts that all was done "for Pharaoh" – to remind us that it was Pharaoh behind this elaborate plot.[7]

However, as such a secluded monarch, he needed a figurehead to be involved in the active governance of the land. This person would be his link to the people. In that role, this viceroy would present all royal decrees to the people and was responsible to ensure they were fulfilled. Therefore, if anyone did not like a rule or wanted to rebel, their anger would be directed at this figurehead and not at the king. Achashverosh selected Haman for this role and even went so far as to make a rule that everyone had to bow to Haman, thus enforcing the perception of the people that Haman was the representative of the king (and the one to show anger at). As such, the king was able to make sure that all his desires were fulfilled, but without risking his rulership. All risk was put on Haman, who had to face the people daily, and all the power and money that Haman attained went to Achashverosh.

In this way, the relationship between Achashverosh and Haman parallels the relationship of Pharaoh and Yosef. With this as backdrop, there are other similarities between Yosef and Haman (such as their both attaining power quickly), that may tie them together. Yosef, an anonymous prisoner in jail, interpreted Pharaoh's dream and became second to the king (*Bereishit* 41:40–41). Haman was similarly described as being raised to the status of second to the king (*Esther* 3:1). Both are given over the ring of the king to symbolize the power that they are given (*Bereishit* 41:42, *Esther* 3:10).

7. This explanation for the additional verses in Ch. 47 gives the reader greater understanding of other details in the story.

First, it helps us understand why Pharaoh would select a non-Egyptian prisoner to the most critical task toward determining the future of Egypt. Pharaoh specifically picked someone who would be an easy scapegoat, whom he could turn against at any moment.

Second, it explains why the *pesukim* specifically state that the Egyptians first went to Pharaoh to demand food and he said "go to Yosef" (*Bereishit* 31:55). Pharaoh was intentionally not getting involved and wanted the people to think that everything was up to Yosef. He didn't want to be blamed for the results at the end when the Egyptians were very unhappy.

According to this understanding of the relationship between king and viceroy, the point of the *perek* (i.e., focusing our attention on the relationship between Pharaoh and Yosef) is bimodal. First, the extra *pesukim* are included in the text to stress the praises of Yosef. Since there were no rebellions by the Egyptians against him, presumably he was able to accomplish Pharaoh's goals of wealth accumulation without overly angering the people. Ramban (*Bereishit* 47:14, ad loc.) highlights this approach to our text – that this story is about the wisdom of Yosef and how he was trusted by king and peasant alike and how he never acted out of his own self-interest.[8] The other option is to highlight the reason for the growing resentment of the Egyptian people to Yosef (and, by extension, his family). Even though there is no immediate rebellion by the Egyptians, there is a simmering hatred towards Yosef and his family that lays the groundwork for *galut Mitzrayim* only a generation later. Exactly as per Pharaoh's plan, the Egyptians blamed Yosef for taking away their money and land. This blame turned to hatred which became directed at the entire Jewish people. As soon as Pharaoh died (and there is nobody left to look out for Yosef's family), their hatred towards the Jews could be acted upon.

Third, this explanation provides context for why, at the end of our *perek*, Yosef moved the Egyptians around the various parts of the kingdom – specifically if he was doing it on Pharaoh's command. There are three possible explanations for why Pharaoh would want to move the people around:

(i) Radak (*Bereishit* 47:21) comments that when you move people into different and unfamiliar land you gain complete control over them. When Pharaoh made them give him twenty percent of the harvest, it was to reinforce the message that they were beneath, and subservient to, him.

(ii) Rashbam (ibid.) explains that by moving the people around, the king ensures that they won't rebel, because they've lost their tactical advantage (knowing the local terrain and familiarity with the environment).

(iii) Ibn Ezra (ibid.) adds that the movement that Pharaoh forced on the people was a move from the urban cities to the fields, in an effort to force more people to work the fields and make more food and money for Pharaoh.

8. See Ramban (ibid., 47:14):

    להודיע מעלות יוסף בחכמה בתבונה ובדעת, וכי היה איש אמונים שהביא כל הכסף בית פרעה ולא עשה לעצמו אוצרות כסף...אבל נתן למלך הבוטח בו...ומצא חן גם כן בעיני העם כי ה' הוא המצליח את יראיו.

B. Yosef the "Real" Leader

As mentioned above, there is another way to view the relationship between Pharaoh and Yosef, which requires that we re-evaluate our *pesukim*. Not only is Pharaoh's name mentioned twelve times in these verses, Yosef's name is also mentioned (and underlined in the text above!) eleven times. This could be an allusion to the active role Yosef took – no less involved than the king himself. As such, the goal of our *perek* is to highlight the immense power that Yosef accumulated. This *perek* is the pinnacle of a remarkable career of power growth for Yosef, who started as a child dreaming of ruling his brothers, and with God's help, became the most powerful person in the world.[9]

From this vantage point, the text can be read to illustrate the nature of the relationship between Pharaoh and Yosef.[10] Pharaoh was clearly impressed by Yosef's natural gifts, which he attributed to God's providence over Yosef, and therefore wanted Yosef to assist him by ruling over Egypt. Pharaoh claimed *"ain navon ve-chakham kamokha,"* that there is no one like Yosef in intelligence and understanding (*Bereishit* 41:39). At that point, Pharaoh elevated Yosef's status, giving him his ring, dressing him in royal garb, and insisting that Yosef ride on the king's chariots (ibid., 40–44). Yosef, on the other hand, seemed able to manipulate Pharaoh into conceding to him whatever it was he wanted. And while it is true that Yosef requested Pharaoh's permission before moving his family to Goshen (*Bereishit* 47:5–6), a full two *perakim* earlier Yosef told his brothers to come down to Egypt and that they would live in Goshen (*Bereishit* 45:9–11). This clearly shows that he had no doubt that he would be able to manipulate Pharaoh into allowing him to bring down his family and give them Goshen. He also told his brothers exactly what to tell Pharaoh to ensure that he'd agree to their plan (*Bereishit* 46:31–34). Rashi (ibid., 34) highlights the instructions Yosef gives his family (that they claim to only know about shepherding), so

9. There are numerous times in the text that Yosef was able to go from anonymity to a powerful position in a short space of time; in Potiphar's home and again in jail (*Bereishit* 39:6, 39:22).

10. Interestingly, in a similar vein, one can read the story of *Megillat Esther* as one in which Achashverosh, the drunken king, is pushed around by Haman, who is the mastermind behind killing the Jews.

that Pharaoh would have no personal use for them and would put them in Goshen, which was a land good for shepherding. Rashi continues (while commenting on *Bereishit* 47:2) to elaborate on Yosef's plan by asserting that Yosef intentionally selected the five weakest brothers as representatives to speak to Pharaoh so that he would not want them for his army.[11] In this context, the role of our *perek* is to magnify Yosef's greatness and power. Our *pesukim* describe how he is able to usurp all of the wealth and land from the Egyptian people.[12]

By focusing on Yosef's power, our *perek* might be teaching the reader an additional lesson about Yosef – that even with all this power, Yosef still associated himself with the Jewish people and his family. Precisely toward this point, Rashi (*Bereishit* 47:21) asserts that Yosef moved the Egyptians to different lands so he could make the move to Egypt more comfortable for his brothers.

To summarize, we now see that these *pesukim* that appeared – at first glance – superfluous, helped present two distinct caricatures of Yosef. The first is of Yosef as puppet who did everything Pharaoh told him. The second is of Yosef the righteous, the powerful, who accomplished the king's work, but in a style that did not anger the Egyptians and highlights his selflessness.

III. SIMILAR STORIES ELSEWHERE IN *TANAKH*

Until now, we have evaluated our *pesukim* through the prism of the *perek* and other stories about the main characters in the text. We will now consider them in light of other characters in *Tanakh*. In fact, the experiences of *Yosef* are mirrored by two episodes in *Tanakh*: (A) Mordechai and Esther and (B) Daniel. Both of these other narratives involve a Jewish

---

11. See also Radak, *Bereishit* 46:33, who says that Yosef coached his brothers on how to talk to Pharaoh to ensure a desired outcome.

12. These collective experiences of Yosef introduce the student of *Tanakh* to the leadership qualities and abilities of Yosef, which he appears to pass on to his progeny. Many of our future leaders will come from Yosef, including Yehoshua (who is from Efraim), most of the *shoftim* (Devorah, Gidon, Yair, Yiftach, and Avdon account for one hundred and nineteen years of leadership), and many kings of Shomron (starting with Yeravam ben Nevat).

person in exile who is forced to navigate the upper echelons of power (and specifically the king) to help the Jewish people. In this context, the 'superfluous' *pesukim* in our *perek* are included to teach critical illustrations of how Yosef associated with a non-Jewish society and monarchy. Specifically, Yosef exercised the power granted him to ensure both the success of the monarch and the well-being of his family.

A. Mordechai / Esther

The textual and thematic similarities between Yosef's experiences and the story in *Megillat Esther* are numerous. Both Yosef and Mordechai are treated as king; both were given the ring of the king (*Bereishit* 41:42, *Esther* 8:2), were dressed up in king's garb (*Bereishit* 41:41, *Esther* 8:15), and were led on the king's chariot through town while their praises were proclaimed to all those listening (*Bereishit* 41:43, *Esther* 6:11). Both men earned (and received) significant power in the governance of the kingdom after proving themselves worthy to the king (*Bereishit* 41:41, *Esther* 8:2). Both were feared and respected by the rest of the kingdom (*Bereishit* 41:44, *Esther* 9:3). And finally, both used their political capital to save the Jewish people. Mordechai saved the Jews from persecution and Yosef saved them from starvation. Both put the Jews in a situation where they would not only survive, but flourish and grow.

A seemingly unnecessary *pasuk* is found near the conclusion of *Megillat Esther*, when the *Megillah* informs the reader that Achashverosh imposed a tax on the land and isles of the sea (*Esther* 10:1). This *pasuk* seems to parallel our extra *pesukim* in *Vayigash*, discussing the political and economic happenings of the reigning nation. However, the *Megillah* juxtaposes that *pasuk* to a discussion of Mordechai's power. *Malbim* (*Esther* 10:1), by connecting these points, suggests that the economic tax is included in the *Megillah* precisely to show us the successes of Mordechai, who was able to collect taxes for Achashverosh from the distant islands. The text is stressing how the honor and money Achashverosh received was due in no small part to Mordechai. This sounds very similar to the text in *Vayigash* that stresses how Yosef helped Pharaoh. Two *pesukim* later, the *Megillah* concludes (*Esther* 10:3) by reporting that Mordechai's power was used to help his own people. Again, this sounds just like the verses in our *perek*.

B. Daniel

Turning to *Sefer Daniel*, there are many similarities to our *perek*. The first is the placement of the main character in captivity, which occured to Daniel during the exile of King Yehoyakim, when King Nevuchadnetzar took children, including Daniel, into captivity. Next, Daniel, like Yosef, seemed to find favor with all who meet him (*Daniel* 1:9, *Bereishit* 39:4, 21). Third, both men lived through hard situations. For Yosef, this entailed living through the experience of being thrown into a pit and then jail (*Bereishit* 37:24, 39:20), and for Daniel it was being thrown into fire (*Daniel* 3) and then a lion's den (*Daniel* 6). Fourth, and most uniquely, each of these men is endowed with the ability to interpret dreams and each ends up interpreting a critical dream for the king (*Bereishit* 41, *Daniel* 2). In both contexts, there is a king with a bothersome dream who was looking for a dream-interpreter and rejected all of his interpreters' explanations for the dream. Similarly, in both situations this was resolved when a servant of the king told him about the Jew who is able to interpret dreams, and brought him to the king. Again, in both stories, the interpretation affected major events within the destiny of the nation among whom the Jews were living. In the case of Yosef, it was the famine that promised to destroy Egypt, and for Daniel, the death of the king. Because of these interpretations, the kings were able to veer off the course of history implied by the dreams; Pharaoh collected food during the years of plenty and Nevuchadnetzar repented (thus delaying his punishment for a year). After the dream was translated by Daniel and Yosef respectively, the king appeared to have the same twofold response. First, each king seemed satisfied with the interpretation and admitted that the interpreter had tremendous understanding and must be a Godly person and, second, the king placed the interpreter in a position of power (*Bereishit* 41:38–44, *Daniel* 2:47–49).[13]

The three stories of *Parashat Vayigash*, *Megillat Esther*, and *Sefer*

---

13. Interestingly, both Daniel and Yosef themselves have dreams that teach them about events in the future (and, specifically, regarding rulership). Yosef's dreams are about his rulership over his brothers (*Bereishit* Ch. 37). Daniel's first dream is about the four empires that will rule the world, followed by the Jewish people (*Daniel* 7), and the second dream is about the kingdom of Persia splitting into four smaller kingdoms (*Daniel* 8).

Daniel, present a consistent theme. In each one, a major figure in Jewish history is put in a position of power in a non-Jewish world. Instead of associating themselves with the non-Jewish nation and going after the power, they remain loyal to the Jewish people, using their power to help save their nation. They give credit to God for all their ideas and abilities, making the kings of the non-Jewish nations also recognize the Jewish God. To this point, the *pesukim* in *Parashat Vayigash* show the exemplary character of Yosef. He could leave the Jewish people and forget about his family, but instead, he forgoes that legacy, and remains 'just' one of 12 tribes.

Concluding where we began, it should now be clear that these 13 *pesukim* in *Parashat Vayigash* fit most consistently with *Chazal's* axiom. If *Chazal* presumed that each part of the Torah be filled with importance and meaning for us, the readers, it is clear these *pesukim* fit that standard. We have attempted to analyze these *pesukim,* to see how they inform the broader Pharaoh/Yosef relationship (which, in turn, may affect the whole Egypt/*Benei Yaakov* relationship), and finally, see how they serve as a model for other *galut* experiences. In sum, the ideas presented above represent an attempt to show how this brief section in the Torah is full of meaning and significance.

Rabbi Mordechai Willig

ויחי: Yehudah and Jewish Survival

YEHUDAH – WHAT'S IN A NAME?

Our people are called *Benei Yisrael* (Israelites) in the Torah. In *Megillat Esther* and since, we are called *Yehudim* (Jews). This change can be explained historically. After the ten tribes were exiled, the tribe of Yehudah comprised the majority of *Am Yisrael*. As such, all of us are called *Yehudim*. However, the Targum Yonatan in *Parashat Vayechi* (*Bereishit* 49:8) offers a different explanation. He explains that *Yaakov Avinu* blessed Yehudah, "Your brothers will acknowledge you (*yodukha*)" as their ruler (a point also made by Rashbam), and that this blessing is a reward for Yehudah's response to Tamar. "Yehudah," the Targum has Yaakov telling his son, "you admitted to the story of Tamar. Therefore, your brothers will acknowledge you (*'yodun achayikh'*) and will be called *Yehudim* after your name." The Targum thus links Yehudah's admission of his sin to his being acknowledged by his brothers.

Perhaps these two explanations, the historical explanation, as well as the *peshat* of the Targum, can be reconciled. We are called *Yehudim* ever since the time that the ten tribes were scattered, because most Jews that were left from that time forward descended from the tribe of

Yehudah. The reason the tribe of Yehudah is the one that survived is because they admitted to their mistakes. Admitting to mistakes enabled Yehudah himself to be acknowledged as the ruler of the family, and it also enabled his descendants, who followed his example, to survive.

One example of the historical phenomenon of the Jewish ability to admit to our mistakes is found in the very story of Esther. Why did the Jews of that time deserve extinction? According to the Talmud, it was because they partook of the party of the wicked Achashverosh (*Megillah* 12a). However, they were spared when they repented after Haman's decree (*Yalkut Shimoni, Esther,* 4:16; see *Mikhtav Me-Eliyahu,* Vol. 1, p. 77). Admitting their mistake and repenting enabled the *Yehudim* to survive and return to *Eretz Yisrael* by the decree of Esther's son Darius (Rashi, *Chaggai* 1:1). The ten tribes, by contrast, have not yet returned.

A third association with Yehudah's name, besides that of admission and acknowledgement, is that of thanks. When Yehudah was born to Leah as her fourth child, Leah said "This time I will thank *Hashem.* Therefore, she called his name 'Yehudah'" (*Bereishit* 29:35). As Rashi explains, Leah was saying, "This time I took more than my share. Hence I must thank [*Hashem*]."

Combining these themes of admission, acknowledgement, and thanks, we learn a valuable lesson. Only by admitting one's mistakes and shortcomings can one be in position to give proper thanks. Otherwise, our feelings of gratitude are hindered by a feeling of entitlement. Only by realizing our imperfections and our sins can we express the proper thanks and gratitude and thereby be worthy of acknowledgement by others (see R. Yitzchak Hutner, *Pachad Yitzchak, Chanukkah* 2:5).

REALIZING OUR LIMITATIONS

On the verse in Yaakov's *berakhah* to Yehudah discussed above, "*attah yodukha acheikha,*" Targum Onkelus has a very interesting explanation. He explains the pasuk as meaning "Yehudah, you admitted and were not ashamed. [Therefore] your brothers will acknowledge you" (Targum Onkelus, *Bereishit* 49:8). How could Yehudah not have been ashamed to admit to his heretofore unknown paternity? Furthermore, isn't shame, especially in intimate matters, a praiseworthy hallmark of our people (*Yevamot* 79a)? How was it that Yehudah did not feel shamed?

The key to answering these questions is the realization that we only feel shame when we fall short of our expected standard of behavior. No one is ashamed of their inability to fly. Yehudah, aware of the fact that "there is no person who does not sin" (*Kohelet* 7:20), was thus able to admit his sin without shame. Also, although intimate matters are usually supposed to be kept private, that value is outweighed when one has the opportunity to save someone else from harm. Thus, Yehudah admitted his paternity in an effort to save Tamar's life (Rashi, *Bereishit* 38:25). Asked to recognize his personal effects and admit his paternity of Tamar's unborn children, Yehudah, as Rashi puts it, was called upon to "recognize [his] Creator." When one recognizes and realizes that it is the will of *Hashem* to admit when one falls short and sins, the shame of a public confession like the one Yehudah experienced can be eliminated. For these realizations, Yehudah deserved to be a ruler and to have our entire nation called *Yehudim*.

A DYNASTY OF KINGS

Just as Yehudah's leadership and our people's survival resulted from admitting mistakes, so too was the Davidic dynasty preserved in this manner. Like his ancestor, *David Ha-Melekh* admitted his mistakes immediately (*Yoma* 22b, see Maharsha and HaRav Y.D. Soloveitchik, *Kol Dodi Dofek*, "*Hakhmatzat Ha-Sha'ah*"). Shaul, in contrast, did not do so when faced with his mistake in not wiping out Amalek, and his dynasty was discontinued.

The ability to admit mistakes requires humility. Like Yehudah, David possessed humility, which enabled him to confess. "I am like a worm, not a man" (*Tehillim* 22:7). Humility not only enables one to admit one's shortcomings, but it also allows one to accept rebuke, and even to maintain silence when faced with provocations.

In the *haftarah* of *Parashat Vayechi*, David tells Shlomo, "Shim'i ben Gera cursed me a powerful curse" (*Melakhim* I 2:8). In fact, Shim'i had called David a murderer (*Shemuel* II 16:7) and pelted him with stones (ibid., 6). However, David protected Shim'i from Avishay, who wanted to kill him (ibid., 9–10), explaining: "*Hashem* told him to curse. Perhaps *Hashem* will repay me with goodness instead of the curse" (ibid., 11–12). *David Ha-Melekh*, in demonstrating such humility, was in fact following in the footsteps of the greatest prophet and the humblest of men, *Moshe Rabbenu*. When Yehoshua told Moshe to imprison the prophets who were prophesying Moshe's demise (Rashi, *Bemidbar* 11:27–28), Moshe rebuffed him (ibid., 29). David, learning from Moshe's example, was able to demonstrate humility and maintain his silence in the face of provocation. As a reward, *Hashem* repaid David for his decision to protect Shim'i and elevated David to the heavenly level of the patriarchs, by which David became the fourth wheel in the Divine Chariot (R. Yisrael Meir Kagan, *Shemirat Ha-Lashon, Sha'ar Ha-Tevunah* 8).

We know that the Davidic dynasty will culminate in the arrival of *Mashiach*. Bar Kokhba, a descendant of David who was proclaimed *Mashiach* by Rabbi Akiva in Beitar, in the end fell short of expectations by showing a lack in the qualities of David. Bar Kokhba mistakenly thought that Rabbi Elazar Ha-Modai, whose prayers protected Beitar, was a conspirator. In his rage, he kicked and killed him. As a result, Beitar fell and Bar Kokhba was killed (*Midrash Eikhah* 2:4). An angry leader, who lacks the humility and forbearance of David, cannot be the *Mashiach*.

A DYNASTY OF TORAH LEADERSHIP

Torah leadership also requires humility. Hillel, a descendant of David, established a centuries-long dynasty of Torah. He famously retained his patience even in the face of outrageous provocation (*Shabbat* 31a) and *Beit Hillel* admitted when they made Torah mistakes, and upon realizing them, ruled in accordance with *Beit Shammai* (*Eduyot* 1:12, 13, 14). Hillel himself was the personification of humility (*Shabbat* 30b). Famously, in our practice, the *Halakhah* always follows *Beit Hillel* because they not only quote *Beit Shammai*'s opinion, but even cite it before their own (*Eruvin* 13b). Obviously, the law is not decided in *Beit Hillel*'s favor simply because of their ethical behavior, but rather, we hold like them because one who humbly listens to, respects, and quotes another's opinion, will likely reach a more proper conclusion in deciding the *Halakhah* (R. Chaim Shmulevitz, *Sichot Mussar, Sha'arei Chayyim*, Ch. 46).

KEYS TO SURVIVAL BEGIN AT HOME

Yehudah was privileged to have our entire nation named after him because he promptly admitted his mistakes. His illustrious descendants *David Ha-Melekh* and Hillel established dynasties of kingship and Torah, respectively, by following the lead of his humility. Thus, the Jews have survived history because of our adherence to the principles of our namesake, Yehudah. Confessing, acknowledging and thanking, the three related verbal expressions connected with Yehudah himself, are the critical survival skills of our people.

These same concepts are equally critical within a Jewish home and family. The model of Yehudah's own rulership occurred within the context of his own family, and must serve as inspiration for Jewish families forever. The Rambam writes that a husband should be viewed as a king (Rambam, *Mishneh Torah, Hilkhot Ishut,* 15:20). To deserve this treatment, however, he must fulfill the first promise of the *ketubah*: "I will cherish you in the manner of Jewish men (*Yehudain*) who cherish their wives in truth (*be-kushta*)." He must acknowledge his debt to his wife, thank her constantly, and admit his mistakes in recognition of the truth (see Onkelos, *Bereishit* 42:21).

Acknowledgement of one's personal debt to a spouse and appropriate and sincere gratitude, as well as sincere apologies when one makes mistakes, are crucial elements of a proper Jewish home. The phrases "I'm sorry" and "thank you" are integral for the success, and even the survival, of a Jewish marriage. As a community and as individuals, it is not enough to be called Jews. We must live up to the name *Yehudim* to survive, thrive, and merit the ultimate Jewish leader, *Mashiach ben David,* a descendant of Yehudah.

ספר שמות

Rabbi Mark Gottlieb

שמות: Moshe and Us Moderns: A Meditation on Cultural Engagement and Its Discontents

It happened in those days, that Moshe grew up and went out to his brethren and observed their burdens; and he saw an Egyptian man striking a Hebrew man, of his brethren. He turned this way and that and saw that there was no man, so he struck down the Egyptian and hid him in the sand. (Shemot 2:11–12)

Hashem *said to Moshe, "One more plague shall I bring upon Pharaoh and upon Egypt; after that he shall send you forth from here. When he sends you forth, it shall be complete – he shall drive you out of here. Please speak in the ears of the people: Let each man request of his fellow and each woman from her fellow silver vessels and gold vessels."* (11:1–2)

Moshe Rabbenu – our most revered master and teacher, prince of prophets, Divine lawgiver and nation-builder par excellence – has always exerted an almost preternatural fascination on some of the most central narratives of modernity. From African-American spirituals, political reflection and Civil Rights symbolism[1] to Freudian deconstruction of identity and pop-culture iconography,[2] Moshe as Redeemer remains a robust, even towering, figure in the world of ideas and expression outside the walls of the *Beit Midrash*. Most recently, the best-selling author, Bruce Feiler, has declared Moshe "America's Prophet" and "true founding father," arguing that the story of Moshe and the Exodus is "the most American of templates."[3] But beyond the popular and political allusions, Moshe's story may serve to instruct us in the deep structures of choice, identity, and cultural formation, the most significant tropes shaping the modern religious condition. In this reading, Moshe's career as *Moshian shel Yisrael* serves not merely as the embodiment of a narrative of hope and redemption from oppression, but as a moral and theological primer on the choices we face as modern men and women, trying to lead authentic lives of piety and devotion to *Hashem* across multiple identities and worlds of discourse.

I. SLAYING THE EGYPTIAN

The birth and early life of Moshe provide rich material for an examination of the ambivalences and tensions of living with a multiple identity,

---

1. *The Nursing Father: Moses as a Political Leader,* Aaron Wildavsky (University of Alabama, 1984). See also, *Exodus and Revolution,* Michael Walzer (Basic Books, 1986).
2. Freud's idiosyncratic reconstruction of the origins of monotheism, *The Man Moses and the Monotheistic Religion* (1939) has received some recent critical treatment. See, especially, Susan Handelman, *The Slayers of Moses: The Emergence of Rabbinic Interpretation in Modern Literary Theory* (SUNY, 1982), Jan Assman, *Moses the Egyptian: The Memory of Egypt in Western Monotheism* (Harvard, 1997), and Richard J. Bernstein, *Freud and the Legacy of Moses* (Cambridge, 1998). See also Rabbi Jonathan Sacks, "Pesach, Freud and Jewish Identity," in *Rabbi Jonathan Sacks's Haggadah* (Continuum, 2007), pp. 15–19.
3. Brude Feiler, *America's Prophet: Moshe and the American Story* (William Morrow, 2009).

a condition that we citizens of late liberal democracy know all too well.[4] *Moshe Rabbenu* – born to slaves, bred and educated in *Beit Par'oh* – must know that his identity is a complex one. Moshe's world-class education makes him especially aware of the personal and ethical burden he bears, giving him both the intellectual and technical skills, as well as the refined sense of moral righteousness, that only a truly liberal education can provide.[5] It is this very deep and broad educational exposure which must have cultivated Moshe's awareness of the complexities of his own self, setting the stage for a decisive choice which will change things for him – and the rest of the world – forever.

Seeing his Jewish brethren suffering at the very hands of those employed by the Royal Household, his own home for the crucial formative years of his young life, Moshe, perhaps for the very first time, is forced to confront a profoundly unsettling question: *"Mi anokhi,* who am I, really?[6] At my most elemental, existential core, am I a favored son of Egypt or a despised son of Hebrew slaves?" Both identities were present under the surface in some blended, inchoate form, but, to date, neither had emerged with a distinctiveness or clarity: *"va-yifen koh va-khoh va-yar ki ain ish"* – "he turned here and there and saw no man" (*Shemot* 2:12). The deep empathy Moshe feels for his nation in witnessing this act of violence creates a connection with people and a coherence of self

4. On the problem of "double life" and contemporary religious identity, see Rav Hutner's now famous letter in *Pachad Yitzchak, Iggerot u-Ketavim,* p. 84.
5. Ibn Ezra (*Shemot* 2:3, ad loc.), catalogs the kind of curriculum the young *Moshe Rabbenu* must have been exposed to, emphasizing both the intellectual and moral advantages Moshe acquired by virtue of his royal education. For a comprehensive treatment of Moshe's pre-calling early career, see Bryna Yocheved Levy, "Moshe: Portrait of the Leader as a Young Man," in *Torah of the Mothers: Contemporary Jewish Women Read Classical Jewish Texts,* eds. Ora Wiskind Elper and Susan Handelman (Urim, 2000), pp. 398–429.
6. Rabbi Jonathan Sacks (above n. 2, p. 15) notes that the very first question Moshe asks *Hashem* when called to assume the role of redeemer is *"Mi anokhi?"* At the level of *peshat*, Rabbi Sacks reminds the reader that Moshe's question is more about personal worthiness – "who am I to stand before Pharaoh?" – than personal identity. Still, the language is suggestive. On the centrality of the theme of identity in *Sefer Shemot*, see also Caroline Peyser, "The Book of Exodus: A Search for Identity," in *Torah of the Mothers* (above n. 5), pp. 379–397.

that had perhaps eluded him to that point. At the very moment Moshe makes the dramatic decision to take a stand against the Egyptian oppressor afflicting his poor Jewish brother, two things occur: in the historical-temporal plane, Moshe slays the taskmaster, setting him at political odds with the Throne that reared him; in the psycho-spiritual realm, Moshe slays the Egyptian prince (*"va-yakh et ha-Mitzri"*) that still lurks uneasily in his heart, submerging this part of his dual-identity in the deep layers (*"va-yitmenehu ba-chol"*) of his sub-conscious mind. Moses, the Prince of Egypt, became Moshe, the radical Other, preparing the way for his prophetic calling. And even though just a few *pesukim* later Moshe will still be identified by his surface appearance as an Egyptian (*"ish Mitzri hitzilenu"*), something has changed, something has been clarified. He cannot simply go back to living in both worlds, the Egyptian and the Hebrew; something must give.

In every age, the faithful Jew must engage the surrounding culture not merely as consumer but, rather, as thoughtful and trenchant critic. When possible, the religiously-driven cultural critic may even turn into a cultural contributor, a partner in creating real artifacts, material and otherwise, informed by a compelling God-centered consciousness and religious worldview. In this way, he must witness against the powers and principalities that run counter to his Divinely implanted Image, offering a more sane and soulful alternative. And while our own religious community has encouraged us – mostly for the better, I believe – to think we can live the life of Both/And, there are critical moments of truth and decision that require a radical choice between Either/Or. When confronted with this choice, the true *eved Hashem* must side with the one necessary thing. *Moshe Rabbenu*, like his and our ancestor and patriarch, *Avraham Ha-Ivri* – the first cultural and religious iconoclast: *"kol ha-olam kulo al tzad echad ve-hu al tzad sheni"* – "the whole world is on one side, and he is on the other" – reminds us that, at its core, religion is a counter-cultural phenomenon, not a space for convenience or accommodation. Sometimes, we must simply choose.

II. EGYPT "DESPOILED"

One of the more challenging passages in the entire narrative of *Yetziyat Mitzrayim*, found in *Hashem's* first revelation to Moshe in *Parashat Shemot*, as well as in subsequent descriptions of the events of the Exodus, is the oft-repeated charge to *Benei Yisrael* to "empty out Egypt" (*Shemot* 3:21–22, 11:2, 12:35–36) of its material riches.[7] Instead of focusing on the moral questions many within our tradition here address, I'd like to look at a specific phrase within this narrative and, in light of our treatment of Moshe and the challenges of living with a dual-identity, offer another interpretation for the need of a special entreaty or request (*"daber na"*) in the context of this particular command of taking the spoils of Egypt.[8]

There is a strand of traditional commentary which understands the Gold and Silver of Egypt that the Jews were commanded to take as the spoils of their slavery sojourn in more than a material sense.[9] In this reading, the treasure of precious metals and fabrics are allusions to the intellectual capital, the repository of worldly wisdom, which was worthy of "redeeming" from the most advanced civilization the world had

7. For a comprehensive survey of some of the classical responses in *parshanut* to this difficult passage, see Yaakov (Gerald) Blidstein, "The Despoiling of Egypt in Rabbinic Sources" (Heb.), *Sinai*, vol. 67, *Av-Elul* 5730. More recently, see R. Elchanan Samet, "The 'Borrowing' of Vessels from the Egyptians" found at www.vbm-torah.org/parsha.63/15bo.htm (accessed 3/15/10). An unabridged Hebrew version of the shiur can be found at www.vbm-torah.org/hparsha-7/hparsha7.htm.

8. Rashi, based on the traditional exegetical understanding of *"ain 'na' ele lashon bakashah"* suggests that the gravity of God's command – this would, after all, be a fulfillment of Hashem's promise to *Avraham Aveinu* at the *berit bein ha-betarim* (*Bereishit* 15:14) – is what generates the petitionary plea of *"daber na."* Our reading speaks more to the way in which Moshe *personally* needs to be encouraged to carry out this difficult charge rather than the more general consideration of helping honor a Divine directive.

9. Rav Tzadok HaKohen, *Pri Tzadik, Vayigash*, 12. See also, R. Elijah Benamozegh, *Israel and Humanity*, trans. Max Luria (Paulist Press, 1995), pp. 72–3. In the Christian exegetical tradition, both Origen and Augustine see the "Gold and Silver of Egypt" as allegories for the pagan wisdom traditions that are proto-Christian and have since been "redeemed" by the revelation of Jesus. See, now, Joel S. Allen, *The Despoliation of Egypt in Pre-rabbinic, Rabbinic, and Patristic Traditions* (Brill, 2008). For a fascinating modern use of this motif, see Thomas Guarino, "'Spoils from Egypt:' Contemporary Theology and Non-Foundationalist Thought," *Laval theologique et philosophique*, vol. 51, no. 3 (1995), pp. 573–87.

yet seen. From the dross and decadence that had engulfed Egypt,[10] this newly-formed Jewish nation was to take what was true, what was good, and what was beautiful from their surrounding culture.[11]

As challenging as this requirement to elevate the "holy sparks" within Egyptian culture was for the common man from a former nation of slaves, Moshe's role in this particular command is especially complicated.

Moshe, after having made the stark, deliberate choice to slay the Egyptian taskmaster, setting him on a path of personal and spiritual self-discovery consciously at odds with the cultural hegemony that was *Mitzrayim*, must now re-engage those very same intellectual and cultural forces, in a kind of spiritual reclamation project. This command to mine the intellectual, spiritual and cultural treasures of Egypt must have presented a deeply challenging charge to the very personal identity Moshe so consciously cultivated in his wilderness wanderings. *Hashem* has to ask Moshe to, once again, open himself up to a world he has fundamentally rejected. This is potentially a perilous task, requiring both the special blessing and entreaty of Hashem (*"daber na be-aznei ha-am"*) and the practical wisdom of this spiritual titan (*"gam ha-ish Moshe gadol me'od be-Eretz Mitzrayim"*). Moshe does indeed fulfill the Divine will and promise, but the work of cultural (re-)engagement is arduous, requiring a degree of discernment and self-mastery that is anything but simple or natural.

We self-conscious moderns are, willy-nilly, denizens of an age of radical choice, desperately trying to fashion a coherent religious identity out of the welter of ideas and experiences that have shaped us. As we negotiate the challenges and confusions of modernity, *Moshe Rabbenu* remains, as ever, our most profound teacher.

---

10. Cf. *Vayikra* 18:3. Generally, *Chazal* and our *Mesorah* understand *Mitzrayim*/Egypt to be a repository of some of the crudest forms of culture. See especially, Maharal, *Gevurot Hashem*, Ch. 28 *supra*. For a contemporary treatment of *Mitzrayim*, informed by traditional tropes, see R. Chaim Friedlander, *Siftei Chayyim, Moadim* 2, p. 86.

11. On the theme of *Am Yisrael* as a synthesizer of the spiritual and cultural values of the nations of the world, see R. Avraham Yitzchak HaKohen Kook, *Orot*, p. 130. Note also the comment of R. Haim Baharier (cited in the journal *Emor* 1: January 2010, p. 13) that – based on the presence of the letters *gimmel* – *lammed*, which are present also in *agol*, circular – *Am Segulah* is "the people which guarantees the circulation of values."

Rabbi Ozer Glickman

וארא: *Chakham Adif Mi-Navi*: The Evolving Nature of Spiritual Leadership

> *God spoke to Moshe, saying to him: "I am YHVH. I appeared to Avraham, Yitzchak, and Yaakov as* Kel Shaddai *but was not known to them by My Name YHVH."* (Shemot 6:2–3)

Something has changed with the revelation to Moshe. God has made Himself known by His Name, the Tetragrammaton that is so revered that its very pronunciation is restricted. So many questions give us pause: Was the Name of God really unknown to the *Avot*? How do we account for the many times the Torah uses the Tetragrammaton in previous *parashiyyot*? How is the revelation to Moshe qualitatively different from earlier revelations to the *Avot*? Is it superior, inferior, or just different? What significance might this have for understanding our own relationship to God?

WAS THE TETRAGRAMMATON UNKNOWN TO THE *AVOT*?

For one cohort of commentators, including, notably, Rashi, Rashbam, Ramban, and the Ibn Ezra, it is not the Name itself that was unknown to the *Avot*, but rather the experience of the aspect of God represented by this Name. The Tetragrammaton denotes the constancy of God in history and His trustworthiness. The promises made to the *Avot* would be fulfilled under Moshe's leadership. He and *Am Yisrael* would experience the faithfulness denoted by His Name firsthand, knowledge that was impossible for the *Avot* who lived earlier, when the promises were first made.

This accounts for the appearance of the Tetragrammaton in earlier exchanges between God and the *Avot*. It is not the Name but the fulfillment of the promises represented by the Name, that the *Avot* did not experience. It is not their deficiency in faith or prophetic vision that prevented their perception of this quality of God, but rather logical necessity: one cannot know the future fulfillment of a promise until its time has come.

The revelation to Moshe is not necessarily qualitatively superior. In fact, it may be argued that it is actually an inferior revelation, dependent as it is on signs and wonders. So we find in many rabbinic sources, including the *Midrash Ha-Gadol* on this verse:

> R. Eliezer the son of R. Yosi Ha-Gelili says: There is a difference between the prophecy of the *Avot* and the prophecies of Moshe and the other prophets. When the Holy One Blessed be He was revealed to the *Avot* to speak with them, He was revealed neither through the image of celestial beings nor the Heavenly chariot, nor via any other distinctions, but the *Shekhinah* would rest upon them.

Note the references to two of the greatest of *Am Yisrael's* prophets: Yeshayahu and Yechezkel. The former saw the vision of the celestial beings (*chayot*) and the later pictured the Heavenly chariot (the *Mer-*

kavah). The surprising feature of the passage, as we shall see below, is the inclusion of Moshe together with them. In relation to the *Avot*, they are all lesser prophets.

This motif is very popular throughout midrashic literature and appears in several other places including the *Sefer Ha-Kuzari* (*Ma'amar* 11:2):

> God revealed Himself to Moshe and Yisrael in such a way that He left no doubt that the Creator of the Universe was creating these new phenomena such as the plagues against Egypt, the splitting of the *Yam Suf*, the manna, the *amud ha-anan*, etc. He did this for them not because they were greater than Avraham, Yitzchak, and Yaakov, but because they were numerous and doubts had arisen in their hearts. The *Avot*, on the other hand, had absolute faith and were pure of heart.

The *Avot* were intimate with God in a way never achieved by Moshe or other prophets. It is the immediacy of the experience of transcendence that was lost to later generations.

WAS NOT MOSHE SUPERIOR TO OTHER PROPHETS?

During the incident of Aharon and Miryam and their rebuke by God for maligning Moshe's marriage, God Himself testifies to the superiority of Moshe's prophecy (*Bemidbar* 12:6–8):

> And He said: "Hear now My words: if there is a prophet among you, I the Lord make Myself known to him in a vision; I speak with him in a dream. Not so with My servant Moshe; he is the most trusted in all My house; with him I speak mouth to mouth, demonstrably rather than enigmatically; he sees the image of the Lord. Why then were you not afraid to speak against My servant, against Moshe?"

Whereas in the *Midrash Ha-Gadol*, Moshe is grouped with the other prophets of Israel, in these verses he is distinguished from them due to the superiority of his prophecy. We must wonder if these verses are not enough to reconsider Moshe's status relative to the *Avot*. Moshe is adjudged as superior to later prophets. What about those who preceded him?

One answer may be found in Rambam's preamble to the Laws of Idolatry in the *Mishneh Torah*. Avraham's acceptance of God flowed neither from direct revelation nor sacred history, but rather, from the power of his own intellect. For Rambam, *Avraham Avinu* came to monotheism by realizing that there must be an organizing principle that explains the existence of the universe. Avraham's experience of God was primarily speculative and intuitive, rather than historical and empirical. He did not need signs and wonders to lead him to belief; the existence of the universe was more than sufficient.

Rambam does not ignore the praise of *Moshe Rabbenu* in *Bemidbar* Ch. 12. He refers to it directly in the *Mishneh Torah* in Ch. 7 of the Foundational Principles of the Torah. Rambam describes there the exceptional nature of Moshe as a prophet, the only prophet who receives direct verbal communication from God. Among the examples of other less direct communication are revelations to Avraham and to Yaakov. Rambam even uses the same word for "difference" used by the *Midrash Ha-Gadol*, the Hebrew word "*hefresh.*" Unlike the *Midrash Ha-Gadol*, however, he does not use it to describe the difference between the *Avot* and all other prophets but between *Moshe Rabbenu* and all other prophets.

It seems, then, that we have two different approaches to our verse in *Shemot* Ch. 6. According to one, the revelation to Moshe is less intimate than the revelations to the *Avot*, even as it is confirmation of God's trustworthiness to which they were never privy. According to the second, it is more direct and objective than the revelations to the *Avot* who, like other prophets, experienced God through visions and allegorical representations.

CAN THE TWO APPROACHES BE MEDIATED?

Following the *Midrash Ha-Gadol*, we envision the *Avot* as experiencing the Divine presence directly and not through the medium of history. They were enveloped by the *Shekhinah*, perhaps in the way we sense on the back of our necks the presence of another walking up behind us.

There was a sense of immediacy and intimacy. Their experience created in them a feeling of alterity that estranged them from the pagan and violent society in which they lived.

In this they are unique in Jewish history. They surpass all other prophets, including Moshe, through the intensity and immediacy of their perception of God's Presence.

Moshe, on the other hand, experienced the Divine more concretely. His prophecy is specific and more dependent on the cognitive than the intuitive. In this he surpasses all prophets, including the *Avot*. For Rambam, the legal philosopher, it is no surprise that he emphasizes the second approach, for it accords with *Moshe Rabbenu*'s role as lawgiver. Language and meaning do not rest upon linguistic convention, but upon the determinacy of Divine communication. The rule of law begins with an experience of objective meaning at Sinai. Only later will it become interpretive. Without objective meaning, we can only aspire to the bounded objectivity of interpretive communities, to borrow language from the jurisprudence of Owen Fiss.

With the destruction of the *Beit Ha-Mikdash* in the first century of the Common Era, the centrality of law was firmly established in contemporary religious experience. The Talmud describes the change in *Bava Batra* 12a:

> R. Avdimi from Haifa said: "Since the *Beit Ha-Mikdash* was destroyed, prophecy has been taken from the prophets and given to the sages." Is then a sage not also a prophet? What he meant was this: although it has been taken from the prophets, it has not been taken from the sage. Ameimar said: "*Ve-chakham adif mi-navi*" ("a sage is even superior to a prophet").

R. Avdimi cannot conceive of religious leadership devoid of prophecy. It is the model of spirituality that pertained to God's very first communication with the *Avot*. In Moshe, both models of spirituality were present – he was prophet and teacher. It is, however, as a teacher that he is principally remembered, for his prophecy was framed in legal terms. As Rambam notes in his Commentary to *Chullin* (Ch. 7), our lives are framed by the teachings of *Moshe Rabbenu* even in the commandments that hearken back to events in the lives of the *Avot*. Our experience of the Divine is through observance of the *mitzvot* rather than palpable experience of the *Shekhinah*.

Ameimar notes that in a post-prophetic age, the words of the sage carry more force than the words of the prophet. Our spiritual lives are built around the experience of the Divine through the study and observance of His law. The superiority of the sage is due to historical circumstance, just as *Moshe Rabbenu* surpassed the *Avot* in the knowledge of the Tetragrammaton due to the time in which he lived, the days in which its meaning was realized.

WHAT DOES THIS MEAN FOR CONTEMPORARY RELIGIOUS EXPERIENCE?

In the discordant cacophonous world in which we live, even the most extraordinarily sensitive ear cannot make out the Still Small Voice. We do not perceive the *Shekhinah* at our backs as the *Avot* did. We cannot hear even the first two commandments from the Almighty. We may yearn to huddle under the wings of the *Shekhinah* in troubled times, but feel estranged and alone.

There are moments, though brief and unexpected, when we may sense the eternity of the Divine Promise. They occur in the exchanges between teacher and student, parent and child, *rav ve-talmid*. Then we perceive the constancy of the Divine Essence, the Name of God, vouchsafed to an eternal people whose everlasting destiny was promised to its earliest ancestor in the ancient city of Ur.

Dr. Shira Weiss

בא: The Hardening of Pharaoh's Heart

At the beginning of *Shemot*, a new Pharaoh rises to power in Egypt. Feeling threatened by the strength and number of the Children of Israel, this new king devises a plan to enslave *Benei Yisrael*, thereby ensuring that they will not rebel and usurp control of his throne.

Early on in *Shemot* (2:24), God listens to the afflicted outcries of the Children of Israel and summons Moshe to go to Pharaoh in an effort to liberate His nation. Before carrying out this mission, God, however, explains to his emissary that Pharaoh will not free the Jews upon his request, since "I (God) will harden Pharaoh's heart" – "*va-ani achazzek et libo*" (ibid., 4:21). When Moshe then asks Pharaoh to grant the Children of Israel permission to travel on a three day journey to worship their God, Pharaoh refuses, "as God had spoken" (ibid., 7:13). Moshe appears before Pharaoh repeatedly prior to the onset of each of the first five plagues, but despite the afflictions Pharaoh endures, he obstinately refuses to heed Moshe's request. After each of the first five plagues, the Torah writes: "and Pharaoh's heart was hardened" – "*va-yechezak lev Par'oh*" or "and Pharaoh hardened his heart" – "*va-yakhbed Par'oh et libo.*" After the sixth plague, however, a literary shift appears in the text in which, instead of Pharaoh hardening his own heart, God is explicitly mentioned as hardening Pharaoh's heart – "*va-yechazek Hashem et lev Par'oh*" (ibid., 9:12). Subsequently, God continues to harden Pharaoh's heart in later plagues,[1] and on two additional occasions following Israel's exodus from Egypt. God hardens Pharaoh's heart, thereby motivating Pharaoh to pursue Israel through the desert (ibid., 14:8) and one final time, which prompts Pharaoh's army to follow Israel into the Red Sea (ibid., 14:17–18).

A number of philosophical questions that arise from the text have been discussed by Jewish philosophers from the medieval period to contemporary times.

1. Does Pharaoh, in fact, have free choice throughout the narrative?
2. If Pharaoh is simply a Divine puppet, in that God deprives him of his free choice by the end, how can Pharaoh be held responsible (and punished) for what he was compelled to do? In other words, how can God's hardening of Pharaoh's heart be reconciled with Divine justice?
3. A key Jewish value, often emphasized in liturgy, is God's desire for man to repent. Until man's dying day, God is said to accept man's return in repentance. Was Pharaoh afforded such an opportunity if God hardened his heart?
4. If Pharaoh was not able to liberate the Jews after (some of) the plagues, why did God insist that Moshe go through the motions of repeatedly appealing to Pharaoh to free his people?

Two medieval philosophical approaches, those of R. Moses Maimonides and R. Joseph Albo, have been perceived as being in opposition to each other. While they differ in their respective interpretations of the hardening of Pharaoh's heart, these two views, I will attempt to show, are more consistent than would appear at first glance, for both deny that God deprives Pharaoh of free choice and of an opportunity to repent.

---

1. With the exception of plague seven (*Shemot* 9:34), (*Shemot* 9:35) which will be dealt with in note 13.

Thus, both Maimonides and R. Albo hold Pharaoh responsible for his 'hardened' actions, thereby maintaining Divine justice in this narrative.

R. Moses Maimonides (1138–1204 CE), in two of his works, the *Mishneh Torah* and *Shemonah Perakim*, interprets this perplexing text. In the *Mishneh Torah*, Maimonides constructs the parameters of the legal category of repentance and uses the hardening of Pharaoh's heart as an illustration of the limits of repentance. In *Shemonah Perakim*, Maimonides is more concerned with the human disposition and its need for free choice, which Pharaoh abuses and is ultimately justifiably denied. In both sources, Maimonides uses the verses from *Shemot* to illustrate a legal category (repentance) and a philosophical concept (free choice). In the *Mishneh Torah, Laws of Repentance* (5:1), Maimonides asserts,

> Free choice is granted to all human beings. If one desires to turn himself to the path of good and be righteous, the choice is his. Should he desire to turn to the path of evil and be wicked, the choice is his.[2]

Similarly, in the beginning of the final chapter of *Shemonah Perakim*, Maimonides reaffirms the foundational belief of human free choice by expressing the Torah's consistency with Greek philosophy, which supports the contention: "that man's conduct is entirely in his own hands, that no compulsion is exerted."[3] Maimonides further argues (*Laws of Repentance*, 6:1–2) that just as man has free choice to sin, so too, he has free choice to repent from his wrongdoing. Maimonides, however, qualifies his general assertion in the following *halakhah* (ibid., 6:3), and articulates the rare occasions when one may be deprived of choice and an opportunity to repent, as a punishment for willful sins. He identifies Pharaoh there as such a sinner.

> A man may commit so great a sin or such numerous sins that

---

2. Maimonides. *Mishneh Torah*: A New Translation with Commentary and Notes. (New York: Moznaim Publishing, 1989), p. 114.
3. Maimonides. *The Eight Chapters of Maimonides on Ethics*, Trans. J. Gorfinkle. (New York: AMS Press, 1966), p. 88.

justice requires of the true judge, as the penalty to be exacted from this particular sinner for the sins, committed by him voluntarily and of his own mind, that repentance shall be withheld from him and liberty to turn from his wickedness shall not be accorded him, so that he may die and perish in the sins which he committed… Hence also, it is written in the Pentateuch, "And I will harden Pharaoh's heart" (*Shemot* 4:21). Because Pharaoh sinned on his own impulse and ill-treated the Israelites who sojourned in his land, as is said "Come let us deal shrewdly with them, so that they might not increase" (*Shemot* 1:10), justice required that repentance should be withheld from him till retribution had been visited upon him. God, accordingly, hardened his heart.[4]

Maimonides explains that there are certain situations in which God makes it impossible for a sinner to escape his well-deserved punishment for a heinous sin that he committed freely. He distinguishes between man's power to freely choose between sinning and not sinning and his power to freely choose between repenting from sin and not repenting from sin. In the case of the former (which is a matter of justice), God will never interfere; in the case of the latter (which is a matter of mercy), God may occasionally interfere. Maimonides identifies the time at which God hardens Pharaoh's heart as an instance of repentance, not sin, and therefore, Maimonides justifies God's intervention.

Maimonides continues his explanation by arguing that this type of punishment was not unique to Pharaoh. Sichon, too, because of his previous sins, was punished by being prevented from repenting, (as *Devarim* 2:30 states: "*ve-lo avah; Sichon melekh cheshbon, ha'avirenu bo ki hiksheh Hashem Elokekha et rucho, ve-imetz et levavo, lema'an tito ve-yadkha, ka-yom ha-zeh*" – "But King Sichon of Cheshbon refused to let us pass through, because God, your Lord, hardened his spirit and strengthened his heart…"). Additionally, the Canaanites, because of their abominable acts, were prevented from repenting so that they would wage war against Israel: "*Ki me'et* Hashem *haytah lechazek et libam likra't ha-milchamah et Yisrael, lema'an hacharimam, le-vilti heyot lahem techinah.*

4. Ibid., p. 140.

Ki lema'an hashmidam, ka'asher tzivah Hashem *et Moshe"* – "This was inspired by *God*, to harden their hearts so that they should come against Israel in battle in order to utterly destroy them and wipe them out, as the *Lord* had commanded Moses" (*Yehoshua* 11:20). The Israelites, too, during the period of Elijah, committed many sins which were also punished by withholding the option of repentance: *"Aneni Hashem, aneni, ve-ed'u ha-am ha-zeh, ki atah Hashem ha-Elokim. Ve-atah hasibota et libam achoranit"* – "...You have turned their hearts backwards" (*Melakhim* I 18:37).

Maimonides concludes that what is common to all of these cases is that God did not decree that Pharaoh should harm the Israelites, that Sichon should sin in his land, that the Canaanites should perform abominable acts, or that the Israelites should worship idols. Rather, they all sinned on their own initiative, and they deserved to have their repentance held back.

If this was a Divine punishment, Maimonides asks, then why then did God send Moshe to Pharaoh requesting the liberation of the Jews? God had already told him that Pharaoh would not release them! Maimonides responds that God made Moshe go through the motions of appealing to Pharaoh, despite God's intention to harden Pharaoh's heart, in order to make known to all of the inhabitants of the world that when God prevents a sinner from repenting, he cannot repent, but will die because of the wickedness which he initially committed willfully. As God said, "[But for this purpose, I have maintained you...] so that My Name will be proclaimed throughout the earth" (*Shemot* 9:16). As a result, Pharaoh and the Egyptians taught sinners not to continue in their ways with the expectation of a future opportunity of repentance.

According to Shaul Magid's interpretation of Maimonides, the Exodus achieved three goals: 1) to liberate Israel from slavery, 2) to show non-Israelites the power of God and 3) to make Israel realize that the covenant with God which they are about to enter, while based on reciprocity, includes the provision that God can punish them by eliminating their ability to repent. Pharaoh's motivation for enslaving the Jews was to thwart Israel's mission by destroying them in Egypt and thereby overcome God's will to liberate them. This attempt to reverse the power structure within a covenantal relationship constitutes an abuse of reciprocity and justifies the dominant partner's (God's) removal of the power of reciprocity (free choice). Maimonides codifies a rabbinic dictum to deal with abuses of reciprocity: "If one would say 'I will sin and then I will repent' (abusing the power of repentance to justify sinful behavior) God will make sure that individual has no opportunity to repent."[5]

Nachmanides (1194–1270 CE) begins his commentary on *Shemot* 7:3 by echoing Maimonides' approach through a reference to *Shemot Rabbah* (5:6). The *Midrash* explains that when God warns an individual on three occasions and he does not turn from his ways, God closes the door of repentance on him in order to punish the offender for his sin. Nachmanides argues that such was the case with Pharaoh, who was warned five times (before each of the first five plagues), but neglected to turn from his evil ways. As a result, God said to him: You have stiffened your neck and hardened your heart; I will double your defilement. Nachmanides then cites the question of the Rabbis in the *midrash* regarding the nature of Pharaoh's sin and the justice of God's punishment and offers two explanations in response. The first answer, similar to that of Maimonides, is that Pharaoh, in his wickedness, had unjustifiably perpetrated such great evils against Israel that justice required that the ways of repentance be withheld from him. He was judged according to his wickedness which he had originally committed of his own choice. Nachmanides then proceeds to offer an alternative approach. He explains that Pharaoh endured half of the plagues because of his transgressions, for in connection with them it is only said: "and Pharaoh's heart was hardened; and Pharaoh hardened his heart." Thus Pharaoh refused to recognize the glory of God and free the Israelites as a result of such recognition. Nachmanides, however, continues,

> But when the plagues began bearing down upon him and he became weary to suffer them, his heart softened and he bethought himself to send them out on account of the onslaught of the plagues, not in order to do the will of his Creator. Then God

---

5. Shaul Magid. "Pharaoh's Hardened Heart: Cruel and Unusual Punishment and Covenantal Ethics." *The Journal of Scriptural Reasoning* 2.2, (2002), p. 13.

hardened his spirit and made his heart obstinate, so that His name may be declared [throughout all the earth]. [6]

Nachmanides explains God's foretelling to Moshe, "and I will harden his heart, and he will not let the people go" (*Shemot* 4:17), as merely His warning to Moshe of that which He would do to Pharaoh in later plagues, similar to when He told Moshe, "and I know that the king of Egypt will not give you leave to go" (ibid., 3:18). God later explains His motivation for hardening Pharaoh's heart, "I will harden his heart so that My wonders may be multiplied in the land of Egypt" (ibid., 11:9), in order to demonstrate His omnipotence to both the Egyptians, as well as to Israel.

R. Joseph Albo (c. 1380–1444 CE), in his *Sefer Ha-Ikkarim* (Book of Principles) (IV:25), elaborates upon Nachmanides' second interpretation and stresses that God's hardening of Pharaoh's heart constituted a preservation of his free choice, not a deprivation as suggested by Maimonides and Nachmanides' first approach. R. Albo turns the tables on previous commentators. They had spoken about Pharaoh's repentance as a free act and the hardening as a coerced act, whereas R. Albo argues the very opposite: Pharaoh's repentance was coerced and the hardening of his heart was free. He develops Nachmanides' second approach, which does not discuss "choice" and "coercion," by identifying Pharaoh's repentance as an instance of coercion and his hardened act as an instance of choice.

R. Albo elucidates his theory in the context of his discussion of repentance, where he distinguishes between repentance from love and repentance from fear. R. Albo further subdivides the latter into repentance from fear of God and repentance from fear of punishment. He argues that while repentance out of love is superior, repentance out of fear of God still achieves atonement. Repentance that is motivated solely by fear of punishment, however, does not constitute true repentance at all. He compares this last type of penitent to a rebellious slave who begs his master for forgiveness while his master is beating him, but then reverts to disobedience once his suffering has ended. R. Albo identifies

---

6. Moses ben Nachman (Nachmanides). *Commentary on the Torah: Shemot* 7:3, Trans. Chavel. (NY: Shilo Publishing House, 1971), p. 79.

Pharaoh as this type of penitent, since by the end of the first five plagues, the multitude of afflictions began to have a debilitating effect that he could barely withstand. Only as long as the afflictions from the plagues were upon him would he proclaim, "I have sinned this time; the Lord is righteous, and I and my people are wicked" (*Shemot* 9:27). As soon as his suffering was alleviated, he hardened his heart again as before, thus reverting back to his original bad behavior.

So, since a decision by the king to liberate the Jews would have been coerced by the severe pain and fear of the punishment, it would not have constituted a free act, and would not have been regarded as repentance. God, therefore, hardened Pharaoh's heart after each of the remaining plagues, by suggesting to him alternative causes to explain such calamities other than Divine providence – chance, accident, or nature – in order to remove the softening effect of the suffering, so that Pharaoh could make a free, non-coerced, sincere decision to repent or not repent. According to R. Albo, then, God hardened Pharaoh's heart in order to preserve, not deprive him of, his free will, and allow his true self to be restored.

> Then it may be found out whether his repentance was free or not. Now since, when the yoke of the plague was removed from Pharaoh, his choice was evil, God said: "I hardened his heart," i.e., I removed from his heart the softening effect which came from the plague and restored him to the natural state of freedom; while he, owing to his wicked attitude, when in a state of freedom, sought various causes and excuses to which he might ascribe the plagues so that they might seem accidental.[7]

Had Pharaoh repented out of fear of God, with the acknowledgment of God's might even in times of respite and with the recognition that all things (even natural events) come from God, he would have been forgiven. Pharaoh, however, freely refused to liberate the Jews after the sixth, seventh, eighth and ninth plagues. Even after the Jews left Egypt follow-

7. R. Joseph Albo. *Sefer Ha-Ikkarim* [Book of Principles] IV:25, Trans. Husik. (Philadelphia: The Jewish Publication Society of America, 1946), p. 227.

ing the deaths of the firstborn, Pharaoh continued to willfully ascribe God's wonders to accident, and pursued Israel into the Sea, thereby coming to deserve his ultimate downfall. R. Albo is suggesting that the plagues caused cowardice, whereas choice requires courage. God, then, hardened Pharaoh's heart in order to afford him courage, which would enable him to overcome the softening effect of the plagues and arrive at a free decision whether or not to repent. Therefore, R. Albo writes, after the suffering from the plagues were alleviated, Pharaoh took courage (*"nitchazek"*) and pursued the Israelites, thereby proving that his initial repentance (liberation of the Israelites) was due to the compulsion of his punishment (*"be-ones u-mechamat ha-makkot"*), and was not a result of free choice (*"bechirut"*).

R. Albo similarly interprets God's 'hardening' of Sichon's heart (*Devarim* 2:30) by explaining that Sichon was guilty of his wickedness, but feared to come into conflict with Israel because of the miracles he had heard that God had performed for Israel against past enemies. As a result, God imposed circumstances to remove the softening effect from his heart and to leave him solely to his freedom. That, according to R. Albo, is why God made Israel turn away from Edom when its king refused Israel permission to pass through its borders. When Sichon saw this, he assumed that Israel's past successes were not due to Divine providence, and that he could refuse them entry as Edom and Moab had done. This removed the softening effect of Sichon's fear and allowed him to make a free decision whether or not to let Israel pass through his land. The responses of Sichon and Pharaoh in the height of their fear, according to R. Albo, do not constitute repentance. He, however, who repents as a result of fear that stems from a recognition that every event is the result of Divine providence, and does not seek pretexts and extraneous explanations for God's ways, *is* considered a penitent.

While R. Albo's argument that God's hardening preserved Pharaoh's free choice seems to oppose Maimonides' approach that God's hardening deprived Pharaoh of his free choice, a deeper analysis of Maimonides' view may reflect commonality between the two interpretations. In light of other references within Maimonides' philosophy, his interpretation of God's hardening of Pharaoh's heart need not be understood as direct Divine intervention, resulting in the withholding of his free choice. In fact, medieval philosophical interpretations of the Bible often reflect a largely naturalistic perspective, including Maimonides' conceptions of God's prophecy, providence and miracles in *The Guide of the Perplexed*.[8] According to Maimonides, God fixed nature, which reflects Divine wisdom and providence and allows for minimal supernatural intervention. Therefore, God commands man to engage His providence by freely choosing virtue over vice in an effort to develop himself and achieve human perfection. In the *Guide* (II:48), Maimonides explains that while human actions are, in fact, free, they are often attributed by the prophets to God, since He is the First Cause of all things, including human actions (but such an attribution does not denote Divine intervention).

> It is very clear that everything that is produced in time must necessarily have a proximate cause, which has produced it. In its turn that cause has a cause and so forth till finally one comes to the First Cause of all things, I mean God's will and free choice. For this reason all those intermediate causes are sometimes omitted in the dicta of the prophets, and an individual act produced in time is ascribed to God, it being said that He, may He be exalted, has done it.[9]

So too, in his interpretation of God's hardening of Pharaoh's heart, Maimonides may not have been arguing that God intervened in order to exact a deserved punishment upon Pharaoh which deprived him of his free choice and ability to repent, thus forcing him to do evil. Rather, the "punishment" alluded to in the *Mishneh Torah* may have been referring to the natural consequence of Pharaoh's actions. Indeed, Nehama Leibowitz (1905–1997), in her *Studies in Shemot*, conceives of Maimonides' theory of God's hardening of Pharaoh's heart in a more naturalistic manner that reflects Pharaoh's self-choice. In a psychological explanation, she

8. Maimonides, *The Guide of the Perplexed*, II:32–48 (prophecy), III:17–23, 51 (providence), II:29 (miracles).
9. Moses Maimonides. *The Guide of the Perplexed*. Trans. Pines. (Chicago: University of Chicago Press, 1963), p. 409.

argues that man initially has complete freedom to choose to do good or evil. As soon as he makes his first choice, however, his options are no longer as equal. For instance, if he chooses evil, even though at first his alternatives of good or evil were evenly balanced, as he persists on the evil path, it becomes progressively more difficult for him to revert back to choose good. Technically, however, his freedom of choice is not affected and no external force is coercing his decision. Leibowitz interprets the hardening of Pharaoh's heart in similar terms.

> God did not force Pharaoh to choose evil. It was Pharaoh's own doing. Once he persisted in his course of action it became more and more irresistible. God had built this response, as it were, into man's make-up. The more he sins, the more his sins act as a barrier between him and repentance.[10]

Thus, Pharaoh's punishment was not Divinely caused, but was rather the natural result of his earlier free choices. Pharaoh's initial free decision to afflict the Jews altogether was exacerbated by his continuous self-willed refusals to release the Jews after each of the first five plagues. Pharaoh is, therefore, morally responsible for his actions which caused his unavoidable predicament in the latter half of the narrative. Such a modern reading actually reflects an ancient Aristotelian influence. Aristotle (384 BC–322 BC) argues in *Nicomachean Ethics* 111:5 that an individual is responsible for his character and his unavoidable bad actions that result from his previous choices.

> If it is manifest that a man is the author of his own actions, and if we are unable to trace our conduct back to any other origins than those within ourselves, then actions of which the origins are within us, themselves depend upon us, and are voluntary... Men are themselves responsible... they acquire a particular quality by constantly acting in a particular way. Therefore, only an utterly senseless person can fail to know that our characters are the result

10. Nehama Leibowitz. *Studies in Shemot.* (Jerusalem: World Zionist Organization, 1976), p. 157.

of our conduct; but if a man knowingly acts in a way that will result in his becoming unjust, he must be said to be voluntarily unjust…this by no means implies that he can stop being unjust and become just merely by wishing to do so…When you have thrown a stone, you cannot afterwards bring it back again, but nevertheless you are responsible for having taken up the stone and flung it, for the origin of the act was within you. Similarly the unjust and profligate might at the outset have avoided becoming so, and therefore they are so voluntarily, although when they have become unjust and profligate it is no longer open to them not to be so.[11]

As a result, Pharaoh's free initial decisions cause his later inability to repent, for which he is appropriately held accountable. While Leibowitz does not address the Scriptural language of Divine causality, she implies that since God does not intervene, the ascription of the hardening of Pharaoh's heart in later plagues to God refers to God's creation of the psychology of man such that, the more he sins, the more his evil decisions seem irresistible, even though there is no external compulsion. Nahum Sarna (1923–2005) more explicitly articulates God's role in this naturalistic approach in his *JPS Commentary on Shemot* 4:21. Sarna explains that from the Biblical perspective, the heart is considered the source of the intellectual, moral and spiritual faculties that determine one's actions. The "hardening of the heart" reflects a state of "arrogant moral degeneracy, unresponsive to human reason." In the aftermath of each of the first five plagues, the hardening of Pharaoh's heart is self-willed, and only thereafter ascribed to God. Similar to Leibowitz, Sarna argues that the attribution to Divine causality does not imply Divine intervention, but rather is the "biblical way of asserting that the king's intransigence has by then become habitual and irreversible; his character has become his destiny. He is deprived of the possibility of relenting

---

11. Aristotle, *The Nicomachean Ethics*. Trans. H. Rackman. (Cambridge: Harvard University Press, 1956), III:5, p. 149.

and is irresistibly impelled to his self-wrought doom,"[12] even though no external force compels his action. This naturalistic interpretation can also explain the lesson that Egypt and Israel were to learn from God's hardening of Pharaoh's heart, namely, not to perpetuate sin with the expectation of a future opportunity to repent. According to this reading, Pharaoh's self-willed downward spiral could serve as a lesson for Egypt and Israel not to underestimate the powerful impact of sinful behavior upon future actions, even without external coercion. The Egyptians and Israelites needed to learn from Pharaoh's example that they may not have the ability to reform from their wicked conduct, not because God deprives sinners of free will or ability to repent, but due to the irresistible pressure of their habitual corruptive actions.

In light of the naturalistic reading, Maimonides' interpretation is no longer in opposition to that of R. Albo, for both maintain that Pharaoh had free will throughout the narrative.[13] In response to the

---

12. Nahum Sarna. *JPS Torah Commentary: Exodus.* (Philadelphia: The Jewish Publication Society, 2004), p. 23.

13. There is a clear distinction between the first and second half of the plagues as reflected in the shift in language, in that, according to both R. Albo and a naturalist reading of Maimonides, the debilitating effect of the progression of the first five plagues took a toll on Pharaoh. In the first five, according to both opinions, Pharaoh hardened his own heart and was thereby responsible for his decisions. By the sixth, according to R. Albo, the debilitating effect of the plagues caused the softening of Pharaoh's heart, which motivated God to suggest alternative sources of the plague to allow Pharaoh to make a non-coerced decision. According to (naturalist) Maimonides, Pharaoh's habitual decisions in the first five determined his decision in the sixth.

Note that in the following plague (number seven, as alluded to in note 1), the language reverts back to Pharaoh hardening his own heart. R. Albo might explain this brief shift back to the language of self-hardening as an attempt by the text to demonstrate that God did not supernaturally compel Pharaoh's decision in plague six, and will not be doing so in plagues eight and onward. Rather, according to R. Albo, Pharaoh himself chose an alternative explanation for the plagues, even when the debilitating pressure of the plagues would have motivated him to acknowledge their Divine source; hence, he acted freely. A parallel explanation of plague seven is available to Maimonides. According to the naturalist interpretation of Maimonides, Pharaoh's earlier free choices made his later decisions irresistible, without any external compulsion. So his choices were his own responsibility even though in the latter plagues he could not have chosen otherwise.

questions posed earlier, both Maimonides' and R. Albo's views agree that Pharaoh's initial decision to afflict Israel, and the subsequent choices he made as a result of the hardening of his own heart as well as God's hardening of his heart – these reflect his own free choices, and therefore God was justified in holding him responsible for his wrongdoing. Pharaoh was, in fact, a malicious tyrant (and not a Divine puppet), since he was afforded numerous opportunities to recognize God's omnipotence (but he neglected to do so of his own volition), and was never deprived of the ability to repent. Moshe needed to appeal to Pharaoh numerous times throughout the narrative in order to give Pharaoh the opportunity to retreat from his evil. Pharaoh's failure to do so could then serve as a lesson for the Egyptians and Israelites regarding the nature of free choice and repentance.

God has given humanity the privilege of free choice which comes with moral responsibility. As a result, man must lead his life in a manner in which he exercises free choice carefully in pursuit of religious values, instead of exploiting such freedom, as Pharaoh did (which led to his corruption). As Chief Rabbi Sir Jonathan Sacks writes in *To Heal a Fractured World: The Ethics of Responsibility*,

The God who gave us the gift of freedom asks us to use it to hon-

---

The language of plague seven, then, enables the reader to realize that God did not and will not supernaturally remove Pharaoh's free choice even when the Bible says that *God* hardened Pharaoh's heart. Having made Pharaoh's freedom and responsibility clear by its language in plague seven, the *Chumash* could simply say in the subsequent plague narratives (and in the narrative about his pursuing the Israelites to the Sea) that God hardened Pharaoh's heart and the reader would understand that Pharaoh was responsible for those decisions. Obviously, this treatment of plague seven is pure conjecture, and a loose end that can be tied up only by speculating. Note, however, that no matter what theory of hardening one adheres to, plague seven is an anomaly (why would God in this one case not harden Pharaoh's heart?), and therefore any theory of hardening will necessitate a conjecture about why the text attributes Pharaoh's resistance in plague seven to Pharaoh and not God.

For a different explanation of how a Maimonidean might explain the anomaly of the seventh plague, see David Shatz, "Freedom, Repentance and Hardening of Hearts." *The Jewish Philosophy Reader*, Ed. Daniel Frank, Oliver Leaman, and Charles Manekin (New York: Routledge, 2000), p. 56.

our and enhance the freedom of others. God, the ultimate Other, asks us to reach out to the human other. More than God is a strategic intervener, He is a teacher. More than He does our will, He teaches us how to do His. Life is God's call to responsibility.[14]

This was precisely Pharaoh's failure, and this is the lesson we must internalize by exercising our free choice in a morally responsible manner to actualize the potential for which we were created.

14. Jonathan Sacks, *To Heal a Fractured World: The Ethics of Responsibility* (N Y: Schocken Books, 2005), p. 3.

I am grateful to Professors David Shatz, Zev Harvey and Charles Manekin for their correspondence regarding ideas in this article.

Rabbi Netanel Wiederblank

בשלח: Free Will and the Exodus: Is It Ever Too Late to Turn Around?

INTRODUCTION

> וחזקתי את לב פרעה ורדף אחריהם ואכבדה בפרעה ובכל חילו וידעו
> מצרים כי אני ה'.

And I will harden Pharaoh's heart, and he will chase after them; and I will be honored through Pharaoh and all his host; and the Egyptians shall know that I am God. (*Shemot* 14:4)

Few religious doctrines have sustained as many attacks as free will. It has been questioned both by non-Torah sources, from ancient philosophers to modern psychologists and neuroscientists, and from within, through grappling with the seeming contradiction between Divine foreknowledge and free will. Nevertheless, the notion of free will is clearly articulated by the Torah[1] and is the basis for moral responsibility as well as reward and punishment.[2] Let us then consider one of the most potent critiques of free will: cases where the Torah itself seems to indicate that a particular agent or agents have lost their free will.

This inquiry touches on another thorny theological issue – *teshuvah*. Those cases where God seems to remove the free will of a sinner call into question the notion that the gates of repentance are never sealed. Thus, let us also consider, is it ever too late to turn around?

There are numerous cases where the Torah, at least according to some interpretations, seems to indicate a loss of free will. These deal with individuals[3] as well as large groups of people, and include both Jews[4] and non-Jews.[5] We will focus, however, on the person who is most overtly and frequently[6] described as a target of manipulation – the Egyptian king Pharaoh.[7]

While the verses in this week's *parashah* explicitly state God's motivation in hardening Pharaoh's heart – so that the entire world will

1. "I [God] have set before you life and death, blessing and curse: therefore choose life" (*Devarim* 30:19). See Ch. 5 of Maimonides' *Hilkhot Teshuvah* for numerous other verses.
2. See Maimonides, *Hilkhot Teshuvah*, Ch. 5: "This matter [of there being a free will] is a very important principle, and is the pillar of the Torah and *mitzvot*." It is beyond the scope of this article to consider Jewish thinkers who may have limited free will.
3. See, for example, *Devarim* (2:30) regarding Sichon and *Shemuel* I (2:25) regarding the sons of Eli.
4. See *Melakhim* I (18:37) regarding the people during the time of Eliyahu; *Yeshayahu* (6:10) regarding the people of his generation; and *Divrei Ha-Yamim* II (36:16), referring to the people during the time of Tzidkiyahu. Note, in each of these cases the verses do not explicitly state that free will was removed. Rambam in the sixth chapter of *Hilkhot Teshuvah* sees all of the aforementioned examples as instances of Divine hardening. See Radak on *Yeshayahu* (6:10) for alternative explanations.
5. See *Yehoshua* (11:20) regarding the Canaanites.
6. See *Shemot* (4:21; 7:3; 9:12; 10:1, 20, 27; 11:10; 14:4, 8, and 17).
7. Even in the case of Pharaoh not all commentaries agree that the phrase "hardening of the heart" implies intervention in Pharaoh's decision-making process. *Akeidat Yitzchak* Ch. 36 understands that God simply provided a break between plagues which allowed Pharaoh to withstand the pressure of the plagues. Likewise, see *Emunot Ve-De'ot* IV:6.

know of God's existence[8] – we are still left wondering how to justify God's intervention in light of the tenets of free will and *teshuvah*. In this article, we will explore four possible approaches to the vexing problem. Before beginning, however, consider reading Dr. Shira Weiss's excellent article "The Hardening of Pharaoh's Heart" on *Parashat Bo* of this volume, where she addresses these issues as well, though from a different perspective. Reading both articles will hopefully benefit the reader by offering dual and somewhat differing perceptions.

THE FIRST APPROACH: FREE WILL AS A GIFT

We generally conceive of free will as a given – something which is automatic and, absent intervention, irrevocable. Rambam, in the sixth chapter of his *Hilkhot Teshuvah*, informs us that we may be hasty in making this assumption. While generally humans are granted free will, this freedom is a gift and an opportunity, one which makes us, as it were, God-like,[9] and can bring us to lofty heights. However, like all opportunities, it can be revoked if not deserved. Thus, Rambam argues, if someone sins in a particularly egregious manner, as was the case with Pharaoh, then the gift of free will can be taken away.[10]

Rabbi Simeon ben Tzemach Duran, or Tashbetz (1361–1444 CE),[11] goes even further. Even though a person's nature is ostensibly shaped by

8. "And I will harden Pharaoh's heart, and he will chase after them; and I will be honored through Pharaoh all his host; and the Egyptians shall know that I am God." (*Shemot* 14:4).

9. Rambam writes that the textual source for our freedom of will is the verse "Behold, the man has become like one of us, knowing good and evil." According to Rambam this means, "there is only one mankind in the world and that there is no other type with respect to this matter such that he alone with his intellect and thoughts knows what is good and bad, and he can do all that he wishes, and there is nothing that will prevent him from doing good or evil." I believe that this notion is integral to refuting the critique to free will based on neuroscience. If one accepts that there is nothing more to a human than the cells that comprise its body, then indeed there is little room for free will. We, however, believe, that the root of our decision making process is our spiritual, and non-physical, soul.

10. Of course, Pharaoh was not held responsible for the decisions made after he lost his free will. Rather, his loss of free will, as well as the suffering he experienced thereafter, were punishments for the sins he made volitionally.

11. *Teshuvot Tashbetz* 2:1.

his characteristics and nurture, a person still has freedom to go against his natural inclinations.[12] However, this does not happen automatically. On the contrary, it only can happen if a person lives and acts thoughtfully and actively. Absent this, a person can go his entire life making decisions deterministically, based on his nature, without truly exercising his free will. Essentially, a person can choose whether or not to tap into his free will. Put differently, we have free will to have free will.

Interestingly, psychological studies show that people who believe they have free will tend to act with greater freedom than fatalists and determinists who deny their ability to control their destiny. For example, people who believe that self-control is nearly unlimited (e.g., "I can change my eating and be a better person, it just takes willpower") tend to be much more successful at fulfilling resolutions than people who believe that we all are born with a limited amount of self-control (e.g., "I can't help myself from eating all this chocolate – I inherited the 'chocolate gene' from my mom!").[13]

We can now understand why loss of free will was an appropriate punishment for Pharaoh. This is because, according to the Bible, Pharaoh hardened his *own* heart for the first five plagues. It was only during the latter plagues that God hardened Pharaoh's heart.[14] What does it mean that Pharaoh hardened his own heart? Presumably, this suggests that he refused to acknowledge what was patently clear. The first five plagues demonstrated God's existence and power to any objective observer. Pharaoh nevertheless ignored this evidence. It was precisely this act of self-deception which warranted the punishment of loss of free

12. He writes:
והדרך הפילוסופי הוא שההכנ' המזגי' המזגיי' [humors] הם מסודרו' מפאת הגרמים השמיים ועל זה תראה משפט אחד יגזור פ' יוליד בנים או בנו' כך וכך ויהיו כ"ו ויתחתן עם פ' וזה קודם היצירה זמן מרובה ואע"פ שהאדם בחירי לבטל זאת הגזרה אם יתנהג ע"פ שכלו אבל אם יתנהג לפי טבעו הגזרה היא מתקיימ'.
13. Mukhopadhyay, A. & Johar, G.V. (2005). "Where There Is a Will, Is There a Way? Effects of Lay Theories of Self-Control on Setting and Keeping Resolutions." *Journal of Consumer Research*, 31, pp. 779–786.
14. See *Shemot Rabbah* 13:3.

will – the ultimate *middah keneged middah* – Pharaoh did not utilize the gift of freedom, so it was removed.[15]

Frequently, we fall prey to this very flaw, albeit to a lesser extent. By not living introspectively or refusing or consider certain types of experiences, we, as it were, are hardening our own hearts. Along similar lines, the lifestyle choices a person makes will oftentimes create a limiting force on his free will. Rambam gives an example of this in *Hilkhot De'ot* (6:1): Because a person is significantly shaped by his surroundings, if he lives in an environment which supports bad behavior he will almost inevitably be influenced; therefore, his only option, should he wish to remain untainted, is to move. If such a person stays, he will be effectively removing his own free will (with respect to that particular vice).[16] Pharaoh did exactly that – he became so set in his evil ways that he could not retract; he became so habituated in his evil behavior that he did not see goodness as an option. True, he once had free will (with respect to persecution of the Jews), but now he no longer saw two

---

15. See D. Shatz, "Freedom, Repentance and Hardening of the Hearts: Albo vs. Maimonides," *Faith and Philosophy* (1997, 14:4) for a similar explanation of Rambam.

16. Whether Rambam would go so far as to say that such a person has virtually no choice but to sin is unclear. On the one hand, Rambam states that a person always has absolute freedom, even about things which seemingly are not in a person's control such as wisdom and/or intelligence (see *Hagahot Maimoniot, Hilkhot Teshuvah* 5:2). At the same time, Rambam acknowledges the invariable influence of one's surroundings to the point where he advises a person to move to a desert if he cannot find a wholesome environment. Choosing to remain in one's place and resist the influence of one's surroundings is not a feasible option even for Rambam. R. Eliyahu Dessler is most famous for adapting the limited approach and acknowledging that there are areas that are beyond a person's purview of freedom – *nekudat ha-bechirah* (*Mikhtav Me-Eliyahu* Vol. 1, *Kuntress Ha-Bechirah, Chelek Aleph*, Ch. 1–2, pp. 111–114). For example, we do not truly consider certain options based on our nature and nurture. With this understanding, we can comprehend the other instances in the Bible when free will was removed. As R. Dessler explains, oftentimes something is initially within our purview of freedom (*nekudat ha-bechirah*) but we remove it from that window through the choices we make (such as where we live). Likewise, in all of the other cases in which the Rambam mentions free will was removed, the parties had sunk so low in their wickedness that they did not see goodness as an option – they abused their own free will, and therefore as a punishment it was revoked. Thus Rambam sees *"hashmein leiv ha-am ha-zeh"* (*Yeshayahu* 6:10) as a reference to a loss of free will.

options. He had taken away a portion of his own free will, and thus as a punishment God took away the rest.[17]

According to Tashbetz, we can consider going even further. Perhaps the removal of Pharaoh's free will was not an external punishment, as Rambam suggests, but was a naturalistic expression of his own failure to tap into his own free will. Perhaps Pharaoh became so set in his course that free choice, with respect to freeing the Jews, became impossible for him – he could no longer consider going against his nature because his nature became so entrenched.[18] At an earlier stage, Pharaoh may have

17. Dr. Shira Weiss in "Hardening Pharaoh's Heart" goes even further, arguing that Maimonides and R. Joseph Albo should be understood as more consistent theories than would appear at first glance, in that "both deny that God deprives Pharaoh of free choice and of an opportunity to repent. Thus, both Maimonides and R. Albo hold Pharaoh responsible for his 'hardened' actions, thereby maintaining Divine justice in this narrative." While our theories agree that according to Rambam, Pharaoh should be held responsible, we differ in our understanding of the extent to which God revokes his free will. This is primarily based on the text of sixth chapter of *Laws of Repentence*, which, to me, indicates that free will was actually removed as a punishment for Pharaoh's egregious sins. The Rambam writes:

> It is possible to commit a great sin or a number of sins until one comes before the true judge for judgment, but one's *punishment* will be according to the sins which one had committed knowingly and willingly, which hinder repentance and do not allow one to return from one's wickedness, so one will therefore die and be destroyed because of one's sin…Therefore, the Torah says, "And I will harden Pharaoh's heart" – because he *initially* sinned willingly and caused bad for the Jews living in his country, as it is written, "Come, let us deal wisely with them" [note how Rambam assumes here that he was the same king], the law permitted the suppression of his repentance until it was denied to him. Therefore, the Holy One, Blessed Be He, hardened his heart (translation by Immanuel O'Levy).

These words preclude the type of explanation that we will suggest for Tashbetz and that is stated explicitly by Meiri, because they indicate that Pharaoh's free will was actually removed as a punishment for his initial sins (done volitionally), of enslaving and murdering the Jews who lived in his country. Thus, even if Pharaoh is ultimately a Divine puppet, this does not detract from his undoubtedly being a malicious tyrant for his murderous reign of terror.

18. This is reminiscent of Yirmiyahu's charge: "No man repented of his wickedness, saying: 'What have I done?' Everyone turns away in his course, as a horse that rushes headlong in the battle" (*Yirmiyahu* 8:6). One way to understand this statement is that the prophet laments that the Jewish people are like horse charging into battle,

still had the presence of mind to reconsider, but after the fifth plague this was no longer possible.[19] Along similar lines, Meiri, in *Chibbur Ha-Teshuvah*, denies that Pharaoh actually lost anything at all.[20] He understands the phrasing of God's hardening his heart to mean that Pharaoh chose his path entirely on his own, but this is ascribed to God, since by choosing to refrain from transcending his evil nature, he retained that nature which God had initially instilled in him, and we therefore ascribe this to God, even though he had actually been perfectly capable of choosing to be good.[21]

THE SECOND APPROACH: REDEFINING FREE WILL

Imagine the following scenario: John tells Tom that he is going to twist his arm until he says, "uncle." Initially, Tom refuses, but when the pain becomes overwhelming he says "uncle." Did Tom act freely? In one sense, of course he did – he could have refused. On the other hand, he did not desire to do what he did. After all, he did not want to say "uncle;" he only did so because he felt compelled.

According to Ramban,[22] a similar thing happened in Egypt. Pharaoh really did not want to allow the Jews to leave. He was able to follow through on this decision for the first five plagues. As the plagues wore on and the pressure intensified, Pharaoh's heart grew faint and he was no longer able to withstand the pressure of the plagues. He was going to relent, not because he wanted to allow the Jews to leave, but because he felt compelled to act against his free will. At that moment God stepped in and strengthened Pharaoh's heart, which means, according to this understanding, that He gave him the fortitude to withstand the pain

whose momentum is so great that there is almost no choice but to continue going forward. Likewise, see *Mesilat Yesharim* (Ch. 2), who derives from this verse the importance of always living introspectively.

19. This leaves open the interesting question of whether eventually Pharaoh did freely release the Jews.

20. My thanks to R. Yitzchak Grossman for informing me of this source.

21. This explanation is troubling both textually (the *pasuk* implies an active intervention) and theologically (did God give Pharaoh an evil nature). Further thought is required.

22. *Shemot* 7:3, second explanation.

and carry out his plan of refusing to allow the Jews to leave.[23] This fits perfectly with the text of the *pasuk* which states *"va-yichazek Hashem et libo,"* literally "and God strengthened (and not hardened) his heart."[24]

Had God not given him this dose of anesthesia, Pharaoh would have relented and freed the Jews. This, according to Ramban, would not have been considered free will – on the contrary, it would have been coercion. Meaningful free will, from a theological perspective, is the choice to choose between right and wrong. Pharaoh almost lost that choice. He wanted to do wrong, but could not until God stepped in and strengthened his heart. Ironically, in order to preserve free will, God had to harden Pharaoh's heart.

Conceptually, Ramban is suggesting that free will is defined as the ability to choose between right and wrong, and not merely the ability to choose x or y. While we perhaps cannot always choose between the morally inconsequential x or y, we are always guaranteed the choice between good and evil.[25]

23. Here too we may wonder whether eventually Pharaoh freely release the Jews or whether his decision was a result of coercion from the plagues.
24. R. Yigal Sklarin pointed out to me that this matter relates to R. Elchonon Wasserman's treatment of the halakhic exemption from the violation of a prohibition in which one acted against his will, i.e. the concept of *ones*, which can be defined as a situation when one's actions and intentions aren't congruous. R. Elchonon (*Kovetz Ha'arot* 49:3) asks what is the reason we exempt one who is forced into violating the Torah: is it because he was forced, and the Torah exempts him, and therefore we view his forbidden act as a permitted one; or is it because his actions and intentions don't match up that he is exempted? A difference between these two possibilities would be if someone was forced to act a certain way, but would have proceeded in the same way on his own accord. Based on the former explanation, the exemption of *ones* would be applied, while according to the later explanation, one would still be held accountable for his actions, even though they were forced. God didn't want Pharaoh to free the Jews against his will through *ones*, therefore, God would only allow Pharaoh to free the Jews when his actions would be compatible with his desires.
25. Along similar lines, Radak explains (*Shemuel* 1 2:25, ad loc.) that when the verses indicate that the sons of Eli were not allowed to repent from their misdeeds, it does not mean that they lost free will. Rather, it means that they lost their ability to feign repentance. Had they intended to repent sincerely, they would have been granted the opportunity.
   ואפילו ירבה הרשע לחטוא אם שב אל ה׳ בכל לבבו ומראה לבני אדם גם כן תשובתו שלימה ואוחז הדרך

THE THIRD APPROACH: KINGS ARE DIFFERENT

King Solomon wrote: *"Palgei mayim lev melekh, be-yad Hashem; al kol asher yachpotz yatenu"* (*Mishlei* 21:1). In other words, just as a farmer might direct the flow of a stream to irrigate his fields, so God directs the heart of the king. While regular people may always be granted free will, this verse indicates that kings may be different. Interestingly, two reasons are given for the reason why kings are particularly subject to Divine influence. Rabbenu Yonah and Ralbag attribute this to the immense impact of the decisions of kings. It would be reckless for God to grant full freedom of choice to a leader, as this may subject his subjects to his irrational whims.[26] A second rationale for why God might suspend the freedom of choice from leaders is for teleological reasons.[27] If there is purpose, direction, and providence within history, then, at times, God may limit the freedom of influential people to carry out a particular plan.

This approach fits particularly well with the *pesukim* in our *parashah* which indicate that God hardened Pharaoh's heart in order to beget the plagues and the splitting of the sea. These events were essential in order to display God's existence and power to the entire world.[28] As

---

הטובה בכל נפשו ובכל מאודו בכל מאודו באמת תקובל תשובתו שלימה ויהיה לו סיוע אלקי בתשובה אבל בוחן לבבות יודע האמת וראה בבני עליו כי לא היה לבבם שלם ואפילו ישמעו לקול אביהם ויסורו מדרכם הרעה ידע כי לא יעשו זה בכל לבם לפיכך חפץ שלא ישמעו לקול אביהם ויענשו וימותו ברשעם כדי שיאמרו בני אדם רשעים היו אלה וראוים היו לעונש הזה ויצדיקו עליהם את הדין.

Thus, like in the Rambam's explanation, the ability to choose between right and wrong is always maintained – they wished to choose wrong, and therefore one particular avenue of wrongdoing was removed from their arsenal of decisions.

26. Rabbenu Yonah writes: מפני שהדברים תלויים במלך.

   Ralbag writes:

   הנה לב המלך ורצונו הוא ביד ה' כמו פלגי מים שיוכלו להטותם אל אשר יהיה שמה החפץ כן יטה הש"י לב המלך אל כל אשר יחפוץ והנה העיר בזה כי פעולות המלך ומחשבותיו הם מוגבלות מהש"י והוא כמו שליח הש"י במה שיעשהו מדבר המלכות וזה כלו הוא מיושר החכמה האלהית כי אילו היה פועל המלך באלו הדברים מסור לבחירתו בשלימות כדרך המס' לבחירתו פעולותיו בעצמו היה זה זה הענין סכנה נפלאה אל העם אשר תחת המלך ההוא ולזה לא עזב הש"י כל זאת ההנהגה למלך כי גבוה מעל גבוה שומר...

27. See *Derekh Hashem* 8:2.

28. Regarding the plagues it says in the beginning of *Parashat Bo* "'Go in unto Pharaoh; for I have hardened his heart, and the heart of his servants, that I might show My signs in their midst; and that you may tell in the ears of you son, and of your son's son, what I have wrought upon Egypt, and My signs which I have done among

Ramban explains at the end of last week's *parashah*, the miracles of the Exodus serve as the basis for our absolute belief in His existence and involvement in the world.[29] Accordingly, it was necessary to harden Pharaoh's heart in order to bring these events about.[30]

THE FOURTH APPROACH: WHO IS THE REAL ME?

Studies show that a remarkable number of people make New Year's resolutions each year, and an equally remarkable number of people fail to follow through on their resolutions.[31] Why do so many people regret the choices they made, sincerely promise to do better, and then carry out the very same poor choices the next year? According to the Maharal, such a phenomenon exists because most people really want to be good.

Why don't they succeed? According to the Maharal,[32] it is because they are overtaken by desire, emotion and passion. But, argues Maharal, this is the basis for why *teshuvah* is possible. When doing *teshuvah*, a person tells God that the person who sinned was not the real me – the real me wants to do what is right. What I did – that did not reflect my truest

them; that you may know that I am God.'" Regarding the splitting of the sea it states: "And I will harden Pharaoh's heart, and he will chase after them; and I will be honored through Pharaoh all his host; and the Egyptians shall know that I am God.'" (*Shemot* 14:4).

29. Thus, the statements such as "in order that you know that I am God," or "I am God on the land," or "that there is no other power like Me" prelude each group of plagues. Likewise, there are numerous *mitzvot* which commemorate the Exodus to remind us of this once in history display of Divine force.

30. R. Hershel Schachter (*Mi-Peninei Ha-Rav*, p. 104) has written in the name of the Rav a similar explanation regarding how the *gedolim* advised people to stay in Europe before the Holocaust. God distorted their decision making process in order to bring about His plan:

כמה צדיקים וגדולי תורה יעצו לחסידיהם שלא לעזוב את אירופה קודם למלחמת העולם השנייה, ולבסוף יצא שנהרגו כולם בידי הנאצים הארורים, ימח שמם. ופעם בדרשה התבטא רבנו על כל אותם הצדיקים שהיה ענין זה בבחינת "משיב חכמים אחור ודעתם יסכל". [וכוונתו היתה על פי הגמ' בגיטין פרק הניזקין (נו:) שרבי יוחנן בן זכאי ביקש מאספסיינוס שלושה דברים בלבד: תן לי יבנה וחכמיה וכו', קרי עליה רב יוסף ואיתימא ר' עקיבא, "משיב חכמים אחור ודעתם יסכל", איבעי למימר ליה לשבקינהו הדא זימנא (היה לו לבקש: הניח להם בפעם זו)].

31. Miller, E.T. & Marlatt, G.A. (1998). How to Keep Up with Those New Year's Resolutions: Researchers Find Commitment Is the Secret of Success. Retrieved online: www.washington.edu/newsroom/news/1997archive/12–97archive/k122397.html

32. *Netivot Olam, Netiv Ha-Teshuvah*, Ch. 1.

desires; I was overtaken by passion. Why should I be held accountable for those actions that did not reflect the real me? If a person is sincere when making such a declaration, then God forgives him, essentially by relating to the "real" person.

However, if someone sins using his intellect – not because he truly wants to do what is right and is overtaken by passion, but because he chooses evil knowing that it's evil – then *teshuvah* is impossible, because he can no longer say that was not the "real" me.[33] Accordingly, avers Maharal, *teshuvah* was impossible for Pharaoh, as it is for the truly wicked. By refusing to allow the Jews to leave after the first five plagues, Pharaoh demonstrated that it was not passion, or desire, or emotion that held him back from freeing the Jews – he had intellectually, and not just emotionally, chosen the path of evil – and thus the gift of *teshuvah* was impossible.

CONCLUSION

Thank God, most of us are not like Pharaoh. Whatever approach we take to understanding the hardening of Pharaoh's heart, we can feel confident in our own free will. Should we take advantage of this gift, it can prove enormously powerful: "every person has the potential to be as righteous as Moses our Teacher, or as wicked as Jeroboam" (Maimonides, *Hilkhot Teshuvah*, Ch. 5). The responsibility is immense. Let us then always remember God's ultimate exhortation – choose life: "*U-vecharta ba-chayyim le-ma'an tichyeh atah ve-zar'ekha*" (*Devarim* 30:19).

---

33. This presumably does not mean that they cannot change their ways; it simply means that their past decisions cannot be erased.

Rabbi Benjamin Blech

יתרו: Why There Are No Ten Commandments

Would you be shocked if I told you that for Jews there is no such thing as the Ten Commandments?

Yes, of course, central to Judaism is the belief that at Mount Sinai God spoke directly to the Jewish people and entrusted them with his covenant of law. Yes, of course, God wrote the 172 words of the Decalogue on two tablets of stone and gave them to Moshe so that they might serve as a guide for the spiritual mission of the Jews to the rest of all mankind.

But the Decalogue was never meant to be called the Ten Commandments – and for a very important reason. The word for "commandment" in Hebrew is *"mitzvah,"* and nowhere in the entire Torah are the ten laws that appear on the two tablets ever referred to as the "ten *mitzvot"* – *"Aseret Ha-Mitzvot."* Instead they are called the *"Aseret Ha-Dibrot"* or the *"Aseret Ha-Devarim"* – the ten words or sayings. And that difference of name is crucial for an understanding not only of their real meaning, but also for a remarkable change of law with regard to the daily prayer service.

We know that according to the Rabbis, prayer today is an attempt on our part to create a substitute for the sacrificial system practiced in the *Beit Ha-Mikdash*. The synagogue as we know it was necessitated by the destruction of the *Beit Ha-Mikdash* and the abolition of animal sacrifice. Prayer, in the eyes of the Talmud, was primarily an inferior alternative to the practice described in the book of *Vayikra*. Yet, in spite of this, the Talmud tells us that even in the days of the *Beit Ha-Mikdash* there were some prayers so basic to an understanding of our relationship with God, that they were recited by the priests as part of the sacrificial service. And remarkably enough, one of these prayers, at a time when institutionalized liturgy as we know it was almost nonexistent, was the recitation of the *Aseret Ha-Dibrot*.

It certainly made sense to give these words of God such prominence. When the *siddur* did not yet exist, and words of the lips took second place to animal offerings, we nonetheless realized that what God personally conveyed to us at Sinai needed to be repeated and reaffirmed on a daily basis. The prayer book in the *Beit Ha-Mikdash* may have been exceedingly small compared to the one in use today, but it recognized that the Decalogue could never be omitted from our meetings with the Almighty. How strange it is, then, to realize that today this is no longer true for us. Our prayer book has expanded to hundreds of pages but it no longer contains the words inscribed by God on the two tablets of law!

Indeed, there are other portions of the Torah that we have chosen to recite on a daily basis. The song that the Jews sang to praise God after miraculously splitting the waters of the Red Sea and then drowning the Egyptians is part of the morning service. So too, a selection of *Tehillim* of King David forms a goodly part of our prayers. The "*Shema Yisrael*" (Hear O' Israel the Lord is our God the Lord is one), is prominently featured morning and evening. But somehow the Decalogue didn't make it!

How can we explain this omission? How can we understand that a part of the Bible considered so crucial to our spiritual development that, when almost nothing else was said, was our verbal focus in the *Beit Ha-Mikdash*, is now deemed superfluous and cast out of our book of holy prayers?

The Talmud explains how it happened. In the tractate *Berakhot* (12a), we're told the people wanted to recite the Decalogue outside of the *Beit Ha-Mikdash* as they had been accustomed to doing for years.

But in a cryptic phrase the Talmud tells us, "the Rabbis negated the daily recitation of the Ten Sayings because of the libels of the heretics."

Who were these heretics? What was the libel they spread that could have had such powerful consequences? The Talmud does not elaborate. Rashi, the master talmudic commentator in the texts we study today, identifies the heretics with one word: *"ha-minim"* – the generic term for heretics (Rashi, *Berakhot* 12a, ad loc.). That still leaves us none the wiser. It doesn't clarify the men or their motives. Fortunately, modern scholarship has discovered an older original version of Rashi's manuscript that is much more specific. What Rashi had written before Christian censors altered his text was *"talmidei Yeshu"* – the disciples of Jesus. These were the early Christians. And it was the way in which they misunderstood the meaning of the Decalogue that represented a libel so serious to Jewish theology that the Rabbis actually felt it was preferable to remove its daily recitation. To put it succinctly, it was Christianity that turned the *Dibrot* into Commandments.

Let me explain. Judaism, as a religion of law, always emphasized that the total number of *mitzvot* was 613. The Torah makes clear that we are not permitted either to add to, or to diminish from, that number. Indeed, the constitutional principle of Jewish law is that "all *mitzvot* are created equal." The *mishnah* in "The Ethics of the Fathers" teaches that we must "be as careful in the performance of a light *mitzvah* as a difficult *mitzvah*, for you do not know the reward granted for the performance of any mitzvah." Anytime we speak of Commandments we never limit them to ten; the phrase is always *"taryag mitzvot"* – 613 Commandments.

How then was it possible for God to select ten out of the immutable and irreducible number of 613 for special emphasis? For Christianity, the answer was that 613 laws obviously included many that were not crucial to human service of God. If ten were singled out, then these indeed must be the most important. These, and these alone, were the ones God chose to personally transmit to the Jewish people. These were the ones God wrote on the tablets of stone. With an eye to spreading their religion, Christianity found an easy way to excise *kashrut*, circumcision, laws of family purity and a host of other seemingly onerous Biblical commands. Religion was made far more appealing by removing its multitude of restrictions and diminishing its massive amount of commands. Christians simply pointed out that by not being included in the list of the Ten Commandments, the remaining 603 laws surely could not have been considered very significant by God and therefore might easily be dismissed by those willing to serve Him. Indeed, this is the mantra of all those who justify their laxness of observance of law with the defense that, "I may not observe all the laws of the Torah but at least I keep the Ten Commandments."

But Jews have another answer to why God selected just these ten for such prominence. Clearly, it could not be because they are superior to laws not included in this list. We know that we dare not play the game of *mitzvah* favoritism. And we know that all 613 of the *mitzvot* have the same Divine source as the ten on the tablets. So why *did* God single out the ten of the Decalogue? The answer becomes obvious when we take note of the fact that they are called *dibrot* and not *mitzvot*. They are, in fact, *not* Commandments but *categories*. They are meant to be understood as the major principles and concepts that underlie all the 613 *mitzvot* of the Torah. They are the seeds from which all of Jewish law sprouts. Take the number 613, some have noted, and add its component parts, 6+1+3, and you will get a total of ten; all 613 laws have their source in what we should henceforth refer to only as the "Ten Sayings," or "Ten Principles."

It was Saadia Gaon (882–942 CE) who clarified this concept in a remarkable little book called *Sefer Azharot*. Under each one of the Ten Principles he enumerated all the laws that emanated from it, and explained the connection. For example, embarrassing someone in public is a grave sin. It is a law found in the Torah but seemingly not on the tablets. Why was it ignored? Because it is a derivative of the sixth principle forbidding murder, which in Hebrew is called *"shefikhat damim"* – the shedding of blood. When one person kills another, the victim has been deprived of life. When someone embarrasses another publicly, the humiliated party may wish he or she were dead and might even have preferred physical extinction to public shame. The Talmud teaches that when a person shames another publicly, God makes the blood rush from the latter's face. That too is a way of shedding blood, and it is viewed as a derivative of the principle, "thou shalt not murder." Maxi-murder and mini-murder are equally forbidden. There is more than one commandment implicit in the sixth *dibbur*, or principle.

Similarly, if one were to ask where in the Decalogue are the all-important holidays of Yom Kippur, Passover, *Shavuot* or *Sukkot*, we need only to look at the principle which captures the conceptual meaning of these days. *Dibbur* number four, "Remember *Shabbat* to keep it holy," teaches us the idea that God may be recognized not only in space, but also in time. Time is holy. *Shabbat* is to be used to reflect upon God as both creator and architect of history. Once we accept this concept on a weekly basis, we may readily grasp the need to develop and extend it in such a way that all significant dates associated with major incidents of the past are to be celebrated on an annual basis as well. The *Shabbat* principle is the seed from which all holidays flower.

In the United States, the Bill of Rights plays a central role in American law and government. There are no more than ten amendments to this crucial legislation, yet it represents a fundamental symbol and synopsis of the freedoms and culture of this nation. From these ten rights emanate the countless laws that define our democratic way of life. They are not Ten Commandments that obviate the need for any other additional laws, rather they are ten principles that validate our entire judicial system. That is very much what God intended at Sinai when he taught us the *Aseret Ha-Dibrot*.

To understand this is to know why Jews do not share the same problem troubling Catholics and Protestants with the "first commandment" that caused them to come up with a different list for the ten that make up the Decalogue.

One might assume that Catholics, Protestants and Jews all agree on the content of something that basically has its source in a clear section of the Torah (*Shemot* Ch. 20; *Devarim* Ch. 5). The words are not subject to dispute. What is interesting, though, is that the "Commandments" are not numbered in the text. The verses themselves do not resolve the issue – some sentences have more than one "Commandment" and some "Commandments" require more than one verse. That leaves room for the three religions to disagree about the actual list.

For Jews, the first of the ten is "I am the Lord your God who took you out of the land of Egypt, the house of bondage." But Catholics and Protestants both object. How could this be the first of the Ten *Commandments* if it doesn't *command* us to do anything? It is merely a statement rather than a directive. So Catholics and Protestants consider this as a simple prelude to what follows. The Commandments themselves, for them, begin with the words that appear next in the text: "You shall have no other gods before me." What for us is number two is for them only number one in the Decalogue.

Catholics and Protestants are, however, well aware that the Bible refers to this as a grouping of ten. Eliminating the first leaves them one shy and each one of them finds a different solution. For Catholics, the final "commandment" serves double duty. The law forbidding one to covet is number nine, "you shall not covet your neighbor's house," and number ten focuses on "you shall not covet your neighbor's wife" – two Commandments with one and the same idea, differing only with regard to the object of sin.

Protestants have a different way of solving the problem created by the elimination of "I am the Lord" as the first Commandment. For them, the Decalogue denounces idolatry by way of two separate laws: "You shall have no other gods before me" is the first and "You shall not make for yourself a graven image, you shall not bow down unto them or serve them" is the second. Following that, the Protestants continue on, using the same numbering system as the Jews.

What stands at the core of the dispute is whether we are dealing with Commandments or principles. Since for Catholics and Protestants these are the Ten *Commandments*, the opening sentence that proclaims "I am the Lord your God" can't be counted as the first; it is no more than a statement. But from the Judaic perspective that these are *dibrot* rather than *mitzvot*, it very readily serves as the first principle. From this principle expressing our need to acknowledge the reality of God stem numerous laws, such as prayer, which come to actualize the concept of belief in the Almighty. Principles *lead* to Commandments – and that is why there's no problem with "I am the Lord" heading the list of a group of ten whose very definition is to serve as the principles from which all of Jewish law emanates.

Catholics and Protestants see in the Decalogue a diminution of the 613 laws of the Torah; Jews see in the Ten Principles a summary of the 613 that magnificently captures their essence.

We've already noted how the Rabbis in the days of the Talmud recognized the danger implicit in an over-emphasis on the Decalogue – the fear that by stressing these ten one might mistakenly reject all the others. For that reason they forbade reciting this portion of the Torah on a daily basis. Their concern was precipitated by the heretical views of the early Christians. I don't think it's misplaced to assume that this fear that the Ten Principles might be misunderstood as the Ten Commandments ought to be considered a threat even in our own times. Without sufficient scholarship, there are indeed many Jews today who believe they can fulfill the demands of their spiritual heritage if they but follow "ten laws for living" that represent the *summum bonum* of Sinai. Their error has serious consequences. It leads to a Judaism without *kashrut*, without the laws of family purity and without all the other fundamentals of our religion that are implicit in the ten concepts etched in stone.

"Well at least I keep the Ten Commandments" is the foolish notion of one who takes pride in following ten out of a required 613 obligations mandated by God. And it is perhaps the most convincing proof that we ought to never again be guilty of using that terribly misleading term, "The Ten Commandments."

Rabbi Yona Reiss

מבשפטים: The Ethics of Emancipation

The weekly portion of *Parashat Mishpatim* provides a plethora of statutes and ordinances relating to humanity's obligations towards the Almighty and towards each other. *Moshe Rabbenu* is told that these are the ordinances *"asher tasim lifneihem"* – "which you should place before them" (*Shemot* 21:1). Rashi comments that the laws should be set like a *"shulchan arukh"* – a fully prepared table, meticulously arranged in a manner ready for human digestion.

Interestingly, the very first of the multitude of laws described in the *parashah* deals with the treatment of the *"eved ivri,"* the Hebrew servant who is sold into servitude by the *Beit Din* in order to make restitution for his thievery (as explained by Rashi, *Shemot* 21:2; there is a separate description in *Parashat Behar* of the laws of the *eved ivri* who sells himself into slavery). We are told that such a bondsman is not to be kept for eternity but rather must be released after six years. If he wishes to stay longer, he must become a *"nirtz'a"* – have his right ear pierced next to a door (see Rambam, *Hilkhot Avadim* 3:9 for a detailed description of the ritual). The choice of *eved ivri* as the cornerstone for *Parashat*

Mishpatim raises an obvious question. Why begin arranging the table with such an unusual place setting?

The Chizkuni explains that since the Jewish people had just been emancipated from their own slavery, the Torah juxtaposes the laws of *eved ivri* in order to emphasize the commandment of not similarly enslaving their own brethren, but rather treating them humanely and releasing them from servitude after six years. In other words, the rationale for setting the table first with the law of *eved ivri* was to underscore the responsibility of the newly freed nation not to inflict upon each other the hardship they had just endured from their Egyptian oppressors. At the incipient moment of their freedom from servitude, they were ideally poised to appreciate the need for sensitivity towards others who might be in a similarly subjugated state.

Based on this insight of the Chizkuni, we can understand the significance of the inclusion at this juncture of the laws regarding the *nirtz'a*. Rashi quotes the statement of R. Yochanan Ben Zakkai, that the servant who wishes to remain in servitude at the expiration of his six year term is punished through the piercing of the ear because he failed to heed what he heard at Mount Sinai when told *"ki li Benei Yisrael avadim ve-lo avadim le-avadim"* – that he was to be a servant to God and not to anybody else (*Kedushin* 22b). This insight should have special resonance for the recently freed servant, who can appreciate the reminder that that there is not only a duty to refrain from subjugating others, but also a responsibility to avoid further enslavement by others. As the experience in Egypt should have taught him, freedom is too precious a commodity to forfeit.

When an individual has suffered in life, these are two critical perspectives that ought to inform his outlook towards the future. First, he should not repeat the cruelty wrought upon him by others. Rather, he should learn from his experience to treat others who may be in similarly vulnerable situations with sensitivity and kindness. Second, he should avoid repeating the actions and tendencies that would place him again in the same position of vulnerability. Instead, he should identify the weaknesses that contributed to that state and overcome them in the future.

Sometimes people can be impeded from self-growth based on a failure to heed these messages. Individuals with persecution complexes, who are never able to overcome the sense of outrage regarding the oppression they have received from others, can be the worst persecutors themselves, as they lash out against a world from which they refuse to be emancipated, and victimize a world perceived by them as comprised of potential oppressors. Similarly, individuals who have overcome other forms of servitude, such as self-destructive addictions or the entrapment of a materialistic lifestyle devoid of Torah values, can lapse into a repetition of similar behavior patterns if they do not sufficiently demonstrate appreciation to God for the magnitude of their personal victories by undertaking to distance themselves from their previous tendencies.

Conversely, those who are able to harness their ability to overcome difficult chapters in life by using such episodes as catalysts to demonstrate greater sensitivity towards others and to gain a stronger appreciation for their newfound opportunities, can appreciate the true meaning of freedom, as expressed by *Chazal* in their teaching *"charut al ha-luchot – al tikra charut ela cheirut"* (*Avot* 6:2) – the ability to be released from other bonds and freed to fulfill the *mitzvot* of the Torah is the greatest realization of emancipation.

In this vein, the entrée of *eved ivri* opens up the possibility of the lavish table that is described in *Parashat Mishpatim.* A close look at the *parashah* reveals an admixture of ordinances between man and his fellow man (e.g., tort law, sensitivity towards converts and widows, principles of justice, laws of returning lost articles, etc.) and ordinances between man and God (e.g., not mixing meat and milk, observing the *shemittah* year, *Shabbat* and the holiday seasons). Through the fresh outlook possessed by a freed slave, the newly emancipated Jewish nation was capable of embracing both types of laws. They had learned to display sensitivity towards the weak and vulnerable in society, and to appreciate their capacity to serve God without being beholden to others.

May we all capitalize upon the *"shulchan arukh"* of *Parashat Mishpatim* to appreciate this vital message of our continued freedom from the slavery of Egypt, and to maximize the potential that we have, through internalizing the message of emancipation in the context of our own life experiences, to improve all facets of our Torah observance.

Rabbi Meir Goldwicht

תרומה: The Ark of the Testimony and the Tablets: the Written Torah and the Oral Torah[1]

The first vessel mentioned in the construction of the *Mishkan* (Tabernacle) is the *Aron Ha-Edut*, the Ark of the Testimony.

(י) ועשו ארון עצי שטים אמתים וחצי ארכו ואמה וחצי רחבו ואמה וחצי
קמתו: (יא) וצפית אתו זהב טהור מבית ומחוץ תצפנו ועשית עליו זר זהב
סביב: (יב) ויצקת לו ארבע טבעת זהב ונתתה על ארבע פעמתיו ושתי
טבעת על צלעו האחת ושתי טבעת על צלעו השנית:

10. And they shall make an ark of acacia-wood: two cubits and a half shall be the length thereof, and a cubit and a half the breadth

---

1. This article was translated by Tuvia Brander from the Hebrew original.

thereof, and a cubit and a half the height thereof. 11. And thou shalt overlay it with pure gold, within and without shalt thou overlay it, and shalt make upon it a crown of gold round about. 12. And thou shalt cast four rings of gold for it, and put them in the four feet thereof; and two rings shall be on the one side of it, and two rings on the other side of it. (*Shemot* 25:10–12)

The question immediately arises as to why the Torah introduces the Ark with a plural verb, "*ve-asu*" – "and they shall make", unlike the rest of the vessels of the *Mishkan* (Tabernacle) for which the Torah utilizes the singular verb, "*ve-asot*" – "and you shall make." *Chazal* answer (*Shemot Rabbah* 34): "R. Yehudah the son of R. Shalom said: 'God said everyone should come and toil in the construction of the Ark in order that they may merit Torah [knowledge].'"

Alas, this is even more perplexing; how does involvement in the construction of the Ark – merely the vessel that holds the Torah – entitle you to partnership in the Torah? It would be understandable if it referred to one who actually labored on the Torah itself, like someone who wrote a letter of a Torah (for without which the entire scroll is invalid). It is possible that this type of action could merit a partnership with Torah. However, a partnership with Torah through the construction of the vessel that held it – how is it possible?

Another question which emerges from the passage on the Ark, is the duplication of the command to put the *luchot* (Tablets) in the Ark. Consider the following verses (*Shemot* 25:16–21):

16. And thou shalt put into the ark the testimony which I shall give thee. 17. And thou shalt make an ark-cover of pure gold … 18. And thou shalt make two cherubim of gold … 21. And thou shalt put the ark-cover above upon the ark; and in the ark thou shalt put the testimony that I shall give thee.

As Rashi comments, (*Shemot* 25:21, ad loc.):

I do not know why it is repeated for it has already said: "You shall place in the ark, the Testimony!" It may be said that it comes to teach that when the ark is alone, without the cover, he should beforehand place the Testimony in it and only afterwards place the cover on it.

Rashi suggests that the answer might be that at the moment they made the Ark, despite its covering still not being ready, they were commanded to place the *luchot* in the Ark even without its cover.

An additional point of inquiry is the lack of clarity as to the nature of the *"keruvim"* ("cherubs"). In our *parashah*, Rashi explains (*Shemot* 25:18) that they had the likeness of a child's face. However, in *Bereishit*, on the verse (3:24): "And He drove the man out, and He stationed from the east of the Garden of Eden the *keruvim*," Rashi explains *keruvim* as angels of destruction. How can the *keruvim* have 'double faces,' on the one hand appearing as children, and on the other hand being like angels of destruction?

MODA'AH RABA LE-ORAITA

In the Talmud (*Shabbat* 88a), it is recorded:

> "They stood at the bottom of the mountain": R. Avdimi bar Chama bar Chasa said: [This] teaches that the Holy One, Blessed is He, covered them with the mountain as though it were an upturned vat. And he said to them: "If you accept the Torah, fine. But if not, your burial will be there!" R. Acha bar Yaakov said: "From here stem strong grounds for a notification of coercion (*moda'ah*) regarding acceptance of the Torah." Rava said: "Nevertheless, they accepted [the Torah] again in the days of Achashverosh, as it is written: 'The Jews established and accepted;' they established in the days of Achashverosh that which they had already accepted in the days of Moses."

At the time the Jews accepted the Torah, *Ha-Kadosh Barukh Hu* forced the Jews to accept the Torah. When they responded in the affirmative, the Israelites essentially gave over a *"moda'ah"* that nullified the entire agreement. According to the laws of the *Shulchan Arukh*, giving over a *moda'ah* nullifies an agreement; for example, if a man who is coerced into selling his possessions, prior to the sale, in front of two valid witnesses, gives over a *moda'ah* stating that the transaction is occurring against his will, even if the sale contract is written 100% correctly, the entire transaction is null and void. Similarly, during *Matan Torah*, the Jews gave over a *moda'ah* that the acceptance of the Torah was under extreme duress, as a mountain was held above their heads. Only after many years, in the days of Mordechai and Esther, the nation of Israel reaccepted the Torah – this time not under duress, but fully of their own will.

The Ramban, in his commentary (*Shabbat* 88a, ad loc.), asks:

> It is difficult for me, for what does this acceptance do from the end of the world to the beginning (i.e., from the days of Mordechai and Esther to Mount Sinai); if before Achashverosh they were not commanded, why were they punished? And if you say they violated the decree of the King – this *moda'ah* was [certainly] nullified.

In other words, if before the days of Achashverosh, the *moda'ah* was valid, why, then, were the Jews punished for not keeping the Torah – didn't the *moda'ah* nullify their commitment obligating them to uphold the Torah? And if you say that they were punished because of what they committed at *Har Sinai* (Mount Sinai) and thus violated the decrees of the King, what is the value of this *moda'ah* – it was never valid!

The words of this passage in the Talmud require explanation.

In order to answer these questions, let us understand the nature of the "*berit*" – "covenant" – the relationship between *Ha-Kadosh Barukh Hu* and the Jewish people – established at *Matan Torah*.

THE VISIBLE *BERIT* AND THE HIDDEN *BERIT*

The visible *berit* was a mutual agreement; the Jewish people pledged to be servants of God and not worship idolatry, and in exchange God promised to single out the Jewish nation as the chosen people and to give to them the Land of Israel, as it is written in the *pesukim* (*Shemot* 19:5–6):

> 5. Now therefore, if you will hearken unto My voice indeed, and keep My covenant, then you shall be Mine own treasure from

among all peoples; for all the earth is Mine; 6. and you shall be unto Me a kingdom of priests, and a holy nation. These are the words which thou shalt speak unto the Children of Israel.

Thus, for many years, this *berit* continued – each side upholding their side of the agreement. All until the Jewish people sinned and turned to worship other gods. Then, *Ha-Kadosh Barukh Hu* exiled us from our land. At that time, the Jews concluded that the *berit* was terminated. Assuming that again there was no connection between them and *Ha-Kadosh Barukh Hu*, the Jews turned to the prophet Yechezkel (*Yechezkel* 20:9) and asked "our teacher Yechezkel, a slave whose master sold him... do they have any claim on each other?" (*Sanhedrin* 105a). Does a slave that was freed from his master have obligations to his former master? God freed us from his service – since He exiled us from the Land of Israel and we are no longer the chosen nation, how are we obligated to fulfill the *mitzvot*?

The prophet Yechezkel answered that, aside from the visible *berit* at *Matan Torah*, there was an additional part – a hidden component to the *berit* God forged with the Jewish people. At *Matan Torah*, there were two elements of the *berit*. The first part was the overt, known-to-all component, as it is written in *Devarim*: "Hashem came from Sinai, and rose from Seir unto them; He shined forth from Mount Paran, and He came from the myriads holy" (33:2). The other was a hidden, secret part, as it says in *Shir Ha-Shirim* (2:4) "He has brought me to the banqueting-house, and his banner over me is love," referring to *Ha-Kadosh Barukh Hu* having brought the Jewish people to his "banqueting-house," a place concealed from all, and making a covenant with them at *Matan Torah*.

The visible covenant was the giving of the Written Torah, while the hidden *berit* was the Oral Torah – the Oral Tradition. As the *midrash* explains on the *pasuk* in *Shemot* (34:27): "And the Lord said unto Moses: 'Write thou these words [this is the Written Torah], for after the tenor of these words [this is the Oral Torah], I have made a covenant with thee and with Israel.'"

Chazal explain (*Gittin* 60b): "R. Yochanan said: The Holy One, Blessed is He, established a covenant with Israel only on the basis of the Oral Teaching. As the verse states: 'For on the basis of these words I have established a covenant with you (Moshe) and Israel.'"

Ultimately, this insight also arises straight from the *pesukim* (*Shemot* 34:28): "And he was there with the Lord forty days and forty nights; he did neither eat bread, nor drink water. And he wrote upon the tables the words of the covenant, the ten words." Is it possible that it took forty days to write two tablets of stone? Rather, during that period of time, Moshe learned the entire Oral Tradition directly from God. As *Chazal* describe (*Vayikra Rabbah* 22:1): "[Even] that which an old student was destined to say before his teacher, all of it was told to Moses on [Mt.] Sinai."

The hidden *berit* was never nullified, and never will be. Even in times of extreme anger, when *Ha-Kadosh Barukh Hu* exiles His children and they are given to their oppressors and it appears that the *berit* has been abrogated – this is only the visible *berit*. The hidden covenant continues forever, and thus *Ha-Kadosh Barukh Hu* will never reject His children, as it is written (*Vayikra* 26:44): "And yet for all that, when they are in the land of their enemies, I will not reject them, neither will I abhor them, to destroy them utterly, and to break My covenant with them; for I am the Lord their God."

Therefore, the prophet Yechezekel responds: the visible, publicized *berit* forged over the Written Torah was indeed severed and on that was there a *moda'ah*. However, even in times of destruction and exile, the private, invisible *berit* sealed over the Oral Torah continues and is still binding!

HIDDEN *BERIT* STANDS REVEALED

The *berit* that exists between *Ha-Kadosh Barukh Hu* and Israel, even in times of destruction, is visible to all. The *keruvim* symbolize this *berit* between *Hashem* and the Jewish people. As the Talmud relates (*Bava Batra* 99a): "At a time when Israel does the will of the Omnipresent... [the cherubim] stood with their faces toward one another... and at a time when Israel does not do the will of the Omnipresent... their faces were pointed towards the House."

However, a passage in *Yoma* is quite astonishing; the Talmud there relates (*Yoma* 54b):

Reish Lakish said: When the gentiles entered the Sanctuary, they saw the cherubim joined together. They took them to the mar-ketplace, and they said, "These Jews – whose blessing is a bless-ing and whose curse is a curse – should be involved in these mat-ters?!" Immediately, they debased them, as it says, "All who once respected her, debased her, for they saw her nakedness."

The question is obvious! How is it possible that at the pinnacle of destruc-tion and anger – as *Ha-Kadosh Barukh Hu* is exiling His children and destroying His Temple – the faces of the *keruvim* are embracing one another, a position that exemplifies a strong love between *Ha-Kadosh Barukh Hu* and His children?

The Maharsha explains that the hug between the *keruvim* revealed to everyone that even when *Ha-Kadosh Barukh Hu* is angry at His chil-dren, destroys His Temple, and abandons the visible *berit*, that is only an outward appearance. Inwardly, the hidden *berit*, the intimate love shared by *Ha-Kadosh Barukh Hu* and the Jewish people, spawns a strength to survive the exile, through the fulfillment of the Oral Torah, that will lead to the reestablishment of the visible *berit* and, ultimately, the redemption.

Ha-Kadosh Barukh Hu broadcasts this idea to all the nations of the world. Yet, the message is not comprehended by all.

Haman the wicked "cast lots" (*Esther* 3:7); as the words of the Talmud are well-known (*Megillah* 13b):

A Baraitha taught: When Haman saw that the lot fell on the month of Adar, he rejoiced greatly. For he said, "the lot fell for me on the month in which Moshe died"...However, Haman did not realize that while [Moshe] died on the seventh of Adar, he was also born on the seventh of Adar [Rashi explains: For it says "I am a hundred and twenty years this day" (*Devarim* 31:2) – 'this day' completed my days and years; worthy is the birth that atones for the death].

Prima facie, there is an obvious question: how does the earlier birth atone for the death that occurs after it (i.e. how does Moshe's birth atone for his death if his birth happened long before his death)? The explana-tion is that *Moshe Rabbenu* represents the Written Torah; he wrote it

תרומה

and accepted it from the heavens. Hence, Haman thought that the day Moshe died, the *berit* of the Written Torah dissolved, terminating the connection between *Ha-Kadosh Barukh Hu* and the people of Israel, and as such, Haman was free to do as he desired. However, he did not know that on that day the hidden *berit* of the Oral Torah was also born. This hidden *berit* atones for the violation of the visible one, and its strength enables all who grasp it to return to the visible *berit*.

THE ARK OF THE TESTIMONY AND THE *LUCHOT*

It is written in the *Midrash Ha-Gadol*:

> "And make for me a sanctuary;" here is the *mitzvat aseh* (positive commandment) to make a house for *Hashem* – to be [a place] to bring sacrifices and to celebrate in it three times a year. And these are the main components of the structure of the Temple: they make in it the *Kodesh*, the *Kodesh Kodashim* and, before the *Kodesh*, the courtyard – and [together] they were called the *Heikhal*. And they made another long partition around the *Heikhal* and it was called the *Azarah*. And they made in it 7 vessels: the altar and *its ramp* to ascend it, the laver and its bases to sanctify from it, the altar of incense, the *menorah* (candelabra), and the table. But the Ark is for the *luchot*, it is not a vessel of the Temple.

The table is a vessel to hold the showbread, and the laver is a vessel to wash from; yet different from them is the Ark. The Ark is not a mere vessel in which to put the *luchot*; rather, the Ark itself is the Torah. The Ark is the Oral Torah, and in it we place the *luchot* that are the Written Torah.

Returning to our original questions, then, when they built the Ark, the Oral Torah, even before they finished its cover, they immediately needed to put the *luchot* into the Ark, because the learning of the Written Torah must be accompanied by the Oral Torah.

Additionally, for every law in the Oral Torah there must be a source in the Written Torah. If there is no explicit source, no logical justification will work no matter how clear the rationale is. As an example of this principle, the Talmud states (*Shabbat* 145b): "Say to wisdom: You are my sister (*Mishlei* 7:4), if a matter of law is clear to you as the fact that your sister is forbidden to you, you may repeat it; but if not, you may not repeat it!" Meaning, the Torah prohibits one from marrying his sister. There is a special derivation from the *pasuk* for one's maternal sister – the daughter of one's mother – and a different one for one's paternal sister – the daughter of one's father. How do we know that one is also forbidden to marry one's sister, the daughter of both one's mother and father? There is therefore an explicit derivation from the *pasuk*, and we do not learn it by way of any logic or rationale. But isn't it a simple *kal va-chomer* (a fortiori)? If the daughter from your mother is forbidden and the daughter of your father is forbidden shouldn't it be that all the more so the daughter of both your mother and father is forbidden?! The Talmud's answer is that the prohibition can't be derived from the *kal va-chomer*, because punishment is not given based on logic, however convincing that logic may be. From here we learn only things that are explicit like "the fact that your sister is forbidden to you" (ibid.) – and that have a textual source for the prohibition – are acceptable to be said. Every law of the Oral Torah must have a source from the Written Torah.

This idea is thus expressed in the Torah's commandment "to make" (plural) – "*ve-asu*," the Ark – "everyone should come and toil in the construction of the Ark in order that they may merit Torah [knowledge]" (*Shemot Rabbah* 34). The Ark in the Holy of Holies was not merely a vessel that held the Torah; rather, it itself was the Torah – the bond between the Oral Torah and the Written Torah. Labor on the Ark is equivalent to work on the connection between the visible *berit* and the hidden *berit* – between the Written Torah and the Oral Torah.

With this in mind, we can understand a wonderful aphorism found in the tractate of *Yoma* (72b): "'From within and from without you shall cover it,' Rava said: any Torah scholar whose inside is not like his outside is not a [true] Torah scholar."

If there is no connection between the hidden *berit* and the visible *berit*, between the interior and the exterior, then the individual has not attained the wholeness required to be a true *talmid chakham* (Torah scholar).

Now, we can understand the 'two-faced' *keruvim*. The status of the relationship between *Ha-Kadosh Barukh Hu* and the nation of Israel is measured by the face of the *keruvim*. At times where there is a strong connection between the hidden *berit* – the Oral Tradition, and the visible *berit* – the Written Torah, the faces of the *keruvim* are likened to a baby: like a baby grows up and develops amidst purity and happiness, so too, the learning of Torah grows and increases. However, when the relationship is compromised, the *Keruvim* appear as angels of destruction.

CONCLUSION

The hidden *berit* between *Ha-Kadosh Barukh Hu* and the Jewish nation is a source of solace and engagement in the hopes of better days.

Ha-Kadosh Barukh Hu commands the prophet Yirmiyahu, on the eve of the destruction of the Holy Temple, to buy fields and houses and to preserve the deeds in earthenware vessels buried in the ground; as it is written (*Yirmiyahu* 32:44,14): "Men shall buy fields for money, and subscribe the deeds, and seal them, and call witnesses ... and put them in an earthen vessel that they may continue many days."

This action seems absurd and incomprehensible! With the imminent destruction of the Temple upon them and the rupturing of *berit*, why would anyone invest in houses?

Perhaps, the answer lies in precisely what we are talking about. The eternality of the hidden *berit* leads to this improbable conclusion. The certainty that the future will bring God's redemption to His children and return the captives of His nation to their land ensures that these houses, bought on the eve of the exile, will eventually see use.

The key to the twofold *berit* is now clear: we must observe the Oral Tradition, for it has the strength to bring to fruition the visible *berit*, the *berit* of the Written Torah. Observance of both the Written Torah and the Oral Torah is thus the ultimate guarantee to the renewal of the twofold *berit* and the complete redemption.

Rabbi Dovid Miller

תצוה: Consistency and Commitment

My father, Rabbi Israel Miller *zt"l*, was fond of quoting a *midrash* on our *parashah* which is found in the introduction of the editor of the *Ein Yaakov*, the anthology of the aggadic statements of the Talmud. The editor (in his *Hakdamat Ha-Kotev*) writes that he found the following *midrash*: Ben Zoma says that the verse that expresses the most fundamental principle of the Torah is *"Shema Yisrael, Hashem Elokeinu Hashem Echad"* – "Hear O Israel: The Lord is our God, The Lord is One" (*Devarim* 6:4). Ben Nanas says there is a verse that expresses a broader principle: *"Ve-ahavata le-rei'akha kamokha"* – "You should love your neighbor as yourself" (*Vayikra* 19:18). Ben Pazi says there is a *"pasuk kollel yoter,"* a verse that expresses an even broader principle: *"Et ha-keves ha-echad ta'aseh ba-boker, ve-et ha-keves ha-sheni ta'aseh bein ha-arbayim"* – "You shall offer one lamb in the morning and the other lamb you should offer in the afternoon" (*Shemot* 29:39). Rav Ploni stood on his feet and stated that the *halakhah* is like Ben Pazi, as it says *"ke-khol asher ani mareh otkha be-har et tavnit ha-mishkan ... ve-khen ta'asu,"* meaning, "according to all that I show you, the structure of the *Mishkan* ... even so you shall

199

make it" (*Shemot* 25:9) [The Maharal of Prague also quotes this *midrash* verbatim in his *Netivot Olam, Netiv Ahavat Re'ah*, Ch. 1].

We generally view *Parashat Tetzavveh* as the *parashah* of Aharon and his sons, containing the detailed description of the "*bigdei kahunah*," the holy garments worn by them, the special sacrifices of the consecration of the *Mishkan*, the "*karbanot milu'im*," and the description of the "*mizbeach ha-zahav*," the altar of incense. The *parashah* is now thrown into the limelight for containing the verse ruled to be the most basic principle in the entire Torah.

What is the meaning of this *midrash*? Everyone would understand the opinion of Ben Zoma that *Shema Yisrael* is the credo of a Jew, proclaiming allegiance to God and proclaiming His oneness. This is the verse recited by every Jewish father immediately prior to his son's entering into the covenant of Avraham, the *berit milah*. This is the verse recited as our final statement before leaving this world, on our deathbeds. This is the verse cried out by myriads of Jewish martyrs throughout our history before they were murdered "*al kiddush Ha-Shem*." *Shema* is the ideal of *devekut*, cleaving to God with one's entire being, and all the other *mitzvot* can be viewed as 612 ways to achieve this goal. Thus, according to Ben Zoma, *Shema* is the most fundamental verse.

We can also readily understand the opinion of Ben Nanas. We all know the story in *Massekhet Shabbat* (31a) of the non-Jew who insisted on being taught Torah while standing on one foot as a condition for his conversion, and Hillel teaching him that the entire Torah is but commentary to the practical application of "*ve-ahavta le-rei'akha kamokha*," namely, that which is hateful to you, desist from doing to the other (see Rashi on the Talmud's second explanation). We were brought up singing the statement of R. Akiva (*Sifre Vayikra* 19:18, *Yerushalmi Nedarim* 9:4) that "*ve-ahavta le-rei'akha kamokha*" is the "*klal gadol ba-Torah*," to which Ben Nanas subscribes. The Maharal, when quoting the *midrash*, explains the opinion of Ben Nanas, that the love of a fellow Jew is the fulfillment of our being a *tzelem Elokim* in the fullest sense, by recognizing that we share that inner value with all the members of our covenantal community [with this explanation, the Maharal combines the two opinions found in the *Sifre* and *Yerushalmi*, those of R. Akiva and Ben Zoma, into one, "*ve-ahavta le-rei'akha kamokha*" and "*zeh sefer toledot adam* ... (this is the book of the generations of humanity on the day that God created man, in the image of God He created him)" (*Bereishit* 5:1), are two sides of the same coin, the latter being the theoretical underpinning of the former]. Thus, according to Ben Nanas, "*ve-ahavta le-rei'ekha kamokha*" is a broad, fundamental principle of the Torah.

What, however, is the meaning of the opinion of Ben Pazi, and why was it chosen in the *midrash* as the most correct of the options? What is the unique principle underlying the *mitzvah* of bringing the *korban tamid*, the daily sacrifice?

My father, *zt"l*, suggested (and I later found this thought in the Maharal as well) that the uniqueness of "*et ha-keves ha-echad…*" lies specifically in its lack of grandeur and specialness. "*Shema*" and "*Ve-ahavta*" respectively represent spiritual peaks of religious ecstasy and human empathy. There are individuals who succeed in "rising to the occasion," but this is not the overriding principle which engenders spiritual growth. Rather it is to be found in the daily sacrifice, the routine, the small increments, the step by step, the continuous, steady, consistent commitment that cements a true relationship with God, creating a genuine *eved Hashem*.

The question can still be raised – there are many *mitzvot* that are daily commitments; even the *mitzvah* of reciting *keriyat Shema* is twice daily. Why then did Ben Pazi choose the specific *mitzvah* of the daily sacrifice as his paradigm of the importance of the maintenance of a daily routine?

Mori Ve-Rabi, Rav Aharon Lichtenstein, offered the following insight. The daily sacrifice, the *korban tamid*, is mentioned twice in the Torah in almost identical verses: in *Parashat Tetzavveh* and in *Parashat Pinchas*. In *Parashat Pinchas* it is mentioned in the context of all time related sacrifices including those of *Shabbat*, *Rosh Chodesh*, and *Yom Tov*. In *Parashat Tetzavveh* it is brought in the context of the building of the *Mishkan*. There is a deep significance to this doubling. The daily sacrifice as a *mitzvah*, as one of the 613, is found in its context in *Parashat Pinchas*. In that context, it is no different than many daily commitments. In *Parashat Tetzavveh*, however, we find the daily sacrifice as a necessary component of the structure of the *Mishkan*. It is not enough to have walls and vessels. The building of the *Mishkan* is not complete without the *korban tamid*. Ben Pazi posits that if the daily sacrifice is that which gives ultimate meaning and completion to the structure of the *Mishkan*, it can serve as the paradigm of that which will give ultimate meaning and fulfillment to the structure of a Jew. Thus the consistency and routine of the *korban tamid* is the model for that which will mold a Jewish personality, namely performing all *mitzvot* with a sense of consistency and routine.

The context of *"et ha-keves ha-echad..."* (*Shemot* 29:39) in the *parashah*, is that it is the factor which enables *"ve-shakhanti be-tokh Benei Yisrael"* – "I will dwell within the Children of Israel" (ibid., 45). If this is true of the *Mishkan* and the *Mikdash*, it is certainly true within each of us. *"Be-levavi mishkan evneh"* – "I will build a dwelling place for the *Shekhinah* in my heart;" each Jew is a living *Mishkan* and potentially a living embodiment of the *Shekhinah*. Consistency and routine are the catalysts creating that spiritual reality. In my humble opinion, this can be seen in the proof text that Rav Ploni brings in the *midrash* for stating that the *halakhah* is like Ben Pazi: the verse *"ke-khol asher ani mareh otkha...ve-khen ta'asu"* – "according to all that I show you the structure of the *Mishkan*...even so you shall make it." The stress is in *"ve-khen ta'asu"* – "like so, you shall make it" – the blueprint, the structure of the *Mishkan* is the blueprint and the structure of man. The daily sacrifice that is the center of the Mishkan has to be replicated in man, *"ve-khen ta'asu."* That same consistency in *mitzvah* performance will help us reach the same goal of *"ve-shakhanti be-tokh Benei Yisrael,"* that God will dwell within us.

We have seen that man's spiritual growth is not determined by the unusual, but by the day to day; not by the peaks, but by the routine. This principle is also emphasized by the Rambam in his commentary on the *Mishnah*. In *Pirkei Avot*, towards the end of Ch. 3, the *mishnah* states: *"ha-kol lefi rov ha-ma'aseh"* – "all is determined by the majority of one's deeds" (*Avot* 3:15). The Rambam stresses that the determining factor in man's personality growth is not *"godel ha-ma'aseh"* – "the greatness of one's deeds," but rather, *"rov ha-ma'aseh"* – "the number of one's deeds." The Rambam gives the example of the individual who has two alternatives open to him: he can give $1,000 to one cause, or give $10 one hundred times to a hundred different causes. The latter alternative, insists the Rambam, is the correct one. Only "*rov ha-ma'aseh*," the repetition of acts, will build and transform the individual into a generous person.

In my humble opinion, I think we can find another dimension in the *korban tamid* to explain why Ben Pazi chose it specifically as his model of daily commitment. The *korban tamid*, the daily sacrifice, is a *korban tzibbur*, it is a communal sacrifice. The Ramban, in his commentary on *Chumash* (*Vayikra* 1:2), stresses that a communal sacrifice is not a sacrifice offered by partners, even if the partners will consist of all the Jews in the world. A sacrifice of partners, *korban shutafim*, is a sacrifice of diverse individuals, a '*korban yachid*.' A communal sacrifice, a *korban tzibbur*, represents the community as a whole, the collective soul of the Jewish people. We are all limbs of one body in bringing a *korban tzibbur*; we are one unit. Perhaps that's why a *korban tamid* was chosen to be the core (of the identity) of the structure of the *Mishkan*. Not only because it represents the daily consistent commitment, but because it is also the means of creating and reinforcing our identity as a communal whole, twice daily. Ben Pazi, in his search for a verse that would serve as the broadest fundamental principle of the Torah, chose "*et ha-keves ha-echad*," which stresses both the daily consistency and the overriding goal of linking into God not only on the individual, but also on the communal, level.

It is also important, however, to recognize the inherent danger in stressing the importance of routine. The daily commitment, the continuous repetition, the consistency, can easily turn into rote. We can find ourselves losing excitement and one can reach the point where one is simply going through motions. In the language of *Chazal*, our *mitzvot* can turn into what the prophet Yeshayahu calls "*mitzvat anashim melumadah*" (*Yeshayahu* 29:13), a habitual ritual, devoid of emotion and spirituality.

One must stress retaining a sense of freshness and excitement within the consistency. Perhaps this is why the Torah, while stressing the importance of the concept of the *korban tamid*, placed the verses of the daily sacrifice immediately following the verses describing the *korban milu'im*, the one time sacrifices that inaugurated and consecrated the *Mishkan*. Just as those *korbanot* were full of excitement, joy, and awe, so should those same emotions accompany the *korban tamid* for generations.

In the beginning of *Parashat Beha'alotekha*, Aharon is commanded to light the *menorah* in the *Mishkan*, and the verse states that he lit it "*ka'asher tzivvah Hashem*" (*Bemidbar* 8:3). Rashi comments that Aharon was deserving of praise "*she-lo shinah*," he didn't deviate from *Hashem's* instructions. Many commentators were bothered why that should be a source of "*shevach*," of praise; wouldn't that be expected? The Ishbitzer, in his *Mei Ha-Shiloach*, explains that "*lo shinah*" means "*lo shanah*," he didn't allow the lighting to turn into rote, into habit. He always performed the *mitzvah* as though it was being performed the first time, with the same joy and enthusiasm (the *Sefat Emet*, year 5655, has a similar explanation).

Rav Shlomo Wolbe in his book *Pathways*[1] points out that every morning we pray to God "*yehi ratzon mi-lefanekha…she-targileinu be-Toratekha*" – "may it be Your will, *Hashem* our God…to habituate us in your Torah." This prayer is, however, always preceded by the *birkat ha-Torah* in which we ask *Hashem* – "*ve-ha'arev na…et divrei Toratekha*" – "to sweeten the words of Torah in our mouth." Torah and *mitzvot* need consistency – "*et ha-keves ha-echad*," but that consistency should always be accompanied with sweetness.

---

1. R. Shlomo Wolbe, *Pathways* (Feldheim, 1993) pp. 43–44.

Rabbi Hayyim Angel

כי תשא: Chur and Pharaoh's Daughter: Midrashic Readings of Silent Heroes

INTRODUCTION

Certain characters in *Tanakh* receive significant attention, riveting readers of all ages. Other characters, however, are relatively minor, leaving little impression on casual readers. Chur and Pharaoh's daughter are two of the latter such characters in *Sefer Shemot*. Both play significant enough roles to warrant mention, but neither is developed and both vanish shortly after they appear. Various *midrashim* explore and exploit the sparse Biblical evidence about them to create more comprehensive portraits.

In his recent book-length midrashic reading of *Moshe Rabbenu*, Rabbi Mosheh Lichtenstein sets out a working definition of *peshat* and *derash*. *Peshat* explicates the text itself, whereas *derash* explains dimensions beneath or beyond the simple meaning of the text. While *peshat* looks for correspondence to the text, *derash* seeks internal coherence that does not contradict the text.[1]

1. Rabbi Mosheh Lichtenstein, *Moses: Envoy of God, Envoy of His People* (KTAV-Yeshivat

In *Midrash Aggadah*, there exists a blurred boundary between *Chazal* as interpreters reading beneath the text, *Chazal* as transmitters of received oral traditions, and *Chazal* as *darshanim* who teach their own lessons (*derekh ha-derash*) without impacting on the *peshat* in *Tanakh*. In this essay, we will focus on strands of what *Chazal* may be attempting to teach regardless of whether they derived their particular readings from the text, tradition, or were using their own midrashic creativity.

CHUR

From the beginning of Moshe's tenure as Israel's leader, three people stood by his side: his brother Aharon, his disciple Yehoshua, and Chur. Who was Chur? From the Torah's scant evidence at the level of *peshat*, Ibn Ezra aptly remarks that "we do not know who he is" (Ibn Ezra, *Shemot* 24:14).

First, let us consider the explicit references to Chur in the Torah. During Israel's battle against Amalek, Moshe ordered Yehoshua to lead the troops. Moshe, Aharon, and Chur ascend the hill, and Aharon and Chur ultimately support Moshe's tiring arms:

> Yehoshua did as Moshe told him and fought with Amalek, while Moshe, Aharon, and Chur went up to the top of the hill. Then, whenever Moshe held up his hand, Israel prevailed; but whenever he let down his hand, Amalek prevailed. But Moshe's hands grew heavy; so they took a stone and put it under him and he sat on it, while Aharon and Chur, one on each side, supported his hands; thus his hands remained steady until the sun set. (*Shemot* 17:10–12)[2]

Chur is never given a "proper" introduction, but clearly is among the highest echelons of the nation's leadership.

Har Etzion, 2008, pp. 221–227). See also my review of his book, "A Modern Midrash Moshe: Methodological Considerations," *Tradition* 41:4 (Winter 2008), reprinted in Angel, *Revealed Texts, Hidden Meanings: Finding the Religious Significance in Tanakh* (Jersey City, NJ: KTAV-Sephardic Publication foundation, 2009), pp. 48–64.

2. Translations of Biblical passages (with minor modifications) were taken from the new Jewish Publication Society *Tanakh* (Philadelphia, 1985).

This impression is confirmed as Moshe ascends Mount Sinai to receive the Torah. Again, his three associates occupied important positions. Yehoshua waited for his master at the base of the mountain, while Moshe delegated the leadership to Aharon and Chur:

> To the elders he had said, "Wait here for us until we return to you. You have Aharon and Chur with you; let anyone who has a legal matter approach them." (24:14)

It is surprising, then, that when the people despaired of Moshe's return from Sinai they clamored to Aharon and built the golden calf:

> When the people saw that Moshe was so long in coming down from the mountain, the people gathered against Aharon and said to him, "Come, make us a god who shall go before us, for that man Moshe, who brought us from the land of Egypt – we do not know what has happened to him." (32:1)

Similarly, Moshe found Yehoshua at the base of the mountain, right where he had been waiting (*Shemot* 32:17–18). Mysteriously though, Chur disappears from the narrative, and we never hear about him again. Where did he go? On the textual level, we will never know.

We are left to the world of *midrash*, which capitalizes on any and all information it can glean from *Tanakh*. The portrait of Chur is developed there in different layers.

> Chur arose and rebuked them: You brainless fools! Have you forgotten the miracles God performed for you? Whereupon they rose against him and killed him. They then came to Aharon…and said to him: We will do to you what we have done to this man. When Aharon saw the state of affairs, he was afraid. (*Shemot Rabbah* 41:7)[3]

---

3. Translations of passages from the Talmud and *Midrash Rabbah* (with minor modifications) are taken from Soncino.

This *midrash* casts Chur as a religious martyr. His sudden disappearance in the text lends itself to this interpretation.[4] This reading helps explain Aharon's willingness to build the calf, and also provides *someone* in the camp who opposed the calf while Moshe was atop the mountain.

The next layer of Chur's midrashic portrait derives from the construction of the *Mishkan*. God designated Betzalel as the chief artisan in the construction:

> See, I have singled out by name Betzalel son of Uri son of Chur, of the tribe of Yehudah. (*Shemot* 31:2)

Why would the Torah trace Betzalel back to his grandfather Chur? One *midrash* states that since Chur martyred himself during the calf episode, God rewarded him by choosing his grandson Betzalel as the chief artisan:

> Why is Chur mentioned here? Because when Israel was about to serve idols, he jeopardized his life on God's behalf and would not allow them to do so, with the result that they slew him. Whereupon the Holy One, blessed be He, said: I assure you that I will repay you for this. (*Shemot Rabbah* 48:3)

In *Divrei Ha-Yamim*, *Chazal* found another clue. In the genealogy of the tribe of Yehudah, Kalev son of Hetzron married Efrat, who gave birth to Chur:

> Kalev son of Hetzron had children by his wife Azuvah, and by Yeriot; these were her sons: Yesher, Shovav, and Ardon. When Azuvah died, Kalev married Efrat, who bore him Chur. Chur begot Uri, and Uri begot Betzalel. (*Divrei Ha-Yamim* I 2:19–20)

---

4. *Tanchuma Tetzavveh* 10 spells out the textual derivation from Chur's mention in *Shemot* 24:14 and subsequent absence in the golden calf narrative. Cf. *Sanhedrin* 7a. *Or Ha-Chayyim* (on *Shemot* 32:1) suggests that the Torah omits Chur's martyrdom since its inclusion would serve only as a stain on Israel's record, whereas the calf episode is primarily intended to teach the power of repentance and atonement.

Whether this Kalev son of Hetzron (a son of Peretz son of Yehudah) should be identified with Kalev son of Yefuneh on the level of *peshat* is dubious (see Ibn Ezra's short commentary on *Shemot* 24:14). However, several *midrashim* identify them as the same person on the level of *derash*. Kalev son of Yefuneh was the most heroic spy during that disaster, stalwartly opposing his collegues and the entire nation and demanding that they have faith in God. The nation threatened to stone him (*Bemidbar* 13:30; cf. *Bemidbar* 14:6–10, where Yehoshua also acts heroically alongside Kalev). Perhaps the *midrashim* that depict Chur's heroic martyrdom during the calf episode derive in part from the story of Kalev. By creating this conceptual father-son relationship, the midrashic story of Chur's martyrdom becomes even more poignant. Kalev and Chur are cast as the two courageous men of faith who opposed everyone else during Israel's two greatest desert sins. Kalev almost was killed by the mob, whereas Chur was killed.

One final layer of *derash* interpretation exists. Who was Efrat, Chur's mother (*Divrei Ha-Yamim* I 2:19–20)? A *midrash* identifies her with Miriam:

> The king of Egypt spoke to the Hebrew midwives (*Shemot* 1:15): Rav and Shemuel [differ in their interpretation]; one said they were…Yocheved and Miriam; and [the other said] they were Yocheved and Elisheva (Aharon's wife, see *Shemot* 6:23)…And because the midwives feared God, He established households for them (*Shemot* 1:21): Rav and Shemuel [differ in their interpretation]; one said they are the priestly and Levitical houses, and the other said they are the royal houses. One who says they are the priestly and Levitical houses: Aharon and Moshe; and one who says they are the royal houses: for also David descended from Miriam, as it is written: When Azuvah died, Kalev married Efrat, who bore him Chur. Chur begot Uri, and Uri begot Betzalel (*Divrei Ha-Yamim* I 2:19), and it is written: Now David was the son of that Ephrathite etc. (*Shemuel* I 17:12). (*Sotah* 11b)

In the Torah, Miriam watched over baby Moshe's ark. The associations of the midwives Shifrah and Puah with Yocheved and Miriam (or Elisheva)

in this talmudic passage further underscore the midrashic characterization of Miriam as a risk-taker as she defied Pharaoh's murderous decrees.

By having Chur's midrashic parents as Kalev son of Yefuneh
(identified with Kalev son of Hetzron) and Miriam (identified with
Efrat and possibly also with Puah), Chur's parents both put their lives
on the line for God and their people. As a bonus, these associations
would make Chur into Moshe's nephew. The two individuals supporting Moshe's tired arms in the battle against Amalek would be Moshe's
brother and his sister's son.

The texts in *Shemot* and *Divrei Ha-Yamim* give us precious few
hints to Chur's character, despite his being so prominent a leader at the
time of the Exodus. At the level of *peshat*, we know that Chur was from
the tribe of Yehudah (*Divrei Ha-Yamim* I 2:19–20), and was the grandfather of the artisan Betzalel (*Shemot* 31:2). The various *midrashim* we
have considered expand him into a religious hero and martyr, son of
the elite of the desert generation: Kalev and Miriam. Chur thereby is
brought to life through these midrashic expansions.

PHARAOH'S DAUGHTER

> The daughter of Pharaoh came down to bathe in the Nile, while
> her maidens walked along the Nile. She spied the basket among
> the reeds and sent her slave girl to fetch it. When she opened it,
> she saw that it was a child, a boy crying. She took pity on it and
> said, "This must be a Hebrew child." Then his sister said to Pha-
> raoh's daughter, "Shall I go and get you a Hebrew nurse to suckle
> the child for you?" And Pharaoh's daughter answered, "Yes." So
> the girl went and called the child's mother. And Pharaoh's daugh-
> ter said to her, "Take this child and nurse it for me, and I will pay
> your wages." So the woman took the child and nursed it. When
> the child grew up, she brought him to Pharaoh's daughter, who
> made him her son. She named him Moshe, explaining, "I drew
> him out of the water." (*Shemot* 2:5–10)

The story of Pharaoh's daughter seems simple enough. Pharaoh's daughter knew Moshe was an Israelite either because he was circumcised, or

because mothers do not normally float their babies down a river. There also is something delightfully ironic about Miriam getting Pharaoh's daughter to pay Moshe's mother Yocheved to nurse Moshe.

Perhaps the most curious element in the *peshat* is that Pharaoh's daughter names the baby "Moshe" since "I drew him out of the water" (*"ki min ha-mayim meshitihu"*). How did Pharaoh's daughter know Hebrew to make such a wordplay? Chizkuni and Abarbanel were so bothered by this question that they espoused a forced reading that Moshe's mother named him. A more likely interpretation, adopted by Shadal and Netziv, is that "Moshe" was an Egyptian name, meaning "son." The Torah makes a *"derashah"* on this Egyptian word into a Hebrew wordplay. At the level of *peshat*, then, Pharaoh's daughter serves as an agent of Moshe's rescue and adoptive mother, and then disappears from the narrative.

Midrashim, however, exploit several details in this brief account that would not have bearing in *peshat*. For example, one *midrash* asks why Pharaoh's daughter would go to the river to bathe. Were there no baths in the palace? Its answer: Pharaoh's daughter was using the river as a *mikveh* in order to banish paganism from herself, thereby essentially converting to Judaism (*Sotah* 12a).

The Torah reports that *"she* spied the basket among the reeds." Were there not also maidservants present? Perhaps the Torah should have said that *they* spied the basket. One *midrash* concludes that of course everyone physically saw the basket. However the Torah distinguishes between the mindset of Pharaoh's daughter and that of her maidservants. When Pharaoh's daughter wanted to save Moshe, her maidservants critically reminded her that her own father had made the decree (*Sotah* 12b)!

A third example: the Torah notes that Pharaoh's daughter "made him her son." Why add this seemingly superfluous phrase? One *midrash* concludes that Pharaoh's daughter hugged and kissed Moshe as though he really was her own child (*Shemot Rabbah* 1:31).

The foregoing questions and responses are not likely to be raised by *pashtanim*, but they still may have bearing on the textual account of Pharaoh's daughter. At one level, there is something remarkable in the courage of Pharaoh's daughter who defied her own father and her society. In addition, several *midrashim* assume that Pharaoh's daughter must have learned Hebrew in order to name Moshe using a Hebrew etymology. Midrashically, this combination points to some form of "conversion" from the paganism and immorality of her father, associates, and entire society.

On a different plane, the Torah reports that a grown Moshe left the palace endowed with an incredible moral sense. In short order he killed an Egyptian taskmaster, intervened in an Israelite quarrel, and heroically stepped into a struggle among Midianites at the well. Where did this moral fortitude come from? Seemingly, it came at least partially from Pharaoh's daughter. Moshe's defiance of Pharaoh and society paralleled the heroism of his adoptive mother. Moshe also instantly identified with his brethren, the Israelites. Perhaps Pharaoh's daughter, who could have raised him as an Egyptian, reminded him who he really was.[5]

As Moshe left the palace as a young adult, Pharaoh's daughter forever lost her beloved adopted son whom she had raised as her own. She likely was heartbroken, but also incredibly proud. She had raised a child who shared her vision of looking beyond the pagan immorality that characterized Egyptian society.

We never will know who Pharaoh's daughter was or even her name from the Torah. But her moral courage in rescuing Moshe against her father's orders and in the presence of her maidservants, her love of Moshe and her nurturing his moral and Israelite identity changed the world by rescuing and then raising the greatest individual who ever lived. We may view Pharaoh's daughter's break from Egyptian immorality as a form of "conversion" from all Egyptian society from Pharaoh down to the maidservants.

Turning to *Divrei Ha-Yamim*, we find a named daughter of Pharaoh in the Judah genealogy: "These were the sons of Bitiah daughter of Pharaoh, whom Mered married" (*Divrei Ha-Yamim* 1 4:18). Midrashically, this woman is identified with Moshe's rescuer. The name Bitiah is understood as "*bat Ya-h*," or "the daughter of God." One *midrash* remarks, "God told Pharaoh's daughter: Moshe was not your child, yet you treated

---

5. Offering an alternative possibility, Joseph H. Hertz surmises that Moshe's formative years nursing with his mother enabled Yocheved to teach Moshe all about his Israelite identity (*The Pentateuch and Haftorahs*, [London: Soncino Press, 1968], p. 210).

him as you would your own son. Even though you are not My daughter, I will call you My daughter" (*Vayikra Rabbah* 1:3).

People often act heroically though they might be forgotten from conscious memory. However, their impact can transform individuals and change the world. The silent yet powerful impact of Chur and Pharaoh's daughter in the Torah, fleshed out by various midrashic traditions, represents this type of greatness.

Rabbi Ezra Schwartz

ויקהל: The Moral of Mishkan Reiteration

*P*arashat Vayakhel seems to be completely superfluous. There simply is no need to go through all of the details regarding the instructions Moshe gave of how to construct the *Mishkan* and the way those instructions were carried out. The Torah could have simply said, "Moshe instructed the Jews to perform all that *Hashem* had told him and the Jews faithfully carried out these instructions." The uncharacteristic verbosity of the Torah regarding the construction of the *Mishkan* is quite puzzling.

There are a number of other *parashiyyot* in the Torah which at first glance seem to be overly verbose and full of meaningless repetition. Yet upon deeper reflection, each of these repetitions underscores a different dimension and contributes a great deal to our understanding. The *korbanot* of the *nesi'im* (*Bemidbar* Ch. 7) are repeated a full twelve times. The Torah could have simply stated that each *nasi* brought the same *korban* as his predecessor. That repetition is, however, far from meaningless, and according to *Chazal* is pregnant with inner meaning. The *Midrash* writes at length to show that although the outward manifestation of each *nasi's korban* was the same, each *nasi* brought a unique set of sublime ideas to accompany his individual *korban*. The lesson is that external similarity must not be overblown. Homonyms are not synonyms. Ideas may sound the same, but in reality there may be a completely different set of values that lie beneath the surface of each seemingly identical notion.

This notion of not being carried away by external similarity does not seem to govern the repetition of the *parashah* of the *Mishkan*. In fact, if we look carefully at the *parashah* of the *Mishkan* we will note a number of nuanced differences between the command *Hashem* gave Moshe, the instructions Moshe delivered to Betzalel, and the command for the Jews to bring the items to Moshe. *Chazal* noted these differences and amplified the fact that Moshe and Betzalel disagreed as to whether the *Mishkan* should be constructed before the *keilim* or *vice versa* (see *Berakhot* 55a). In this respect, the repetition of the *parashah* of the *Mishkan* is not akin to the repetition of the *korbanot ha-nesi'im*.

This may have been what impelled Ramban (*Shemot* 36:8, ad loc.) to note that the repetition of the *parashah* of the *Mishkan* is in fact similar to the expansive telling and retelling of the story of Eliezer the servant of Avraham. In that instance, the same story is repeated, with slight variances and differences. It seems to parallel the repetitions of the *parashah* of the *Mishkan*. Ramban maintains that the many repetitions of the *parashah* of the *Mishkan* come to increase the reward of the one who engages in its study. In effect it is similar to the *parashah* of "*ben sorer u-moreh*" that was written to enable the one who studies it to glean much reward.

It is generally understood, however, that the reason why the story of Eliezer the servant of Avraham is repeated is in order to teach a moral lesson.[1] Minutiae of the *Halakhah* are best transmitted in a concise, even apodictic manner. However, matters of the spirit, emotions and attitudes are best conveyed through elaboration. This explains why Chassidic lore is so expansive and full of so many detailed stories. Training in matters of faith or in the more aptly termed 'duties of the heart,' requires such elaboration. This forces us to confront a different question. The construc-

---

1.   See R. Mayer Twersky's essay at http://www.torahweb.org/torah/2000/parsha/rtwe_chayeysara.html for a nice development of this idea.

tion of the *Mishkan* seems to fall into the category of matters of the mind, rather than the heart. Why should it be so expansively elaborated upon?

Some have argued that the many repetitions of the *Mishkan* teach a halakhic lesson. The Talmud (*Shabbat* 49b) cites an opinion that the source for the 39 prohibited *melakhot* on *Shabbat* is the number of instances that the word *melakhah* occurs in the Torah. This approach serves to maintain the halakhic nature of the *Mishkan*, but still maintain that the repetitions are not for naught. Rather, each repetition effectively creates a new category of prohibited labor on *Shabbat*.

I am more inclined, however, to maintain that the *parashah* of the *Mishkan* in fact is repeated time and time again in order to convey a moral lesson. The Ramban notes in his introduction to *Sefer Shemot*, that the *Mishkan* represents the culmination of *ge'ulah*. *Sefer Shemot* marks the transition we undergo as a people from slaves to free men. However, that transition is incomplete until we attain an ongoing, intimate relationship with *Hashem*. The *Mishkan* represents the physical attainment of this ongoing relationship with the Transcendent. As a place of ongoing *hashra'at ha-Shekhinah*, it is the paradigm for *ge'ulah*, literally bringing us back to our ultimate source. Perhaps we can suggest that the many repetitions of the *parashah* of the *Mishkan* underscore that attaining such an intense relationship is, in fact, a possibility. Man may believe that a *Mishkan* is beyond the realm of possibility. For this reason the Torah repeats it time after time, to teach that in fact construction of such a sacred space is within the realm of possibility. The fact that everyone contributed to the *Mishkan* and that the talents of each individual were used to build this sacred space further this point. The nuances of difference between the various retellings highlight the fact that there are slightly different ways of attaining this *hashra'at ha-Shekhinah*; however, they all must be grounded in the same general framework: doing what *Hashem* commanded Moshe.

Dr. Aaron Koller

פקודי: Building the Tabernacle, Building a World

ביום החדש הראשון באחד לחדש תקים
את משכן אהל מועד (שמות מ:ב)

On the day of the first month, on the first of the
month, set up the Mishkan. (Shemot 40:2)

The date given situates us on two clocks. On the mundane clock, it has been nearly a year since the Exodus. On the sacred clock, the completion of the *Mishkan* is linked to the Creation at the beginning of *Bereishit*.[1]

---

1. The *Tanna'im* debated whether the world was created in Tishrei or in Nisan (see

I. THE *MISHKAN* AS CREATION

As we read through the end of the book of *Shemot*, there are a number of *pesukim* which are further reminiscent of the Creation story at the beginning of *Bereishit*.

Bereishit 1:31–2:2	Shemot 39–40
וירא אלהים את כל אשר עשה והנה טוב מאד (בראשית א, לא)	וירא משה את כל המלאכה והנה עשו אתה כאשר צוה ה׳ כן עשו (לט, מג)
ויכלו השמים והארץ וכל צבאם (ב, א)	ותכל כל עבדת משכן אהל מועד (לט, לב)
ויכל אלהים ביום השביעי מלאכתו אשר עשה (ב, ב)	ויכל משה את המלאכה (מ, לג)
ויברך אלהים את יום השביעי (ב, ב)	ויברך אתם משה (לט, מג)
ויקדש אתו (ב, ב)	וקדשת אתו ואת כל כליו והיה קדש (מ, ט)

The two narratives are connected by some of their most important vocabulary: God/Moshe *saw* that the work was done well; the work (*"melakhah"*) was *completed*; God/Moshe blessed the result; the work is sanctified (*"kadosh"*). These verbal similarities serve to connect the construction of the *Mishkan* to the Creation of the world.

    Chazal also point to this connection, in a number of ways. The work done by Betzalel on the *Mishkan* is compared in one passage to the work done by God in creating the world: "R. Yehudah said in the name of Rav: Betzalel knew how to combine the letters through which the heavens and earth were created" (*Berakhot* 55a). The *Midrash Tanchuma* on our *parashah* (*Pekudei*, 2) makes a similar point, pointing to the verbal parallels between Creation and the construction of the *Mishkan*, and drawing the conclusion that "the place of the *Mishkan* is equivalent to the creation of the world."

especially *Rosh Ha-Shanah* 10b–11a). What became the dominant view is that Tishrei marks the birth of the world (*ha-yom harat olam*), but calling Nisan "the first month" harks back to Creation whether or not it was the same month of the year.

In what follows, it will be suggested that there are at least two implications of the connection between the Creation and the construction of the *Mishkan*. First, within the realm of *Halakhah*, the connection will grant us insight into a central aspect of the laws of *Shabbat*; second, on a literary-theological plane, it will point to one of the structuring themes of all of *Chumash*.

II. THE CONNECTION BETWEEN
SHABBAT AND THE *MISHKAN*

The list of the thirty-nine *melakhot* which are forbidden on *Shabbat* is, as is well known, tied to the *Mishkan*. This linkage appears in a number of contexts. In *Shabbat* 49b, R. Chanina b. Chama is quoted as making the point explicitly: "That which we learned, that there are one less than forty *melakhot*, corresponds to what? R. Chanina b. Chama said to them: corresponding to the *melakhot* of the *Mishkan*." A Baraitha is then quoted:

אין חייבין אלא על מלאכה שכיוצא בה היתה במשכן: הם זרעו ואתם לא
תזרעו; הם קצרו ואתם לא תקצרו....

One is not liable for doing *melakhah* except for a *melakhah* which was done in the *Mishkan*: they sowed, so you may not sow; they harvested, so you may not harvest....

Having established that a *melakhah* had to have been "done in the *Mishkan*" in order to be prohibited on *Shabbat*, we ought to ask: what does it mean that a particular act was done "in the *Mishkan*"? This question arises when "baking" is listed among the prohibited actions. Rashi (*Shabbat* 73a s.v. *ofeh*) comments, "baking did not exist in the *Mishkan*, since it only applies to bread, and there was no bread in the construction of the *Mishkan* (*melekhet ha-mishkan*)." One may ask, though, why does Rashi not simply point to the showbread, the *lechem ha-panim* which was baked weekly for the *Mishkan*? Apparently, Rashi's view is that in order to be prohibited on *Shabbat*, an act had to have been done in the *construction* of the *Mishkan*.[2]

2. Compare similarly the comments of the Ramban on *Shabbat* 74a. For further discus-

פקודי

What is the logic to this position? It seems that Rashi is following
Chazal in intuiting a complex, triangular relationship between *Shabbat*,
the *Mishkan*, and Creation. The construction of the *Mishkan* is, as we
have seen, a conceptual re-incarnation of the Creation process. *Shabbat*
is presented as the opposite, as the (temporary) repudiation of the Creation process. By extension, then, *Shabbat* stands in opposition to the
construction of the *Mishkan*, as well. It is for this reason that *Shabbat*
was re-commanded immediately after the directive to build the *Mishkan*
(*Shemot* 31:12–17), and then again before the narration of the construction (*Shemot* 35:2–3). *Chazal* point out this textual connection, and draw
the conclusion that the construction of the *Mishkan* does not supersede
the construction of the *Mishkan*. What can be added is that the linkage is
not merely a surface-level conflict between construction and a prohibition of construction. Instead, the conflict runs to the deepest level: the
building of the *Mishkan* was designed to embody the Creation process,
and *Shabbat* was designed to renounce the act of Creation.

The connection between *Shabbat* on the one hand, and Creation
and the *Mishkan* on the other is seen also in the terminology used to
describe the actions performed. Both Creation and the *Mishkan* are
specifically called *melakhah*; *Bereishit* (2:2), for example, reports that
"*va-yekhal Elokim ba-yom ha-shev'i melakhto asher asah*" – "and on the
seventh day God finished His work which He had made," and we read
in *Shemot* (40:33) that "*va-yekhal Moshe et ha-melakhah*" – "and Moshe
finished the work." And it is *melakhah* which is forbidden on *Shabbat*.

The difference between *melakhah* and *avodah* is discussed in
detail by R. Yaakov Zvi Meklenburg (1785–1865) in his *Ha-Ketav Ve-
Ha-Kabbalah*.[3] He argues that *melakhah* is creative, but not necessarily
laborious, whereas *avodah* is laborious, but not necessarily creative. For
example, writing two letters is *melakhah*, but would not be classified as
avodah. Running a marathon and carrying furniture upstairs, on the other
hand, are laborious *avodah*, but not *melakhah*, and are therefore permit-

sion, see R. Yaakov Neuberger, "Mekor Lamed-Tet Avot Mel'akhot," *Beit Yitzchak*
37 (2005), pp. 148–155.
3.   R. Yaakov Zvi Meklenburg, *Ha-Ketav Ve-Ha-Kabbalah* (Frankfurt am Main: Kauff-
man 1880 [originally 1839]), on *Shemot* 35:2.

ted on *Shabbat*. R. Meklenburg thus explains the difference between *Shabbat* and the festivals: on *Shabbat* all *melakhah* is forbidden, but on the festivals only *melekhet avodah* is forbidden. The difference between the two categories, he explains, is reflected in the law regarding cooking, which is creative but not laborious; cooking is therefore not included in *melekhet avodah* and not forbidden on the festivals.

But why, we may ask R. Meklenburg, is it specifically creative acts – *melakhot* – which are prohibited on *Shabbat*? What does this say about the nature of *Shabbat*? Simple, he may say: *Shabbat* is precisely the opposite of the Creation-*Mishkan* matrix, which is all about creative *melakhah* and the formation of new world orders. So of course it is *melakhah* – creating anything new in or about the world – which is prohibited on *Shabbat*. The *Mishkan* was the creation of a new world, and therefore anything done in the construction of the *Mishkan* is forbidden on *Shabbat*.

III. THE FIRST PART OF *CHUMASH*: CREATION TO CREATION

These textual and thematic connections between *Bereishit* Ch. 1 and *Shemot* Ch. 39–40 were recognized in modern times by Martin Buber.[4] In Buber's reading, the *Mishkan* shows that – to borrow a talmudic phrase from a different context – "man has become God's partner in the creation process" (*Shabbat* 10a and elsewhere). In the Creation in *Bereishit*, God creates, alone. He thinks, He executes, He approves. After Sinai, however, God thinks, God shows Moshe the plan, and then Moshe instructs the people and the people do. Buber points out that the verb "to do" appears more than 100 times in the story of the *Mishkan* being built: the people are very much *doing*. This is highlighted by one of the parallels above: whereas in Creation "*God* sanctified [the *Shabbat*]," when the *Mishkan* is completed the people are charged, "*you* shall sanctify it and its vessels."

This is not an unambiguously positive development. There are

4. Mordecai (Martin) Buber, *Darko shel Mikra: Iyyunim Be-Defusei Signon Ba-Tanakh* (Jerusalem: Bialik, 1964), pp. 55–57; I thank Professor Barry Eichler for this reference. See also Benjamin Sommer, *Bodies of God and the World of Ancient Israel* (Cambridge: Cambridge University Press, 2009), pp. 110–111.

advantages to having God be the craftsman. Buber draws attention to the difference between what is "seen" in *Bereishit* and what is "seen" in *Shemot*. "God saw all which He did, and lo, it was very good" (*Bereishit* 1:31), but "Moshe saw all the work, and lo, they did it, as God commanded so did they do it" (*Shemot* 39:43). It cannot be said that it is "very good;" this is reserved for work done by God.

But compensating for whatever diminution from perfection there may have been is the fact that humans, God's treasured creation in whom He invested so much hope and who had always held out so much promise, had finally learned from their Master and *created*. And they created a home for the Master, no less, to allow him to permanently dwell amongst them.

It is no accident that the allusions detected in the *Mishkan* narrative which point back to Creation point specifically to the first Creation story (*Bereishit* 1:1–2:3). This is the narrative analyzed by R. Yosef Dov Soloveitchik as describing Adam the First.[5] This is the model of the human who is empowered to subdue the earth and to develop it, to be creative, innovative, and inventive. Crucially, this is also the "man" said to be created in the image of God.

It is also not an accident, of course, that these parallels connect the beginning of *Bereishit* to the end of *Shemot*. While the Ramban insightfully discussed the theme of the book of *Shemot* as a literary unit,[6] it was Joseph Blenkinsopp who drew attention to the motif discussed here, which provides a structural frame for the first two books of *Chumash* together as a single unit.[7] One could say, then, that the end of *Shemot*

5. R. Yosef Dov Soloveitchik, *The Lonely Man of Faith* (New York: Doubleday, 1992 [originally 1965]).
6. See the Ramban's introduction to *Shemot*. In what follows I am assuming, conceptually, that the Ramban is correct that the *Mishkan* is designed as an ideal of sorts, as opposed to the view of Rashi (and perhaps the Rambam) that the *Mishkan* is necessary as a correction after the golden calf. Besides Rashi on *Shemot* 31:8 (and the implication of Maimonides, *Guide to the Perplexed* III:46), see also the beautiful comments of Rashi on *Shir Ha-Shirim* 1:13–15. For the polemical potential (and possibly motivation) of Rashi's interpretation, which is very different from that of the Rambam, see Elazar Touitou, "Peshat Ve-Apologetica Be-Perush Ha-Rambam Le-Sippurei Moshe Ba-Torah," *Tarbiz* 51 (1982), pp. 235–237.
7. Joseph Blenkinsopp, *CBQ* 38 (1976), pp. 275–291.

brings to a close the first large unit of the *Chumash*, which began with the Creation story and concludes when the *Mishkan* is erected.

Three important transitions can be seen within this two-book unit, which explain why this part can now come to an end. First, God has, so to speak, handed off to mankind the job of creation, as Buber said. Second, and in what may be a related development, the focus has shifted from sacred time to sacred space. When God's act of creation is described, what He completes and what He blesses is a fragment of time; when human creation is narrated, they create, complete, and give sanctity to a fragment of space.

Third, God has found His home. It has been observed that elsewhere in the ancient Near East, when a god is said to have created the world, the immediately following aftermath is that a temple is constructed for him or her. In *Chumash*, these expectations are foiled.[8] God's own Creation, full of such order and promise in *Bereishit* Ch. 1, crashed in the face of the reality of Eden in *Bereishit* Ch. 3, again in Noah's generation in *Bereishit* Ch. 6, and again in the valley in Shin'ar in *Bereishit* Ch. 11. The entire first part of *Chumash* may be read as God's search for man, or, more precisely, God's search for a sacred space among man.

He abandoned His plans, so to speak, for a perfect world governed by all of mankind, and focused His attention on shepherding one family into a sacred space, promising them a land of their own. Finally, in the second half of *Shemot*, though still outside that Promised Land, man has – on the orders of God – created a space within their own space for God Himself. This first act of the grand drama ends on a crescendo of accomplishment, and yet with the promise of an even more transcendent future: now that the *Mishkan* is built, "the cloud of God" will live among man forevermore.[9]

---

8. See especially Moshe Weinfeld, "Shabbat U-Mikdash Ve-Hamlakhat Hashem," *Beit Mikra* 22 (1977), pp. 188–193.
9. On the literary continuity between the end of *Shemot* and the beginning of *Vayikra*, see Sommer, *Bodies of God*, p. 73.

ספר ויקרא

Rabbi Shmuel Hain

וַיִּקְרָא: Making Sense of the Sacrifices

I. INTRODUCTION: THE SACRIFICES AND THEIR SIGNATURE FEATURES[1]

The intricate and seemingly arcane laws of the various sacrifices constitute the entire reading of *Parashat Vayikra*. These details can, at times, overwhelm the reader unfamiliar with the sacrificial service and as a result, the rites of the *korbanot* and their rich theological significance are often overlooked. This essay will analyze one of the sacrifices, the *korban asham* – the guilt offering, with an eye towards uncovering its thematic thrust, a message which is relevant even in an era bereft of the Temple and its sacrificial service.

The key to understanding the essential nature and goal of a *korban* is to examine its name along with what makes its sacrificial service

1. For an overview of the sacrifices from a Biblical perspective, see Joshua Berman, *The Temple: Its Symbolism and Meaning Then and Now* (Jason Aronson, 1995). See also the first chapter of *Shiurei HaRav Aharon Lichtenstein: Zevachim*. For conceptual analyses of specific sacrifices, see volumes I and VI of Yeshiva University's Kollel Elyon Journal, *Kol Zvi*.

unique. *Parashat Vayikra* delineates the distinctive element of three of the four primary animal sacrifices:

1. *Olah*: The opening section describes how the *korban olah* (elevation or burnt offering) is burnt completely on the Altar. This signifies the "gift" or appeasement motif of the *olah*. Although the Torah does invoke atonement in its description of the *olah*, the vehicle for that atonement is the *ritzui* – or appeasement – expressed through the gift of an entire sacrifice to God (see *Vayikra* 1:4).

2. *Shelamim*: The third chapter describes the *korban shelamim*, the peace or whole offering. This sacrifice is characterized as *zevach* (feast) *shelamim*, underscoring the covenantal feast aspect of the sacrifice. As such, the Torah projects the theme of covenantal feast by mandating that the meat of the *shelamim* be shared by God via the Altar (the *Mizbeach*, which comes from the root *zevach*), the priests and the owner of the sacrifice. The Torah omits any reference to atonement in the context of *shelamim*, indicating that it does not atone; rather, it celebrates the ongoing covenantal bond shared between God and Israel.[2]

3. *Chatat*: The trademark feature of the sin, or cleansing, offering is the sprinkling of the blood on the altar. The blood of a *chatat*, unlike all other sacrifices, is sprinkled on top of and on all four corners of the altar (see *Vayikra* 4:30, *Zevachim* 52b) and the blood is not merely poured onto the Altar, it is sprinkled via the priest's finger (*Zevachim* 13b). According to the Talmud (ibid., 6a), the ceremonial sprinkling of the blood of a sacrifice achieves atonement. The *chatat*'s unique sprinkling indicates that its blood achieves a halakhic state of atonement for a specific transgression by cleansing the effects of the transgression. Once again, the sacrifice's trademark feature highlights its essence.

However, the fourth and final category of animal sacrifice described in our *parashah*, the *korban asham*, has no distinguishing feature in its sacrificial service. The sprinkling of its blood is not like the comprehensive sprinkling of a *chatat*, nor is its meat distribution like the singular distributions of *olah* and *shelamim*. More strikingly, the Torah, in its discussion of *asham* (*Vayikra* Ch. 5), does not even offer a basic

---

2. For an in-depth analysis of *korban shelamim* and its centrality in the world of *zevachim*, see the article on *shelamim* in *Kol Zvi*, vol. VI.

description of how an *asham* is sacrificed![3] Deepening the mystery, it is not clear from the Torah why specific situations and transgressions trigger the bringing of an *asham*.[4] What, then, is the essential nature of *asham* and why is it offered in very specific, and infrequent, circumstances?[5]

3. Only later on in *Parashat Tzav* (Ch. 7) when the specific instructions on sacrificial procedures are transmitted to the priests is the actual service of the *asham* described. It is striking that we find no such description in *Parashat Vayikra* which describes the essence of the sacrifices for all of Israel from the perspective of the ones offering them, suggesting that the service is ancillary or superfluous.

4. Altogether, there are six *ashamot*. Three of them are triggered by actual transgressions: 1) *Asham Gezeilot*: If someone owed money, whether for a loan, theft, article in safekeeping, or any other reason, and took an oath denying that he owed the item, he must make restitution, add a surcharge of one-fifth, and bring an *asham* to atone. 2) *Asham Me'ilah*: If one unintentionally used for himself objects that were consecrated to the Temple, he must make restitution, add a fifth, and bring an *asham*. 3) *Asham Shifchah Charufah*: This refers to a woman who is half-slave and half-free who is betrothed to a Hebrew servant. Should another man have relations with her, he is not subject to the standard capital punishment for adultery but is instead liable to bring an *asham* to atone for his sin. A fourth, *Asham Talui*, is offered when one is in doubt about whether he has become liable for a *chatat*. *Asham Nazir* and *Asham Metzora* are offered in response to certain circumstances and not in response to sin. The relationship between the latter two and the other *ashamot* is a very complicated one and is beyond the scope of this essay. It should also be noted that only *Asham Talui*, *Me'ilah* and *Gezeilah* appear in *Parashat Vayikra*.

5. At first glance, *asham* appears to be very similar to *chatat*. Like *chatat*, it is triggered by specific transgressions and it, too, cannot be brought voluntarily. In addition, the Torah projects the theme of atonement in the sections dealing with *korban asham* by concluding each section with the phrase, "and the priest shall provide atonement, and it shall be forgiven him," the same concluding phrase used for *korban chatat*. Furthermore, Ramban notes (*Bemidbar* 8:13, ad loc.) that an inaugural *korban asham* was not offered at the time of the dedication of the altar even though all of the other types of sacrifices were offered (including a one-time only voluntary *chatat*). The Ramban explains this fact by underscoring the close link between *chatat* and *asham*: "The sin offering and the guilt offering are the same thing, have the same purpose, and there is one law for them." Since a *chatat* had been offered, Ramban states, there was no need to bring its sister *korban*. Yet, there are certain elements of *asham* which mimic *olah*. The sprinkling of its blood is not like *chatat*'s but like *olah*'s, indicating that the sacrifice is not focused on atonement for a specific transgression. Ramban himself notes (*Vayikra* 3:1, ad loc.) that the gender of the animal used for *olah* and *asham* is male, while the *chatat* must be a female: "The guilt offering must be a male because the sin offering is brought for those transgressions which, if committed willfully, incur excision, in order that 'the soul return to

II. *ASHAM*: A LOOK BACK

We can begin to understand the nature of *korban asham* from a comment of Ramban about the significance of the term *asham* when it appears earlier in the Torah (*Bereishit* 42:21). When the brothers experience difficulties upon their arrival in Egypt, they connect their travails with their mistreatment of Yosef. The brothers admit to one another, "'*Aval asheimim anachnu*,' indeed we are *guilty* concerning our brother inasmuch as we saw his heartfelt anguish when he pleaded with us and we paid no heed; that is why this anguish has come upon us."

Ramban notes that the brothers' sense of guilt was not due to the act of throwing Yosef into the pit, nor was it due to the act of selling Yosef. Rather, the source of their deep-felt shame was their cruelty towards him in ignoring his pleas for mercy throughout the ordeal. The realization of this character flaw, and not the specific acts of throwing him in the pit or selling him, was the focus of their repentance. *Asham*, then, is associated with the guilt upon recognizing one's underlying flaws that cause one to sin, unlike *chatat/cheit*, which focuses on specific acts of transgression.[6]

III. THE SINS OF *ASHAM*

In light of the brothers' suggestive invoking of the word *asham*, we can appreciate the very specific, and infrequent, instances which trigger the sacrifice. How do we account for certain transgressions obligating an *asham*, while others require a *chatat*? Ramban and Netziv, in their commentaries on our *parashah*, present opposite approaches to this question.

According to Ramban (*Vayikra* 5:15, ad loc.), the severity of the sin

---

God' ('*she-tashuv ha-nefesh el ha-Elokim*'), but the guilt offering is not brought for those transgressions for which one incurs excision, and therefore it is as if it were for 'a pleasing odor' ('*reiach nichoach*') just like the burnt offering.'" According to Ramban, the nature of a *korban* dictates its gender. *Chatat*, inspired by a severe sin and designed to atone for that sin, must be female, while *asham* and *olah*, triggered by lesser transgressions and attempting to bring the penitent closer to God, must be male.

6. See the commentary of *Tzeror Ha-Mor* on the initial section in the Torah about *korban asham* (*Vayikra* 5:15). He explicitly links the atonement of *korban asham* with the brothers' admission of guilt, "*aval asheimim anachnu*."

distinguishes *chatat* from *asham*: "...it appears to me that the term *asham* denotes some serious deed for which the person who did it deserves to be *shamem* (desolate) and destroyed because of it...the word *chatat* denotes something that has merely turned aside off the way." Ramban then describes at length why each one of the transgressions and circumstances of *asham* is more severe than *chatat*.

Netziv (*Vayikra* 5:9, ad loc.), however, suggests the exact opposite reason for a distinction: the transgressions of *asham* are less severe in comparison to *chatat* transgressions and therefore require a different *korban*.

To fully explain the nature of *korban asham*, I would suggest that Netziv and Ramban are both correct. On one plane, Netziv is correct. The punishments for transgressions that obligate an *asham* are less severe than for those that demand a *chatat*. A *chatat* is offered when one unintentionally transgresses a sin with the punishment of *karet*, or excision. However, *asham*'s sins pale in comparison: the sins of falsely swearing about a stolen object, inappropriate use of Temple property and relations with a partial maidservant do not entail a punishment of excision. Some of these are even questionable as acts of transgression. While clearly inappropriate, relations with a *shifchah charufah* are not defined explicitly as illicit. Robbery is not necessarily permanent; returning the stolen goods can rectify, and perhaps eliminate retroactively, the transgression. The prohibition of benefiting from consecrated property is a more specialized, and subtler, act of robbery from consecrated goods. Finally, *asham talui* is not even triggered by an actual transgression; it is offered only when one is *unsure* about whether he has transgressed a *chatat*-inducing prohibition.

At the same time, Ramban is also correct: These transgressions, due to their questionable status as acts of transgression, may reveal a much deeper flaw in one's religious personality that entails a sense of *shemamah* (desolation or shame).[7] Taking advantage of a handmaid, precisely because it is not illicit, demonstrates a disregard for the halakhic system. It suggests that the transgressor does not take seriously

---

7. It is noteworthy that the *ashamot* for robbery and for relations with a handmaid are brought when the transgressions are intentional.

the prohibition due to its relatively mild punishment. Likewise, stealing money via a false oath abuses the judicial system and ignores the One who is the true provider of material possessions. *Me'ilah* indicates a lack of clarity between items that are holy and those that are not. *Asham talui* demonstrates a total lack of caution and awareness of one's actions.[8]

Thus a *korban chatat*, due to the severity of the sin as an objective act (albeit committed unintentionally), can and must only atone for the actual transgression. The transgressions that result in a *korban asham*, due to their questionable status as acts of transgressions and to the fundamental flaw in one's character that they reveal, allow and encourage room for the penitent to transcend atonement for the particular sin that was committed.

IV. *ASHAM*'S UNIQUENESS: IT'S ALL ABOUT THE ADMISSION

If the sins and circumstances of *asham* are unique, why does the *korban* lack a unique feature in its sacrificial service? Moreover, how does the process of offering an *asham* facilitate its goal to transcend the specific transgression and address the underlying character flaw at the root of the sin? To answer these questions, we must determine what *is* unique to *asham*. Ramban (*Bava Metzia* 3b, s.v. *elah*) observes that to obligate

---

8. In his discussion of the severity of *asham* transgressions, Ramban includes the *ashamot* offered by a *nazir* and a *metzora*, *ashamot* that are not offered in response to a sin. Though this essay has focused on the *ashamot* offered in the context of sin, *asham nazir* and *asham metzora* could be viewed in a similar manner. A *nazir* and a *metzora* offer both an *asham* and *chatat* in order to become ritually pure. Perhaps their respective sin offerings are offered as a specific response to the state they are in (like a regular *chatat* that is offered to neutralize a specific sin). At the same time, their respective guilt offerings are brought to focus on the underlying reasons for why they are in this situation (like a regular *asham* that is brought to inspire a reevaluation of one's religious self). Ramban in this context also groups the *oleh ve-yored chata'ot* (variable *chatat* offerings) with the *ashamot*. The connection between *asham* and *chatat oleh ve-yored* (a *chatat* that is determined by the financial status of its owner) is a complicated one. Though they are defined as *chata'ot*, the Torah consistently refers to the sacrifice as an *asham*. From its placement in the Torah between the sections about *chatat* and the sections dealing with *asham*, it appears that *chatat oleh ve-yored* is on the border between these two sacrifices.

an *asham,* unlike a *chatat,* an explicit confession by the transgressor is required. Why should personal admission be indispensable for an *asham* but not for a *chatat*? Ramban explains:

In the context of *asham,* "and he shall confess" (*"ve-hitvadah"*) is written, because it is the confession which generates the obligation and he cannot be obligated without a confession, even if Eliyahu were to testify. This is not comparable at all to eating *chelev* and similar situations of *chatat.* In the context of *chatat,* the eating generates the obligation for the *korban* and the witnesses merely reveal the facts, whereas the obligation for an *asham* is only generated by, and at the time of, his confession.

Chatat is offered in order to neutralize a specific transgression. A statement of the facts by two witnesses without protestation by the sinner proves that the act was committed. Therefore, there is no need for an explicit admission in order to trigger the sacrifice whose service will erase the effects of the act. An *asham,* on the other hand, can only be created through an explicit admission of guilt. Its goal is not to merely erase a transgression, but to parlay the sin into a positive force for a repentance that recognizes and uproots the underlying character flaws that caused the transgression. To access this unique opportunity to rehabilitate one's entire self, a realization of guilt along with a concomitant admission of wrongdoing are critical.

Asham, like *chatat,* is triggered by a particular sin, but its ultimate goal is to inspire a reassessment of the owner's character. The owner's sense of *shemamah* (guilt and desolation) and the requirement to articulate one's guilt, account for *asham's* singular ability to transform the penitent in a more comprehensive fashion. To invoke the distinction of the language of the Gemara in *Zevachim* (89a–89b), *chatat* is a sacrifice that "atones," while *asham* is a *korban* that is "derived from the power to atone."

We can now understand why *asham's* sacrificial service has no distinguishing element and why the Torah omits a description of the service in our *parashah.* In contrast to *olah, shelamim,* and *chatat,* the actual sacrificial service of an *asham* is secondary. *Chatat's* goal is to achieve atonement for a specific sin. The means for achieving that goal is the sprinkling of the blood. Therefore, *chatat's* special feature is its multifaceted sprinkling of the blood. *Olah's* purpose is to bring man closer to God. It accomplishes this through a gift of an entire *korban* to God.

ויקרא

Therefore, *olah* is the only sacrifice that has all its meat burnt on the altar. *Shelamim* celebrates the ongoing covenantal relationship between God and Israel via a shared feast. *Asham's* focus is on man's realization of an underlying flaw in his religious personality. Its trademark, a mandatory admission of wrongdoing, encourages a thorough reevaluation of one's character. Thus, there is no need for a special feature in the actual sacrificial service of an *asham*.[9]

The centrality of an admission of guilt explains another feature unique to *asham*. The Talmud, in several places (see, for example, *Zevachim* 5a), differentiates between *asham* and the other sacrifices based on the fact that *asham* can only be offered by an individual. *Chatat, olah,* and *shelamim* function, in certain instances, as communal offerings. Why is *asham* the only one of the sacrifices that is offered exclusively by an individual?

The respective themes of *olah, shelamim* and *chatat* are not limited to an individual. The entire nation as a whole can use the *chatat* to eradicate a specific communal wrongdoing. Likewise, the Jewish people can collectively offer a gift to God via an *olah* or celebrate its covenantal relationship by offering a *shelamim*. Conversely, the theme of *asham*,

9. In light of the ancillary role that the sacrificial service plays, we can suggest an alternative explanation to Ramban's question about why an *asham* was not offered when the Altar was dedicated. Ramban attributes this phenomenon to the fact that *chatat* and *asham* are, fundamentally, one and the same. Based on our analysis, the lack of an *asham* at the Altar's inauguration is due to the fact that an *asham* without an admission of wrongdoing is not an *asham*. The service itself is not what makes an *asham* as evidenced by its lack of a distinguishing feature, so there was no need to initiate the Altar with the sacrificial service of the *asham*.

Viewing the actual sacrificing of an *asham* to be of secondary importance may also help explain a problematic comment of Ra'avad. In *Hilkhot Shevuot* (10:20), Ra'avad explains that since a decree of the Geonim that eliminated the use of God's name in vows, there is no penalty of a fifth nor is a *korban asham* offered when someone swears falsely about a stolen object. Radvaz (ad loc.) correctly points out that from the time the Temple was destroyed, the *korbanot* ceased. Why, then, does Ra'avad attribute elimination of *asham* to the decree of the Geonim? According to our analysis of the primacy of admission, perhaps even after the *asham* was no longer sacrificed on the Altar, there was a custom to articulate a verbal confession and a symbolic setting aside of funds for the *korban*. This very unlikely possibility could only exist for an *asham* due to the secondary role played by its sacrificial service.

236

highlighted by its demands for personal reflection and admission of guilt, is only applicable to an individual.[10]

V. *ASHAM* AS *TESHUVAH* PARADIGM

Asham's singular requirements of an explicit admission and confession of guilt form the backbone of Rambam's general obligation to repent. Rambam (*Hilkhot Teshuvah* 1:1) formulates the commandment to repent as follows: "If a person transgresses any of the commandments of the Torah...*when* he repents and turns away from his sin, *he must confess* before God..." For Rambam, the decision to repent does not appear to be obligatory. Rather, when one embarks on the path of repentance, there is an obligation to confess one's sins. What are we to learn from this counterintuitive formulation?[11] Perhaps Rambam is highlighting the aspiration of repentance. It is not enough to merely redress the sin that was committed. The obligation to repent entails much more than that; Rambam mandates a verbal admission of guilt to indicate that the act of repentance must be approached as an *asham*-like opportunity for an evaluation of one's spiritual personality and character flaws.

A *korban asham*-like admission of guilt, a critical component of Rambam's view of repentance, underscores another element of an ideal form of *teshuvah*. By requiring an admission of guilt, this manner of *teshuvah* fosters a more comprehensive repentance and allows the penitent to uncover new spiritual forces within his soul. The goal of this repentance, unlike a *korban chatat*-style repentance, is not just to erase the sin. Rather, the sin and the subsequent feelings of guilt combine to create a chance to rectify and elevate one's sins. The *asham* model of repentance does not entail making a clean break with the past. On the contrary, sin must be remembered. The intensity of sin and the sense of guilt and shame that overwhelms man in its wake, infuse man with a burning

---

10. Another unique feature of *asham* may be related to its ambitious goal of a comprehensive repentance of an individual. *Asham*, unlike all other *korbanot* has a minimum cost. The *mishnah* in *Zevachim* (90b) states that the *ashamot* that are offered to atone must be worth a minimum of two silver shekels. Perhaps this minimum requirement relates to *asham's* attempt to transcend atonement for the specific transgression to atone for the entire person. See *Shiurei HaRav Aharon Lichtenstein: Zevachim*, p. 13.

11. There are of course a number of alternative explanations to this Rambam.

desire to transform his religious personality.[12] These forces can elevate the character of the penitent to a state even higher than before sinning.[13]

A careful study of *korban asham*, then, presents us with an ambitious approach to repentance, one that is particularly meaningful in a post-sacrificial era. Ultimately, *korban asham* teaches us that the realization of the underlying causes of sin can transform the individual and propel the penitent to new spiritual heights.

12. Viewing sin as a constant force to drive man to greater heights can help explain a seemingly strange position of Rambam (following R. Eliezer Ben Yaakov in *Yoma* 86b). Rambam (*Hilkhot Teshuvah* 2:8) rules that even if one has confessed for a specific sin on a previous Yom Kippur and has not transgressed that particular sin since, he should still confess his sins on future Yom Kippurs. Why should we recall our past failings that we have already atoned for in previous years? Indeed, the *Tanna Kamma* holds that one should not confess for these sins again and compares it to a dog frolicking in his own waste. The verse used to support this ruling answers this question while capturing the essence of *korban asham*, "My iniquity I know and my sin is before me always" (*Tehillim* 51:5). We are not to dwell negatively on our past. Yet, we must derive inspiration from our sins to continually soar to new spiritual heights.

13. HaRav Yosef Dov Soloveitchik (*Al Ha-Teshuvah*, pp. 149–187) uses a similar approach to explain the difference between repentance out of love, which can transform intentional sins into merits, and repentance out of fear, which merely change intentional sins into unintentional ones (see *Yoma* 86b).

While the Rav focuses on repentance for sins between Man and God, Emmanuel Levinas uses similar language to describe the ideal form of reconciliation between man and his fellow man (Emmanuel Levinas, *Totality and Infinity*, pp. 282–283): "The paradox of pardon lies in its retro-action; from the point of view of common time it represents an inversion of the natural order of things, the reversibility of time… Active in a stronger sense than forgetting, which does not concert the reality of the event forgotten, pardon acts upon the past, purifying it. Forgetting nullifies the relations with the past, whereas pardon conserves the past in the purified present. The pardoned being is not the innocent being. This does not mean that innocence is above pardon; [we] discern in pardon a surplus of happiness, the happiness of reconciliation, the *felix culpa*…"

Rabbi Michael Taubes

צו: As If One Has Sinned

The Torah concludes its presentation of many of the details concerning the various sacrifices by declaring, "*zot ha-Torah*" – this is the law – "of the *olah*, of the *minchah*, and of the *chatat* and of the *asham*, and of the *milu'im* and of the *shelamim* offering (*Vayikra* 7:37). In a famous exposition of this verse, Reish Lakish, as cited by the Talmud (*Menachot* 110a), and apparently prompted by the reference to Torah in this phrase (see Rashi there, s.v. *mai dekhtiv*), teaches that whoever engages in the study of Torah is considered as if he has offered an *olah*, a *minchah*, a *chatat* and an *asham*. In a similar vein, the Talmud there subsequently quotes R. Yitzchak as understanding from other verses in our *parashah*, which likewise refer to *Torah* in the context of the sacrifices (*Vayikra* 6:18, 7:1), that whoever engages in the study of the Torah of a *chatat* is considered as if he has offered a *chatat*, and whoever engages in the study of the Torah of an *asham* is considered as if he has offered an *asham*.

Some commentators are troubled as to what it is that R. Yitzchak is adding to the teaching of Reish Lakish, other than presenting different verses as his source. One possibility is that, whereas Reish Lakish is discussing the study of Torah in general, asserting that one who studies any part of Torah is regarded as though he has offered a sacrifice, due, perhaps, to some kind of relationship between Torah learning and the sacrificial rites, R. Yitzchak maintains that this credit is given only to one who studies specifically the laws dealing with the Temple service (see Rashi there, s.v. *ein tzarikh* and s.v. *be-torat*). As an interesting aside, there is a discussion among later authorities, which may possibly (though not necessarily) relate to this dispute to some extent, about whether one who engages in the study of the Torah of any *mitzvah* is regarded as though he has performed that particular *mitzvah*. The *Chafetz Chayyim* (in his *Likkutei Halakhot* to *Menachot*, ibid., s.v. *ein tzarich*, in his *Zevach Todah* there, s.v. *amar Rava*, and at greater length, in his *Ma'amar Torah Or*, especially Ch. 2) contends that the kind of Torah study which atones for one's sins, hence accomplishing the same thing as a sacrifice, is Torah study which focuses on the laws of sacrifices. This would have no bearing, though, on any other *mitzvah*. The Mabit (Introduction to *Kiryat Sefer*, Ch. 7), however, as well as the *Shelah*, cited by the *Sha'arei Teshuvah* (*Orach Chayyim* 300:1) and others, suggest that even with regards to other *mitzvot* one may (under certain circumstances) learn specifically about their laws as a substitute for their actual performance (see also *Va-Yaged Moshe* on the *dinim* and *minhagim* of the *Pesach Seder*, 24:40 and the discussion in *Megillah* 4a regarding Purim on *Shabbat*, with the commentaries there, especially Ritva, s.v. *dorshin*).

The Maharsha on *Menachot* (ibid., s.v. *mai dekhtiv*), however, offers a different approach to understanding the flow of the Talmud and the lesson taught by R. Yitzchak. His suggestion is predicated on the fact that the two sacrifices which R. Yitzchak mentions, the *chatat*, the sin offering, and the *asham*, the guilt offering, are sacrifices which are brought, and may only be brought, in connection with the commission of certain specific transgressions; unlike other offerings, they can never be brought on a voluntary basis (see Rambam, *Hilkhot Ma'aseh Ha-Korbanot* 14:8; it should be noted, though, that according to some, one type of *asham* offering may be brought voluntarily, as pointed out by the *Mishneh Le-Melekh* there and by the *Beit Yosef* to *Orach Chayyim* 1, s.v. *ve-achar*, among others). By singling out these particular offerings, R. Yitzchak is thus asserting that when one studies the laws relating to these sacrifices, it is not that he accrues whatever benefit, in the general sense, that he would accrue by offering the sacrifices themselves, but rather that one is regarded not only as if he brought these sacrifices, but as if he became *obligated* to do so, for that is in fact the only way that he could have brought them. In other words, one is considered as though he has actually sinned and has brought the requisite offering to atone for the sin.

This analysis obviously requires some further investigation. Why would one want to be considered as though he has committed a transgression? With regards to other sacrifices, such as the *olah*, the *minchah* and the *shelamim*, it is understandable that one who learns their laws would want to be viewed as having offered them on the altar. These offerings can be brought voluntarily and he who brings any of them is deserving of some credit; one who studies the Torah relating to these sacrifices has volunteered to do what he can do in order to get some of the credit that he would have gotten had he indeed offered them. Why, however, would one want to be viewed as having offered a *chatat* or an *asham* which relate exclusively to sin? Would it not be better for a person *not* to have to offer these sacrifices at all?

It is true that the Talmud in both *Ta'anit* (27b) and *Megillah* (31b) reports that *Hashem* told *Avraham Avinu* that the right of his descendants to hold on to the Land of Israel depends upon the offering of the sacrifices which brings them atonement, and that Avraham, prophetically anticipating an era when this would not be possible, asked in what merit they would retain their claim to the land at that time, and was told that whenever they read about the offerings, they will be considered as having brought them and will thus be forgiven. Similarly, the *Midrash Tanchuma* to our *parashah* (#14) relates that when *Hashem* instructed the prophet Yechezkel to teach the Jewish people in Babylonia about matters concerning the *Beit Ha-Mikdash* specifically while they were in exile, Yechezkel's initial reaction was that this seems unfair. Why tease the people by informing them of facts and laws that they would be unable to observe? *Hashem* responded by saying that He considers the act of reading about everything which relates to the *Beit Ha-Mikdash* to be tantamount to the act of building the *Beit Ha-Mikdash*. Learning about *all* the sacrifices, including the *chatat* and the *asham*, then, does indeed have value and significance. But why would one want to be regarded as actually having sinned and then brought a sacrifice, as the Maharsha implies, when one studies about certain offerings?

A simple explanation may be that what R. Yitzchak really means to convey is that one who studies the laws of the *chatat* and the *asham* is considered as though he has sacrificed them *if he indeed was required to do so*. A possible parallel to this idea may be found in a ruling of the *Tur* (*Orach Chayyim* 1), who records the practice of reciting, on a daily basis, the verses from the Torah relating to the different categories of sacrifices, followed by a "*yehi ratzon,*" a brief prayer that this recitation be accepted by *Hashem* as though the petitioner has in fact offered that particular sacrifice itself. He notes, though, that one does not recite this petition after quoting the verses concerning the *chatat* because one cannot volunteer to bring that sacrifice; it is brought only by one who has definitely committed a sin. One who is not required to bring a *chatat* may not do so and thus should not request that he be regarded as if he has done so. The *Bach* (ibid., s.v. *ve-achar*), however, cites the Maharshal, who says that one may simply modify the petition to state that one's recitation of the verses concerning the *chatat* should be viewed as though he has actually offered a *chatat* if he is indeed obligated to offer a *chatat*. This, then, may likewise be the position of R. Yitzchak here, as understood by the Maharsha. But aside from certain inherent difficulties in this ruling of the Maharshal (see *Magen Avraham*, ibid., #11), the problem is that the Maharsha did not say that one who studies the Torah pertaining to the *chatat* is credited as having offered a *chatat* if he is indeed obligated to bring one; he said that the person is considered to have in fact sinned and then offered the *chatat* to atone for the sin. Our question thus still stands: why would one want to be regarded as having sinned if he did not actually do so?

It would seem, then, that there is possibly some positive benefit in being considered as having committed a sin and then having repented and atoned for it. This may be understood from several perspectives. First, there is the oft-quoted comment of Talmud that "in the place where people who have repented stand, even the completely righteous do not stand" (*Berakhot* 34b). The Rambam explains that these people are on such a high pedestal because they have tasted sin, but have then managed to overcome their inclinations, which is a tremendous accomplishment that the completely righteous have never had the opportunity to achieve (*Hilkhot Teshuvah* 7:4). The *Ba'al Ha-Tanya* (*Likkutei Amarim*

Ch. 7) speaks of the unique yearning for closeness to *Hashem* experienced by one has been distanced from Him due to sin, but then wishes to repent; this powerful desire for *deveikut*, for cleaving to *Hashem*, is not like anything felt by those who have always been completely righteous. Whatever the exact explanation, it is apparent that one who has sinned and then repents is, in at least some sense, on a unparalleled exalted level; one who studies the Torah of the *chatat* offering, by virtue of being considered as having sinned and brought the requisite sacrifice as part of his repentance, is perhaps regarded as having attained that level as well.

Beyond that, we may also gain some insight by examining the nature of true atonement following sin. Offering the appropriate sacrifice(s) is certainly part of the process, but its importance rests not in the sacrifice itself but in what it represents. As expressed by the Ramban, one who brings a sacrifice should view himself as though he personally is actually being consumed on the altar, as that, strictly speaking, is what he deserves because of his transgressions (Commentary to *Vayikra* 1:9). It is due only to the kindness of *Hashem* that He accepts some other offering instead. Based on a statement of the Rambam (*Hilkhot Ma'aseh Ha-Korbanot* 3:15), however, Maran HaRav Yosef Dov Soloveitchik (*Al Ha-Teshuvah*, p. 168) stresses that one actually brings about his atonement not merely through the offering of the sacrifice, but through his repentance – through his confession of his sin and his sense of self-sacrifice, his total submission of himself before *Hashem*. A person offering a sacrifice begins to realize that, in truth, whatever he has belongs to *Hashem*; even his very self is not really his own. Perhaps this same level of subservience to *Hashem*, achieved by one who has offered a sacrifice after having sinned and who has thereby recognized that truly everything he has, including his own self, belongs to *Hashem*, is attained as well by one who studies the laws of the sacrifice and is thus viewed as having sinned and offered that sacrifice.

Finally, an examination of the talmudic passage which presents the famous teaching of Reish Lakish that proper repentance can transform intentional violations into unintentional violations and, when done in a certain manner, even into meritorious deeds (*Yoma* 86b), can offer us another solution. That intentional sins can become considered as unintentional sins is understandable; when a person returns to *Hashem* properly, *Hashem* accepts his repentance, and his transgressions are "dropped" to a lower level. But why, even with an appreciation of the great power of repentance, should we say that one's sins can become considered like good deeds? Surely his actions were not positive! Rav Soloveitchik (ibid., pp. 174–187) develops the idea that it is because such a person can serve *Hashem* and perform *mitzvot* with a kind of strength and power never evidenced before. The very same energy, effort, desire and passion that one applied in the past towards sin can now be applied towards *mitzvot*, towards good deeds, and towards serving *Hashem*. (It may be noted that such was the life experience of Reish Lakish himself; see *Bava Metzia* 84a with *Tosafot*, s.v. *iy hadart*.) When he repents properly, the individual's past sins thus become elevated, because they are now, in a way, contributing to his development as a God-fearing person, and as a result, the individual himself becomes elevated (see Rambam, *Hilkhot Teshuvah* 7:6–7). It may thus be suggested that this same transformation of one's character traits, resulting in a person having a greater drive for the service of *Hashem*, may also be accomplished through the study of the laws of the sacrifice which is part of the repentance process.

It is clear from the above that Torah study can lead a person to the highest possible spiritual heights, bringing about the unique benefits usually reserved for one who has offered sacrifices and repented sincerely before *Hashem*. With this thought in mind, we can perhaps better understand the advice of the Talmud (*Sukkah* 52b) which suggests that if one is tempted by the evil inclination, he should go to the *Beit Ha-Midrash*. Where one has the opportunity to study Torah, all his drives and desires can be channeled in a positive direction, resulting in his attaining those exalted heights.

Prof. Deena Rabinovich

שמיני: Initiation and Innovation: Midrashic Views of the Death of Nadav and Avihu

The *parashah* opens in the middle of the narrative (*Vayikra* 8:1–10:20, the only extended narrative in the entirety of *Sefer Vayikra*) which describes the dedication and inauguration of the *Mishkan* (the Tabernacle) that served as the sanctuary for the Israelites during their years of wandering in the desert and beyond. The narrative relates back to the detailed description of the building of the Sanctuary and its furnishings, which comprises the final third of *Sefer Shemot*. In line with the standard view of *Chazal* that God ordered the building of the *Mishkan* as a corrective for the sin of the golden calf[1] (*chet ha-egel*), the dedication

---

1. This is, of course, not the view of Ramban: see the Ramban's Introduction to *Parashat Terumah*.

ceremonies were planned to reassure the Jewish people that God indeed dwelled in their midst. The tragic death of Nadav and Avihu in the course of the dedicatory ceremonies, though, tempered the joy that the people felt and introduced an element of fear and uncertainty alongside the mood of confidence and hope with which our narrative opens.

The dedication narrative is situated immediately after the detailed textual description in *Vayikra* (1:1–7:38) of the various offerings that are to be brought in the sanctuary. This "Torah" (*Vayikra* 7:37), or teaching, regarding the burnt offering, the gift offering, the sin offering, and so on, had been revealed to Moshe at *Har Sinai* (*Vayikra* 7:38)[2] and its presentation here is out of its chronological order. Let us return then, briefly, to the story of the construction of the *Mishkan* which serves as the backdrop for our story.

According to the rabbinic tradition preserved by Rashi (to *Shemot* 31:18, apparently from the *Tanchuma*), *chet ha-egel* (*Shemot* 32) preceded the command to build the *Mishkan* (*Shemot* 25:1 *et seq*). According to this tradition, the shattering of the *Luchot Ha-Berit*, the denouement of the *chet ha-egel* story, took place on the seventeenth day of *Tammuz*, of year one in the desert. Eighty days later, on the tenth of *Tishrei*, after Moshe spent forty days in prayer and forty days receiving the second tablets, God forgave the people and the very next day the donations for the *Mishkan* began, culminating some six months later with its dedication.[3]

2. There is an obvious question here since *Vayikra* 1:1 indicates that what follows was spoken by God to Moshe from the *Ohel Mo'ed*, not from *Har Sinai*. The Talmud (*Zevachim* 115b) cites two tannaitic views: R. Yishmael held that basic principles were revealed at Sinai while the detail were presented only later, while R. Akiva held that all of the details were also revealed at Sinai, but were repeated at the *Ohel Mo'ed* and then repeated again on *Arvot Moav*, the plains of Moab, shortly before the people entered the Land of Israel. Of the laws set out in the first seven chapters, only those of *Vayikra* 6:12–16 are specifically related to the dedication narrative.

3. The dates of the dedication ceremonies are themselves subject to disagreement. What has become the standard view (*Seder Olam* Ch. 6; *Shabbat* 87b, *Mekhilta de Milu'im* [see, Menahem Kahana, "The Halakhic Midrashim," in *The Literature of the Sages: Midrash and Targum*, eds. S. Safrai et al., (Assen: Royal Van Goreum-Fortress Press, 2006), p. 85, n. 412]) is that the actual construction of the *Mishkan* concluded on the 23rd of Adar. The seven days of *milu'im* (installation) (*Vayikra* 8:33) began on the same day, culminating in the dedication ceremonies of the "Eighth Day"

The sin and its aftermath bring a structural change to the encampment. God was prepared to destroy the entirety of the nation and begin a new people with Moshe himself. Moshe has managed to save the people but cannot win complete exculpation: those who sinned are indeed punished (they are cut down by the loyal men of the tribe of Levi) and, as set out in the *midrashim*, some element of the punishment is reserved for each future generation. In addition, Moshe's tent is relocated to a position outside of the camp (*Shemot* 33:7–11):

(ז) ומשה יקח את האהל ונטה לו מחוץ למחנה הרחק מן המחנה וקרא לו אהל מועד והיה כל מבקש ה' יצא אל אהל מועד אשר מחוץ למחנה: (ח) והיה כצאת משה אל האהל יקומו כל העם ונצבו איש פתח אהלו והביטו אחרי משה עד באו האהלה: (ט) והיה כבא משה האהלה ירד עמוד הענן ועמד פתח האהל ודבר עם משה: (י) וראה כל העם את עמוד הענן עמד פתח האהל וקם כל העם והשתחוו איש פתח אהלו:

Now Moses used to take the tent and to pitch it without the camp, afar off from the camp; and he called it the tent of meeting. And it came to pass, that every one that sought the Lord went out unto the tent of meeting, which was without the camp. And it came to pass, when Moses went out unto the Tent, that all the people rose up, and stood, every man at his tent door, and looked after Moses, until he was gone into the Tent. And it came to pass, when Moses entered into the Tent, the pillar of cloud descended, and stood at the door of the Tent; and [the Lord] spoke with Moses. And when all the people saw the pillar of cloud stand at the door of the Tent, all the people rose up and worshipped, every man at his tent door.[4]

(*Vayikra* 9:1), that is the first day of *Nissan*, and the beginning of Year Two. There is an alternative tradition, though (Ibn Ezra, *Shemot* 40:2; *Vayikra* 9:1; D.Z. Hoffman *Sefer Vayikra* Vol 1, p. 191, citing alternative versions of *Sifre* and the Talmud), which takes *Shemot* 40:1 in its plain sense that the *Mishkan* was completed on the first of *Nissan* and that, accordingly, the dedication ceremony took place on the eighth of *Nissan*.

4. All *Tanakh* English translations taken from the JPS 1917 Translation.

Moshe's tent, which had been the *situs* of God's presence in the camp, is now separated from the camp. Perhaps this helps to explain the alacrity with which *Benei Yisrael* respond to Moshe's appeal to donate goods for the construction of the *Mishkan,* which will symbolize the return of the *Shekhinah* to the camp (*Shemot* 25:1–9).

> (א) וידבר ה' אל משה לאמר: (ב) דבר אל בני ישראל ויקחו לי תרומה...
> (ח) ועשו לי מקדש ושכנתי בתוכם: (ט) ככל אשר אני מראה אותך את
> תבנית המשכן ואת תבנית כל כליו וכן תעשו:

And the Lord spoke unto Moses, saying: 'Speak unto the children of Israel, that they take for Me an offering; of every man whose heart maketh him willing ye shall take My offering … And let them make Me a sanctuary, that I may dwell among them. According to all that I show thee, the pattern of the Tabernacle, and the pattern of all the furniture thereof, even so shall ye make it.'

As *Rosh Chodesh Nissan* draws near, *Benei Yisrael* have witnessed the various stages of construction of the *Mishkan.* For the last few months, since the day after Yom Kippur, they have donated raw materials in the form of gold and copper for the various utensils. These have been weighed and stored, as has the silver collected during the taking of the census, and are now used to fashion the sockets that held the very pillars of the *Mishkan* erect. For the past seven days, they have watched from afar as Aharon and his sons have undergone special preparations to enable them to enter the *Mishkan* and begin performing the *avodah.* Finally, the eighth day, *Rosh Chodesh Nissan,* draws nigh (*Vayikra* 9:1–6):

> (א) ויהי ביום השמיני קרא משה לאהרן ולבניו ולזקני ישראל: (ב) ויאמר
> אל אהרן קח לך עגל בן בקר לחטאת ואיל לעלה תמימם והקרב לפני ה':
> (ג) ואל בני ישראל תדבר לאמר קחו שעיר עזים לחטאת ועגל וכבש בני
> שנה תמימם לעלה: (ד) ושור ואיל לשלמים לזבח לפני ה' ומנחה בלולה
> בשמן כי היום ה' נראה אליכם: (ה) ויקחו את אשר צוה משה אל פני אהל
> מועד ויקרבו כל העדה ויעמדו לפני ה': (ו) ויאמר משה זה הדבר אשר צוה
> ה' תעשו וירא אליכם כבוד ה':

And it came to pass on the eighth day, that Moses called Aaron and his sons, and the elders of Israel; and he said unto Aaron: 'Take thee a bull-calf for a sin-offering, and a ram for a burnt-offering, without blemish, and offer them before the Lord. And unto the children of Israel thou shalt speak, saying: Take ye a he-goat for a sin-offering; and a calf and a lamb, both of the first year, without blemish, for a burnt-offering; and an ox and a ram for peace-offerings, to sacrifice before the Lord; and a meal-offering mingled with oil; for to-day the Lord appeareth unto you.' And they brought that which Moses commanded before the tent of meeting; and all the congregation drew near and stood before the Lord. And Moses said: 'This is the thing which the Lord commanded that ye should do; that the glory of the Lord may appear unto you.'

The *kohanim* gathered the animals and brought them to the Tent of Meeting where the whole community gathered and stood before the Lord. Moshe said: "This is what the Lord has commanded that you do, that the Presence of the Lord may appear to you."

(ט:כב) וישא אהרן את ידו על העם ויברכם וירד מעשת החטאת והעלה והשלמים:

And Aaron lifted up his hands toward the people, and blessed them; and he came down from offering the sin-offering, and the burnt-offering, and the peace-offerings.

At this moment of high drama, Aharon prepares the offering, blesses *Benei Yisrael*, and waits for the response from God in the form of fire. He waits, but nothing happens until Moshe joins his brother:

(כג) ויבא משה ואהרן אל אהל מועד ויצאו ויברכו את העם וירא כבוד ה' אל כל העם: (כד) ותצא אש מלפני ה' ותאכל על המזבח את העלה ואת החלבים וירא כל העם וירנו ויפלו על פניהם:

And Moses and Aaron went into the tent of meeting, and came

out, and blessed the people; and the glory of the Lord appeared unto all the people. And there came forth fire from before the Lord, and consumed upon the altar the burnt-offering and the fat; and when all the people saw it, they shouted, and fell on their faces.

Moshe joins Aharon, and the two together bless *Benei Yisrael*. At this juncture, God sends down a fire that consumes the offering. Recognizing the fire as a sign of the Divine presence, *Benei Yisrael* rejoice in the knowledge that God has indeed forgiven them for *chet ha-egel* and has validated their efforts to atone. As the Ramban notes (*Bereishit* 18:1 s.v. *be'eilonei mamrei*), this is one of the few times in the Torah in which there is a Divine revelation not so that God can teach or command, but to show that God approves of the people's actions.

וזה גילוי השכינה אליו למעלה וכבוד לו, כענין שבא במשכן ויצאו ויברכו את העם וירא כבוד ה' אל כל העם (ויקרא ט כג) כי מפני השתדלותם במצות המשכן זכו לראיית השכינה. ואין גלוי השכינה כאן וכאן לצוות להם מצוה או לדבור כלל, אלא גמול המצוה הנעשית כבר, ולהודיע כי רצה האלקים את מעשיהם.

Now this revelation of the *Shekhinah* came to Abraham as a mark of distinction and honor, even as it is said in connection with the dedication of the Tabernacle, 'And they came out, and blessed the people, and the glory of the Eternal appeared unto all the people,' as it was on account of their effort in fulfilling the commandment of building the Tabernacle that they merited seeing the *Shekhinah*. Now the revelation of the *Shekhinah* here and there was not at all for the purpose of charging them with some commandment or to impart some communication. Instead, it was a reward for the commandment which had already been performed, and it informed them that their deeds have God's approval.[5]

5. Translation taken from Charles B. Chavel, *Ramban: Commentary on the Torah, Bereishit* (New York: Shilo, 1975), p. 232.

At this point in the text, we are told of the actions of Nadav and Avihu, the two oldest sons of Aharon. In interpreting these verses, we wonder if, once again, the Torah is telling us the story out of order.

(י:א) ויקח בני אהרן נדב ואביהוא איש מחתתו ויתנו בהן אש וישימו עליה קטרת ויקריבו לפני ה' אש זרה אשר לא צוה אתם:

And Nadab and Abihu, the sons of Aaron, took each of them his censer, and put fire therein, and laid incense thereon, and offered strange fire before the Lord, which He had not commanded them.

The sons bring a "strange fire" before God which the Lord has not commanded, and they use the fire to consume the incense (*ketoret*) that they have brought, also without having been commanded to do so. This is a serious infraction for which they pay with their lives. The Divine reaction is to send another unscheduled fire which consumes them "before God."

(ב) ותצא אש מלפני ה' ותאכל אותם וימתו לפני ה':

And there came forth fire from before the Lord, and devoured them, and they died before the Lord.

What could have prompted Nadav and Avihu to act so precipitously? Then, again, what was so wrong with their offering that it resulted in such an immediate and fatal punishment? *Vayikra* (10:1–2) leaves much unsaid and the *midrashim* attempt to round out the narrative.

One suggestion in the *Yalkut Shimoni* (*Shemini*, 10) looks at their transgression in light of the prevailing mood of the nation as the *Mishkan* is inaugurated.

ויקחו שני בני אהרן נדב ואביהוא אף הם בני אהרן בשמחתם כיון שראו אש חדשה שירדה משמי מרום ולחכה על המזבח את העולה ואת החלבים עמדו להוסיף אהבה אהבה על אהבה שנאמר ויקחו ואין לקיחה אלא שמחה.

"Aharon's two sons, Nadav and Avihu, took" – They, too, were rejoicing because they saw a new fire from the heavens above that came down and licked the Altar, eating the *olah* and the *chalavim*. They thought to add love on top of love, for it says: 'they took' and the term 'took' always implies rejoicing.

Wishing to contribute to the celebratory atmosphere, Nadav and Avihu bring their own fire to the proceedings. Why, though, the additional choice of *ketoret* for the celebration?

[תנחומא, תצוה טו] הקטורת אינה באה לא על החטא ולא על העוון ולא על האשם אלא על השמחה. הוי: "שמן וקטורת ישמח לב". חביבה הקטורת לפני הקב"ה...כשעשה משה המשכן וכליו וכל המלאכה והקרבנות, לא ירדה שכינה עד שהקריבו קטורת...אמר הקב"ה לישראל: בני, היזהרו בקטורת יותר מכל הקרבנות שאתם מקריבים לפני, שעל ידי הקטורת אתם מתכפרים בעולם הזה ואף לעתיד לבא.

The *ketoret* is not brought to atone for sin, for iniquity, or for the guilt, only for rejoicing. Behold: "Oil and *ketoret* will gladden the heart." The *ketoret* is beloved before God...when Moshe made the *Mishkan* and its vessels and all the work and the sacrifices, the *Shekhinah* did not descend until the *ketoret* was offered...God said to Israel: 'My children, be more careful with the *ketoret* than all the sacrifices that you bring before me, for it is the *ketoret* that will atone for you in this world and the world to come.'

The *Tanchuma* points out that the *ketoret* has unique qualities. It is dear to God, so much so that it was only after the *ketoret* was offered that the Divine presence rested upon the *Mishkan*. Yet the punishment for misusing it is severe, as seen in the *pesukim* alluded to by the *Tanchuma* which discuss the command to bring the *ketoret*. [6]

The death of Nadav and Avihu is tragic and at odds with the celebration of the day. There are other such days of joy where people could have been punished for one transgression or another, yet God chooses

---

6. See *Shemot* 30:37–38, Rambam (*Hil. Bi'at Ha-Mikdash* 9:4 and *Hil. Kelei Ha-Mikdash* 2:9).

to delay the punishment for another time.[7] If their motivation was sincere and their goal was to increase the level of *simchah,* could not the punishment of Aharon's sons also have waited for another day? Does the fact that God punished them instantaneously suggest that their motivation was impure?

Perhaps it is these questions that lie behind the different reading of the narrative suggested in *Vayikra Rabbah,* where the discussion centers on which types of transgression can result in a speedy and unexpected death. R' Eliezer posits that immediate death, without any warning signs of debilitation, is also effected in the case of a student who proclaims the law in the presence of his teacher. Nadav and Avihu should have asked their father and uncle if it was appropriate to bring the offering they were considering:

[ויקרא רבה (וילנא) פרשה כ:ו] תני ר' אליעזר לא מתו בניו של אהרן
אלא ע"י שהורו הלכה בפני משה רבן, ומעשה בתלמיד אחד שהורה לפני
רבו ר' אליעזר אמר לאימא שלום אי לאשתו של זה אינו מוציא שבתו
לא באת שבתו עד שמת נכנסו חכמים אצלו א"ל נביא אתה אמר להם
(עמוס ז) לא נביא אנכי ולא בן נביא אלא כך מקובלני כל המורה הלכה
לפני רבו חייב מיתה.

R' Eliezer taught: The sons of Aharon died only because they pronounced a rabbinic ruling in the presence of their teacher Moshe. There was an incident involving a student who ruled in the presence of his teacher. R' Eliezer said to [his wife] Imma Shalom, "Woe to the wife of this one as he will not live out the week." And indeed the student died within a week. The sages visited [R' Eliezer] and asked, "Are you a prophet?" He responded, "I am neither a prophet nor the son of a prophet. But I have received this tradition: anyone who issues a rabbinic ruling in the presence of his teacher is liable to die [at the hands of Heaven]."

As the day of dedication proceeded, the sons wondered where the fire which would consume the various offerings would come from. They

7. As seen in the *Yalkut Shimoni* of *Parashat Shemini* discussed later on.

wished to complete the ceremony by ensuring the presence of the *Shekhinah*.

[מכילתא דמילואים פרשה א, כב, מד ע״ד] כיון שראו בני אהרון שקרבו כל הקרבנות ונעשו כל המעשים ולא ירדה שכינה לישראל, אמר לו נדב לאביהוא: וכי יש לך אדם שמבשל תבשיל בלא אש, מיד נטלו אש זרה ונכנסו לבית קדשי הקדשים, שנאמר ״ויקחו שני בני אהרון נדב ואביהוא איש מחתתו ויתנו בהם אש״.

As soon as Aharon's sons saw that all the sacrifices had been brought and all their acts had been performed and the *Shekhinah* had not descended, Nadav said to Avihu: "Is there anyone who cooks without fire?" Immediately they took a strange fire and entered the Holy of Holies, as it says: "And the two sons of Aharon, Nadav and Avihu took their fire pans and put fire in them."

Nadav and Avihu, then, may only have been trying to move the process along. They saw their father, Aharon, in a potentially embarrassing moment. He had prepared the sacrifices, following the laws as presented by God – but where was the fire? Where was the Divine presence? If the "strange fire" was brought at that point in time, when the Jewish people awaited a sign of Divine approval, then one can defend the sons as looking out for Aharon's honor (although one might also be struck by a certain uncomfortable similarity to the description in the *midrashim* of a certain priest of *Ba'al* who, in the course of the confrontation with Eliyahu at *Har Karmel*, tried to surreptitiously light a fire under the offering).

Other *midrashim*, though, are more critical of the mindset of Nadav and Avihu. One *midrash*, for instance, focuses on a procedural error that the sons committed, while a second, relying on a close reading of a verse in *Bemidbar*, undermines the ostensible motivation for their action.

[ויקרא רבה (וילנא) פרשה כ:ח] בר קפרא בשם ר׳ ירמיה בן אלעזר אמר בשביל ד׳ דברים מתו בניו של אהרון על הקריבה ועל הקרבה על אש זרה ועל שלא נטלו עצה זה מזה, על הקריבה שנכנסו לפני ולפנים ועל ההקרבה

שהקריבו קרבן שלא נצטוו על אש זרה אש מבית הכניסו ועל שלא
נטלו עצה זה מזה שנאמר שם (במדבר יז) איש מחתתו איש מעצמו עשו
שלא נטלו עצה זה מזה.

Bar Kapara said in the name of R. Yirmiah ben Eleazar, "For four transgressions Aharon's sons died: because they approached [a holy space], because of their sacrifice, because of the strange fire, and because they didn't take advice one from the other. 'On coming close,' because they entered the innermost chambers, 'on the sacrifice,' because they brought a sacrifice that was not commanded, 'on the strange fire,' because they took a fire from the stove-top, and 'because they didn't take advice from one another,' as it is said: 'each took his pan for himself,' meaning they didn't take advice from one another."

Nadav and Avihu went where they were not supposed to go (into the Holy of Holies), took what they were not supposed to take (the holy fire), to use in preparation of that which they were not allowed to bring as individuals (the *ketoret*), and did not even consider that entry into the most hallowed area was an action of such moment that it required seeking a second opinion. They were so sure of their status – based on their family tree coupled with the events of the Seven Days of *Milu'im* in which they were prepared for their special role – that they felt that they had the right, perhaps even the duty, to enter every corner of the newly consecrated *Mishkan* and to bring any offering that they could imagine. This point, perhaps, emerges from examination of the parallel account in *Sefer Bemidbar* (3:1–4) which contains a genealogical listing of the sons of Aharon.

(א) ואלה תולדת אהרן ומשה ביום דבר ה' את משה בהר סיני: (ב) ואלה
שמות בני אהרן הבכר נדב ואביהוא אלעזר ואיתמר: (ג) אלה שמות בני
אהרן הכהנים המשחים אשר מלא ידם לכהן: (ד) וימת נדב ואביהוא לפני
ה' בהקריבם אש זרה לפני ה' במדבר סיני ובנים לא היו להם ויכהן אלעזר
ואיתמר על פני אהרן אביהם:

Now these are the generations of Aaron and Moses in the day

that the Lord spoke with Moses on Mount Sinai. And these are the names of the sons of Aaron: Nadab the first-born, and Abihu, Eleazar, and Ithamar. These are the names of the sons of Aaron, the priests that were anointed, whom he consecrated to minister in the priest's office. And Nadab and Abihu died before the Lord, when they offered strange fire before the Lord, in the wilderness of Sinai, and they had no children; and Eleazar and Ithamar ministered in the priest's office in the presence of Aaron their father.

In this account, the salient detail added is that Nadav and Avihu died without having any children. This helps create the backdrop for the following *midrash*:

> [ויקרא רבה (וילנא) פרשה כ:י] ר' לוי אמר שחצים היו הרבה נשים היו יושבות עגונות ממתינות להם מה היו אומרים אחי אבינו מלך אחי אמנו נשיא אבינו כהן גדול ואנו שני סגני כהונה אי זו אשה הוגנת לנו...

R' Levi said: "[The sons of Aharon] were haughty. Many women were remaining unmarried and were waiting for [the sons of Aharon to wed them]. What did they [the sons] say? Our father's brother is the king, our mother's brother is a prince, our father is the Kohen Gadol and we are the two assistants – what woman could possibly be worthy of one of us?"

Not only did they feel superior to the masses, but they felt that they were even better than the nation's leaders and could not wait until that old leadership (their father and uncle) died so that they could assume the mantle.

> [סנהדרין נב.] וכבר היו משה ואהרון מהלכין בדרך ונדב ואביהו מהלכין אחריהן וכל ישראל אחריהן. אמר לו נדב לאביהו: אמיתי ימותו שני זקנים הללו ואני ואתה ננהיג את הדור. אמר להן הקדוש ברוך הוא: הנראה מי קבר את מי?

Moshe and Aharon were walking and Nadav and Avihu were walking behind them, and all Israel were walking behind them. Nadav said to Avihu, "When will these two old men die and you and I will lead the generation!" Thereupon the Holy One, Blessed is He, said [of] them: "We shall see who shall bury whom."

Perhaps this is one way of understanding the "*horu halakhah*" of R. Eliezer: they presumed to see themselves as those deserving to be in charge and, as such, would not deign to seek advice. Perhaps this helps to explain the very public and very dramatic death with which they were punished.

In contrast to those *midrashim* which depict Nadav and Avihu as pompous popinjays, there is a school of thought that presents Nadav and Avihu in a more positive light. One midrashic comment, disagreeing with what is cited above, insists that the sons were guilty of only a single offense, that of bringing the "*eish zarah*."

[ויקרא רבה (וילנא) פרשה כ:ח] א״ר ירמיה בן אלעזר בד׳ מקומות מזכיר מיתתן של בני אהרן ובכולן מזכיר סורחנן כל כך למה להודיעך שלא היה בידם אלא עון זה בלבד א״ר אלעזר המודעי בא וראה כמה מיתתן של בני אהרן יקרה לפני הקב״ה שכל מקום שמזכיר מיתתן מזכיר סורחנם כל כך למה להודיעך שלא יהא פתחון פה לבאי עולם לומר מעשים מקולקלים היו בידם בסתר שעל ידי כן מתו.

R' Yirmiah b. Eleazar taught: "[The Torah] mentions the death of the sons of Aharon in four places and each time their infraction is recalled. Why the repitition? To inform the reader that they had committed no other sins." R' Eleazar ha-Modai taught: "See how precious the death of the sons of Aharon is before God. For in each place their death is discussed, their infraction is mentioned. Why? To inform the reader and so that there will be no room for those in later generations to say that their deeds were secretly corrupt and that was what caused their death."

How do Moshe and Aharon react to the death of Nadav and Avihu?

[ויקרא י:ג] ויאמר משה אל אהרן הוא אשר דבר ה׳ לאמר בקרבי אקדש ועל פני כל העם אכבד וידם אהרן:

Then Moshe said to Aharon, "This is what the Lord meant when

He said: Through those near to Me I show Myself holy, And gain glory before all the people." And Aharon was silent.

In this *pasuk*, the words of note are "*hu asher dibber Hashem*." When precisely (and to whom) did God utter these words? And how is the concept of "*bi-krovai ekadesh*" meant to comfort the distraught father? The *Yalkut Shimoni* fills in the gap: God had said these words to Moshe at Sinai, but Moshe had not grasped their meaning until now:

דבר אחר ויאמר משה הוא אשר דבר ה' לאמר בקרובי אקדש זה דבור
נאמר למשה בסיני ולא ידעו עד שבא מעשה לידו וכיון שבא מעשה לידו
א"ל משה לאהרן אהרן אחי לא מתו בניך אלא בשביל קדושת שמו של
מקום שנאמר ונועדתי שמה לבני ישראל ונקדש בכבודי.

Moshe said, "This is what *Hashem* meant when he said, 'by those close to me I am sanctified.'" This is what was said to Moshe on *Har Sinai* and it was not understood until the circumstances occurred, and once the circumstances came about, Moshe said to Aharon, "Aharon my brother, your sons only died for the sanctification of God's Name, as it is said, 'I will become known there, to *Benei Yisrael* and I will be sanctified by those who honor Me.'"

These words also help to give another perspective to the entire incident. The deaths of Nadav and Avihu are associated with the sanctification of God's name and, as such, their lives become infused, retroactively, with meaning and significance.

Do these words help Aharon deal with his grief? According to the continuation of the *Yalkut Shimoni*, Aharon's subsequent silence, an exquisite literary touch in the text, is an indication of his acceptance of this lesson imparted by Moshe:

וכיון שידע אהרן שבניו ידועי המקום הן שתק וקבל שכר על שתיקתו,
מכאן אמרו כל המקבל עליו ושותק סימן יפה לו.

And when Aharon learned that his sons were considered beloved of God he was silent and subsequently received a reward for this silence. From here we learn that one who accepts in silence that which has been decreed – it is a good sign for him.

In this vein, Nehama Leibowitz quotes the noted *maskil*, Naftali Hertz Weisel:[8]

רב נפתלי הירץ ויזל, "ביאור" - ולדעתי ניחם משה את אהרון, שלא יצטער
לחשוב שהיו בניו חלילה חוטאים בסתר, ועל כן בערה בם אש ה', אלא
מקרובי ה' היו, מן הקדושים אשר בארץ, ובעבור גדולתם נענשו, כי כן דרכו
של הקדוש ברוך הוא להיקדש בקרובים אליו...כי דקדק עמהם מאוד
על חטא שחטאו מתוך געגועי אהבה, למען דעת כי ה' קדוש ומרומם
על מחשבת בני האדם שמדרך אדם לחוס על קרוביו ונושא להם פנים
מאהבתו אותם, וה' נוהג להפך.

In my opinion, Moshe assured Aaron not to harbor the dreadful thought that God has punished his sons with His consuming fire because they had sinned covertly. On the contrary, they were holy men, close to God, whose downfall was a result of their greatness, for it is God's way to be sanctified through those near unto Him…God dealt with them sternly for an offence prompted by the love of and yearning for God. Thus, they exemplified the lesson that God is holy and beyond the notions of man. Men tend to spare and favor those near and dear to them, but God pursues the opposite course.

Don Isaac Abarbanel disagrees:

[ויקרא פרק י'] וידום אהרן. כתב הרב רבי משה בר נחמן שהיה אהרן בוכה
וצועק במר רוחו וכאשר דבר משה שתק ולא בכה עוד ואינו נכון שירים
קולו ויצעק לפני האלקים ביום חתונתו וביום שמחת לבו. אבל פירוש וידום
אהרן הוא שנהפך לבו והיה דומם ולא נשא קולו בבכי ובמספד כאבל

8. Nehama Leibowitz. *Studies in Vayikra* (Heb). (Jerusalem: World Zionist Organization, 1976), p. 108; *New Studies in Vayikra* (English). (Jerusalem: World Zionist Organziation, 1993) p. 131.

אב על בנים. גם לא קבל תנחומים ממשה כי לא נותרה בו נשמה והדבור
אין בו ולכן אמר וידום אהרן שהוא מלשון דומם ושותק.

"Va-yidom Aharon" – Nachmanides explained that Aharon was
crying and shouting with a bitter spirit but when Moshe spoke,
he became quiet, crying no more. This is not correct, though, for
he would not have raised his voice and shouted [in pain] before
God [on such a joyous occasion] when the *Mishkan* was being
dedicated. Rather the correct explanation of *va-yidom* is that Aharon's heart was turned, it became like an inanimate stone; he did
not raise his voice to cry, or to eulogize like a mourner mourning
for his sons. Nor did he accept consolation from Moshe, because
his spirit was gone, and he could not speak. Therefore it says *va-
yidom*, from the words "inanimate" and "silent."

What, then, can we conclude about the incident? Were Nadav and Avihu
motivated by a desire to help their father avoid embarrassment? Or were
they tempted to overreach by a sense of superiority? Either way the
result is the same. Any misstep in the *Mikdash* results in death. Rank and
social standing do not allow one greater license in the *Mikdash*. Rather,
those who are chosen to work in the *Mikdash* must be even more careful
about following the rules and are sometimes swallowed into its holiness.

In his discussion of the death of Nadav and Avihu, R. Samson
Raphael Hirsch notes that the primary role of a *kohen* is to perform his
functions as "executed through the accomplishment of God's ordinances,
not by inventing new ways of worship":

> The Jewish priest is part of the nation, and his position is not an
> isolated one before God, but one that he occupies only within
> and through the nation…even though some of the acts of the
> offering had not been forbidden, their not having been com-
> manded would have sufficed to forbid them…The closeness of
> and approach to God, which we seek with every offering, may
> only be found through obedience to and acceptance of God's
> will…Self-devised sacrifices would destroy the truth which is
> meant to achieve man's submission to it by the very sacrifice,

and would mean the glorification of arbitrary subjectivity and placing it on the throne which should be dedicated wholly and exclusively to obedience to God...[9]

We may understand the death of the sons of Aharon, on the eighth day of their consecration, as a warning to future generations of priests to avoid personal and subjective predilections and ordinances of their own invention in their approach to the service in the Sanctuary which belongs to God and which is governed by His law (and not by any newfangled innovations introduced into the order of service). Only by observance of the precepts of the Torah can the priest of Israel remain true to his principles. Or, to quote Chief Rabbi Sacks,

> To be true to God's purposes, there must be times and places at which humanity experiences the reality of the Divine. Those times and places require absolute obedience. The most fundamental mistake – the mistake of Nadav and Avihu – is to take the powers that belong to man's encounter with the world, and apply them to man's encounter with the Divine. Had Nadav and Avihu used their own initiative to fight evil and injustice they would have been heroes. Because they used their own initiative in the arena of the holy, they erred. They asserted their own presence in the absolute presence of God. That is a contradiction in terms. That is why they died.[10]

9. R. Samson Raphael Hirsch, *Sefer Vayikra* 10:2 (London: Judaica Press, 1966) p. 253.
10. *Covenant and Conversation – Shemini* 5767.

Rabbi Dr. Edward Reichman, M.D.

תזריע: *Parashat Tazria* and Childbirth: An Open and Shut Case

INTRODUCTION: MEDICINE IN RABBINIC LITERATURE[1]

This volume is replete with creative and insightful words of Torah from some of the greatest minds in the Orthodox Jewish community. We have undoubtedly been treated to novel analyses and interpretations utilizing rabbinic literature from the Talmud up to the present day. While not privy to the manuscript prior to publication, I suspect that few, if any, of the essays herein have significant medical or scientific content. This is, of course, not a medical work, but a book on the Torah portion of the week. However, throughout the centuries, rabbinic commentators have often used their works as a vehicle or springboard for medical and

---

1. The definitive work on Biblical and talmudic medicine remains Fred Rosner, trans., Julius Preuss, *Biblical and Talmudic Medicine* (New York, 1978). See also the many works of Dr. Fred Rosner on this topic, including his *Encyclopedia of Biblical and Talmudic Medicine* (Jason Aronson, 2000), which includes an essay by this author reviewing the literature on this topic entitled "Biblical and Talmudic Medicine: A Bibliographical Essay."

scientific discussion, sometimes in the service of textual Biblical interpretation; other times simply as narrative tangent. The Torah portion
of *Tazria*, where human childbirth and its associated laws are addressed,
is the Biblical source of many medical discussions in rabbinic writings
throughout the centuries. Appreciating the diversity and historical context of these writings is our essay's objective.

The *Midrash* expresses a foundational idea about the creation of
the world: "*Ha-Kadosh Barukh Hu histakel be-Oraita u-bara alma*" – literally, God looked into the text of the Torah and created the world. In
essence, the Torah is the Divine blueprint for the creation of the world.
I would submit that the converse is true for man. *Adam histakel be-alma
u-bara Oraita* – man examines the world around him and creates, in a
figurative sense, the Torah. When man delves into the workings of the
world through the study of medicine and science, he brings the Torah to
life and gains an appreciation of God's role in the creation of the world.
The crowning glory of God's creation is man himself. To understand the
creation of man, the process of conception and birth, is to understand
man's Creator. Therefore, man in every generation has sought to gain
greater insight into the science of human reproduction. These yearn-
ings are reflected in the rabbinic discussions on the portion of *Tazria*.

Regarding the very creation or birth of the human being, the
Talmud informs us of the origin of a minor anatomical feature of major
consequences, called the philtrum – the small infra-nasal indentation.
According to tradition, the fetus learns the entire corpus of Torah *in utero*.[2] Just prior to birth, however, the baby receives the touch of an angel,
who causes the indentation of the philtrum. This afflicts the child with
transient amnesia, causing the child to forget all he has learned, neces-
sitating years of laborious effort to restore this lost knowledge. What
could be the possible benefit to the child of such a seemingly cruel act?
Many have suggested that the very process of reacquiring the Torah
through years of struggle and tireless effort (*yegi'ah*) will lead to a more
meaningful and everlasting relationship with the Torah and its creator.

Man can then, theoretically, with proper devotion and effort,
ultimately return to his state of knowledge *in utero*, when he had mas-

2. *Niddah* 30b.

tered the entire Torah. What of the study of science, however, and the understanding of human physiology? Does the individual child learn the intricacies of medicine and science *in utero*, only to forget and subsequently relearn them all with proper effort? Assumedly not, at least not as an individual. In fact, while it is theoretically possible for one person to learn the entire corpus of Torah teachings, this is decidedly not the case for science and medicine. While throughout the ages we have been blessed with Torah sages who have been the repositories of all extant Torah knowledge, no such analogue exists in science. There is no one human being who possesses all knowledge of medicine and science. The greatest minds in the history of medicine and science knew only the minutia of their specific fields. Einstein knew little about human physiology.

Science, by definition, is a collective endeavor, advanced only through the conglomerate efforts of thousands of great minds across the span of time. Perhaps, analogous to man as an individual working to restore his lost knowledge of the Torah, all of mankind works tirelessly to restore the knowledge of the scientific workings of the world that was known at the time of creation, attempting to reverse our global amnesia. This endeavor has progressed slowly, with each generation adding incrementally to our collective knowledge of science and medicine, and thus our appreciation of *Ha-Kadosh Barukh Hu*.

Some advances have incorporated and built on pre-existing theories, while others have rejected or supplanted previous notions. This evolution of the understanding of medicine is reflected in the rabbinic literature throughout the centuries.

Biblical commentaries of past centuries can often be challenging to interpret. However, persistence coupled with consultation of additional *sefarim* is often rewarded with a better understanding of the difficult passages. There are, however, certain medically related passages for which the conventional approach will not yield fruits. A cursory review of the major commentaries on the first few verses of the portion of *Tazria*, for example, will leave the 21st century reader utterly bewildered. Search as one may in standard *sefarim*, one is unlikely to reach any clearer perceptions or achieve any greater wisdom. One will encounter in pre-modern rabbinic commentaries a number of notions on reproductive physiology and anatomy that simply defy or elude modern understanding. Some of these notions are a product of their historical period and reflect the evolution of science, while others are uniquely Jewish in nature. This brief essay discusses some of the medically related passages in rabbinic literature on the portion of *Tazria* and is but a small contribution to the vast and evolving field of medicine and science in rabbinic literature.

MEDICAL PASSAGES IN THE RABBINIC DISCUSSIONS ON OUR *PARASHAH*

On the first section of our *parashah* we find a number of rabbinic discussions relating to human reproduction. The discussions cover a number of topics, including anatomy, physiology and embryology, each of which will be treated separately below. We will cite representative primary sources for each section, though the same medical notion, or variation thereof, may be expressed in other sources.

Anatomy

Human anatomy, in all its gloriously detailed intricacies, is well understood today. There are no debates about the configuration or structure of the parts of the human body. All the parts have been identified and labeled, and the occasional anatomical variants have been categorized. The human uterus is of course amongst them. There are indeed some variations of this pear-shaped, single chamber structure, and sometimes the chamber can even be partially divided in two. However, the description found in the *Da'at Zekeinim Mi-Ba'alei Ha-Tosafot* below does not seem to correspond to any known anatomical variant.[3]

> And some say it is found in the Book of Nature that the womb of a woman has seven chambers – three on the right, three on the left, and one in the center. If the seed enters the right chambers, she will beget a male child; if it enters the left chambers, she will beget a female child, and if it enters the center chamber, it will

---

3. *Vayikra* 12:2.

result in the birth of a *tumtum* (ambiguous genitalia) or *androgenus* (hermaphrodite).

Here, the *Da'at Zekeinim Mi-Ba'alei Ha-Tosafot* is not referencing an idea of his own, or of specifically rabbinic origin for that matter, but one he explicitly cites from contemporaneous medical literature. Was the uterus of this historical period indeed comprised of seven chambers? If not, how could such a notion gain currency when even the most cursory inspection of the body would dispel it? These questions can only be answered with an understanding of the history of anatomical dissection. Prior to the Renaissance, the study of the human body was not systematic. Anatomical teachings were often based on animal dissection. Moreover, theory and philosophy superseded rigorous scientific analysis. The theory of the seven chamber uterus was based on the former.

The so-called doctrine of the seven chamber uterus is nowhere to be found in the Talmud, and in fact, only arose in the Middle Ages. The doctrine was disproved when anatomical dissection became a scientific discipline in the Renaissance, though it was perpetuated for some time thereafter. The doctrine of the seven chamber uterus is found not only in Biblical commentaries, but in many areas of rabbinic literature over a span of eight centuries.[4]

Embryology[5]

Human embryology is the branch of biology that deals with the formation, early growth and development of the human being. The *Midrash*

4. For more on this topic, and for references on the history of anatomy in rabbinic literature, see Edward Reichman, "Anatomy and the Doctrine of the Seven-Chamber Uterus in Rabbinic Literature," *Hakirah* 9 (Winter, 2010), pp. 245–265. Parenthetically, the Talmud contains discussions on female reproductive anatomy, inasmuch as it relates to the laws of *niddah*, and uses metaphorical terms for its anatomical descriptions. While many have tried to correlate these terms with modern anatomical understanding, the exact identifications elude consensus. For references see aforementioned article at n. 5.

5. For references to embryology in Jewish sources, see David I. Macht, "Embryology and Obstetrics in Ancient Hebrew Literature," *John Hopkins Hospital Bulletin* 22, 242 (May, 1911), pp. 1–8; W.M. Feldman, *The Jewish Child* (London, 1917), pp. 120–44; W.M. Feldman, "Ancient Jewish Eugenics," *Medical Leaves* 2 (1939), pp. 28–37;

Rabbah on this portion contains a magnificently detailed embryological description of the fetus *in utero*.

> How is the fetus positioned in its mother's womb? Folded and resting like a notebook (*pinkas*). Its head is positioned between its knees; its hands on the sides of the head ... the mouth is sealed and the navel (umbilicus) is open. It receives nourishment from what its mother eats, and drinks from what she drinks. It does not excrete waste lest it kill its mother. When it exits ... the closed passages open and the open passages close.[6]

This description is as accurate today as it was then. There is, however, an embryological passage in the Talmud, related to this portion, which requires further discussion. The beginning of *Tazria* details the periods of purity and impurity that a woman is required to observe upon the birth of a child. The total combined periods of purity and impurity for the birth of a female child, eighty days, are double that for the male child, forty days. While this difference has spawned many homiletic interpretations, R. Yishmael posits an embryological basis for this differentiation.

> R. Yishmael says if she miscarried on the forty-first day following conception, she must observe the *tum'ah* laws of a male birth ... And if she miscarried on the eighty-first day following conception, she must observe the *tum'ah* laws of a female birth, for the basic form of a male embryo is completed by the forty first day and the basic form of a female embryo is completed by the eighty first day.[7]

Samuel Kottek, "Embryology in Talmudic and Midrashic Literature," *Journal of the History of Biology* 14:2 (Fall, 1981): pp. 299–315; H.J. Zimmels, *Magicians, Theologians and Doctors* (London, 1952), pp. 62–64; Julius Preuss, *Biblical and Talmudic Medicine* (New York, 1978), pp. 41–138; Pieter Willem Van Der Horst, "Sarah's Seminal Emission: Hebrews 11:11 in the Light of Ancient Embryology" in *Greeks, Romans and Christians: Essays in Honor of Abraham J. Malherbe*, edited by David Balch et al. (Minneapolis, 1990): pp. 287–302.

6.   *Vayikra Rabbah* 14:7.
7.   *Niddah* 30a.

The Sages attempt to refute R. Yishmael by citing an experiment performed by Cleopatra on her maidservants who were condemned to death. She sacrificed them forty days after they had conceived in order to examine the anatomical composition of the fetuses. Inspection revealed that both the male and female fetuses were formed by forty days. R. Yishmael's response to the results of this experiment is instructive.[8]

> I bring you a proof from the Torah and you bring me a proof from imbeciles?[9]

While the Sages marshal support from sources external to the rabbinic tradition, R. Yishmael maintains that his embryological approach has "proof from the Torah." While some medical and scientific traditions may be co-opted from contemporaneous medicine, this may not always be the case. It should be noted that the notion of the disparate growth and formation rates for the male and female fetus was espoused in antiquity by a number of writers, with the formation of the female fetus believed to take longer than that of the male.[10] However, the exact numbers forty and eighty for the embryological formation of the two genders is not mentioned in external sources.

The period of forty days appears in another related passage in the Talmud that cites our Torah portion. It discusses the propriety of praying for the gender of a child after the woman has already conceived.

---

8. The talmudic exchange about the validity and possible shortcomings of the experiment is remarkable and reflects sensitivity to the experimental method we utilize today. It should be noted that the Talmud records another version of the experiment with different results. For more on the experiment of Cleopatra see, J. Needham, *A History of Embryology* (New York, 1959), pp. 65–66 and Samuel Kottek, pp. 299–315.
9. *Niddah* 30b.
10. These authors include Empedocles, Asclepiades and Hippocrates. See Preuss and Kottek. While the exact numbers of forty and eighty do not appear in known sources from talmudic times, Thomas Aquinas later claimed that male embryos were 'ensouled' at about 40 days, while female embryos were not 'ensouled' until about 80 days in the womb.

> If his wife is pregnant and he said, "May it be Your will that my
> wife give birth to a male," this is a prayer in vain.[11]

The Talmud challenges the assumption that prayer will not help by citing the story of the birth of Dinah. As the Talmud records, Leah was
pregnant with a male child, and based on her concern for the role of
her sister Rachel in the birth of the twelve tribes, she prayed to God
that her child should not be male. The Talmud relates that her prayers
were answered and a male child was converted to a female child *in utero*.[12]

The Talmud considers whether the case of Leah was a miraculous or natural event, and posits that perhaps Leah's prayer took place
within the first forty days of gestation, when the gender of the fetus is
not yet determined.

While some have attempted to interpret this passage in light of
contemporaneous medical history, others have attempted to explain
it in light of modern science. I cite two examples of the latter, the first
being one of the earliest examples from the modern era, and the second
being one of the most recent contributions.

The following passage, referring to the talmudic discussion on
the ability to pray for the gender of a child within forty days after conception has occurred, appeared in *Medical Leaves*, a journal dedicated
to the study of Jewish medical history and contemporary Jewish medical problems, in 1939.[13]

> This utterly fantastic speculation assumes considerable interest in
> the light of the very recent researches … which shows that even
> such an apparent absurdity is not altogether outside the realm of

11. *Berakhot* 60a.
12. On the many versions of the story of the birth of Dinah, including an analysis of the
    contemporary halakhic ramifications of this story in cases of surrogate motherhood,
    see this author's forthcoming "Midrash, Miracles and Motherhood: The Birth of
    Dinah and the Definition of Maternity – *Tzarich Iyun l'Dinah*," *Rapo Yerapei*, vol. 2
    (in press).
13. W.M. Feldman, "Ancient Jewish Eugenics." Between 1937 and 1943, five volumes of
    the journal *Medical Leaves* were published. W.M. Feldman himself wrote about this
    very passage earlier in his *The Jewish Child* (London, 1917), p. 140.

scientific possibility. As is well known, every early embryo is primarily bisexual, in that it possesses both Wolffian and Mullerian ducts, which are the precursors of the male and female genital organs, respectively. The chromosomal influence of the particular fertilizing spermatozoon determines which of these pairs of ducts shall ultimately atrophy. Atrophy of the Mullerian ducts results in a male child, and atrophy of the Wolffian ducts produces a female child...Hence, although sex is normally determined at the moment of conception by the chromosome constitution of the fertilizing sper-matozoon, this gametic influence may, in cer-tain cases, and under non-understood and un-controllable circumstances, as well as in varying degrees, be overcome.

The next citation appeared in the 2009 issue of the journal *B'Or Ha-Torah* on science and Judaism,[14] and is, in essence, a scientifically updated version of the above passage.

A well-known passage in the Talmud states that parents can pray for the gender of their unborn child only during the first forty days of pregnancy. Another passage states that the female identity of an embryo takes eighty days to be formed.

At first blush, this appears to be contradictory to the basic facts of reproductive biology. Isn't the gender of the embryo determined at the moment of conception? A more careful analysis reveals that the chromosomal makeup of the fertilized egg, XX or XY, is not the only factor determining the embryo's gender. The successful expression of the SRY gene located on the short arm of the Y chromosome is another crucial factor.

In fact, it takes approximately forty days from the time of conception for male gender to become irreversibly determined and about eighty days for female gender to be determined.

One can only wonder at the prophetic insight of the Talmud

14. L. Poltorak, "On the Embryological Foresight of the Talmud," *B'Or Ha-Torah* 19 (2009): pp. 19–24. I thank Dr. Poltorak for sending me a copy of her article.

Sages, who pinpointed the precise time frame for the formation of gender – long before the science of genetics was developed.

Physiology

Another aspect of biology that is found in the Biblical commentaries of this portion is the physiology of conception, in particular, the respective contributions of the man and woman to the fetus. Ramban, for example, himself a physician, comments on this topic on the verse "if a woman is *tazria* and gives birth to a male child." The root of the word "*tazria*," *zera*, implies the presence of a reproductive seed of the woman. It is this very issue that Ramban addresses in his comments.[15]

> ... although it says "when a woman emits seed"... the implication is not that the fetus is made from the female seed. For even though a woman has ovaries (*beitzim*) analogous to those of the male (*beitzei zachar*) [testicles], either no seed is made there, or the seed has nothing to do with the fetus. Rather the term "*mazra'at*" refers to the uterine blood... that unites with the male seed. In their opinion (*Niddah* 31a) the fetus is created from the blood of the woman and the white [semen] of the man, and both of them are called seed[16]... and likewise is the opinion of the physicians regarding conception. The Greek philosophers believed that the

15. For an analysis of this Ramban and discussion of the rabbinic understanding of the female contribution to conception, see David Feldman, *Marital Relations, Birth Control and Abortion in Jewish Law* (New York, 1974), esp. Ch.'s 6 and 7; Edward Reichman, "The Rabbinic Conception of Conception: An Exercise in Fertility," *Tradition: A Journal of Orthodox Thought* 31:1 (Fall 1996), pp. 33–63. See also Kottek; Van Der Horst; S.F. Koren, "Kabbalistic Physiology: Isaac the Blind, Nahmanides and Moses De Leon on Menstruation," *AJS Review* 28:2 (2004), pp. 317–339.

16. This refers to the passage in *Niddah* (31a) that there are three partners in the formation of man – God, the father and the mother. On this passage, see Marvin Gold, "Genetic Imprinting and Gene Silencing," *B'Or Ha-Torah* 16 (2006), pp. 19–31, as an example how modern science is used to reinterpret rabbinic passages on medicine. See also R. Kiperwasser, "Three Partners in a Person: The Genesis and Development of Embryological Theory in Biblical and Rabbinic Judaism," *Lectio Difficilior* 2 (2009).

entire body of the fetus is formed from the menstrual blood and the [seed of the] man gives form to the matter.

As Ramban explicitly mentions medical theories from external sources, appreciation of these sources in their historical context is warranted. Ramban alludes to a major debate that raged since antiquity. Since the female seed was not visible to the naked eye, and was not emitted externally, its very existence was a matter of conjecture until modern times. As a result, two competing theories evolved in antiquity that coexisted until pre-modern times. Aristotle, the Greek philosopher to whom Ramban refers, denied the existence of a female seed, claiming that only the male possessed seed. This seed provided the "form" and the "principle of movement" to the fetus, whereas the female provided the material from which the fetus was formed, i.e. the menstrual blood. Galen (130–200 CE), on the other hand, following in the footsteps of Hippocrates (4th-5th centuries BCE), maintained that both the male and female contributed seed. The exact identity of the female seed was in question, but he conjectured it might be located in the uterus. He also claimed that the male semen provides the material for the development of the nerves and the walls of the arteries and veins, whereas the menstrual fluid is the source of the blood. Ramban, citing the talmudic passage (*Niddah* 31a), aligns the rabbinic tradition with the two-seed theory.

Gender Determination

Our final section addresses the issue of gender determination as reflected in a passage from the Talmud.

> R. Yitzchak said in the name of R. Ami: If the woman emits seed (*mazra'at*) first, she bears a male; if the man emits seed first, she bears a female, as it is stated: *"ishah ki tazria ve-yaldah zachar"* ("When a woman emits seed and bears a male, etc.").[17]

As discussed briefly above, the very word *"mazra'at"* for the woman is a matter of debate. While the word *"mazria"* for the male unequivocally

17. *Niddah* 31a.

עתזרת

refers to the emission of male seed, the analogous term for the female was not traditionally interpreted in a parallel fashion.[18]

This notion of gender determination associated with the prec-edential emission of reproductive seed appears to be uniquely rabbinic. While scientists since antiquity have struggled to solve the mystery of gender determination, a study of contemporaneous medical theories of antiquity does not reveal this specific notion. Furthermore, the notion appears to be driven by the linguistic phrasing of the Biblical verse. Maharal elaborates upon this in his *Gur Aryeh*.[19] In explaining why the verse *"ishah ki tazria ve-yaldah zachar"* is used as a source for the notion that if a woman emits seed first, a male child will result, Maharal asserts that the Torah could have written, "when a woman emits seed, if it is a male child then certain laws apply; if it is a female child then certain laws apply." The fact that the Torah writes, "when a woman emits seed and begets a male child," it means that if she emits seed first, she will, with certainty, beget a male child.[20]

Commentators over the centuries have posited explanations for the talmudic principle based on the medical knowledge of their time. Examples include the commentaries of Seforno (16th cent.),[21] *Keli*

18. In pre-modern times, when the identity and function of the woman's contribution to the fetus was in question, *mazra'at* was understood by many to refer to the female climax. On this passage, see D. Feldman; Fred Rosner, "Sex Preselection and Pre-determination," in his *Biomedical Ethics and Jewish Law* (KTAV, 2001), pp. 165–173; A. Korman, *Ha-Adam Ve-Tivo Be-Mada U-Ve-Yahadut* (Tel Aviv, 5763), pp. 112–118; Preuss, pp. 390–391; N. Kass, "Sex Determination: Medically and in the Talmud," *Koroth* 7:11–12 (June, 1980), pp. 293–301; Yaakov Levi, "Isha Ki Tazria," *Koroth* 5:9–10 (July, 1971), pp. 716–17.
19. *Vayikra* 12:2.
20. The talmudic principle that a woman's emitting seed first is associated with the birth of a male child has a corollary principle in Biblical interpretation that male children mentioned in the Torah are associated with their mothers, while female children are associated with their fathers. See *Niddah* 31a, Rashi on *Genesis* 34:1 and 46:15. For an analysis of these passages in Rashi, and their relationship to the nature of Dinah's birth discussed in the talmudic passage above, see Reichman, "Midrash, Miracles and Motherhood: The Birth of Dinah and the Definition of Maternity – *Tzarich Iyun l'Dinah*," *Rapo Yerapei*, vol. 2 (in press).
21. *Vayikra* 12:2.

Yakar (17th cent.),[22] *Sefer Ha-Berit* (19th cent)[23] and the *Torah Temimah* (early 20th cent.).[24]

The modern era is no exception. In light of advances in the under-standing of reproductive physiology in the modern era, this passage has been reinterpreted. Dr. L.B. Shettles observed that the Y chromosome travels faster than the X chromosome, so that if a woman ovulates prior to marital relations, there is a greater likelihood that the Y chromosome will reach the egg first, resulting in a male child.[25] This observation led to the reinterpretation of the talmudic passage. The word "*mazra'at*" could refer to ovulation, the emission of the female seed, analogous to the emission of the male seed. Thus, if a woman emits seed first (i.e., ovulates), she will beget a male child. This reinterpretation of the rabbinic passage was known even to Shettles himself and is found repeatedly in works of Jewish medical ethics.

Whether the Shettles method has scientific merit remains a matter of debate. The opinion that the timing of ovulation bears on the subsequent gender of the progeny cannot be easily proved or disproved. While it seems anachronistic to interpolate this understanding into the talmudic passage, written some 1500 years prior to the identification and visualization of the egg and the physiological understanding of ovulation, one cannot discount the possibility of a *mesorah* for this notion which is only now better understood in light of modern medicine. Just as man learns the Torah forgotten *in utero* only later in life, perhaps mankind, over generations, is gradually learning the forgotten secrets of medicine and human reproduction.

CONCLUSION

In this essay we have discussed some selections from rabbinic lit-erature on the portion of *Tazria* that relate to medicine, in particular, human reproduction. We have interpreted some passages in light of

22. *Vayikra* 12:2.
23. (Warsaw, 5629), Part 1, Section 17, Ch. 2. I thank Dr. Abe Lipshitz for this reference.
24. *Vayikra* 12:2.
25. L.B. Shettles and D.M. Rorvik, *Your Baby's Sex* (New York, 1970), p. 56. He also takes into account the nature of the acidity of the secretions of the reproductive tract during climax and around the time of ovulation.

contemporaneous medical history. This approach can be applied to other medically related passages in rabbinic literature, but it must be applied judiciously. Clearly when the rabbinic authorities of earlier centuries themselves refer to external medical sources, as is the case for the seven chamber uterus and the theories about the contributions of the male and female to the fetus, a review of those sources and their context is beneficial in understanding the interpretations. However, there are some areas where the rabbinic medical discussions are not in consonance with known contemporaneous medical doctrines. In these areas one cannot simply attribute these notions to ancient doctrines. In addition, there may be an element of *mesorah* at play in these cases, as is perhaps the case with the position of R. Yishmael cited above and the talmudic approach to gender determination. In some instances, modern advances have led to fresh interpretations and perhaps vindication of the pre-modern rabbinic sources. Some of these interpretations are convincing, others less so. Nevertheless, those who consider all pre-modern rabbinic passages on medicine as erroneous and antiquated relics of the past are mistaken, as are those who vigorously defend all such passages as medically correct. Each passage requires independent analysis. But we must always exercise humility, awe and respect for the words of *Chazal* as we continue to search and explore these areas.

In the aforementioned description of the fetus *in utero* from the *Midrash Rabbah*, it states that when the baby exits the womb and enters the outside world, the previously closed passages open, and the open passages shut. The same expression is applied to the study of Torah in general. Sometimes opening one avenue of analysis closes another, and vice versa. Navigating the maze of the openings and closings of the medical passages in rabbinic literature is a challenging and oft-times rewarding task. Satisfactory resolution of some of these challenges, however, may not be forthcoming until we exit this world and enter the World to Come.

Rabbi Yonason Sacks

מצורע: *Badad Yeisheiv:* Appreciating *Kedushat Yisrael*

Each member of *Knesset Yisrael* is endowed with an inherent *kedushah* that manifests itself both individually and collectively. A true *oved Hashem* not only strives for personal piety and religious growth, but also concerns himself and identifies with the aims and needs of others.

The Torah ascribes added significance to a *mitzvah* by virtue of its collective nature. Hence, should an individual lose a close relative during a festival, his personal obligation to mourn is suspended until the conclusion of that festival in order to allow him to fulfill the obligation of *simchah* (rejoicing). Explaining the priority given to *simchat Yom Tov*, the Talmud (*Mo'ed Katan* 14b) states: *"Atei aseh de-rabbim u-dachi aseh de-yachid"* – "a positive collective commandment comes and takes precedence over a positive individual commandment." The Rambam maintains that both of these obligations, mourning the loss of a relative and rejoicing on a festival, are Biblical commandments. Hence, even from a Biblical perspective, preference is shown to a collective obligation. Furthermore, *Tosafot* assert that even a collective rabbinical obligation can override a personal Biblical prohibition.

The distinction between individual and collective obligations is often evident in the Torah's formulation of the *mitzvah* itself. Whereas individual commandments are often stated in the plural, collective imperatives are formulated in the singular, thus emphasizing the collectivity as a whole. An example of the latter is the obligation of counting the *Yovel* (Jubilee) cycle. Unlike the *mitzvah* of taking a *lulav* on *Sukkot* which is formulated in the plural, "*u-lekachtem lakhem*" – "and you shall take for yourselves" (*Vayikra* 23:40), here the Torah states, "*ve-safarta lekha*" – "and you shall count for yourself" (*Vayikra* 25:8). For this reason, the *Sifre* (ad loc.) comments, "'*ve-safarta lekha'* – *be-veit din*" – "'and you shall count for yourself' – in a rabbinical court," limiting the obligation of counting the *Yovel* years to the highest court which represents the people of Israel as a whole.

Another example is the obligation of counting the *Omer* which, although initially rendered in the plural, "*u-sfartem lakhem*" – "and you shall count for yourselves" (*Vayikra* 23:15), is later repeated in the singular "*tispar lakh*" – "count for yourself" (*Devarim* 16:9). Accordingly, the Torah requires each individual to count the *Omer*, thereby accounting for the initial plural formulation of this commandment. However, basing himself on the second singular formulation, R. Eliezer argues (*Menachot* 65b) that the counting must be "*tiluyah be-beit din*," dependent on the highest court as well. Hence this court, the collective representative of Israel, must determine when the counting begins. The *Sifre* on *Devarim* (16:9) requires that the *Omer* be counted twice, once individually and a second time collectively, by the highest court.

Appreciating this two-fold *kedushah* is essential to properly understand the significance of *tzara'at*. The many restrictions imposed on the *metzora*, as well as the detailed process of his purification, underscore the uniqueness and severity of *tzara'at*. Unlike other forms of *tum'ah*, which prevent an individual from entering various parts of the *Beit Ha-Mikdash*, the *metzora* is forced to leave the entire *machaneh Yisrael* (camp of Israel).

The Talmud in *Erakhin* (16b) links this isolation with the very cause of *tzara'at* itself. "*Mah nishtanah metzora she-amrah Torah, 'badad yeisheiv mi-chutz le-machaneh moshavo'*? *Hu hivdil bein ish le-ishto, bein ish le-re'eihu, lefikhokh amrah Torah, 'badad yeisheiv'"* – "Why is a *metzora* different that the Torah states, 'He shall dwell alone; outside the camp shall be his dwelling'? He [through his slander] separated a husband from his wife, a man from his neighbor, therefore the Torah says, 'He shall dwell alone.'"

The slanderous *metzora* who, through his behavior, fails to value the harmony of the community, must live in isolation.

The laws governing the *metzora*, however, extend far beyond his sequester. Based on the verse, "*begadav yihyu frumim ve-ro'sho yihyeh faru'a ve-al safam ya'teh*" – "his garments shall be torn, the hair of his head shall be unshorn, and he shall cloak himself up to his lips" (*Vayikra* 13:45), the Talmud in *Mo'ed Katan* (15a) explains that a *metzora* must tear his garment and cover his head, as well as refrain from cutting his hair and greeting others.

The common theme linking these *halakhot*, implied by the Talmud and stated explicitly by the Rambam (*Hilkhot Tum'at Tzara'at* 10:6), is *aveilut*. The *metzora* is an *aveil* and is thus bound by the many obligations and restrictions of mourning. In what sense, however, is a *metzora* an *aveil*? Why is it that he must observe the traditions of *aveilut*?

Each member of *Knesset Yisrael* possesses a two-fold *kedushah* – as an individual and as a vital part of the collectivity of *Benei Yisrael*. A *metzora*, through his callous slander, severs his bond with the collective *kedushah* of *Benei Yisrael*; it is as if part of him has died. Indeed, the Talmud states (*Nedarim* 64b) "*arba'ah chashuvin ke-met* – *ani u-metzora...*" – "four [types of people] are as if they are dead – a poor man, a *metzora*...." Accordingly, the Torah mandates *aveilut*; the *metzora* mourns himself.

The onset of *Yom Tov*, however, marks a clear contrast between the *aveil* and the *metzora*. Whereas the commencement of *Yom Tov* cancels *aveilut*, the Talmud (*Mo'ed Katan* 14b), states "*noheg tzara'ato be-regel*" – "the laws of the *metzora* apply on *Yom Tov*." How do we understand this distinction? The ability of *Yom Tov* to suspend *aveilut* stems from the communal nature of *Yom Tov*: "*Atei aseh de-rabbim* [*Yom Tov*] *u-dachi aseh de-yachid* [*aveilut*]" – "let the public commandment of *Yom Tov* come and supersede the individual commandment of mourning." A *metzora*, however, has severed his bond to the community. For him, the communal nature of *Yom Tov* cannot suspend the obligations and restrictions of *tzara'at*.

The plight of the *metzora* highlights the privilege and responsibility of *kedushat Yisrael*. May we be the worthy beneficiaries of this transcendent gift.

Rabbi Shmuel Goldin

אחרי מות: The "Sent Goat"[1]

At the center of the Yom Kippur Temple service lies the mysterious ritual of the *"se'ir ha-mishtaleach"* – "the sent goat":

> And from among the Children of Israel he [Aharon] shall take two he-goats as a sin offering… and stand them before the Lord, at the entrance of the Tent of Meeting. Aharon shall place lots upon the two he-goats: one lot for the Lord and one lot for Azazel. And Aharon shall bring near the he-goat upon which the lot for the Lord has been drawn and shall make it a sin offering. And the he-goat, upon which the lot for Azazel has been drawn, shall be stood alive before the Lord, to affect atonement upon it, to send it to Azazel, in the wilderness.[2]

Further in the *parashah*, the text continues:

---

1. An earlier version of this article appeared in the author's *Unlocking the Torah Text: Vayikra* (Gefen Publishing House and OU Press, NY), 2010.
2. *Vayikra* 16:5–10.

And Aharon will place his two hands upon the living he-goat and shall confess upon it all of the iniquities of the Children of Israel and all of their rebellious sins in all of their sins, and he shall place them upon the head of the he-goat and he shall send it at the hand of a designated man to the wilderness. And the he-goat shall bear upon it all of their iniquities to a desert land, and he shall send the he-goat into the wilderness.[3]

How are we to understand this strange, even troubling ritual of the sent goat which serves as the centerpiece of the service on the holiest day of the year, at the holiest spot on earth, under the direction of the *Kohen Gadol*, acting as the representative of the entire nation?

The questions are manifold.

What is the significance of the simultaneous selection of two goats? This question becomes even more intriguing in light of the mishnaic dictate that the goats chosen should be as similar as possible in stature and appearance.

Why are lots drawn to determine the fate of each goat? Why not simply designate, without resorting to a ceremony of chance?

What is the implication of the confession uttered by the *Kohen Gadol* over the sent goat on behalf of the entire nation? What role does this confession play in the atonement of Yom Kippur? Isn't atonement a private, personal process, best experienced individually rather than communally?

Above all, the very concept of the *se'ir ha-mishtaleach* itself raises a series of troubling concerns. Are the sins of the people truly transferred to the "head of the goat," as the text seems to indicate? Does the animal really become a ritual "scapegoat" for our sins? Such an idea seems completely antithetical to Jewish law and its prohibition of all superstitious practice.[4] Over and over again, the Torah speaks of the doctrine of personal responsibility. We are each responsible for our actions, good or bad. Atonement for sins can only be effected through a wrenching process of *teshuvah*, return, which entails *recognition* of past transgressions,

3. Ibid., 21–22.
4. *Vayikra* 19:26.

remorse over those transgressions and a *commitment* to future change. To suggest now that the *teshuvah* process can somehow be short-circuited through a magical act of transference of sins seems to fly in the face of all that we believe.

Furthermore, where is this goat being "sent"? What is the definition of the term "Azazel"? Why does the Torah mandate that a portion of this ritual be performed off of the Temple Mount? To whom, or to what, is this animal being offered? It seems totally inconceivable that Jewish tradition, founded on the absolute principle of a single, unified God, could suddenly embrace a ritual including an off-site offering to another unknown force.

The Talmud identifies the *se'ir ha-mishtaleach* as a classical legal mystery, one of five halakhic phenomena that earn Satan's scorn due to their illogical nature. From this perspective, the sent goat ritual is a clear example of a *chok*, a law for which no reason is given in the Torah.[5]

Once we enter the realm of *chukkim*, this talmudic source concludes, any attempt at real understanding is pointless. We are challenged, instead, to observe the law even when (or, perhaps, particularly when) the law's purpose remains elusive: "I, the Lord have established [these laws] and you have no right to question them."[6]

Other rabbinic sources, however, while accepting the *se'ir ha-mishtaleach*'s classification as a *chok*, nonetheless find value in the struggle to understand.[7]

A review of the Rabbis' search for answers will take us on a journey to the extremes of rabbinic opinion, from the mystical to the rational. Some of the suggestions offered will seem radical. One classical opinion will venture, in fact, so dangerously close to the edge of acceptability that its proponent will record it only in code, lest it be misinterpreted by those unready to read it. Yet the potential lessons that can be gleaned from the struggle to understand this central Yom Kippur rite make the

5. See my *Unlocking the Torah Text: Shmot; Terumah 3, Approaches A* (Gefen Publishing House, New York), 2007.
6. *Yoma* 67b.
7. *Unlocking the Torah Text: Shmot; Terumah 3, Approaches B–F.*

journey more than worthwhile. First, however, a historical note, under-scoring the depth of the problems.

Later events may well reflect the dangers of misinterpretation associated with the sent goat ritual. The *Mishnah* records that centuries after the inception of the ritual, Babylonian Jews attending the Temple service (the Talmud corrects this to "the Alexandrian Jews") began to pull at the hair of the individual accompanying the sent goat and shout: "Take [our sins] and leave! Take [our sins] and leave!"

Uncomfortable with the desecration of the Temple service result-ing from the peoples' literal interpretation of the sent goat ritual, the Rabbis mandated the construction of an elevated pathway leading from the Temple grounds to the outskirts of Jerusalem. The goat was then led on this pathway, out of the reach of onlookers.[8]

These developments only serve to strengthen our previously raised questions. What explanations can be offered for a ritual which, at face value, seems to contradict so many basic principles of Jewish belief?

Our analysis best begins, perhaps, with an attempt to define the term "Azazel." Who, or what, does this word – describing the ultimate destination of the sent goat – signify?

The broadest consensus among the authorities develops around the definition of Azazel as a geographic location. Numerous scholars, including Rashi, adopt the tannaitic position that the word "*Azazel*" (built on the root word *az*, strong or bold) connotes a wilderness site of exceptional strength and harshness.[9] The goat, they maintain, was led to a desolate mountain in the wilderness where it met its fate, falling over the edge of a sharp precipice.[10]

What possible reason, however, could there be for this procedure? If the sent goat was to be a sacrifice, why was it not offered in the usual manner on the Temple Mount?

Prominent among the rationalists concerning the *se'ir ha-mishta-leach* is, of course, the Rambam who, as is his wont, offers an intellectual-philosophical explanation for this strange ritual. He notes a general pat-

8. *Yoma* 66a–b.
9. *Yoma* 67b.
10. Ibid., 67a–b.

tern in connection with the sin offerings offered as part of the Temple ritual. Unlike burnt offerings, which are consumed in the fire of the Sanctuary's altar, sin offerings brought as atonement for severe transgressions are burned outside the Israelite camp. This ritual distinction, the Rambam suggests, mirrors a deeper philosophical divide. Far from creating the symbolic "sweet savor to God" of the celebratory burnt offerings, the burning of a sin offering reflects the destruction of the negative. Through this ritual, the supplicant makes known his desire that the sin which necessitated the sacrifice be erased, destroyed and eradicated from memory. The Torah, therefore, mandates that specific sin offerings be consumed not on the altar, but outside the camp. Atonement can only be achieved if the people distance themselves from the sins associated with the burning of these offerings.

When it comes to the *se'ir ha-mishtaleach*, the Rambam continues, our tradition goes one step further. So severe are the year-long communal sins represented by this offering, that it is sent as far from the camp as possible, to the desolate wilderness of Azazel.

Above all, concludes the Rambam, the Torah's reference to the placing of the sins of the nation on the *se'ir ha-mishtaleach* cannot be taken literally. "Sins are not physical burdens which can be removed from one man's back and placed upon the back of another."[11] *Rather, the drama of the sent goat ritual is designed to strike fear and awe in the hearts of onlookers and move them towards the difficult task of personal teshuvah.* The message of the ritual is clear: as the goat embarks on its final journey into the distant wilderness, symbolically accompanied by the sins of the people, all present should cleanse and distance themselves from past failures and transgressions by committing themselves to concrete future change.[12]

Other commentaries suggest additional educational layers to the rituals surrounding the *se'ir ha-mishtaleach*.

Ha-Ketav Ve-Ha-Kabbalah, for example, references a phrase concerning idolatry that appears later in *Parashat Acharei Mot*: "And they shall no longer slaughter their offerings to the demons (literally the

11. Rambam, *Moreh Nevukhim* III:46.
12. Ibid.

"he-goats") after whom they stray…".[13] Idolatrous practice at the time included the worship of wilderness demons which often took the form of goats. The dramatic destruction of the sent goat is thus designed to convey to the nation the emptiness and the abhorrent nature of idol worship. As the people witness the graphic, violent end of the sent goat, the detritus of idolatry will dissipate from their souls and they will cleave to their Creator. By prompting the nation to return to their God, maintains *Ha-Ketav Ve-Ha-Kabbalah*, the *se'ir ha-mishtaleach* will functionally "bear upon it all of their iniquities."[14]

Moving in a different, yet equally rational, direction, the Abarbanel, the *Akeidat Yitzchak* and others view the rituals surrounding the *se'ir ha-mishtaleach* as symbolic of the eternal struggle between two twin brothers, Yaakov and Esav, and their progeny. These two towering historical figures emerge from the same womb at the same time. One brother, however, is fated to serve the Lord as the ancestor of his chosen people, while the other is destined to a violent, turbulent existence. So too, two goats, preferably of equal stature and appearance, are selected during the Temple service on Yom Kippur. Through the drawing of lots, God's will is evidenced as their fates are determined. One goat is chosen to ascend the Temple's altar as a holy sacrifice while the other is sent to its destruction in a wild, desolate, barren land. From this perspective, the ritual of the sent goat is specifically fashioned to remind the Israelites, on the holiest day of the year, of their unique destiny and responsibility as the descendants of Yaakov, God's chosen people.[15]

Finally, perhaps the most obvious *peshat*-based explanation for the ritual of the *se'ir ha-mishtaleach* is further offered by the Abarbanel, the *Akeidat Yitzchak*, and elaborated upon extensively by Rabbi Samson Raphael Hirsch. The rituals within the sanctuary on Yom Kippur reflect a fundamental truth central to the very fabric of creation. In order to afford man with free choice, for every good God creates, He necessarily fashions a concomitant evil. The challenge facing each individual witnessing the dramatic ritual of the sent goat is dramatically clear: *Which*

---

13. *Vayikra* 17:7.
14. *Ha-Ketav Ve-Ha-Kabbalah, Vayikra* 17:22.
15. Abarbanel, *Vayikra* 16:1–22.

path will you choose? Will you dedicate your life to the sanctified worship of the Lord; will you "ascend His Altar," or will you, God forbid, allow your base impulses to lead you down the destructive path "to Azazel"?[16]

At the opposite end of the interpretive spectrum from the rationalists are those who approach the entire ritual of the *se'ir ha-mishtaleach* in mystical, midrashic terms. Many of their suggestions, however, seem to raise serious philosophical difficulties.

One tradition in the Talmud and *Midrash*, for example, links the Yom Kippur Temple ritual to a most puzzling passage in the Torah, found towards the end of *Parashat Bereishit*. At the close of a ten-generation genealogical table leading from Adam to Noach, and immediately before the announcement of God's decision to punish the world through the great flood, the text states:

> And it came to pass when man began to multiply on the face of the earth and daughters were born to them; *and the sons of the gods* [alternatively, sons of the rulers] saw that the daughters of man were good and they took for themselves as wives from whomever they chose. The giants were upon the land in those days and also afterward, when the sons of the gods [or sons of the rulers] consorted with the daughters of man, who bore to them. They were the mighty who, from old, were men of name.[17]

Clearly, this baffling passage calls for a full analysis, which is beyond the scope of our current study. Suffice to say, numerous interpretations (again, from the rational to the mystical) are offered by the commentators.

One approach to the text, however, recorded in the Talmud and *Midrash*, identifies the "sons of the gods" as Aza and Azael (in other sources, Shemchazei and Azael), two angels who convince God to send them into the corruption of human society in order to prove their own steadfastness. Upon their descent to earth, however, these angels

---

16. Abarbanel, ibid.; *Akeidat Yitzchak, Vayikra, Sha'ar* 63; Rabbi Samson Raphael Hirsch, *Vayikra* 16:10.

17. *Bereishit* 6:1–2.

immediately rebel against God's will and, in the process, introduce further sexual licentiousness into human experience. The Temple offerings on Yom Kippur – and particularly the *se'ir ha-mishtaleach* – are offered to atone for the sins of these angels (note the similarity between Azael and Azazel) and the subsequent sexual immorality that has followed, across the centuries.[18]

Among the unanswered problems raised by this midrashic tale is the portrayal of angels as independent beings with free choice. This depiction directly contradicts Judaism's general understanding of angels as messengers of God with no free will of their own.[19]

An explanation, perhaps, emerges if we view this *midrash* in figurative rather than in literal terms. The Rabbis use midrashic technique to underscore the grave dangers surrounding potential sins of a sexual nature. So great are the temptations that even "angels" can ultimately fall prey; and so pervasive is the problem in the human sphere that the central Temple ritual on Yom Kippur is dedicated to the atonement of such sins. This *midrash* finds support not only in the many laws within Jewish tradition designed to prevent sexual offenses, but also in a Yom Kippur practice which continues to this day. The Torah portion chosen for recitation on Yom Kippur afternoon is specifically the section from *Parashat Acharei Mot* that catalogues the Torah's prohibitions of sexual immorality.[20]

Another midrashic approach to the *se'ir ha-mishtaleach* is so potentially explosive that one of its scholarly proponents is only willing to allude to it "in code." After outlining a number of ideas concerning this mysterious ritual, the Ibn Ezra makes the following baffling statement: "If you have the ability to decipher the secret that is found after the word Azazel, you will know its secret and the secret of its name…. and I will reveal a small portion of the secret in a riddle: 'When you are thirty-three years old, you will know it.'"[21]

A brief, reassuring message to those readers who are thirty-three

18. *Yoma* 67b; Rashi, ibid; *Midrash Rabbah, Devarim.*
19. See my *Unlocking the Torah Text: Bereishit; Vayeitzei 4, Approaches A.*
20. *Megillah* 31a.
21. Ibn Ezra, *Vayikra* 16:8.

years old or older and do not understand this declaration: *don't worry, you are in good company.*

Scholars across the ages have struggled to break Ibn Ezra's code. Among the many solutions offered, the most widely accepted is that of the Ramban, who, tongue in cheek, opens his explanation as follows: "Behold, Rabbi Avraham (Ibn Ezra) is a trustworthy soul who keeps a secret; and I am the talebearer who will reveal his secret; for [it really is no secret,] our Rabbis have already revealed it on many occasions."[22]

The Ramban goes on to disclose the key to the Ibn Ezra's riddle: if you count *thirty-three sentences* in the text from the first mention of the word *Azazel*, you arrive at a statement that we have already encountered in this study: "And they shall no longer slaughter their offerings to the demons [literally the "he-goats"] after whom they stray..."[23]

Apparently, the Israelites actively worshiped demons, angels and other perceived supernatural "forces." The Torah, therefore, expressly prohibits this pointless veneration. Angelic or demonic "forces" are not independent entities worthy of worship. They are simply manifestations of God's will.[24]

As the Ramban continues his analysis of the Ibn Ezra, however, it becomes abundantly clear why the latter might have been hesitant to openly state his position. There is, it seems, an exception to the rule prohibiting gifts to supernatural forces other than God:

> On Yom Kippur, however, *the Holy One Blessed Be He commanded that we send a goat to the wilderness, to the "force" that rules in desolate places*...and from whose power devolves...bloodshed, warfare, violence, strife and destruction...and under whose authority are the demons referred to by the Rabbis as *mazikim*, "destroyers," and in the Biblical text as *se'irim*, "he-goats."[25]

Recognizing the startling nature of his own words, the Ramban

22. Ramban, ibid.
23. *Vayikra* 17:7.
24. *Unlocking the Torah Text: Vayikra; Vayikra 4, Approaches* A.
25. Ramban, ibid.

immediately explains that the *se'ir ha-mishtaleach* is by no means to be understood as an independent offering of our own initiative to this "force" of the wilderness. Such an act would be totally contrary to Torah law and thought – *an open contradiction of our belief in one unified God.* The gift to Azazel must instead be viewed as fulfillment of God's will, best compared to a gift of food given by the supplier of a banquet to a servant at the host's request. The supplier grants nothing directly to the servant, nor does he honor the servant at all. All substance and honor is given only to the host through adherence to the host's directives. So, too, we send the goat to Azazel only in fulfillment of God's command.

This approach, maintains the Ramban, also explains the use of lots in the selection between the two goats. Had the *kohen* chosen the goat to be sent to Azazel, it would have been as if he were worshiping the "force" of the wilderness and offering directly in its name. The ritual as outlined in the Torah, however, calls for both goats to be stood before the sanctuary. Both animals are offerings to God, Who then makes His will known through the drawing of lots. God, not the Kohen, determines the fate of each of the offerings. God selects the gift for Azazel.

In spite of the Ramban's earnest attempts to buffer the blow, however, his explanation of the Ibn Ezra's approach to the *se'ir ha-mishtaleach* strikes with unsettling force. How can we accept a Torah mandate that not only treats angels as independent powers, but enjoins us to extend a "gift" to one such power on the holiest day of the Jewish calendar year? Even if the bequest to Azazel is indirect, this Sanctuary ritual seems to undermine the very essence of our belief in one, and only one, heavenly force.

Perhaps, once again, a solution lies in finding the moral message embedded at the core of this mysterious approach. Yom Kippur, the holiest day of the Jewish year, carries one overarching imperative: *teshuvah,* "return," or, to be more specific, positive behavioral change. *Commitment to such change, however, is doomed to failure without a fundamental recognition of the power of evil and sin.* Year after year, the best of intentions, eloquently expressed over the High Holidays, fall prey to the temptations of the "real world." Our high expectations for ourselves, forged in the rising emotional tide that crests with the cadences of *Ne'ilah* (the dramatic closing Yom Kippur prayer), are soon dashed against the shoals of everyday pressures that inevitably stunt our spiritual growth. Our tradition thus attempts to forestall this eventuality through the message of the sent goat. A gift is given to the "destructive force" of the desert in an apparent effort to direct the power of even that "force" towards our betterment.

And, through this symbolic act, a powerful, personal message is conveyed to all present: *Do not let this holiest of days pass without attaining a healthy respect for the potentially destructive forces that inhabit your world. Above all, recognize the strength of your own personal yetzer ha-ra, your evil inclination, and its unerring ability to undermine your valiant attempts at self-betterment. Denial of its existence has not worked for you in the past and will not work for you in the future. Attempted sublimation of the yetzer ha-ra is, in fact, the surest way to grant it greater power over your actions.*

Adopt, therefore, a different tactic. Acknowledge your "adversary;" respect its strength; then turn that strength to your benefit. Channel the energy that could lead you astray and direct it towards good.

The ritual of the *se'ir ha-mishtaleach* thus emerges as a dramatic reiteration of a fundamental truth which, according to Jewish tradition, is embedded in the fabric of the world's creation.[26] No aspect of man's Divinely created makeup is inherently evil. Good and evil are instead defined, in concrete terms, by how our potential is used. The very internal forces that are so often destructive – lust, ambition, the drive for control and power – can, when properly acknowledged, controlled and harnessed, lead us to the greatest good and accomplishment.

In our search for a proper life path, "Azazel" can and must become our ally.

Our analysis of the sent goat ritual underscores a fundamental truth concerning Torah study, which cannot be stated often enough: even the most difficult, esoteric concepts within our tradition can, upon diligent study, yield extraordinary lessons of immediate relevance to our lives. The treasures of meaning are there for the taking. All that is required is the will and the energy.

26. *Unlocking the Torah Text: Bereishit; Bereishit 1, App. F.*

Rabbi Menachem Genack

קדושים: "You Shall Be Holy"

> *And the Lord spoke unto Moshe, saying: "Speak unto all the congregation of the children of Israel, and say unto them: 'You shall be holy; for I the Lord your God am holy.'"* (Vayikra 19:1–2)

The *Midrash* comments on the phrase "I the Lord your God am holy" – "My holiness is different from yours!" (*Bereishit Rabbah* 90:2). But would we have imagined that a human can rival God's holiness? Could we think that mortal, finite man could achieve the sanctity of Almighty God?

This section from the portion of *Kedoshim* in *Vayikra* continues with a significant pattern that is evident elsewhere in the *Chumash*. Nachmanides (*Shemot* 21:1) points out that the *parashah* of *Mishpatim* is preceded by statements that parallel the first two of the Ten Commandments. "You have seen that I have talked with you from heaven" (*Shemot* 20:19), asserts Nachmanides, corresponds to the first of the Ten Commandments (ibid., 2). The passage preceding *Mishpatim* then goes on, "You shall not make anything to be with Me; gods of silver or gods

293

of gold you shall not make for yourselves" (ibid., 20), which parallels with the second of the Ten Commandments (ibid., 3ff.). *Mishpatim* then commences with laws that correspond to the commandments prohibiting coveting (ibid., 14).

Nachmanides explains that this passage in *Kedoshim* is another instance where a number of directives can be understood as being a reformulated presentation of all the Ten Commandments (Nachmanides, *Vayikra* 19:1). The statement, "I the Lord your God" (*Vakiyra* 19:2) parallels "I am the Lord your God" (*Shemot* 20:2). "[Do not] make cast images for yourselves" (*Vayikra* 19:4) corresponds to "You shall have no other gods before me" (*Shemot* 20:3), the second of the Ten Commandments. "You shall not swear falsely by my name" (*Vayikra* 19:12) is reminiscent of "You shall not take the name of the Lord your God in vain" (*Shemot* 20:7). The command to observe the Sabbath is similarly repeated (*Shemot* 20:8; *Vayikra* 19:3), as is the obligation to respect one's parents (*Shemot* 20:12; *Vayikra* 19:3). The prohibition of murder (*Shemot* 20:13) has its *Vayikra*-parallel: "You shall not stand idly by the blood of your neighbor" (*Vayikra* 19:16). The prohibitions of adultery (*Shemot* 20:13), coveting (*Shemot* 20:14), theft (*Shemot* 20:15) and false testimony (*Shemot* 20:16) also have corresponding commands (*Vayikra* 19:29, 18, 11, 16).

The repetition of the Commandments in *Kedoshim* has a unique lesson. Rabbi Joseph B. Soloveitchik, the Rav, pointed out that the Commandments were said by Moshe to the entire assembly, for the Bible calls the giving of the Law the "day of assembly" (*Devarim* 9:10). As Rashi explains at the beginning of *Kedoshim* (Rashi, *Vayikra* 1:2), this entire passage was also taught in assembly. But in the Hebrew, the Ten Commandments (*Shemot* 20:2–13) are addressed in the singular form. It is *Kedoshim* that uses the plural form, representing a charge to the community as a whole.

Each Jew stood at Mount Sinai and received the Torah, in particular the Ten Commandments, as a member of the Jewish collective. Despite this, the Commandments are in the singular form because each Jew is obligated in them *qua* individual. Even if he were to be the only person in the world, a Jew would still be charged to keep these laws. Additionally, the validity of the Torah's laws does not depend on societal confirmation. Were the collective of humanity to agree that murder is acceptable, each individual would still be obligated to follow the Commandments and not the communal consensus. As the Rav stated, the prohibition of murder did not become nullified at the ovens of Auschwitz.

The restatement in the plural of these Commandments in *Kedoshim* refers to the obligations of the community. Yet the differing details between these two delineations of the law teach a significant message. These distinctions indicate that much more is demanded of the community than of the individual. While the Ten Commandments require one to "Honor your father and your mother" (*Shemot* 20:11), the plural form in *Vayikra* requires the more elevated commandment, "You shall fear every man his mother and his father" (*Vayikra* 19:3). *Shemot*'s "You shall not commit murder" (*Shemot* 20:12) is expanded in *Vayikra* to the more demanding "You shall not stand idly by the blood of your neighbor" (*Vayikra* 19:16). "You shall not covet" (*Shemot* 20:13) emerges as the more exalted "You shall love thy neighbor as thyself" (*Vayikra* 19:18).

Loving-kindness is the essence of the ethical imperative. For this, there must always be a "you," an object of one's kindness. God, however, is entirely independent of the universe. His holiness is manifest in His separation, loneliness, and isolation. God is holy in that He is totally "Other," beyond the universe, hidden by clouds of transcendence, shrouded in infinity. The Rabbis in the *Midrash* feared that man might try to emulate God and attempt to achieve holiness in the same fashion – by being insulated and aloof, cloistered from the world's temptations, potential cruelty and vulgarity. They insisted, therefore, that we achieve holiness within the context of society, involved and engaged with the community. Coupled with the plural form, the higher ethical standard in *Vayikra*'s reformulated Decalogue calls us to holiness, for only by being involved with our neighbors, carrying their burdens, feeling their pain, and rejoicing in their triumphs, can we come close to God.

Human holiness must be achieved not through negation, but through affirmation; not through isolation, but engagement; not by abjuring the world and adopting a monastic life, but by the riskier approach of confronting the world and its imperfections. This approach chances failure, but it brings us to the path of redemption.

Rabbi Shalom Carmy

אמור: From Israelites to Priests: On the Unfolding of *Vayikra's* Teaching

I

Summarizing a text sounds like a jejune piece of schoolroom busywork. Yet the results of such an exercise often reveal a great deal about the reader's tacit understanding of theme and structure. This is particularly true in studying some of the books of the Bible. Traditional readers are often fixated on local phenomena and exegetical difficulties and gravitate to commentaries that address these questions. The need to consider how large units of text hang together and how a book or even an extended section of the Torah unfolds is less frequently addressed. Such subjects play an important role in contemporary study.

Twice in his commentary on *Vayikra*, Abarbanel offers a summary of the book: first in his introduction to the book, and then in his preface to *Parashat Emor*. The differences between his two summaries are instructive; they may be taken to reflect differing ways of looking at the structure of the book.

Abarbanel (Introduction to *Vayikra*) defines the purpose of the book of *Vayikra* to be an exposition of the sanctuary service and how the priests are to serve their God, how they are to atone for Israel, the laws that must occupy the priests in their teaching capacity, and how the priests are to be supported. He then continues:

> Because of their status, He wished them to be distinguished from the rest of the people in dress and character and intellectual standing, and that they not defile themselves through contact with the dead, or shave their heads and beards, and that they not marry any opportune woman who is not appropriate to them in purity, and avoid wine when they serve in the sanctuary, and not to serve with bodily disfigurement or aged, and to be sanctified in all respects, as it says "They shall be holy to their God." And He commanded the people to honor the priest, as it says "And you shall sanctify him."

At the beginning of Ch. 21, Abarbanel alludes to his introductory summary. He writes:

> I already explained in my introduction to this third book that this book of the Divine Torah is about the holiness of His people. For that reason He began with the sanctity of the people and the various offerings and then separated them from the defilement of prohibited foods and bodily lesions and emissions, and then from the impurity of the sanctuary and what is consecrated to it, and then He sanctified them, in sexual relations and the other commandments above. And then He consecrated the priests and then the land (with the Sabbatical year and Jubilee) and dedications of value (*arakhim*) and tithes and dedicated houses at the end of the book. Thus He began with "You shall be holy" and ended "You shall be holy" and this is the continuity of all the sections.

Although Abarbanel's second set of comments explicitly refers to the first set, the differences are salient. The general introduction identifies the sanctuary and the role of the priests as the primary theme of *Vayikra*; one aspect of this is the honor the people must give the priests. This description fits the rabbinic name "*Torat Kohanim*," and the non-Hebrew name "Leviticus." The preface to *Emor*, by contrast, says that *Vayikra* is about the holiness of God's people. The sanctified status of the priests, in this summary, appears late in the book, after many commandments directed to the Jewish people as a whole. The contours of Abarbanel's summary have altered, though he seems unconscious to the fact.

While Abarbanel's obliviousness to the shift is surprising – one wonders whether the phrasing of the general introduction was overly influenced by the opening lines of Ramban's introductory summary to *Vayikra* – the change in his description is not. Like a painting or a musical composition, a text is not seen perpetually from the same perspective. Where you are situated in the text will inevitably affect your description of it, even after many repeated re-readings. Seeing *Vayikra* as one component of the five books of the Torah, in a broad perspective, as it were, the role of the priests stands out. As one progresses through the book step by step, in particular in the transition from *Parashat Kedoshim* to *Emor*, the emphasis on God's relationship with Israel as a people looms larger.

II

Several of the laws directed at the priests in the beginning of *Emor* repeat injunctions already given in *Kedoshim*. "They shall not make a bald patch on their head or shave the fringes of their head, and they shall not make a laceration on their flesh" (*Vayikra* 21:5) were directed to all of Israel in *Vayikra* (19:27–28). The Talmud (*Makkot* 20–21) derives certain details from the two versions of the prohibition, but does not explain why laws that apply equally to Israelites and to *kohanim* are iterated in two separate chapters. This task occupied later commentators, especially those associated with the renaissance of *peshat* study in the 18th-19th centuries. R. Hirsch, *Ha-Ketav Ve-Ha-Kabbalah*, the Netziv, R. David Zvi Hoffmann, in dialogue with earlier writers like N.H. Wessely, to some degree influenced by Rambam's view that these practices were associated with idolatrous priests, and aware of the connections between idolatrous worship and the cult of the dead, suggest the need to emphasize that these prohibitions extend to the priests as well, or especially. Despite their ingenuity, the fact of repetition in the Torah is more salient than the proposed reasons for it, and its impression lingers with the *peshat* student even after the commentators' distinctions are taken into account.

Furthermore, it is not only the repetition that attracts our attention, but its order. Following Abarbanel's general introduction, when we focus on the early *parashiyyot* of the book, we tend to think of *Vayikra* as oriented to the priests. By the time we reach *Kedoshim*, it seems evident that the center of gravity has shifted decisively to the entire people of Israel. Thus it seems odd that *Emor* follows *Kedoshim*, returning, as it were, to the special status of the priests. If the order had been the opposite, we would have said that the Torah began by singling out the priests as holy, and then "democratically," so to speak, bestowed holiness upon the entire nation. In that case, we would understand that the laws sanctifying the body by forbidding its disfigurement as a sign of mourning, applied not only to the priests but to the people as well. With *Kedoshim* coming first, this literary progression is missing; to say that the same prohibitions addressed to Israel also include the priests seems anticlimactic, despite the exegetical reasons for singling them out.

Compound this with another difficulty. In Ch. 21, Moshe is told to speak to the *kohanim*. One would expect the speech to address the priests in the second person. Instead, the message is reported as an indirect discourse in which the *kohanim* are referred to in the third person: "they shall not become defiled to a corpse" (*Vayikra* 21:1) and so forth. When the Torah eventually uses the second person, the addressee is not the priest, but the community of Israel: "And you shall sanctify him, for he offers up the bread of your God" (ibid., 8). From a grammatical point of view, Moses is not to speaking to the priests, but about them.

The last problem may provide a key to the clarification of the others. As Abarbanel noted in his preface to *Emor*, *Vayikra* can be read as a book about the holiness of the Jewish people, in which the role of the priests is subservient to that of Israel. If that is the case, then the point of the opening section in Ch. 21 is not simply that the *kohanim* are required to accept certain restrictions in keeping with their position, but that the people are to sanctify the *kohen* because of his function in the service of God. The status of the priest is not merely the consequence of Divine election. It is also formed by the priest's own conduct and through the honor expressed by the people. This idea is best articulated after the holiness of the people has already been developed in *Vayikra*, initially at the end of *Shemini*, where adherence to the Torah's dietary laws is the mark of sanctification (*Vayikra* 11:44–45), but most prominently in *Kedoshim*, with its wealth of ethical commandments.

If this is true, the movement from *Kedoshim* to *Emor* exhibits the sanctity of the priests as a facet of the sanctity of Israel, rather than presenting the sanctity of Israel as an aspiration to the status of the priests. Had the Torah placed *Emor* first, we would have considered the *kohanim* as the truly elect. The people would be on a lower level, and "democratization" would have meant that the people adopt some of the privileges and restrictions of the priests. Instead the Torah begins with the idea that the entire nation is intended to be a "kingdom of priests and a holy nation" (*Shemot* 19:6). The priesthood is a group that is selected from among the people to perform specific functions in the service of God, and whose role is fully defined only in the aftermath of the Golden Calf, where the failure of the people necessitated this selection, a failure that crucially redefined the relationship of God and His people, as Seforno and R. Meir Simcha of Dvinsk have maintained. The difference between these two ways of thinking about the Israel-priest nexus is substantial. It is the difference between an initial elitism that is, to some measure, extended to others, on the one hand, and what the Torah in fact teaches: a priesthood of all Israel that is modified at a secondary level.

Thus our reflection on the Abarbanel's seemingly casual summaries of *Sefer Vayikra* has led us to a more robust sensitivity as to the plurality of perspectives on *Vayikra*'s structure. This awareness then helped us to see in a new light some striking and fundamental problems regarding the organization and content of *Vayikra*, particularly the connection between *Kedoshim* and *Emor* and the puzzling repetition of laws. The theological upshot of our discussion is a keener sense of the role played by the *kohanim* in the formation of Israelite holiness.

Rabbi Dr. Hershel Reichman

בהר: Humble Strength

The *parashah* begins: "*Va-yeddaber Hashem el Moshe be-Har Sinai*" – "God spoke to Moshe on the Mountain of Sinai, saying" (*Vayikra* 25:1). On this, Rashi comments saying,

> מה ענין שמיטה אצל הר סיני והלא כל המצוות נאמרו מסיני אלא מה
> שמיטה נאמרו כללותיה ודקדוקיה מסיני אף כולן נאמרו כללותיהן
> ודקדוקיהן מסיני.

Why does the Torah connect the *mitzvah* of *shemittah* – the seventh year – with Mount Sinai, weren't all the *mitzvot* said at Sinai? In order to teach that just like all the general and specific principles of *shemittah* were said at Sinai, so too were all the laws of the Torah said at Sinai.

However, despite Rashi's comments, we are still left with the question: why did the Torah choose to highlight this principle – that all of the Torah commandments come from Sinai – via the *mitzvah* of *shemittah*? What does *shemittah* especially have to with Mount Sinai?

The *Shem Mi-Shmuel* presents a fascinating and profound answer:

We read in *Sefer Shemot*, in describing the Jew's arrival at *Har Sinai*: "*Va-yavo'u midbar Sinai va-yachanu ba-midbar, va-yichan sham Yisrael neged ha-Har*" – "They came to the desert of Sinai. They camped in the desert. Israel camped there opposite the mountain" (*Shemot* 19:2).

On the word "*va-yichan*" – which is in the singular – Rashi comments, "*Ke-ish echad be-lev echad*" – "Like one person with one heart."

Why did the Torah make this point when it mentioned the *har* at the end of the verse, and not when it mentioned the *midbar* at the beginning of the verse?

Chazal (*Megillah* 29a) say that all the mountains were inferior to the Mountain of Sinai, which embodied humbleness, whereas the other neighboring mountains, though taller and more impressive, embodied haughtiness. The Almighty sought a humble place to give the Torah. He therefore chose the Mountain of Sinai.

But if Sinai was humble because it was a low mountain, why didn't God give the Torah on the flat plain of the barren desert?

The idea of the Talmud is that every physical place also carries a certain spiritual quality. Some places breed haughtiness, other places bequeath humility. Sinai bred humility and this was critical for the Jews to receive the Torah.

The Torah was to be given to the entire Jewish people. The people had to first be a simple nation, and then they would be worthy to be the nation to receive the Torah. The way to unity is lack of strife, and strong bonding among individuals. The Jewish people are particularly susceptible to internal strife and disputes.

The main cause of strife among us is our strong opinions and convictions. Jews are blessed with very strong intellects – "*koach ha-sekhel*." Therefore, oftentimes Jews quarrel with one another, trying to impose their own set of opinions on their fellow Jew. In order for Jewish unity to exist, people have to be humble – to be able to hear and consider the other's point of view and to sometimes concede one's own position. Humility is the foundation of unity.

However, there is genuine humility and false humility. False humility takes two forms. Sometimes "humility" is nothing but a front for the self-centered person to disarm others. This is very destructive.

Another bad form of humility is one which contains elements of depression and helplessness. This is equally terrible.

Proper humility is a balance wherein the individual recognizes his or her strengths and the worth of their views and opinions, but also realizes their limitations and fallibilities. It is a difficult balance to attain.

The concept of worthwhile humility was succinctly stated by the great Torah sage Hillel, who said: *"Im ein ani li mi li, u-ke-she-ani le-atzmi mah ani"* – "If I am not for myself who will be for me, if I am only for myself who am I?" (*Pirkei Avot* 1:14).

This paradoxical dialectic of self-reliance and dependence is the symbol of *Har Sinai. Har Sinai* was a mountain, but a humble one. It had strengths and rose high over the desert, but did not compare to the other gigantic peaks. Thus, it spiritually represented humble strength, the quality the Torah wanted for the Jewish people. That's why the Torah emphasized that the unity of the Jewish people was formed at the base of Mount Sinai, and not previously.

Shemittah is a *mitzvah* which requires humble strengths. On the one hand, this self-denial by the typically self-reliant, independent landowner requires great inner strength. It requires strength to control his basic human instincts for his own personal property and wealth. Thus, in *shemittah*, we find the perfect and typical Torah values of strength and humility. This is one experience and character lesson received at *Har Sinai*, and that is why, as the *Shem Mi-Shmuel* says, *shemittah* is the model *mitzvah* taught to the Jewish people at Sinai.

In learning Torah, one must have strength and humility – confidence in one's own understandings of Torah, combined with the humility to learn from others, including teachers, peers, and students. Everything the Torah asks of us is a combination of humble strength – to do what's right firmly, and with conviction, but to realize we are only God's creatures and messengers of His exalted will. This humble strength is at the core of Jewish unity and love of Israel.

Rabbi Zevulun Charlop

בחוקותי: The *Shoah* and the Lady Who Wasn't There

Some while back, a longtime member of my congregation, who was a Holocaust survivor, passed away. In addition to his wife, he left behind two sons, both of whom he sent to the Lubavitch *Yeshiva Ketannah*, which was located in the Bronx at that time – not without some struggle and sacrifice. The struggle to get his boys to want to attend was greater than the financial sacrifice, which he was happy to make. He wanted his children to grow up to be good and proud Jews! His sons, indeed, were fine young men as they progressed through school, but, not unlike many of their peers, were also a bit rebellious. Their friends all around them, mostly Jews, went to public school and seemingly lived without restrictions. They did what they wanted on *Shabbat* and ate what they wanted, wherever and whenever they wanted. The brothers, on the other hand, felt muzzled and leashed to the circumscribing strictures of Jewish observance to which a yeshiva boy was, more or less, expected to adhere. And, upon graduating from yeshiva elementary school, they switched to public high school and were "free at last!"

Nonetheless, I was not prepared for what I was to learn when I went to the deceased's home for *nichum aveilim*. Only one of the sons was there. The other was in Europe on "important business," which, he claimed, did not allow him to come to his father's funeral and, indeed, lasted for the duration of *shivah*. When I came to the mourners' home, I found this incongruous family tableau – the mother sitting on a traditional, low *shivah* bench, while the son was sitting nonchalantly in an easy chair, with his leg dangling over one side. I asked him why he didn't also sit on a *shivah* bench. To my shock, he told me, unabashedly, "I don't believe in the Jewish God: If there was a Jewish God, He would not have allowed the Holocaust and all the massacres and persecutions that have obscenely accompanied us through the long, wretched, and harrowing history of our people." It was then that he introduced his wife and sturdy blond children. And, I was not surprised to learn from him that she was a German *frau* and apparently not Jewish, and that he and she and their children lived in Germany, in a small rural community not too far from where he worked. In fact, he boasted that he was the only Jew in that town and told me how comfortable he felt in his new environs. Never mind that the people of that good, pleasant earth of 60 to 70 years ago, at least some of them, anyway, may have directly participated in the annihilation of one third of his people, including his father's family, or were complicit in this unprecedented beastly carnage by their acquiescence or silence. He claimed that he could not pray to the wrathful God of his fathers, who turned His face from His trumpeted "chosen people" and allowed their near-destruction.

There was no arguing with him at that time and place, but I told him I would like to talk to him, about his new world outlook, which seemed so absolutely reasonable and inevitable to him and so appalling and incredible to me. To my surprise, he accepted my invitation, and we set a time to meet in my office at Yeshiva, an appointment which he faithfully kept.

After some amenities, we got down to the business at hand. He began, belligerently almost, "Rabbi – you seemed to be astonished by the turn of my life, which, to me, is so natural after what happened in World War II, the barbaric and total breakdown of humanity – how can you still believe in a Jewish God – in any God?"

Without beating around the bush, I told him that I can understand where he is coming from, and I do not, at all, make light of his argument. He is not alone in his view, which, at first blush, may appear frighteningly understandable. Nonetheless, I told him, to his visible surprise, that, on the contrary, the Holocaust does not – *chas ve-chalilah* – undo the notion of the existence of God. On the contrary, it affirms His existence – a God who created the heavens and earth and who continues immanently to reign over them, and to whom, therefore, homage and service are owed. For, in the Torah He gave on Sinai over 3,500 years ago, we find that unsparingly detailed litany of woe known as the *tokhechah* in *Bechukkotai* and continuing into *Devarim* – in *Ki Tavo, Vayelekh* and *Ha'azinu* – which leaves nothing to the imagination. He set before us the unspeakable fate that would be ours millennia later – God forbid – if we abandoned Him and His law. This is, in itself, powerful proof that there is an eternal God! *Even as I say this, it does not mean that we understand, or can even presume to begin to understand, why the Shoah was especially visited upon our people, enveloping the tzaddik and rasha – the righteous and the wicked – in the terrible sweep of its indiscriminate fury.*

Curiously, we find in *Ha'azinu* (*Devarim* 32:25) – and I deliberately use the translation of Chief Rabbi J.H. Hertz in the *Chumash* edition bearing his name, which was issued in 1937, two years before the outbreak of World War II and the beginning of the *Shoah* – "*mi-chutz teshakel – cherev u-me-chadarim eimah gam bachur gam betulah yonek*" – "without, shall the sword bereave. And in the chambers of terror, slaying both young man and virgin; the suckling with the man of grey hairs." The word "chambers" has become an awful *leitmotif* – the evil crucible – of the Holocaust.

Moreover, this unvarnished and untempered glimpse into that desperate time of "*Anokhi astir et panai ba-yom ha-hu*" – "I will hide My face on that day" (*Devarim* 31:18), which proved to be abysmally literal, demonstrates the eternal and unquestionable reality of God, even if He is nowhere to be seen or sensed.

What may speak even more surely to His existence and unsunderable relationship to His people, come what may, is that immediately after telling us of His apparent and total concealment, indeed, in the very next verse (*Devarim* 31:19), without a pause almost, it is written: "And now, you shall write this song." Mind you, after *tokhechah*, the Torah is still denominated as a song: "Put it in their mouths, for this song shall be a witness to the Children of Israel." More than this, it is the *tokhechah* itself that is most particularly designated as *shirah*.

In its curious juxtaposition, this call, which defines the darkest moment, may be even less fathomable than the asphyxiating, gaseous flames, which immediately preceded it and indelibly seared our people forever.

However, I came upon a remarkable image of sight and speech, and from an altogether unlikely source. A little over a year ago, one of America's greatest and most controversial painters, Andrew Wyeth, passed away. Among his unique strengths as an artist was his ability to convey, beyond the image on the canvas, figures that are implicit – that the viewer sees, even though they are not there.

One of Wyeth's most famous paintings, "Christina's World," moves its viewers, no doubt, individually and differently, to see what is not in the picture itself, but which they instinctively feel is there. The picture encapsulates Wyeth's prowess and artistic aspiration as a painter. It became an American icon, like Whistler's portrait of his mother or Emanuel Leutze's "Washington Crossing the Delaware."

Christina was crippled from the waist down. To Wyeth, she was a model of dignity who refused to use a wheelchair and preferred to live in squalor rather than be beholden to anyone. In the picture, she is looking at a bare field in a desolate farmland, facing a weather-beaten, empty wooden house – her back to the viewer. This picture has evoked incredible mystery: what does this lady look like, and why is she looking at the house?

Wyeth said that if he were a better artist, he would have painted just that field (without the lady) and have you sense her "without her being there."

Wyeth's ambition may provide us with a perception of "*Anokhi astir*" that is startling, but possibly the beginning of an answer to the still unanswerable.

Hashem was not to be sensed or seen in that terrible time of *tokhechah*'s unfolding! It was "hide and seek." He was hiding, and *Am Yisrael* was seeking and, for a while, could not find or even sense His presence. But, the Supreme artist, if only in retrospect, allowed *nishmat Yisrael* – the soul of Israel – to sense and see Him at once – now and then – even when He did not seem to be there at all!

ספר במדבר

Rabbi Yaakov Neuberger

במדבר: Precarious Lives and Moments of Certainty

Opening *Sefer Bemidbar* brings me back to *seudah shlishit* in the sparsely furnished home of the saintly and vigorous Rav Tzvi Yehudah Kook *zt"l*. For several weeks I had joined his students, who would stream from Kiryat Moshe to Geulah as the *Yerushalayim* sun was setting, in order to bring *Shabbat* to a close amidst heartfelt *niggunim* and the thought-provoking words of their teacher and guide. To Rav Tzvi Yehudah, the *parashiyyot* of *Bemidbar* were the chapters of Diaspora, the wandering, the rootlessness and the restlessness. Every week Rav Tzvi Yehudah would expound on the challenges and opportunities of these episodes, known all too well to contemporary thinking Jews.

No doubt many of us view the journey through the *midbar* in preparation of coming into Israel as a necessary experience, one that perhaps had to complete the *"kur ha-barzel"* (*Devarim* 4:20), the "refinery" that was Egypt. Indeed there is good reason for this, as we are all familiar with the oft-quoted vision of *Yirmiyahu* (2:2): "So says *Hashem*, I recall the kindness of your early years, the love of your wedding period, how you followed me into the desert, into an entirely uncultivated land."

Presumably this kindness is ascribed due to the harsh dangers of desert travel, the relentless fear of thirst and starvation, and the lack of protection from threatening predators, all of which we endured without first questioning.

What would be the benefit of a journey that could endanger all that we had gained in leaving Egypt? Had we not already experienced *Hashem*'s miracles on our behalf, witnessed the empty values of a pagan culture and watched pagan deities fail to protect their people? Nevertheless, now came the moment to act on our newly refined and articulated beliefs by surrendering our nascent nationhood and our very survival into *Hashem*'s hands. With that we would end exile, all the while gaining complete spiritual redemption.

Thus, we have come to expect the desert to be used as a metaphor for desolation and even despair, and that is how Hoshea refers to the *midbar* in the beginning of the *haftarah* of Bemidbar. "Lest I strip her [the unfaithful wife that symbolizes our nation] bare...and I shall set her like a *midbar* and place her like a parched land, and I will kill her with thirst" (*Hoshea* 1:5).

Is it not then surprising to read in the very same *haftarah*, "Therefore, I will seduce her and lead her to the *midbar*, and I will speak to her lovingly. I shall give her vineyards from there and a deserted valley will become a portal of hope for her and she will proclaim from there as in her youthful days and as in the days of her ascent from the land of Egypt" (ibid., 16). We certainly would not anticipate viewing the desert as a romantic place where we would once again relive the freshness or our early relationship with *Hashem* and earn once again *Hashem*'s trust. And yet, it would seem that it is precisely for that reference that Hoshea's words were chosen for the introductory *haftarah* of Bemidbar.

True, the intimidating *midbar* could be an early form of tough love, shaping the young and indistinct nation by fire, forcing us to express our commitment to *Hashem* for all times. Nevertheless, the images employed by Hoshea add that *Hashem* treasured that time and apparently would want us to do so as well. To be sure, the *midbar* was that time when He had us all to Himself, undistracted by civilized surroundings and undiluted by competing cultures. It was this intense *Mishkan*-centered existence which, according to the opening *parashiyyot* of Bemidbar, governed our movements, determining when, where and how we would travel and encamp. Apparently, from those *Mishkan*-anchored years, we would emerge strong, optimistic and ready to fight for *Eretz Yisrael*, and ready to wrest it and settle it as Torah-bound communities.

It would seem to me that this *haftarah* was chosen to highlight what could easily be overlooked in the *parashah*. The count that opens the *parashah*, according to Rashi, is borne out of the love that must be expressed as *Hashem* rests His *Shekhinah* on us. The *midrash* sees in the detailed dates of the events in the *parashah* a sign of the love which insists on remembering and recording every detail. The *midrash* further reports that each tribe, once assigned its numbers and position within the camp, pined for its own flag, and, with great love, *Hashem* assigned each one a flag to establish its separateness.

It is through the words of Hoshea that we come to view the *midbar* as a serene and spiritually secure desert isle, and appreciate its profound promise and perhaps purpose as well. Ultimately, Hoshea's words give us insight into the challenge that the *meraggelim*, according to many, tried to address and the way of life they sought to protect.

Yet there is a more pertinent insight which may be communicated through Hoshea's lens. Perhaps we are being told that we must first be anchored in this desert isle *midbar* before we consider our destiny of establishing a nation-state that will indeed be a light unto all peoples, and that will be worthy of showcasing *Hashem*'s concern and power in our world. Precisely because we came to know ourselves in an environment that defined itself around *Hashem*'s presence and service, we were strong enough to negotiate and teach a world that is often unkind to spiritual pursuits. Possibly only after being nurtured in a culture which is God centered – in values and sense of security – will we appropriately adapt future situations and environs into ones that place *Hashem*'s concerns and values at their core.

Towards the end of the *sefer* we are introduced to a similar idea about this cultivation of the individual. According to *Chazal* (Rashi, *Bemidbar* 27:16), Yehoshua is announced as the successor of Moshe neither because of his military prowess as indicated at the battle with Amalek, nor for any leadership acumen with which he had been tested together with Kalev. Rather, it is because he dedicated himself to the seemingly still and simple life of Moshe's tent that he held all the promise of leading our people on to one of our most complex transformations.

If we were to look back at the words of Yirmiyahu that describe the *midbar* experience we would now see he does include Hoshea's prophetic insight as well. Yirmiyahu (ibid.) refers to *"chesed ne'urayikh ahavat kelulotayikh"* which translates as, "kindness of your early years, the love of your wedding period." Perhaps accepting the precarious life of the desert expresses our kindness, and living alone with *Hashem* is the romance of the early marital years to which Yirmiyahu is referring.

All that we have suggested may be summarized for the contemporary Jew through one opinion in the *Midrash* which actually identifies the *midbar* of the future, the *midbar* that will prepare us for the third commonwealth, as *Midbar Yehudah*, the seemingly barren hills north of *Yerushalayim*. What an insight into our times and challenges! To see some of our finest built homes and gardens, lives and communities, in solitude and in threatening surroundings, with fervor and trust, fully expresses the selflessness of *"chesed ne'urayikh"* and the intense romance of *"ahavat kelulotayikh"* at once.

Dr. Yaakov Elman

נשא: An Excess
of Offerings?

One of the most basic rules of Divine draftsmanship is that of economy: *Hashem* does not waste words, or even letters, in His Torah, let alone verses or *parashiyyot*. And if the Torah does seem to devote an inordinate amount of space to a narrative or exposition, there must be a reason: some lesson – halakhic, theological or moral – that the Torah wishes to impart. As R. Acha observes regarding the narrative of Abraham's servant Eliezer's journey to find a wife for Isaac (*Bereishit Rabbah* 60:8):

א"ר אחא/י יפה שיחתן של עבדי בתי אבות מתורתן של בנים, פרשתו
של אליעזר שנים וג' דפים הוא אומרה ושונה, ושרץ מגופי תורה ואין דמו
מטמא כבשרו אלא מריבוי המקרא, רשב"י אומר טמא הטמא ר"א בן יוסי
אומר זה וזה בראשית רבה (וילנא) פרשה ס ד"ה ח ויבא האיש.

Said R. Acha: "The conversation of the servants of the patriarchal houses is more beloved [before *Hashem*] than the Torah learning of their descendants; [this is apparent from that fact that] the *parashah* of Eliezer is narrated and repeated in two-three columns [in a *Sefer Torah*], while [in regard to the matter of] a dead creeping thing, which is an essential [rule] of the Torah, [the rule that] its blood is as polluting as its flesh [is derived] from a *ribbui* [=a seemingly unnecessary] text [and in this case, one letter]." R. Shimon b. Yohai says: "[It is derived from the extra *heh*] of *tamei/ ha-tamei* [of *Vayikra* 11:29]," [while] R. Eleazar b. Yose says: "[It is derived from the extra *vav*] of *zeh/ve/zeh* [ibid.]."

R. Acha refers to the interesting fact that while the entire narrative of Eliezer's journey to Padan Aram is narrated in the 67 verses of *Bereishit* (24:34–48), the Torah yet quotes Eliezer recounting the events of the journey. His meeting with Rivkah at the well is also recorded in great detail. Both are events that the Torah had already described! Why then the duplication, and why then the length of the narrative in the first place? R. Acha concludes that the doings of the patriarchal household hold a dearer place before *Hashem* than the *halakhot* that *Chazal* would derive from single letters!

R. Acha's dictum can be understood as standing alone: the fact that the Torah devotes this much of its precious space to rehearsing the details of Eliezer's conversation with Rivkah's family demonstrates his high spiritual status, so that even his conversation (*sichah*) is important and/or instructive enough to be recorded in the Torah. Alternately, we can attempt to understand what it was about that conversation that required such repetition and such length. Thus, Abarbanel suggests (as well befits a financier and diplomat) that the Torah here provides a model of the skilled negotiator at work. Or, as the Ramban hints by paraphrasing our *midrash* in *Bereishit Rabbah*, it was the importance of Eliezer's mission – to find a wife for Isaac, a wife who would provide half of the genetic inheritance of *Kelal Yisrael* – that made his mission so important and gave it such a large place in the Torah.

Another observation of R. Acha's indicates that his intention mirrors our first interpretation, for he goes on to say:

ומים לדחוץ רגליו ורגלי האנשים אשר אתו, א"ר אחא יפה רחיצת רגלי עבדי בתי אבות מתורתן של בנים שאפילו רחיצת רגלים צריך לכתוב,

והשריץ מגופי תורה ואין דמו מטמא כבשרו אלא מריבוי המקרא, רשב"י
אומר טמא הטמא ר"א בר"י אמר זה וזה.

"And water to wash the feet of the men who were with him" – Said
R. Acha: "The foot-washing of the servants of the patriarchal
houses is more beloved than the Torah-learning of their descendants, for even their foot-washing had to be recorded, while
[in regard to the matter of] a dead creeping thing, which is an
essential of the Torah, [the rule that] its blood is as polluting as
its flesh [is derived] from a *ribbui* [=a seemingly unnecessary]
text [and in this case, one letter]." R. Shimon b. Yohai says: "[It is
derived from the extra *heh*] of *tamei/ha-tamei* (of *Vakiyra* 11:29),"
[while] R. Eleazar b. Yose says: "[It is derived from the extra *vav*]
of *zeh/ve/zeh* [ibid.]."

Note that in this case R. Acha refers not to speech, which is a reflection
of man's soul, as in Onkelos' translation of "*ruach chayyim*" (*Bereishit* 2:7)
as "*ruach memallelah*," "the spirit of speech," but the phase "patriarchal
servants" in this case does not refer to Eliezer, who, the *Midrash* tells us,
studied under Abraham's direction, but the anonymous servants who
accompanied him, "the men with him."

How then are we to understand the twelve-fold repetition of the
inauguration-offerings of the *nesi'im* in our *parashah*? Eliezer's negotiations were repeated once in detail; the offerings of the *nesi'im*, which
differed not at all, were repeated eleven times, and then summarized a
twelfth time! In the words of the Ramban:

והנכון בטעם הכתוב, כי הקב"ה חולק כבוד ליריאיו וכמו שאמר כי
מכבדי אכבד (ש"א ב ל), והנה הנשיאים כולם ביום אחד הביאו הקרבן
הזה שהסכימו עליו יחד, ואי אפשר שלא יהא אחד קודם לחבירו וכבד
את הנקדמים בדגלים בהקדמת ימים, אבל רצה להזכירם בשמם ובפרט
קרבניהם ולהזכיר יומו של כל אחד, לא שיזכיר ויכבד את הראשון "זה
קרבן נחשון בן עמינדב" ויאמר וכן הקריבו הנשיאים איש איש יומו, כי
יהיה זה קיצור בכבוד האחרים. ואחרי כן חזר וכללם, להגיד שהיו שקולים
לפניו יתברך. וכן אמרו שם בספרי (נשא קס) מגיד הכתוב שכשם ששוו

321

כולם בעצה אחת כך שוו כולם בזכות, קערות כסף שתים עשרה, הן הן
שהתנדבו ולא אירע בהן פסול:

The proper interpretation of the meaning of the verse [is as fol-
lows]: for the Holy One, blessed be He, honors those who fear
Him, as Scripture says: "For I will honor those who honor Me"
(*Shemuel* I 2:30). Now, all the *nesi'im* brought this offering, which
they had all agreed upon, on one day, but it was impossible that
one should not precede his fellow, and [so] He honored those
who were among the earlier flags (i.e., those tribes who marched
earlier) by [mentioning them] on earlier days. But He wanted to
mention them by name and the details of their offerings, and to
mention the day of each of them. He did not wish to mention and
honor [only] the first: "This is the offering of Nachshon son of
Aminadav" and then say: [that] each of the *nesi'im* offered [their
offerings] each on his day, for this would limit the honor of the
others. After that He went back and mentioned them all together
in order to emphasize that they were all equal before Him, may
He be blessed. And so it says in [the *Midrash*] *Sifre*: "Scripture
tells us the just as they were all equal in their plan, they were all
of equal merit, 'twelve gold bowls' that they had donated, and
none of them became invalid [before the time for offering came]."

ועוד בזה טעם אחר במדרשם, כי לכל אחד מהנשיאים עלה במחשבה
להביא חנוכה למזבח ושתהיה בזה השיעור, אבל נחשון חשב בשיעור הזה
טעם אחד וזולתו כל אחד מהנשיאים חשב טעם בפני עצמו, אמרו שחשב
נחשון שיביא קערת כסף שיהיה מנין אותיותיה תשע מאות ושלשים כנגד
שנותיו של אדם, ומשקלה שלשים ומאה כנגד תולדות שהעמיד, וכל
המדרש כמו שכתבו רש"י (פסוק יט):

And there is another reason [given] in their [the Sages'] *midrash*:
It occurred to all of them to bring an inauguration offering for
the altar, and that it should be of such a measure, but Nachshon
understood the measure in one way, and aside from him, each
of the *nesi'im* considered the reason in his own way; [the rabbis]
said that Nachshon thought to bring a gold bowl whose count by

letter was 930, representing Adam's lifetime, and its weight was 130 [to symbolize the age] at which he [began] to have children, all according to the *midrash* that Rashi quotes (v. 10).

או כפי המדרש האחר (במדב״ר יג יג), שהיה מסורת מיעקב אבינו ביד כל שבט ושבט כל מה שיארע לו עד ימות המשיח.... וכן מצאו שם במדרש בכל שבט ושבט טעם מיוחד בקרבנו ובשיעורי הקרבן, ולכך השוה אותם הכתוב לפרט כל אחד בעצמו כאילו לא הוזכר האחר. ואחרי כן כללם כאחד, לדמוז כי בעת אחת עלה במחשבתם להקריב החנוכה ולא קדם אחד לחבירו במחשבה ולא בהבאה לפני המשכן, ועל זה הזכירם הכתוב לכולם בהשואה:

Or, according to another *midrash*, each tribe had a tradition from our Forefather Yaakov as to what would occur to them until messianic times.... And so each tribe found a symbolic meaning for its offering and its measure, and therefore Scripture mentions each separately as though it alone was mentioned, and [only] then were they mentioned together, to hint that they all thought [of this] inaugural [offering] at the same time, and no one thought of it before the other, nor brought it before the Tabernacle [earlier], and it is for this reason that Scripture mentioned them equally.

The Ramban provides three separate explanations for why the *nesi'im* brought the offerings that they did, which can also serve to explain why the Torah took pains to list them. The first is that *Hashem* wanted to honor each *nasi* equally; in order to do this, the Torah gives each of them "equal time," so to speak, and doesn't start with Nachshon and then add a phrase, "and so for all of them." Rather, the Torah described each offering in the same detail as each of the others – even at the cost of having some precede the others. In order to emphasize their equality, the offerings are summarized at the end.

The second, midrashic answer the Ramban gives is that even though all the offerings were identical, each reflected the particular intentions of the *nasi* who offered it. Finally, the Ramban cites a *midrash* that relates each offering to the history of each tribe "until messianic times."

As usual, the Ramban is careful in describing each view. The first he prefaces with the comment that it is "the proper interpretation of the meaning of the verse," while the second he introduces with "and there is another meaning for this in the *midrash*." The third he introduces with "or according to another *midrash*." Why is he careful to present these three views, and what place does each play in his understanding of the entire passage?

It seems to me that the first suggestion is the plain meaning of the *parashah*: clearly, the Torah wished to give proper honor to each *nasi* for his contribution and his initiative in proposing it. But while this may be the plain meaning of the verse, we may well wonder why *Hashem* should accord so much honor to a one-time contribution for a *mitzvah that* was not even meant *le-dorot*, for future generations, since, after all, the Tabernacle was eventually replaced by the Temple, and, besides, the wagons were even more temporary, since they were used only in the wilderness. Should the Torah devote so much space to such an offering? We are right back to R. Acha's dilemma! True, the *nesi'im's* offerings are closer to Torah than Eliezer's conversation with Lavan and Bethuel, but what is the eternal message to be derived from these *parashiyyot*?

Certainly, on one level we can learn the appreciation that we should show to people who provide not only for the public good, but for the good of the spiritual state of *Kelal Yisrael*. Indeed, for those of us in America, where America's individualism is always a danger to the social and spiritual cohesion of Torah society, the importance of working for the public good is always a salutary lesson. But still, do we need 89 verses to teach us that?

Moreover, what are we then to make of the laconic narrative of Yitzchak's life? The major events of his life are the *Akeidah* and Yaakov's taking the birthright, in both of which Yitzchak was relatively passive. The other details of his life are sketchy at best. True, the Ramban occasionally remarks that when the Torah seems to ignore happenings between events about which we are told in detail, or otherwise withhold information, that indicates that nothing important happened then (see for example his comments on *Bemidbar* 16:5, 16:11, 20:21, 32:33, among others). But that rule still seems to give outsized importance to the *nesi'im* and their offerings. Why? And is the need to give due respect to each *nasi* so important as to take up this much space in the Torah?

Our wonderment becomes stronger when we consider other *parashiyyot* that the Torah repeats – but not to such an extent. Take the *Aseret Ha-Dibrot*, for example. The whole passage takes 18 verses in *Shemot*, and 18 verses in *Devarim*! Nothing like the 89 verses here.

The Ramban thus supplements this reason with the symbolic interpretations offered by two *midrashim*. In the first *midrash*, each *nasi* bases his offering on number symbolism based on past events: Nachshon based his on the events of the lives of Adam and Noah, etc. But here too one might well ask: so what? These numbers may commemorate the history of the world as encompassed by the lives of significant Biblical figures, but why devote so much space to information available elsewhere? What do we *learn* from all this?

And so the Ramban cites the second *midrash*, which bases its interpretation of the details of the offerings on the *future*. This explanation then touches on the heart of the matter, as the Ramban emphasizes (in another context, *Bereshit* 12:6 ad loc.),

ויעבר אברם בארץ עד מקום שכם - אומר לך כלל תבין אותו בכל הפרשיות הבאות בענין אברהם יצחק ויעקב, והוא ענין גדול, הזכירוהו רבותינו בדרך קצרה, ואמרו (תנחומא ט) כל מה שאירע לאבות סימן לבנים, ולכן יאריכו הכתובים בספור המסעות וחפירת הבארות ושאר המקרים, ויחשוב החושב בהם כאלו הם דברים מיותרים אין בהם תועלת, וכולם באים ללמד על העתיד, כי כאשר יבוא המקרה לנביא משלשת האבות יתבונן ממנו הדבר הנגזר לבא לזרעו:

"Avraham passed through the land till Shekhem's location" – I will tell you a rule by which you will understand all the passages that follow regarding Avraham, Yitzchak and Yaakov. It is an important matter [which] our masters mentioned only allusively (lit., "in a short manner"), when they said: All that occurred to the Patriarchs is a sign for the[ir] descendents. And that is why the verses expand on (lit., "lengthen") the narrative of the travels, the digging of wells, and other incidents, [which] some may think are extraneous matters which have no [spiritual] purpose. But all of them come to teach us regarding the future, for when an incident occurs to the three Patriarchs as a prophet (that is, he understands the incident in a prophetic manner), he understands from it the matter that is destined to occur to his descendants.

ודע כי כל גזירת עירין כאשר תצא מכח גזירה אל פועל דמיון, תהיה הגזרה
מתקיימת על כל פנים. ולכן יעשו הנביאים מעשה בנבואות כמאמר ירמיהו
שצוה לברוך והיה ככלותך לקרוא את דברי הספר הזה תקשור עליו אבן
והשלכתו אל תוך פרת ואמרת ככה תשקע בבל וגו' (ירמיה נא סג סד).
וכן ענין אלישע בהניחו זרועו על הקשת (מ"ב יג טז-יז), ויאמר אלישע
ירה ויור ויאמר חץ תשועה לה' וחץ תשועה בארם. ונאמר שם (פסוק יט)
ויקצוף עליו איש האלהים ויאמר להכות חמש או שש פעמים אז הכית את
ארם עד כלה ועתה שלש פעמים תכה את ארם:

Thus, you must know that all the decrees of the heavenly beings when [the decree] issues forth by the power of a decree by means of a symbolic action, the decree comes to be in any case. And thus the prophets perform some (symbolic) act [along with enunciating their prophecies] as well, as when Yirmiyahu command Baruch: "When you finish reading this book (i.e., the scroll that Yirmiyahu dictated to him), tie a stone to it and throw it into the Euphrates and say thus: 'So shall Babylon sink'" (*Yirmiyahu* 51:63–64). And so with the matter of Elisha putting his arm on the bow (*Kings* II 13:16–19): "Elisha said: 'Shoot!' and he (i.e., the king) shot [an arrow], and he said: 'This is an arrow of *Hashem's* salvation and an arrow of deliverance from Aram.'" [Elisha then commanded the king to strike the ground with his arrows, but the king struck only three times.] And it is said there: "The prophet (lit., "man of the Lord") was angry, and he said to strike five or six times – then you will [be able] to strike Aram totally, but now you strike Aram three times [they will not be defeated]."

ולפיכך החזיק הקב"ה את אברהם בארץ ועשה לו דמיונות בכל העתיד
להעשות בזרעו, והבן זה...:

Therefore *Hashem* strengthened Avraham in the land, and had him perform symbolic actions regarding all that would happen to his descendents – understand this well.

This can be applied to our case in two ways. Our passage's length is characterized both by its length and its repetitions. In his comments on the *Mishkan*, the Ramban explains why the *parashah* of the *Mishkan* is repeated up to five times; the repetitions betoken its importance. But the *midrash* regarding Eliezer refers also to the amount of detail lavished on the story; the Torah even records the foot-washing of Eliezer and his men! And the answer there is: *Hashem's* preference, or, if you will, his love for the patriarchal family, "*chibbah*," (as the Ramban and most *Rishonim* and *midrashim* put it – Divine love) is expressed by his dwelling on the details of their lives. And so the honor the *nesi'im* were given is that bestowed on them by *Hashem*, and it lasts forever – as does the Torah.

Nevertheless, the Ramban hints at another explanation, and neither contradicts the other. That is, encapsulated in the details of these offerings is the future history of the tribes, and hence, of *Kelal Yisrael*. And that history – also an expression of *Hashem's* love – deserves all the space it gets. However, since we have been granted free will, the Torah will not reveal such matters in any clear way, and so it is hidden in the details of the offerings of the *nesi'im*.

The issue of space and importance works both ways, in the Ramban's view. Thus, he asks (*Bereishit* 12:2) why such a great miracle as Avraham's rescue from Nimrod's fiery furnace is not mentioned in the Torah.

והנה זאת הפרשה לא באָרה כל העניָן, ...אבל הטעם, מפני שעשו אנשי אור כשדים עמו רעות רבות על אמונתו בהקב״ה, והוא ברח מהם ללכת ארצה כנען ונתעכב בחרן, אמר לו לעזוב גם אלו ולעשות כאשר חשב מתחלה, שתהיה עבודתו לו וקריאת בני האדם לשם ה' בארץ הנבחרת, ושם יגדל שמו ויתברכו בו הגוים ההם, לא כאשר עשו עמו באור כשדים שהיו מבזין ומקללים אותו, ושמו אותו בבור או בכבשן האש. ואמר לו שיברך מברכיו ואם יחיד מקללו יואר, וזה טעם הפרשה. אבל התורה לא תרצה להאריך בדעות עובדי עבודה זרה ולפרש העניָן שהיה בינו ובין הכשדים באמונה, כאשר קצרה בעניָן דור אנוש וסברתם בעבודה זרה שחדשו:

Now, this *parashah* does not explain the entire matter..., but the reason [Avraham left Ur Kasdim was] because the people of Ur Kasdim treated him very badly on account of his belief in the Holy One, blessed be He, and he fled from them in order to go to Canaan. [On the way] he lingered in the Charan, [but *Hashem*] told him to leave there also and do as he had originally intended, that his worship should be for Him [=*Hashem*] and he should exhort people of the Chosen Land to [worship] *Hashem*. There his name would become great and those nations would be blessed through him – not as had been done to him in Ur Kasdim, where they denigrated and cursed him, and placed him in a kiln or fiery furnace. And He told him that He would bless those who blessed him [=Avraham], and if an individual would curse him, he would be cursed. And that is the meaning of the *parashah*. But the Torah did not wish to expatiate at length on the opinions of idolators and explain the differences between him and the Kasdim regarding [matters of] faith, just as [the Torah only] briefly [recounted] the story of the generation of Enosh and their reason for inventing the worship of idols.

Indeed, he employs this principle in determining whether the *parashah* detailing the history of the Edomite kings in *Bereishit* (Ch. 36) is meant to be historical or prophetic. Rashi contends that the *parashah* is prophetic and refers to the history of Edom until the time of Sha'ul, but the Ramban objects (*Bereishit* 36:31): Is the "King in Israel" a reference to Sha'ul; is the *parashah* prophetic, or does it refer to Moshe, so that the narrative is *historical*?

ואלה המלכים אשר מלכו בארץ אדום - נכתב זה להגיד כי נתקימה בו
ברכת יצחק שאמר לו ועל חרבך תחיה (לעיל כז מ), כי גברו על בני שעיר
החורי ומלכו עליהם בארצם, ואלה הערים מדינות בארץ אדום, כי בצרה
לאדום היא, כמו שכתוב (ישעיה לד ו) כי זבח לה' בבצרה וטבח גדול
בארץ אדום, וכן ארץ התימני מאדום, כמו שנאמר בו (עובדיה א ט) וחתו
גבוריך תימן למען יכרת איש מהר עשו. וכולם כך המה, אבל ספר הכתוב
כי לא היו מלך בן מלך, כאשר היו בישראל:

ולפני מלך מלך - ימים רבים קודם, ואין טעם "לפני מלך מלך"
שנמשכה מלכות אלה עד מלכות ישראל (ראה רש"י, ורד"ק), אבל לאמר
כי אז לא תהיה להם מלכות, לקיים "ואת אחיך תעבוד" (לעיל כז מ). ויתכן

שאלו כולם בימי משה כבר עברו, כי היו זקנים בעת שהמליכו אותם ולא
האריכו ימים:

"These are the kings who reigned in the land of Edom [before
a king reigned for Israel]" – this was written in order to inform
[us] that Yitzchak's blessing – "by your sword shall you live" –
had been fulfilled, for they [the Edomites, Esav's descendents]
overcame the sons of Seir the Chorite, and ruled over them in
their land, [for] these cities are states in the land of Edom, for
Bozrah is Edomite, as Scripture states regarding it: "for a sacrifice is for *Hashem* in Bozrah, and a great slaughter in the land of
Edom" (*Yeshayahu* 34:6); the land of Yemen is also of Edom, as
Scripture states: "and your warriors will tremble, Yemen, in order
to cut off a man from the Mount of Esav" (*Ovadiah* 1:9). And all
of them are thus [kings], except that the Torah recounts that the
succession did not follow in the same family as it did in Israel.

The expression "before there reigned any king," means
"many years before." But "before there reigned any king" does not
mean that these kingdoms of Edom continued to exist until the
kingdom of Israel. Instead, it means to say that at that time the
Edomites will not have sovereignty, in order to fulfill Isaac's words,
"and thou shalt serve thy brother." It is possible that all these kings
had already passed away in the days of Moshe as they were old
when they crowned them and their lives were not prolonged.

And then, in his comments to verse 40, he makes his intention entirely clear:

ונכתבה הפרשה בדרך הנבואה לדעת רבים (רש"י, וראב"ע, והרד"ק).
ואיננו נכון, כי הנבואה למה תזכיר את אלה, ועד איזה זמן תמנה ותפסיק
בהם. אבל הנכון שכל אלה לפני התורה. ונאמר שמשלו כאחד ויהיה פירוש
למקומותם, שמשל כל אחד במקומו, או שהיה ממשלתם זמן מועט, ושנות
רשעים תקצורנה (משלי י כז):

According to the opinion of many, this *parashah* was written
in a prophetic manner, but this is not correct, for why should

prophecy take notice of these (lit., "mention") [kings, who are spiritually unimportant], and, furthermore, until what time should [this prophecy] count them? [In other words, how far in the future should this narrative be understood as lasting?] Rather, the proper interpretation is that all of these kings [lived] before the Torah [was completed in Moshe's time], and Scripture informs us (literally, "it is said") that they ruled simultaneously, and thus the meaning of "according to their places" is that each one ruled in his place, or their kingship lasted but a short time, [since] "the years of the wicked are short" (*Mishlei* 10:26).

Thus, the fact that the Torah mentions someone or some incident may not mean that the person or incident is of essential importance, or rather, that he or she or it are not important enough to warrant a prophetic word, but only a historical note. In this case, these kings of Edom are mentioned not because of their importance, but only to emphasize that Yitzchak's blessing to Esav was fulfilled. These kings were not important enough in *Hashem*'s scheme of things to be recorded for their own sake, but only for the sake of Yitzchak.

In sum, R. Acha informs us that the Torah has two "speeds," as we might say: halakhic and aggadic, and the aggadic is much "slower." In the halakhic parts of the Torah, the Torah is laconic and compressed; in the aggadic it is expansive. Thus, the 333 verses of *Re'eh*, *Shoftim* and *Ki Teitzei* contain no fewer than 169 *mitzvot* – 27.5% of the *taryag*! At that rate, the 5,845 verses of the entire Torah could contain no fewer than 2,966 *mitzvot*, or, to put it another way, if the Torah had contained only *mitzvot*, *Hashem* could have given us a Torah of 1,207 verses, or a fourth of its current size. Indeed, if we take the 73 *mitzvot* of the 110 verses of *Ki Teitzei* as our model, the Torah could have been as short as 923 verses, or, conversely, it could have included nearly 3,879 *mitzvot*. Again, to take the 100 verses of *Mishpatim* that contain halakhic exposition as our template, 44 *mitzvot* at 100 verses yields a proportion of 2.27 verses/*mitzvah*; compare this to the ratios of the three *sedarot* (1.97) or *Ki Teitzei* alone (1.5).

Of course, there is no need for extra *mitzvot*; we have all we need in 613. But then more *halakhot* could have been included than are now in *Torah She-Bikhtav*.

But of course, as the Rambam informs us (at the end of *Hilkhot Melakhim*, in the censored passage), *Hashem's* thoughts are not ours, and His ways are not ours. He gave us a dual-speed Torah, and somewhat different skills are needed to "drive" them. A sharp, razor-like intellect is needed for the one – along with other skills, as *Avot* enumerates the 48 characteristics needed for the "acquisition of Torah." The other requires a different mode of analysis, and perhaps a greater proportion of human understanding. The metaphor of the "fifth *chelek* of *Shulchan Arukh*" may help us here. There is, of course, no such part of the Jewish Code of Law. Why? Because it would cover human relations that are so complicated that they cannot be codified. It is that *chelek* of which we get a hint in *Naso*. In that *chelek*, human sensibilities are so fine and so fragile, that it is worth expending 89 verses for *Hashem* to cater to them! What a lesson for us as we hurtle through our lives and the lives of others, all but heedless of their presence.

So much for one level of understanding. In the next two levels, the Ramban informs us of how to be more sensitive to others. We are all passengers on a vessel sailing from past to future, and all hands are needed to make the voyage. As has been said, the two Temples were destroyed by baseless hatred – *sinat chinam*; the next one will be built when we take some time to consider our *mitzvot bein adam la-chavero* on the same level as *mizvot bein adam la-Makom*.

Rabbi Elchanan Adler

בהעלותך: Miriam's Rebuke: A Psycho-Midrashic Interpretation[1]

Have we ever stopped to think about the connection between who we are today and our early childhood experiences? About how a poignant feeling or instinct we had in youth continued to resonate within us, consciously or subconsciously, only to manifest itself again many years later? How the nature of our earliest relationships with our parents and siblings became inextricably linked with our self-image?

---

1. This essay is based on a *Shabbat* talk that I gave several years ago. Its thesis, the link between aspects of Miriam's childhood and the episode involving her critique of Moshe *Rabbenu*, is, in effect, a piecing together of disparate midrashic sources. The observation that the Divine rebuke in the latter episode served to reopen an emotional wound from Miriam's youth is based on the comments of R. Zev Wolf Einhorn (Maharzu, *Shemot Rabbah* 1:22), and elaborated on in his treatise *Netiv Chadash* (p. 14).

בהעלותך

Or how a gesture of kindness performed as a child can unexpectedly provide solace for us many years later?

These matters are largely the domain of psychoanalysts who posit that our adult "personalities" – our feelings, tastes, attitudes and interests – can be traced to childhood experiences. While there are some who invest vast resources to probe the origins of their present reality, most of us are content living our daily lives without the need to discover underlying patterns from the distant past.

Yet sometimes we stumble upon a particular incident where the impact of our early personal history is inescapable. I believe that such an example can be found in the Torah at the conclusion of *Parashat Beha'alotekha* in the episode dealing with Miriam's slander against her younger brother, Moshe.[2]

The essence of Miriam's slander was that she equated Moshe's level of prophecy with that of her own: "Was it only to Moshe that *Hashem* spoke? Did he not speak to us as well?"[3] For this insensitive remark, Miriam was chastised by *Hashem*, who made it unequivocally clear that Moshe's prophecy was in a class of its own – qualitatively different from that of other prophets.

In the wake of this Divine rebuke, Miriam was stricken with

The *derashah* raises a number of important issues of *hashkafah*; among them, the balance that must be maintained when analyzing the conduct of *gedolei ha-ummah* – Torah giants whose sanctity and piety defy description. On the one hand, the fact that the Torah does not obscure the mistakes of our leaders suggests a certain license to probe such matters, ostensibly in order to draw inferences that may be of moral value to us. Yet the very enterprise of scrutinizing individuals of enormous spiritual stature carries the risk of introducing biases borne of our small-mindedness and limited understanding. With this in mind, it behooves us not to lose sight of Miriam's prominence within the *mesorah*.

To the extent that our approach helps to illuminate this Torah narrative, it should be emphasized that the dynamics must surely have played out in a far more subtle manner than words can convey. I share this *derashah* in the hope that it will foster an appreciation of *de-kulah bah* – that there is no element of truth regarding human nature that is not alluded to in the Torah.

2. Although both Miriam and Aharon were faulted for the error, since Miriam initiated the conversation, she was the one who was held primarily accountable for the misdeed.

3. *Bemidbar* 12:2.

tzara'at (a skin ailment which was inflicted upon slanderers during Biblical times). Aharon turned to Moshe and implored him to pray on behalf of their sister, and Moshe obliged. *Hashem* responded by ordering Miriam to be secluded outside the camp for seven days. The people postponed their journey for a week until Miriam could rejoin them.

There are two critical aspects to the story that link it to an earlier episode in Miriam's childhood. The first is the topic of Miriam's slander; the second is *Hashem's* introductory remarks before issuing Miriam's sentence of seclusion.

In addition to devaluing Moshe's level of prophecy, Miriam also spoke "about the Kushite woman" (*Bemidbar* 12:1) to whom Moshe was married. As Rashi explains, Miriam was critical of Moshe's separating from Tzipporah. Moshe had done so in order to remain "on call" for prophecy at all times. Though *Hashem* had authorized Moshe's decision, this was not known to Miriam.[4]

In effect, Miriam's critique of Moshe had two components: first, she underestimated Moshe's status as a prophet; second, she considered it wrong for Moshe to deprive himself of a normal family life. These two components were interrelated. Because Miriam failed to appreciate the uniqueness of Moshe's prophecy, she saw no justification in Moshe's decision to separate from his wife. After all, Miriam too was a prophet who nonetheless lived a normal family life. From Miriam's perspective, it was presumptuous and inappropriate for Moshe to be different.

The clue that this story finds its roots deep in Miriam's past can be detected in *Hashem's* statement prior to ordering Miriam into seclusion: "Were her father to spit in her face, would she not be humiliated for seven days? Let her be quarantined outside the camp for seven days, and then she may be brought in."[5] Simply stated, *Hashem* offered a logical justification for His sentence – a rebuke by her biological father would put her to shame for a week's time, so clearly the Divine rebuke, by the

---

4. The comments of Rashi (*Bemidbar* 12:1–2,8), based on *Sifre*, suggest that Moshe's initial separation from Tzipporah was done at God's behest. Other sources (e.g. *Shabbat* 87a; *Yevamot* 62a) indicate that Moshe's decision was arrived at independently and only received Divine sanction subsequently. See also the comments of *Tosafot* to *Shabbat* and *Yevamot*, ibid.

5. Ibid., 14.

Heavenly Father, must entail a punishment no less harsh. But why, we may ask, did *Hashem* use the metaphor of a father's rebuke? Is this analogy merely hypothetical? According to various midrashic and talmudic sources, it is not. It is something that Miriam had actually experienced in her own life.

If we flash back to Miriam at the tender age of six, we find her during one of the cruelest, darkest periods of the Egyptian exile (even the name 'Miriam' is etymologically related to the Hebrew word for bitter). The Hebrew sojourners in Egypt had been transformed into slaves. Originally recruited into building large storage houses for Pharaoh, they gradually found themselves subjected to a daily regimen of back-breaking field labor. Their lot grew increasingly bitter by the day and they were demoralized. To make matters worse, Pharaoh had just issued a royal edict that every newborn Jewish male be cast into the Nile. At this depressing juncture, Miriam's father, Amram, an influential leader in the community, made a fateful decision to divorce his wife, Yocheved. Amram reasoned: What purpose could there be in bringing children into a world where they might be forcibly drowned? His decision sent shock waves through the community and many others followed suit. But soon afterwards, Amram was chastised by his daughter Miriam who argued: "Father, your edict is more drastic than that of Pharaoh! Pharaoh's edict was directed against the Jewish males, yours is directed at the males and females, for you are allowing neither gender to be born."[6] Upon hearing her rebuke, Amram reversed his decision and reunited with his wife. This, in turn, led all those who had divorced their wives to resume their former marital relationships.

What was it that prompted young Miriam to boldly challenge her father? On one level, it must have been a powerful instinct about the profound importance of family life. To Miriam, family was the quintessential symbol of Jewish continuity, and even extraordinary circumstances did not justify breaking up the family unit.

But there was another factor as well – an actual prophecy that

6. *Sotah* 12a, *Pesikta Rabbati* (ed. Ish Shalom), *Piska* 43, puts Miriam's age at six at the time of this episode. (My thanks to Mr. Zvi Erenyi of the Mendel Gottesman Library for his help in locating this source.)

Miriam received at this young age, informing her that her mother was destined to give birth to a son who would eventually become the redeemer of Israel.[7] Indeed, it was out of this "reunion" between Amram and Yocheved that *Moshe Rabbenu* was born.

It should now be obvious how Miriam's critique of Moshe's separation from Tzipporah and her equating of Moshe's prophecy with her own find their roots in the events of Miriam's childhood. As we can see, both of these issues were intertwined with the events leading up to Moshe's birth. It was then that Miriam championed the cause of family in persuading her father to reunite with Yocheved. And it was then that Miriam began her own career as a prophet in predicting the birth of her brother. No wonder that Miriam felt justified in criticizing Moshe on both of these counts.

But the story does not end there. Both of these issues, Miriam's strong feelings for family and her identity as a prophet, were destined to become enmeshed with a third dimension – that of her father's love and acceptance. When baby Moshe was born, the entire house filled with a spiritual light. Amram then turned to his daughter and kissed her forehead, saying: "My daughter, it seems that your prophecy will indeed be realized." But a short three months later when the baby could no longer remain in hiding, Moshe was placed in a wicker basket to virtual abandonment and concealed among the reeds at the bank of the river. At that point, Amram turned again to his daughter, this time in great disappointment, slapped her face and cynically asked: "My daughter, what has happened to your 'so called' prophecy?"[8]

As little Moshe lay in his basket upon the water, a pair of watchful eyes gazed anxiously from afar, waiting to learn the fate of the newborn baby: *"va-teitatzav achoto me-rachok le-de'ah mah ye'aseh lo"* – "And his sister stationed herself at a distance to know what would be done to him."[9]

Miriam, Moshe's eldest sibling, whose tenacity and vision made

---

7. *Sotah* 12b–13a. Miriam is referred to elsewhere as "Miriam the prophet, the sister of Aharon" (*Shemot* 15:20) – because her first prophecy came to her at a time when she was still merely the sister of Aharon prior to the birth of Moshe.
8. *Sotah*, ad loc.; *Shemot Rabbah* 1:22.
9. *Shemot* 2:4.

his birth possible, stood *"me-rachok"* (from a distance), not just distant from the baby in a geographical sense but distant from her father who had snubbed her,[10] distant from her own self who had been so certain that this baby needed to be born – *"le-de'ah mah ye'aseh lo"* – to know not just what would become of the baby but what would become of her prophecy which now hung precariously in the balance. Miriam knew that the fate of this baby was inextricably linked with that of her own – her belief in the preservation of the family unit, her identity as a prophet, and her reconciliation with her father. So Miriam waited as only a loving sister could.

Suddenly Moshe's life was miraculously saved by the most unlikely of sources – Pharaoh's daughter. When Pharaoh's daughter requested a Jewish woman to nurse the baby, Miriam promptly emerged and offered the services of the baby's own mother, Yocheved.[11] Miriam had now found peace with herself and with her father. Her prophecy was authentic after all. Her faith in the power of the family had proved correct. Her father's love would yet return.

This was Miriam as a child. Many years later, these same factors resurface, in *Parashat Beha'alotekha*, but in a different context. Once again, we find Miriam championing the cause of family unity – this time in her criticism of her brother, Moshe, for separating from Tzipporah. And once again, it was Miriam's confidence in her own prophetic status that led her to equate herself with Moshe. This time, however, she was not right. Moshe's situation was different because Moshe was different. And *Hashem* knew that Miriam had to learn this lesson in a painful manner.

When Miriam was stricken with *tzara'at* and sentenced to seclusion for her sin, it reopened old wounds from her past by triggering bitter memories of her estrangement from her father. We may now understand why *Hashem* drew the analogy of her father having spat in her face – *"ve-aviha yarok yarak be-faneha"* (*Bemidbar* 12:14). The Divine rebuke was to Miriam today what her father's slap must have felt like many years before (*Tosafot, Da'at Zekeinim*, ad loc.).[12] Miriam's current feelings of

10. See Maharzu to *Shemot Rabbah* 1:22.
11. *Shemot* 2:7–8.
12. *Da'at Zekeinim*, in the commentary to this verse, suggests that the depiction of

abandonment were, in effect, a reliving of the paternal rejection that she had experienced as a child.

But at the same time that *Hashem* offered rebuke, He also extended a comforting hand: "And the people did not journey until Miriam was brought in."[13] As Rashi explains, Miriam was granted this special tribute of being "waited for" just as she had "waited" in her youth for her baby brother by the riverbank.[14]

Yes, Miriam was grossly mistaken in her criticism of Moshe. Her championing of family values in this case was misplaced. Her equating of Moshe's prophecy with that of her own was fallacious. But her instincts as a young girl were still valid. All that she did to insure Moshe's birth and survival was still valued and appreciated – her standing up to her father, her prophecy, her watchful devotion as a sister. She may not have risen to be a prophet of the caliber of Moshe but she was a prophet none-theless. And her passionate desire to preserve the family was a positive one. It was just that Moshe was exceptional. Miriam remained beloved even at this vulnerable time. All of this was being conveyed to Miriam through the nation's postponement of its journey.

It is truly remarkable to see how Miriam's current experience opened up a window to her past. On the one hand, the Divine punishment reawakened old wounds, images of paternal rejection – "Were her father to spit in her face." At the same time, she was also provided an opportunity to heal her past – "and the people did not journey until Miriam was brought in."

As we go about the business of our daily lives, we all carry within ourselves imprints of our youth. We are, after all, an accumulation of our personal histories. We are, at times, inclined to harbor early feelings and to re-enact deeds prompted by those feelings. Every so often, we become aware of these forces through powerful experiences that reawaken our past. Sometimes, these experiences, like Miriam's, may be traumatic.

her father "spitting in her face" specifically refers to Amram's having chastised his daughter at the time when *Moshe* was cast into the Nile. In addition, *Midrash Mishlei* (Ch. 31) recounts that after slapping her and belittling her prophecy Amram "rose up and spat in her face."

13. Ibid., 15.
14. Rashi ibid., based on *Sotah* 9b.

בהעלותך

But as with Miriam, the suffering can serve to expand our wisdom and consciousness, while also allowing for therapeutic emotional healing. As we struggle through the hurt of old wounds, we can, hopefully, come to realize that despite our disappointments, we remain worthy of God's love. As we strive to sort out right from wrong, we must bear in mind that having erred need not mean that our underlying instincts were inherently suspect. Life is about living and learning, and about healing the past.

Dr. David Shatz

שלח: *Hashkafah* and Interpretation

As numerous commentators observe, *Benei Yisrael's* movement from the desert into the Land of Israel involves a change in the way their lives are governed. They are about to move from what Netziv calls *hanhagah nissit*, a life governed by Divine miracles, to *hanhagah tiv'it*, a life governed by nature and therefore requiring practical endeavor.[1] The former is signified by the manna, the well, and the clouds that guided the people in their travels.

The *nissit/tiv'it* distinction must not be drawn rigidly. In fact, the transition to fighting battles begins before entry to the land – the Jews fight Midian, as well as Sichon and Og. Certainly the tumbling

---

1. Although the terms "practical endeavor" and "practical initiative" are often used interchangeably, Aaron Segal pointed out to me that "endeavor" is the better term in our context. For when God issues a command for the Jews to, e. g., go to battle, the Jews act on God's initiative, not their own. Likewise, if God commands us to heal illness through natural means, or to work for a living, we are engaging in practical endeavor, but do not act on our own initiative. I therefore generally use "practical endeavor," though occasionally I use "initiative."

of Jericho's walls and Yehoshua's stopping the sun, among much else, suggests a salient element of *nes* and Divine intervention even after the nation entered *Eretz Yisrael*. *Sefer Yehoshua* stresses Divine activity: you conquered by God's activity, "not by your sword and not by your bow." Rather, "I have given you a land for which you did not labor, cities that you did not build, and you eat from vineyards and olive groves that you did not plant...."[2] Finally, the Jews' fate in the land and their very ability to remain there are tied in supernatural fashion to their deeds (as in *ve-hayah im shamoa* and the *tokhachot*). Still and all, while we must be wary of overstatement, it is undeniable that after the sin of the *meraggelim*,[3] the Jews were dependent on pragmatic efforts far, far more than they were previously.

But what *religious value* should we assign to *hanhagah tiv'it* and practical endeavor? Is pragmatic endeavor a *lekhatechillah*, or rather a merely acceptable *bedi'avad* – a concession for people on a lower level of religiosity, or perhaps even a punishment for the sin of the *meraggelim*?[4] What is the proper balance between trust in God on the one hand, and human initiative on the other? How does Judaism relate to physicality– are the physical and spiritual in conflict? How do the physical qualities of *Eretz Yisrael*, its agricultural characteristics, relate to its spiritual dimension? *Parashat Shelach* is often taken to bear mightily on these questions. Given the questions' utter centrality in elucidating Jewish life and values, notably in assessing Religious Zionism, it is a welcome fact that, in the words of R. Yehudah Nachshoni, "Of all the *parashiyyot* in the Torah, that of the *meraggelim* is the most expounded (*ha-nidreshet be-yoter*) by commentators and the *derush* literature."[5]

2. *Yehoshua* 24:11–13. See also *Devarim* 6:10–11.
3. As many have pointed out, the dominant word in *Shelach* to describe the people we call "the *meraggelim*" is "*tarim*" (in *Bemidbar*), and in *Devarim* 1:22 the verb used is "*ve-yachperu*." I will refer to them generally as the "scouts," but for my purposes nothing rides on the exact translation and I will not fuss over it.
4. The significance of Adam's being consigned to physical labor with regard to the larger debate about the value of practical endeavor is beyond the scope of this essay.
5. R. Nachshoni, *Hagut Be-Parashiyyot Ha-Torah* (Bnei Brak, 1981), vol 2, p. 609. I am indebted to R. Nachshoni's discussion in my selection of pre-twentieth century commentaries. My essay focuses on the value of practical endeavor, but I have listed other questions because they are similar or related.

Shelach is a case study in how *haskhafah* (religious outlook) and interpretation interact. I will show the hashkafic presuppositions and implications of different approaches to *Shelach*, and will conclude with a general reflection on the role of *derush* (homiletics) and *hashkafah* in our approaches to Bible. My focus will be on how diverging interpretations impact upon Religious Zionism.[6] I will usually cite *mefarshim* by name, but sometimes anonymously; and for ease of exposition I will occasionally blend together comments by different commentators who share the same general viewpoint but diverge over details.

6. Saying that interpreters use "presuppositions" need not unsettle readers. With certain qualifications, there is nothing wrong with an interpreter reading the Bible through the lens of background assumptions, and in fact presuppositions may be necessary to interpret a text. The reading strategies (to use a contemporary term) of medieval rationalists and of kabbalists become unfathomable if we object to interpreting the Torah via presuppositions. The rationale for reading in light of presuppositions is that one wants the Torah to come out true by one's lights. Further, all of us approach narrative texts with presuppositions about human psychology and morality that enable us to interpret the motivations of protagonists and the Torah's assessment of their actions. Likewise many texts, particularly in *nevi'im* and *ketuvim*, require for proper interpretation views about historical context. So presuppositions are not only admissible but often are necessary.

But as I said there are caveats. The interpreter must be open to having his or her presuppositions refuted by the text. While it is often said that, given a sufficiently resolute and ingenious interpreter, every text can logically fit any theory, some interpretations that an interpreter resorts to in defense of a theory will be too far out to merit acceptance. But there is no ironclad rule, since sometimes an interpretation is based on a virtually certain presupposition and the text must be interpreted with the presupposition firmly in place. Thus, Maimonides interpreted all texts that ascribed a body to God in a way that nullifies anthropomorphism because he had a proof that God is incorporeal. Note, as another complication, that an interpreter's "presupposition" may not really be a *pre*supposition but rather might be derived from his or her reading of the very text under discussion. In these cases, obviously the thinker's philosophy does not justify readings of the text that are implausible when taken in isolation.

The relevance of these complexities will become clear later when we assess R. Eliyahu Dessler's readings or potential readings of texts that *prima facie* refute his theory about practical endeavor.

שלח

PRELIMINARIES

The quest for the *parashah*'s meaning is complicated by an ostensibly contradictory account in *Sefer Devarim* (*Devarim* 1:22–46). My discussion assumes that, as many *mefarshim* posit, the *prima facie* discrepancies between *Shelach* and *Parashat Devarim* can be reconciled by positing roughly the following sequence:

- The entire people express to Moshe the desire to send scouts to report on the best path to enter the Land and on the state of the cities' security (*Devarim* 1:22).
- Moshe is either commanded by God to accede to the people's request (*"Shelach lekha anashim ve-yaturu et Eretz Kena'an"*), or (as in the *midrash* [*Tanchuma* 5; see also *Sotah* 34b]) to make his own decision (*"Shelach lekha"*) (*Bemidbar* 13:1–2).[7]
- In either case Moshe approves of the people's requests (*Devarim* 1:23 – *"va-yitav be-einai ha-davar"* – "I approved of the idea").[8]
- Moshe picks the scouts (both *Shelach* and *Devarim*).
- In *Shelach* (*Bemidbar* 13: 17–20), when he charges the scouts, Moshe expands on the people's request (made in *Devarim* 1:22). He elaborates on the questions about the cities' security and defense capabilities, and he asks a new set of questions about whether the land is "good" or "bad" and agriculturally rich.
- The scouts go on their mission.
- They report favorably on the land, but unfavorably on (in a nutshell) the military prospects.[9] Panic and despair follow.

The respective narratives and the differences between the accounts do not end there, but this will suffice for now. Nor will I here seek reasons

---

7. Rashi to *Bemidbar* 13:2 (apparently paraphrasing or building upon this *midrash*) sees the sending of the scouts as a setup – God is giving them the "opportunity" to sin and be denied entry.
8. I will assume that if he was *commanded* by God to send regardless of his own wishes, then *"va-yitav be-einai ha-davar"* would mean "I understood God's reasons," not "I decided God was right."
9. Rabbi Morris Besdin a"h called the *meraggelim*'s word *"efes"* (*Bemidbar* 13:4) the "editorial but."

for the striking differences in narration.[10] We should also note that, although the *parashah* does not wear its import on its sleeve as regards *our* question – the value of practical endeavor – certain lessons and messages are reasonably clear.

- We must not be intimidated by our enemies, for God is with us.[11]
- We must not reject the land that God promised us.
- We betray God and break the covenant when we spurn His gift.[12]
- We are not worthy of that gift unless we value it.[13]
- The land is very good in material terms (*Bemidbar* 14:7).[14]

One can adjust or fine-grain these messages in various ways (e.g., saying that valuing land is one thing, valuing a state another; or saying, with

10. For a close analysis that goes beyond harmonization of sequence, see Rav Chanoch Waxman, "'For I am the Lord that Heals You' (*Shemot* 15:26): Of Spy Stories and Heroic Measures," http://vbm-torah.org/archive/parsha66/37–66shelach.htm.

11. As an aside, I note that fear does not necessarily reflect lack of trust. Knowing you have to swim without your parent actually holding on creates fear, no matter how emphatically the parent announces you will swim successfully – and no matter how much you trust. Fear can be experienced even while watching a movie, where there is no belief that one is unsafe. Phobias involve fear without belief in impending calamity. Therefore, when Moshe orders the people not to fear (*Devarim* 1:29), he is going beyond asking them to trust. And as opposed to mere fear, the people's certainty that they would die in battle and therefore must return to Egypt (see *Bemidbar* 14:3, *Devarim* 1:27–28) – their implication that God would be totally out of the picture – is truly amazing.

12. Admittedly, "gift" may not be the best word, since the Land is given as part of a covenant. See Harry Orlinsky, "The Biblical Concept of the Land of Israel: Cornerstone of the Covenant between God and Israel," in *The Land of Israel: Jewish Perspectives*, ed. Lawrence Hoffman (Notre Dame, IN: University of Notre Dame Press, 1986), 1–23.

13. The people feel something much worse than not valuing it – they think God is giving it to them because He hates them! (See *Devarim* 1:27.)

14. The scouts do not dispute the land's agricultural goodness, and even bring back a sample of the land's bounty. But as *Akeidat Yitzchak* notes, they do not value its spiritual potential (Cf., however, Ramban to *Devarim* 1:25 on whether, as per Rashi, only Kalev and Yehoshua endorsed the land's goodness.) Why Moshe asked about physical virtues, and indeed why the *Chumash* highlights them in general, is an interesting question, but I will not pursue it here except implicitly.

much Biblical support, that God protects us in the land only when we are good – sins lead to exile). But at their core the messages seem easily derivable from the *parashah*, and in fact, I think, are its *main* messages.

What is unanswered is whether the change to practical endeavor is for better or for worse. Those who mine *Shelach* and the *Devarim* narrative for an answer at times elevate that answer to the level of a central message. In truth, any implication the episode may carry vis-à-vis the value of practical endeavor should not eclipse the other, perhaps more crucial messages I identified. With that caveat, I proceed.

THE DEVALUATION OF PRACTICAL ENDEAVOR

As a first example of how *hashkafah* can drive the interpretation of *Shelach*, let us consider R. Eliyahu Dessler. The late Jewish philosopher Eliezer Goldman crisply described R. Dessler's theology as "a frontal attack upon the modern ethos with its emphasis on foresight, calculation, planning, and domination of nature through knowledge of its workings."[15] R. Dessler championed an ethos of *bittachon* that deprecates practical endeavor. The human being must view God as the cause of everything. A person must put in just a *little* effort of his or her own, in order to be *tempted* to believe that it is his or her endeavors that produce results (e.g. *parnasah*, livelihood). To resist that self-created temptation, to see that nature is not a true cause, is to pass a crucial test of faith. One must not view one's welfare as dependent on anything but Divine response to his or her perceptions and deeds.

True to his principles, R. Dessler maintains (in a larger discussion of the balance between trust and practical endeavor) that, once the people requested that scouts be sent (as per the *Devarim* account), once they showed they would not rely on faith and minimal effort alone – then they had done something wrong, or at least non-ideal.[16] Does this mean

---

15. See Goldman, "Responses to Modernity in Orthodox Jewish Thought," *Studies in Contemporary Jewry* 2 (1986), 55.

16. See *Mikhtav Me-Eliyahu*, ed. Aryeh Carmell and Alter Halpern (Jerusalem, 2000), 1:187–95. An English translation is *Strive for Truth*, trans. Aryeh Carmell, Part Two, (New York: Feldheim, 1985), 263–282. The brief quotes I have from R. Dessler are from that translation. R. Dessler's account is characteristically subtle, nuanced and attuned to psychological complexities. The scouts' motive was not proper, he says;

that Moshe erred in sending the scouts? No, for "the level they were now on," R. Dessler says, "made it necessary" for Moshe to act in accordance with their request. The very request showed that they were on a level that required practical endeavor on their part. One might add that this is why Moshe does not rebuke them for their request.

There is thus a triple sin (i) the people wanting scouts in the first place,[17] (ii) the scouts issuing the report they did, and (iii) the people reacting with fear and a desire to return to Egypt. The comments in *The Chumash: The Stone Edition* that precede the *haftarah* of *Shelach* maintain, likewise, that were it not for the sin of sending *meraggelim*, those who entered *Eretz Yisrael* would not have had to fight.

> If the Jewish people had not dispatched a mission to survey the Land, G-d would have permitted them to enter *Eretz Yisrael* without meeting resistance and without requiring weapons…. Since the Israelites erroneously believed that acquisition of the Land would be dependent upon military efforts, they viewed the amassing of strategic information as a necessity. By acting according to this fundamental misconception, Israel indicated that it had lost sight of its manifest destiny… Because the Jews failed to rely on Divine intervention, they were subject to a diminution of Divine guidance, resulting in the obligation to participate actively in securing their inheritance. As a result, Israel had to shoulder its weapons and gird its loins.[18]

but they were deluded about their motives and came up with a rationalization, oblivious of the fact they were succumbing to the *yetzer ha-ra* and tilting toward too much practical endeavor.

17. Again, for the wrong reasons, as per the previous note.

18. Within the devaluationist school, R. Dessler's is not the only understanding of why Moshe consented to the people's request and dispatched scouts. Some suggest that Moshe's command to report back on the strength of the inhabitants and on the security of the cities was an attempt to lead the scouts to appreciate the strength of the enemy precisely so that they will realize that God will create the victory, as it could not occur in the course of nature by human activity. *Eretz Yisrael* is the land God is giving ("*asher ani noten li-Vnei Yisrael*" (*Bemidbar* 13:2)), not one that people are *taking*. The scouts misunderstood Moshe's directive and supposed that victory must come by natural means. Hence their fear and pessimism.

The denigration of *hanhagah tiv'it* and practical endeavor means that the existence that the Jews led in the Land, militarily and possibly agriculturally,[19] was not only spiritually inferior but was a punishment, *middah ke-neged middah*. Efforts to wage battle were antithetical to an ideal spiritual existence, but sin made them necessary.[20]

AN ASSESMENT OF THE DEVALUATION APPROACH[21]

R. Dessler held that his overall philosophy follows Ramban's.[22] But *prima facie*, his understanding of the scout episode conflicts with Ramban's. Ramban sees Moshe's command to examine the military situation, to wage battle using the best means available through nature, as proper and necessary.[23] R. Dessler would likely not wish to contradict Ramban, yet their views ostensibly contrast.

In fairness, though, despite the widespread invocation of Ramban as affirming the propriety of sending scouts, near the end of his comments Ramban seems to reverse course. He quotes *"Da'at rabboteinu"* (the view of *Chazal*) to the effect that the people should have followed the cloud. Ramban's comments need to be reconciled, and one method for harmonizing them is to use R. Dessler's approach, as the latter himself suggests.[24] Furthermore, for a devaluationist other than R. Dessler,

19. For various reasons, the agricultural question is more complex.

20. In *Devarim*, Moshe faults the people for lacking faith in God (*Devarim* 1:32–33). But this point is consistent with a positive approach to practical endeavor, since those who champion such an approach do not rule out Divine guidance operating as well.

21. I call it "devaluationist" rather than "quietist" because R. Dessler, as noted, counsels some minimal practical endeavor, and believes that people on a lower level must resort to it. R. Yitzchak Blau noted another path to devaluation, viz. a moral one, stressing the ethically problematic nature of warfare. See note 39 below.

22. The claim that for Nachmanides all that happens is the result of Divine causation is problematic. See David Berger, "Miracles and the Natural Order in Nahmanides," in *Rabbi Moshe Nahmanides: Explorations in His Religious and Literary Virtuosity*, ed. Isadore Twersky (Cambridge, MA: Harvard University Press, 1987), 107–28.

23. In his discussions of sorcery, divination, astrology and medicine, Ramban regards resorting to pragmatic efforts and the laws of nature as spiritually inferior. See his commentary to *Vayikra* 26:11 and *Devarim* 18:9–15.

24. See *Mikhtav Me-Eliyahu* I:190–99. A key question is whether Ramban is only trying to understand *Chazal*'s reading while adhering to his own as *peshat*. In very helpful correspondence about the seeming discrepancy within Ramban's comments, Mi-

Ramban's holding a contrasting view may not be a powerful problem. Hence critics will have a stronger case if they pose objections from the Biblical text instead of from the commentaries.

A difficulty that is genuinely based on the Biblical text is that Moshe himself, with impunity, later sends scouts to Yazer and battles the Emori there (*Bemidbar* 21:32). He also fights Midian (*Bemidbar* ch. 31), Sichon, and Og at God's command. Perhaps more tellingly – because it *precedes* the sending of scouts – there is another, rather strange incident in *Parashat Beha'alotekha*: we are told about the clouds that guided *Benei Yisrael*, and are informed that "by the word of God they would travel, and by the word of God they would camp" (see *Bemidbar* 9:9–23). Yet, not long after (*Bemidbar* 10:29–34), Moshe asks Yitro (taking "Chovav" to be Yitro) to accompany the Jews and says, "*ve-hayita lanu le-einayim*." Ramban, Abarbanel, R. Hirsch, Netziv and others take this to mean "be for us a scout" – someone with the practical wisdom to lead us on our travels and even (so some of these interpreters mention) our battles. Yitro's non-Jewish lineage suggests he possesses practical wisdom. To some commentators it even seems that had Yitro acceded to Moshe's request (it is debated whether he did), he would have led, rather than the Ark.[25] So we have the cloud on the one hand (*hanhagah nissit*) and Moshe's request to Yitro on the other. The point seems to be that now or eventually the Jews will need to combine guidance by the cloud with practical ways of scouting, and it is natural to take this as a *lekhatechillah*.[26]

chelle Levine noted that in his comment on 13:2, "he does not provide a concluding statement where he goes back to his *peshat* reading, as one might anticipate after his protracted discussion of his own opinion. Nevertheless, just before quoting the opinion of *Chazal*, Ramban concludes that the main sin was that the people themselves asked for the mission, while it should have been Moshe who initiated it. And Ramban appears to be applying his *peshat* considerations as the basis for understanding *Chazal*'s reading of the Israelites' sin." For another context in which Ramban stresses practical endeavor, see his commentary to *Bemidbar* 1:45, concerning the need for a census.

25. Abarbanel writes that "because Yitro, who was a *chakham* and knew the desert paths, did not wish to go with them, the Ark traveled ahead of them...." (*Bemidbar* 10:11, ad loc.).
26. Whether Yitro acceded is not clear, and the answer may make some difference to

Does this objection stymie one who deprecates practical endeavor? Not necessarily. He would say that Moshe knew that the people were not worthy of continued guidance by the cloud, so his request to Yitro was of a piece with his sending of the scouts – a concession born of the realization that this people was not worthy of supernatural guidance. To embellish this account, a devaluationist might note that the request to Yitro is made after the Jews camp in the ill-fated Midbar Paran, giving the request an ominous tone. The later dispatching of scouts to Yazer can be explained similarly – as can Yehoshua's sending *meraggelim* and fighting battles.[27]

This line of reply will frustrate critics. It is beginning to look like the devaluation approach is un-falsifiable, and in particular that it cannot be refuted by appeal to other missions involving practical endeavors. In every case in which Moshe seems to sanction practical endeavor, devaluationists will assert that he did so only because the people were on an inferior level. To critics, this response will seem *ad hoc* and forced. Critics might argue against it *ex silentio* (i.e., no explicit denigration of Moshe's practical endeavors is found in the text), or may argue, more sharply, that it conflicts with the surface, straightforward implication – the plain meaning – of the text. "Plain meaning" here designates the meaning we would assign if we took the text in isolation and read it starting from a philosophically neutral standpoint. The devaluationist can claim a plausible understanding of the Biblical narrative only if he reads it in light of his controlling assumptions about what theological position is correct. His is not the reading one would derive by taking the text in isolation.

"But so what?" a devaluationist might legitimately ask. If you enter an infallible text with a certain theory – in this case, that practical endeavor is bad – and you believe you have strong independent grounds for the theory, you will select from competing interpretations one that

our understanding of events. For example, maybe if he had agreed, the later ill-fated scouting mission would not have been necessary. Better trust the *"einayim"* (eyes) of Yitro than those of the scouts, whose eyes are referred to *Bemidbar* 13:33.

27. Cf. the complex explanation in the *Stone Chumash* (pp. 1184–1185) of the spy mission initiated by Yehoshua.

accords with your view, not one that is inimical. This selection procedure seems reasonable.[28] It is true that if the devaluationist interpreter bases his *hashkafah* entirely on the very text that is being wielded as an objection, it is not compelling to use the hashkafic position as a presupposition in interpreting the text. That procedure would be blatantly circular. So, if a devaluationist bases his devaluation on his construal of the narratives about Moshe and Yitro and about the wars (that Moshe acted as he did only because the people were on an inferior level), it is appropriate to use those texts as an objection. After all, his is not the interpretation one would arrive at by taking those texts in isolation. R. Dessler, however, has what by his lights are ample independent bases for devaluation, that is, bases that do not include the episode of the scouts.[29] So he is reasonable in construing the seemingly problematic episodes as reflecting the people's being on an inferior level. I hasten to add that it is equally reasonable for one who enters the text with a philosophy that values practical endeavor as a *lekhattechillah*, or even one who enters the text with a neutral stance on the issue, to reject R. Dessler's interpretation and to follow the straightforward meaning, based, e. g., on the Yitro episode, that practical endeavor is an acceptable and even laudable step. Nonetheless, R. Dessler cannot be refuted by reference to texts like the Yitro episode or the sending of scouts to Yazer.

But there remains for critics of devaluationist readings the option of discrediting the devaluationist philosophy on logical grounds. And indeed the devaluation approach – as applied to the Biblical episodes – faces logical difficulties. Granted, if one assumes that *every human being* (or every Jew) is capable of rising to a level where he or she devalues practical endeavor, then one can conclude the Jews were at fault for acting in a practical way. But if one assumes that only *special* individuals can rise to these heights, would not God be unreasonable in (supposedly) frowning on the sending of scouts? It would be unreasonable for

---

28. See note 6 above.

29. Aside from citing other Biblical and rabbinic texts, R. Dessler argues that assigning causal powers to anything but God is *avodah zarah*, and that all relations put forth as causal are contingent. For an assessment of these arguments, see my "Divine Intervention and Religious Sensibilities," in my *Jewish Thought in Dialogue: Essays on Thinkers, Theologies, and Moral Theories* (Boston, Academic Studies Press, 2009).

God to expect every human being to ascend to the level required for dispensation with practical endeavor. Perhaps in this regard He simply accepts the inherent limitations of human nature. As Rambam notes in *Guide for the Perplexed* (III:32), if human nature were perfect, God would not have to give *mitzvot* that seek to improve us. *Mitzvot* address a non-ideal situation, but they are obviously not a punishment. God elsewhere makes concessions to human nature and does not punish people for giving in to their nature; think of *eshet yefat to'ar* (*Devarim* 21:10–14). The "concession" view and the "punishment" view thus sit in tension. Punishing people for not doing what they are not equipped to do is not what we would expect of God.

Thus, our conclusion to this point is that the devaluation reading cannot be refuted on purely textual grounds, but its reading of the text is predicated on a philosophy that is logically problematic.

THE INTEGRATIONIST APPROACH

We turn now to those interpreters who value practical endeavor and find that evaluation in the text.

Why should one value practical endeavor? Several commonly heard arguments are not altogether persuasive.

(a) Some who hold practical endeavor in esteem see a lack of practical endeavor as copping out of "responsibility." They see in the Israelites a failure to assume "responsibility" when, after the scouts' report, they fall into panic and dread. It is difficult to see, however, why assuming responsibility must entail *practical* endeavor. Do we not take responsibility by performing or else failing to perform *mitzvot,* or by striving for knowledge of God or *devekut*?

(b) Others note that lack of practical endeavor entails a slave mentality, and argue that *Benei Yisrael* could not enter the land bearing the mindset of meek, oppressed slaves that they bore in Egypt. But this is not wholly convincing either: isn't God our master and we His servants ("*ki avadai hem*" – "they are my servants," *Vayikra* 25:42)? Even though God is our father as well as our master, we must at times exemplify a slave mentality. Furthermore, what we want to know is, in essence, what is wrong with a slave mentality. We cannot explain that just by saying the Bible thinks the mentality is bad. Our question remains – why is practical endeavor valuable?[30]

(c) For Netziv, the people preferred not to live by *hanhagah nissit* because such a system is oppressive and frightening – every act is scrutinized, every violation punished immediately.[31] *Hanhagah tiv'it* is a way of living with less pressure.[32] But couldn't God handle this by not dishing out punishments so readily and consistently?

(d) Certain *mitzvot* require cultivating the land and driving out enemies. But this does not answer the question *why* one should value that activity, that is, why God should command battle and agricultural labor.

The Lubavitcher Rebbe *zt"l* provides an account of *Shelach* that could *both* explain why practical endeavor is valuable *and* construe *Shelach* in a way that is opposite to the devaluation approach.[33] His springboard is two questions: How could the people who had seen God's miracles suddenly despair? And why does Kalev silence the people by saying *"aloh na'aleh ve-yarashnu otah"* – affirming their military capability – rather than arguing from the miracles they had seen in the past? The error of the people, the Rebbe replies, was to think of *hanhagah nissit* and *hanhagah tiv'it* as mutually exclusive, as either-or propositions, and to miss seeing the spiritual dimension of practical endeavor.

The Rebbe's idea is that when the people say *"lo nukhal la'alot,"* they mean: we cannot *ascend spiritually* if we seek to control our destinies

---

30. On slave mentality, see Shalom Carmy, "Why Should a Slave Want Freedom? A Literary and Theological Reflection on *Gittin* 12b–13a," in *Mishpetei Shalom*, ed. Yamin Levy (Jersey City, NJ: KTAV, 2010), 123–38.

31. See *Ha'amek Davar* to *Bemidbar* 13:2.

32. In *Devarim* 5:20–28, the people approach Moshe with the request not to hear God's voice lest they die. This is a different sort of pressure, but the general idea – that they do not want a direct relationship with God – is the same as Netziv's explanation in *Shelach*. In *Devarim* Ch. 5, God approves their request, while one senses that Moshe did not do so before God spoke. I am not sure why the presence of a direct, close nexus between a deed and the doer's welfare is different from what God describes in *"ve-hayah im shamoa"* and the *tokhachot*. True, the latter two involve the collective, but so does Netziv's context.

33. *Torah Studies*, adapted by R. Jonathan Sacks (Third edition, London: The Lubavitch Foundation, 1992), 239–45; from *Likkutei Sichot*, vol. IV, 1041–1047.

by practical wisdom. This is a mistake – a profound one. Here are quotations from the Rebbe's *sichah*, as adapted by R. Jonathan Sacks:

> Their fear was, that a concern to work the land and make a living might eventually leave the Israelites with progressively less time and energy for the service of G-d…Their opinion was that spirituality flourishes best in seclusion and withdrawal…In a land where every benefit had to be worked for, their spirituality might decline and be defeated.

> And yet, the spies were wrong. The purpose of a life lived in Torah is not the elevation of the soul: it is the sanctification of the world.[34]

This, says the Rebbe, is why Kalev did not dwell on God's past miracles when he spoke to the people. The people needed to understand not Divine guidance but rather the value of practical endeavor. And now we can also see how distinguished representatives of their tribes could have sinned. It was their desire for spirituality that led to their error.

With characteristic cleverness, this Chasidic interpretation understands Kalev's words *"aloh na'aleh ve-yarashnu otah"* as follows: the spies thought that *hanhagah tiv'it* is a *yeridah*. In truth, as Kalev recognized, it is a twofold *aliyyah* – elevated physicality and, through that, elevated spirituality. Judaism stands for the celebration of an integrated life, in which physicality rises to the level of spirituality through human striving and action.[35] Our earlier observation about Yitro augments the integrationist approach.

R. Sacks quotes this approach (as "a Chasidic explanation") in the closing paragraph of an essay dealing with the dichotomy drawn by R. Joseph Soloveitchik zt"l between Adam the first and Adam the sec-

---

34. Both quotations are from p. 242 of the *sichah*. The Rebbe here stresses agricultural endeavor, while devaluationists spoke of the scouting mission itself and the battles. The Rebbe's account is not devoid of reference to battles, however, since that was the people's first fear.

35. Why did Kalev challenge the spies and Yehoshua didn't? Some say that Yehoshua remained silent because, as the future leader, he was reluctant to look self-aggrandizing by encouraging entry into the Land.

ond.[36] However large the general theological differences between the Rav and the Rebbe may be, it is fair to draw a comparison. Just as the Rav – so contrary to R. Dessler's deprecation of human endeavor – saw humanity's attempt to create technology, governments, and economic structures, as the fulfillment of a religious mandate, just as he declared that "The Halakhah believes that there is only one world – not divisible into secular and hallowed sectors,"[37] so too the Rebbe does not see practical endeavor as secular. The reason for valuing practical endeavor is that Jews are commanded to hallow the secular – a powerful idea that is accepted across a broad spectrum of the Jewish world.

It is deeply ironic that the perspective on the sin of the *meraggelim* I just sketched is situated in Chasidut. For the integrationist approach would seem to translate into an affirmation of the religious significance of the present State of Israel, something Chasidim are to say the least reluctant to endorse.[38] Though the irony is worth noting, it does not matter for our purposes. My concern is with its content – its potential as an interpretation favorable to Religious Zionism – and not its provenance.[39]

I do not know whether the Rebbe intended his suggestion as

---

36. Jonathan Sacks, "Alienation and Faith," *Tradition* 13:4 and 14:1 (Spring-Summer 1973, double issue), 161. R. Sacks registers disagreements with the Rav, but need not contest my analogy between the Rav and the Rebbe with regard to the sanctioning of practical endeavor.

37. *The Lonely Man of Faith* (New York: Doubleday, 1992), 84.

38. Some Chasidic sources even spiritualized *Eretz Yisrael* to the point where it became a state of mind. See Marc Saperstein, "The Land of Israel in Pre-Modern Jewish Thought: A History of Two Rabbinic Statements," in *The Land of Israel*, ed. Hoffman, 188–209. The Rebbe's approach embraces the land's physicality, tying its *gashmiyyut* to *ruchniyyut*. In the service of Religious Zionism, Rav Kook saw Eretz Yisrael as the meeting place of Heaven and Earth, and viewed the return to the Land, to a physical home, as a *techiyyat ha-metim*, resurrection of the dead. But in "Ha-Milchama" (*Orot* [Jerusalem: Mossad HaRav Kook, 1985]), 14, he expresses the view that Jews should remain withdrawn from politics until politics is no longer ruthless.

39. There are other ways to explain the scouts' error in terms that are *melammed zekhut*. For example, as R. Yitzchak Blau noted, one could attribute to them moral hesitations (of some sort) about waging battle. Cf. Emmanuel Levinas, *Nine Talmudic Readings*, trans. Annette Aronowicz (Bloomington, IN: Indiana University Press, 1994), 51–69. Cf. Yuval Cherlow, *Achararekha Narutzah* (Tel Aviv: Yedi'ot Aharonot and Sifrei Hemed), 199. I thank Warren Zev Harvey and R. Hayyim Angel, respectively,

peshat and, for that matter, where he or other Chasidic interpreters draw the line between *peshat* and *derush* (generally translated as "homiletics").[40] Be that as it may, as *peshat*, the Rebbe's approach – disappointingly to Religious Zionists like myself – seems strained. For its basic implication is that the people feared practical endeavor not because they would fall physically, but because they would fall spiritually. The text, by contrast, suggests a people lacking in spirituality and spiritual aspiration. And would God wax angry at them for wanting spirituality?[41]

CONCLUDING REFLECTIONS

In our time many literary theorists and philosophers regard it as a truism that textual readings reflect an interpreter's background assumptions. This thesis seems to be intended both descriptively (i.e., this is how interpreters do in fact interpret) and normatively (i.e., it is admissible to interpret this way, or even – a bolder claim – this is how interpreters *should* interpret). An interpreter will select a textual reading based on a general religious sensibility, even when in isolation the reading seems less plausible than alternatives. (In note 6 I have offered a more nuanced statement of the point.) Once one may legitimately apply background assumptions to justify a particular reading of a Biblical text, one person's "mere" *derush* (homiletics) will be another's *peshat*.

What we have before us is a case study in this theme. Consider the approach to the episode of the *meraggelim* that sees practical endeavor as a sin that is punished measure for measure by later having to rely on practical endeavor. That approach leaves us, as I wrote earlier, with

for these two references. The Rebbe's motive is presumably to mitigate the severity of the sin of the *dor ha-midbar*, but as I note later, it is extremely difficult to explain God's wrath given his stance.

40. Abundant samples of *derush* are found in sermons, *vertlakh*, and other forms of rabbinic discourse that offer religious and ethical insights without seeming to capture *peshat* or even pretending to. I know that "*peshat* and *derash*" is a more familiar pairing than "peshat and *derush*." But *derush* has its own flavor.

41. It is one thing if God were simply to decide that this generation cannot do the job in *Eretz Yisrael*; it is another for Him to be so angry. In fact, *Akeidat Yitzchak* asks why it should matter to God that they rejected a land with (apparently merely) good physical attributes such as "flowing with milk and honey." His reply is that they did not want to ascend to spiritual heights, which the Land would enable them to do.

a discomfiting feeling about how *Am Yisrael* acted from the moment they entered the land – their activist mode of acquiring the land was not what God ideally wanted – and about how *Medinat Yisrael* conducts its business, from its birth until this very day. The integrationist interpretation – however fiercely Chasidic thinkers would have repudiated this application – essentially supports Religious Zionism. So Religious Zionists would resist the devaluationist reading, and (based on the other cases of Moshe taking initiative) will find the *peshat* in conflict with it, even though R. Dessler has a *"terutz"* (reply) that makes the text logically compatible with his position (viz., the reply that Moshe knew the people were on a lower level and therefore approached Yitro and later sent scouts). We Religious Zionists are able to reject R. Dessler because we value practical endeavor, but were we advocates of his ideology, we could accept his *terutz* concerning the other cases of initiative. So both his reading and our resistance illustrate how *hashkafah* and religious sensibilities affect interpretation. Matters will remain this way unless the general *hashkafah* of one or both interpreters is shown to be wrong on independent grounds, or some decisive, unanswerable textual objection is brought forth to one of the positions. I have suggested a logical objection to the devaluationist position and a textual objection to the integrationist reading of the *parashah*.

To reiterate, close textual reading militates against the Rebbe's interpretation because it is highly implausible that the people were looking for spirituality, and difficult to fathom why God would be angry if they did. Here, I think the textual objection is powerful enough to militate against the Rebbe's reading as a candidate for *peshat*. In his case – unlike R. Dessler's – the thesis that background assumptions validate a reading that is not plausible when the text is viewed in isolation, will not rescue the interpretation as *peshat*. For whereas R. Dessler offers an explanation of those texts that *prima facie* refute him, no suggestion has been made about how the integrationist approach can cope with the textual difficulty that faces it (viz., that the people are not portrayed as seeking spirituality). Also, the fact that spirituality requires practical endeavor does not require, as a corollary, that to opt out of practical endeavor out of a desire for greater spirituality merits divine anger to the degree expressed in the narratives. So, even if (a) *hashkafah* can or must legitimately influence interpretation, (b) one thinks Religious Zionist *hashkafah* is correct, one should admit that the Rebbe's reading of the sin of the scouts and of the people is not *peshat* but rather *derush*.

Let us, however, place these problems with the Rebbe's interpretation in perspective. Rejecting his reading does not invalidate other pro-initiative readings of *Shelach*, those based on inferences from Moshe's earlier and later practical endeavors. Rather, rejecting his reading qua *peshat* merely means that the Rebbe's strongly put thesis that a life without practical endeavor is lacking in spirituality – even if true – is not being expressed by the particular text we are discussing. That an antecedently held thesis is true does not mean that the text expresses it anywhere and everywhere. And at the end of the day – to make a point that readers may have thought of much earlier in this essay – it is not clear that support of Religious Zionism depends on whether practical endeavor is *ideal* (nor even on whether our ancestors were punished for it). *"Ein somekhin al ha-nes"* – "we do not rely on miracles" is an established principle of *Halakhah* – and at the bottom line full endeavor may be required even if practical endeavor is not ideal. Hence, classifying the Rebbe's account as *derush* does not invalidate Religious Zionism.

But I would like to insert one more piece of perspective. Suppose we ask the following question, which applies to all *derush* and not only the Rebbe's: having decided that an explanation is *derush* and not *peshat*, should we teach and disseminate it?

I say yes, but let me explain the question. The Modern Orthodox community, both scholars and laity, have produced brilliant, innovative micro-analyses of Tanakh using the best literary techniques and have drawn large and profound implications. I am an avid follower of this genre and on occasion have ventured outside my primary field (philosophy) and developed my own readings of Biblical texts using such methods. It is a supreme achievement of the Modern Orthodox community that it has made the study and understanding of Tanakh soar to staggering levels of quality and interest. But R. Norman Lamm has lamented the decline of *derush* as an art form and a mode of study.[42] Out-

---

42. "Notes of an Unrepentant Darshan," in his *Seventy Faces: Articles of Faith* (Hoboken, NJ: KTAV, 2002), vol. 2, pp. 94–107.

side of sermons, life cycle events, and certain other contexts, *derush* is at
times denigrated. *"Derush,"* writes R. Lamm, "has, for some, become a
pejorative synonym for a form of rhetoric that is pretentious, superficial,
and lacking in intellectual value or respectability."[43] Indeed, I have often
heard certain attempts at *Chumash* interpretation in public *shiurim* denigrated or dismissed as "mere *derush*." The attitude seems to be: weaving
in *Midrash* – that could be fine;[44] citing or creating *derush* – emphatically
no. I maintain, in contrast, that while we must make clear to listeners
and readers what is *peshat* and what is *derush* (not always an easy line to
draw), we need to use *derush* more – in classrooms and adult education
settings – and to get across that, in R. Lamm's words, it is "a respectable
discipline with its own skills and traditions and methodology as well as
an invaluable asset for the practicing rabbi."[45] We can explain to students
the nature of the genre, bring examples judiciously to colorfully introduce or capture ideas, relate the examples to the outlooks of particular
darshanim, and so on. To repeat, we must identify *derush* as such, so as
not to create the justly lamented mindset that the *Chumash* says that
Abraham smashed his father's idols or Yaakov learned at the yeshivah
of *Shem Ve-Ever.* But let us teach *derush,* clearly identified as such, for its
inspirational value along with its historical importance in our tradition
as a mode of expounding Biblical and rabbinic texts.

Ironically, many accept the value of *derush* as a serious enterprise
without realizing it. The most powerful Jewish analysis of a religious
person's relationship to the modern world is Rav Soloveitchik's *The
Lonely Man of Faith.* The essay is responsive to an important textual
question, and convincing in its basic assertion that *Bereishit* Chs. 1 and

43. Ibid., 95. I add that the very word *"derush"* is now unfamiliar to some or perhaps
many Orthodox Jews (albeit the term "derash" is well known).
44. Actually, some approaches to teaching *Tanakh* resist teaching Midrash as part of
Tanakh study. The focus is exclusively on *"peshuto shel mikra,"* as noted by R. Mosheh
Lichtenstein, "Fear of God: The Beginning of Wisdom and the End of Tanakh
Study," in *Yirat Shamayim: The Awe, Reverence, and Fear of God,* ed. Marc D. Stern
(Jersey City, NJ: The Michael Scharf Publication Trust of the Yeshiva University
Press, 2008), 135–62. His view about *Midrash* and my view about *derush* correspond.
I thank Stuart Halpern for noting the relevance of R. Lichtenstein's article.
45. Ibid., 94. R. Lamm is contrasting the low interest in *derush* with the great interest
in halakhic *shiurim,* while I am referring to two forms of Bible study.

2 refer to two ways of regarding human beings or two aspects of human personality. Yet the idea that Bereishit Ch. 1 can be taken so far as to mandate that humanity must pursue technology, economics, political science, and the fashioning of norms, ultimately is *derush* – of a great and powerful sort. To take next a case that perhaps more clearly ranks as *derush*, when Abraham said to the Hittites, "I am both a *ger* and a *toshav*" (*Bereishit* 23:4), "a stranger and a resident," he did not mean that although different from them he will join in the quest to fight disease.[46] The Rav's well known five *derashot* to Mizrachi in support of Zionism are generally speaking exactly that – *derashot*, though he does provide some non-text-based arguments for his positions too. Yosef was not referring to the development of technology when he dreamt of the moon and the stars, nor was Rivkah referring to a state engaging in "economics, finance, politics, in the technical, scientific and military training of the youth and so on" when she told Yaakov to go out to the field to procure food as part of their plot for fooling Isaac.[47] Seldom is anyone bothered that the Rav's leading ideas are expressed as *derush*, and many day school students study the Rav's writings. Yet people generally do not strive to study other great *darshanim*[48] or create their own *derush* in Modern Orthodox educational settings.

Derush inspires; it provides images and modes of expression that enable Jews to expound their differing views in a way that engages hearts. *Derush* ought to hold our attention and allegiance, and be part of curricula, as a means of identifying and expressing the values that animate us. Adding to this feeling is that not every interpretation that strives for *peshat* includes a striking religious message. That is simply not a necessary condition for a good or even great *pershat* interpretation.

46. See "A Stranger and a Resident," in *Reflections of the Rav*, adapted by Abraham R. Besdin (Jerusalem: The Department for Torah Education and Culture in the Diaspora of the World Zionist Organization), 169–77.
47. See "Joseph and His Brothers," *The Rav Speaks: Five Addresses on Israel, History, and the Jewish People* (New York: Israel Book Shop and Judaica Press for Toras HoRav Foundation, 2002), 25–33, 176–79 respectively. The quotation is from p. 178.
48. It is gratifying that R. Norman Lamm's *derashot*, found on www.yu.edu/lammheritage, have attracted many readers, but the question is whether they are introduced in the classroom.

So we need more "messages," messages that a *peshat* approach does not always supply. But even if I have not convinced you that constructing *derush* to find our values in Biblical texts is a salutary enterprise worthy of inclusion in curricula for its inspirational value, I hope I have convinced you that there is an important issue about directions for Biblical interpretation and education that must be placed on the table. All the while, my love for and fascination with *peshat*-oriented Biblical readings continues unabated.[49]

49. I thank David Berger, R. Yitzchak Blau, Yoel Finkelman, Rachel Friedman, Stuart Halpern, Michelle Levine, Shifra Schapiro, and Aaron Segal for commenting on a draft of this essay. I also thank R. Nati Helfgot, Penny Kraut, R. Reuven Ziegler, and Yael Ziegler for very helpful correspondence and discussion about, *inter alia*, the relationship between the physical goodness of Eretz Yisrael and its spiritual character, and in particular about why Moshe stressed the land's physical assets in his charge to the scouts. For reasons of space, I in the end did not explore here that aspect of the *parashah*. I also benefited from the analyses on the Israel Koschitzky Virtual Beit Midrash website of Yeshivat Har Etzion, although my aim here is different from that of those studies.

Dr. Naomi Grunhaus

קֹרַח: Revelation and Revolution: Korach's Challenge

The Biblical portion of *Korach* is universally known as the *"parashah* of *machloket,"* the paradigmatic chapter of controversy, because of the challenge to *Moshe Rabbenu*'s leadership instigated by Korach (*Bemidbar* Ch. 16–17). Yet, when we review the Biblical account of forty years in the desert, we find numerous instances of the Jewish people challenging Moshe's authority, where they expressed dissatisfaction with the style and substance of his leadership. At one point they declared, "Let us make a captain, and return to Egypt" (*Bemidbar* 14:4). Indeed, Moshe himself often revealed his own frustration or sense of inadequacy or even outright anger at the conduct of the recalcitrant people. He called them "rebels" (*Bemidbar* 20:10), he complained to the Almighty, "Did I bear them that you should say to me, 'Carry them in your bosom as a nurse carries an infant,'" (*Bemidbar* 11:12), and he expressed his fears that "Before long, they will be stoning me!"

Why then does the episode of Korach stand out? Why has Korach garnered such a high degree of infamy, to the extent that there are those who maintain that he and his assembly have no share in the World to Come?[1] In all the other episodes, never do we find *Moshe Rabbenu* "fighting back," entering into the controversy. He spoke out at times to remind the Jewish people that it was God's rule they were rejecting, but he never responded on a personal level, except with Korach. Why? What was so different about this episode that Moshe felt he had to prove his point publicly, or else "it was not the Lord who sent me?"[2]

Korach's challenge to Moshe's leadership had the potential to destroy the purpose for which God had taken the Jews out of Egypt, to thwart the destiny for which they had been chosen. For Korach was essentially undermining the basic premise upon which the entire future and destiny of the Jewish people would be based: he rejected the belief that "the Divine presence was speaking [to the Jewish people] from the throat of Moshe."[3] If the essence of Torah was only the Ten Commandments, which all the Jews had heard at Mount Sinai, if all Jews equally could interpret those commandments as they saw fit – "For all the community are holy" (*Bemidbar* 16:3) – and the entire congregation are all equally qualified (to interpret the Law), then the fundamental basis of Judaism would be negated, its mission crippled.

This aspect of Revelation is so crucial to the character and mission of the Jewish people that it constitutes not just one but two of the Thirteen Articles of Faith, as iterated by Maimonides.[4] Korach rejected the article of faith that the prophecy of *Moshe Rabbenu* is uniquely superior to that of all other prophets (Article 8), by claiming that "all the community are holy," inasmuch as they all heard God's voice at Mount Sinai. Korach also denied that the entire Torah taught to the Jewish people by Moshe was directly from God Himself, without any addition or lacunae (Article 9).

Korach would not accept that God was the one who gave the

1. *Mishnah, Sanhedrin* 10:3.
2. See the commentary of Malbim, *Bemidbar* 16:28.
3. *Zohar, Pinchas* 232.
4. See Maimonides' introduction to *Perush Ha-Mishnayot, Sanhedrin*, Ch. 10.

entire Torah to *Moshe Rabbenu,* an argument that has surfaced often in Jewish history. If the Torah was not wholly of Divine origin but rather (at least in part) a set of regulations devised by Moshe and imposed upon the nation, then other leaders can later change those regulations.[5] Korach said the Torah was not Divine, but rather a human instrument. Echoes of this position can be perceived in the course of Jewish history, in the Sadducean sect and the Karaites, among others.

It is for this reason that Moshe responded so passionately, and called upon God to perform not just a miracle, but to create something entirely new, beyond magic, beyond miraculous, to prove beyond doubt that He had sent Moshe. Only through an act that God alone could perform would the unassailable truth be established – that He had sent Moshe to do all that he did. Let God Himself *now* create a "mouth" for the earth, which would swallow Korach and his cohorts alive. An ordinary death would not suffice to prove that Moshe's authority came straight from God – after all, even the magicians in Egypt had "supernatural" powers. Moshe understood the dreadful danger imminent in Korach's challenge – if Korach were able to convince the Jewish people that he was right, the elemental belief in Torah as the Divine Will would be vitiated. The Jews would not become the bearers of the word of God to the world, and humankind would be robbed of the opportunity to fulfill its destiny as envisaged by the Torah.

For that reason, Moshe reacted so strongly: it was not his own prestige that concerned him, for indeed he was the humblest of men (*Bemidbar* 12:3) and would willingly have had someone else take on his mission. However, once God had appointed Moshe as the messenger from God to the Jewish people (and from them to all humanity), impugning his authority was tantamount to denying the Divine origin of the Torah. And that he could not allow. Therefore, he acted so seemingly

---

5. The boast of Samuel Holdheim, a leading reformer in the 19th century, comes to mind: "The rabbis of the Talmud legislated for their time, and for their time they were right; I am making rules for my time, and for my time I am right." See M.A. Meyer, *Response to Modernity* (New York: Oxford University Press, 1988), 83 n. 81.

out of character, to establish for all time that the Torah is from God and only from God Himself.[6]

A midrashic tradition cited by Rashi (*Bemidbar* 17:13, ad loc.) illustrates the unique status of *Moshe Rabbenu* in Jewish belief. When later in this *parashah* a plague struck the Jews, Moshe instructed Aharon to run quickly, carrying the *ketoret* (incense) in order to halt the outbreak of death. Aharon ran out into the crowd, with the incense on his pan, and confronted the Angel of Death, who was busy killing the Jewish people.

"Stop," he said, "I am sent here to stop you."

"How can *you* tell me to stop, why should I listen to you?" retorted the Angel, "I am acting under orders from God Himself."

"But I am telling you, you must stop." answered Aharon, "and I am speaking under orders from *Moshe Rabbenu*."

"Why should I listen to Moshe, who is flesh and blood," expostulated the Angel, "when I am fulfilling the command of God Himself!"

Whereupon Aharon answered – "Because everyone knows that Moshe does nothing on his own without first clearing it with God. If Moshe sent me, then that is what God wants. And if you doubt this – you can confront Moshe and God, who are both at the entrance to the Tabernacle, and confirm it for yourself!" Indeed, the Torah then tells us, "and the plague was checked" (*Bemidbar* 17:15).

This midrashic tradition further negates the core challenge of Korach and his party: the contention that Moshe's teachings, however sublime, are nevertheless the invention of Moshe (who is ultimately only a superior prophet, but not beyond criticism or error). The doubt cast on the identification of Torah as the direct word of God could not be allowed to fester, as Moshe so starkly expressed in his response: if Korach was wrong, then only God Himself could make that known, by performing a miracle which only the Creator could do. Hence, Moshe threw down the gauntlet – it was either Moshe's way or Korach's way; there could be no compromise (*Bemidbar* 16:29–30).

After the earth swallowed Korach and his band, God commanded that the copper fire pans, used by those who died, be hammered into

---

6. We follow here the interpretation of events according to Malbim on *Bemidbar* Ch. 16, in passim.

plating for the altar as a reminder to the Israelites, "so that no outsider…
should presume to offer incense before the Lord and suffer the fate of
Korach and his band (alternatively: 'let there not be anyone like Korach
and his assembly')" (*Bemidbar* 17:5). Some rabbis understand the last
part of this verse (*"ve-lo yihyeh ke-Korach ve-ka-adato"*) as an actual Biblical commandment – one is forbidden to foment controversy in the community, as did Korach and his assembly.[7] We can analyze the Korach
episode further, to understand the Torah's warning to us.

In *Pirkei Avot* (5:17), the Rabbis define Korach's challenge as
"not for the sake of Heaven." By a straightforward explanation, "not for
the sake of Heaven," means their desired goal was their own power and
self-aggrandizement.[8] According to traditional commentators, Korach
and his followers sought distinct, self-contradictory agendas.[9] Korach
wanted the high priesthood to be given to him, the 250 tribal leaders
wanted the holy service restored to the first-born in each family, while
Datan and Aviram were angry that Moshe had taken the leadership role
(to which they felt their tribe Reuben was entitled) and transferred it to
the Levites and the children of Yosef. This assembly of malcontents who
gathered around Korach was an inherently unstable coalition because
there was no way all of them could reach their objectives at one time;
the only thing that united them was their desire to challenge Moshe's
rule. Their divisiveness, their negativism – these were the engine that
fueled these disparate individuals.

In denigrating the controversy of "Korach and his Assembly," the
mishnah in *Pirkei Avot* contrasts it with the "controversy of Hillel and
Shammai" – the former is "not for the sake of Heaven" and consequently
"will not last," while the latter is seen in a positive light, and "will last." If
the Torah detests controversy, why is one better than the other? What
makes one the paradigm of shameful debate, while the other is desir-
able as "for the sake of Heaven"? Hillel and Shammai strove to uncover
the truth and therefore, their controversy was "for the sake of Heaven."

7. *Sanhedrin* 110a. See also Nachmanides' *Hasagot* to *Sefer Ha-Mitzvot* of Maimonides,
   Shoresh 8.
8. See commentary of Rabbi Ovadia Bartinoro, ad loc.
9. See commentaries of Rashi, Ibn Ezra, and Nachmanides to *Bemidbar* 16:1.

They held opposing views due to their objective understanding of the halakhic issues under question, not because they calculated that it would win them popularity or political advantage.[10] They had no concealed motives. Korach and his cohorts, on the other hand, were not in the least bit concerned with the truth, as is evident from their separate agendas, which were essentially contradictory.

Yet we may glean further insights if we look a bit deeper. Notice that Korach spoke so effectively that virtually the entire Jewish nation was prepared to consider the validity of his claim. He wrapped himself in the mantle of deep concern for the equality of all Jews and passionately asserted that all who stood at Mount Sinai were equal – yet his true goal was to wrest the position of *Kohen Gadol* from Aharon and claim it for himself! This is so typical of those who foment controversy in the Jewish community – they proclaim their righteousness, their devotion to the community, campaigning for certain measures for the "common good," when in truth they are only trying to weaken the leadership so that they themselves can rush in and take control. Perhaps included in the Biblical precaution of *"ve-lo yihyeh ke-Korach ve-ka-adato"* is a warning to the community not to repeat its tragically naïve acceptance of glib "champions" at face value. It behooves us to look beneath the surface and question the motivations of those who want to lead an assault on traditional leadership in the name of acting for the public benefit. The parody of sincerity must never be repeated. Let there never be those who act like Korach, saying one thing, but striving for another, for their ruse can destroy the Jewish people.

10. Commentary of Bartinoro, ad loc.

Dr. Moshe Sokolow

חֻקַּת: What is a *Chok* and How Does One Teach It?

This *sidrah* is justifiably famous for its introduction of the laws of *parah adumah*, the red heifer, whose ashes purify one who has been rendered impure through contact with a corpse, while – enigmatically – contaminating one who performs the purification rite. That is nearly as far as I plan to get into what you probably expect from a *devar Torah* on this *sidrah*. I would like, instead, to focus attention entirely on the word *"chukkat"* and what it can teach us about Jewish education.

ETYMOLOGY AND SEMANTICS – AN INTRODUCTION

A useful pattern to recognize in the Hebrew language is that words generally start out designating something concrete and realistic and, subsequently, denote something abstract or conceptual. Indeed, in this respect, language follows the recognizable lines of development in children who similarly, move from "concrete" to "formal" operations.[1]

---

1. According to Jean Piaget's theory of cognitive development, the former lasts between the ages of 7–11, and the latter extends from 11 through adolescence. Cf. *The Construction of Reality in the Child* (New York: Basic Books, 1954).

For instance, the noun *neshamah*, which denotes the concept "soul," derives from the verb *nshm*, which means to breathe, indicating that the essence of life was identified with autonomous respiration.[2] Its synonym, *nefesh*, derives from the poetic Biblical word for throat,[3] which contains the pharynx, a critical organ of respiration. *Rachamim*, denoting compassion, derives from *rechem*, meaning "womb," signifying that compassion is to be exercised without expectation of recompense, as a mother would treat the fruit of her womb.[4]

CHOK: CHUKKAH

Since the nouns *chok* or *chukkah*[5] (usually translated: statute[6]) denote abstractions, we are advised to seek their origins in a concrete, physical reality.

We find one in the verb *chkk* whose primary meaning is to engrave, carve, or sculpt. In *Tanakh*, we find a paradigmatic usage in Yeshayahu's challenge to Shevna the scribe: "*mah lekha foh u-mi lekha foh ki chatzavta lekha poh kaver chotzvi marom kivro chokeki va-sela mishkan*" – "Who and what are you to have carved here a grave for yourself; to have carved a lofty grave, to have sculpted a residence in the cliffs?" (*Yeshayahu* 22:16). Yechezkel uses it to depict idolatrous art: "*va-avo va-er'eh ve-hineh tavnit remes u-behemah sheketz ve-khol gilulei Beit Yisrael mechukkeh al ha-kir saviv saviv*" – "I came and observed and, behold, all manner of Israelite insect, animal, reptile and abomination was engraved about the walls" (*Yechezkel* 8:10).

We also encounter the participial form: "*lo yasur shevet mi-Yehudah u-mechokek mi-bein raglav*" – "The staff shall not depart from Yehudah, or a *mechokek* from his loins" (*Bereishit* 49:10). Literally an engraver, it appears here (arguably) in its secondary use as legislator, indicating

---

2. With possible significant consequences for the contemporary debate on brain death.
3. Cf. *Yonah* 2:6: אפפוני מים עד נפש and *Tehillim* 69:2: הושיעני אלהים כי באו מים עד נפש.
4. Which is why it should not be translated "mercy," which shares an etymology with merchandise and mercenary, signifying something undertaken for payment.
5. We shall use them interchangeably.
6. From Late Latin *statutum*: law, regulation; past participle of *statuere*, to set up. The noun *statue* shares the same etymology. We shall shortly see the significance of this coincidence.

the same relationship between engraving and legislation that inheres in statute (see note 6). Given that the codes of law of the ancient world were either engraved on stone tablets (such as the *luchot*) or inscribed – with a stylus[7] – on damp clay tablets (like the Code of Hammurabi), the connection seems obvious and logical.

A *chok*, then, is an engraving or, if you please, a groove, with a particular affinity to the inscription, engraving or writing[8] of legal matters.

IM BE-CHUKKOTAI TELEIKHU:
HOW DOES ONE WALK IN A CHOK?

To round out our survey of *chok*, we must look back, as it were, to its appearance in the title of an earlier *sidrah*: *Bechukkotai*.

The first verse of this *sidrah* states: *"Im be-chukkotai teleikhu"* (*Vayikra* 26:3). This is complemented by a following verse: *"Im be-chukkotai tim'asu"* – "If you detest My *chukkim*" (ibid., 15). While the latter usage is understandable – statutes may be objects of loathing – the former just doesn't sit well. How does one walk in a *chok*? A closer reading of these verses is called for.

וְאִם בְּחֻקֹּתַי תִּמְאָסוּ	אִם בְּחֻקֹּתַי תֵּלֵכוּ
וְאִם אֶת מִשְׁפָּטַי תִּגְעַל נַפְשְׁכֶם	
לְבִלְתִּי עֲשׂוֹת אֶת כָּל מִצְוֹתַי	וְאֶת מִצְוֹתַי תִּשְׁמְרוּ וַעֲשִׂיתֶם אֹתָם

By matching the respective nouns and verbs, we come up with the following pairs:

1. statutes (*chukkim*) can either be walked in or rejected;

---

7. Hebrew: חרט, cf. *Shemot* 32:4: ויקח מידם ויצר אתו בחרט ויעשהו עגל מסכה; *Yeshayahu* 8:1: קח לך גליון גדול וכתב עליו בחרט אנוש.

8. Elsewhere, *chkk* extends from engraving to writing, as in: עתה בוא כתבה על לוח אתם ועל ספר חקה – "Now, come and write it with them upon a tablet and engrave it in a book" (*Yeshayahu* 30:8).

2. commandments (*mitzvot*) can either be observed or not per-
    formed;

3. and laws (*mishpatim*) can be despised (or, by implication,
    respected).

We see that while the contrast between the observance and transgression
of the *mitzvot* is given in the objective and relatively value-free terms
of performance ("*ve-asitem*") and non-performance ("*le-vilti asot*") the
contrast regarding the *chukkim* and the *mishpatim* utilizes the highly
value-laden terms of abhorrence ("*tim'asu*") and loathing ("*tig'al*").

Rashi carries this negative evaluation even further. On the earlier appearance of the verb *g'l* (*gimmel, ayin, lamed*) in verse 11, he comments: "Every instance of *g'l* signifies the expulsion of one thing from
within another."[9] According to this interpretation, the accusation leveled
against the Jewish people in verse 15 is not merely nonfeasance, i.e., the
failure to perform the *mitzvot*, but repugnance; loathing the *mitzvot* and
desiring to be rid of them.

In theological terms, this distinction is telling. Whereas the failure to perform, or the transgression of, any individual *mitzvah* has a
stipulated, specific penalty, the abhorrence and rejection of *mitzvot*, *in
toto*, incurs more and more severe penalties, the most severe of which is
God's abhorrence and rejection of the Jewish people. As God states in
verse 30, utilizing the very words of verse 15: "*ve-ga'alah nafshi etkhem*" –
"I shall loathe and reject you" (*Vayikra* 26:15). Illustrating the principle
of reciprocity (*middah keneged middah*), the Jewish people's expulsion
of the word of God from their midst incurs their expulsion from His
midst, i.e., from the Land of Israel.

"ASHER HALKHU IMMI BE-KERI"
HOW DOES ONE WALK IN *KERI*?

Seven times in *Bechukkotai* the word *keri* appears, accompanied – each
and every time – by the verb *hlkh*. The question we posed earlier: "How

---

9. כל געילה לשון פליטת דבר הבלוע בדבר אחר.

does one walk in a *chok*?" now has a counterpart in: "How does one walk in *keri*?"

The noun *keri* derives from the verb *krh*, to befall or occur, and "to go in *keri*" means "to act casually." If the Jewish people regard the presence of God in their midst as mere "happenstance," God – again implementing the principle of reciprocity – threatens: "*af ani elekh imam be-keri*" – "I, too, shall behave casually with them" (*Vayikra* 26:41).

Since the consequences of "walking in *keri*" are identical with those of "abhorring My *chukkim*," we are entitled to assume an identity between the two phrases, which we will now explore and to which we will attach the pedagogical significance we have been seeking.

GROOVE OR RUT? A MEANINGFUL DISTINCTION

A good deal of religious life revolves around regular obligation whose fulfillment often seems to be by way of rote performance. Some religious inspirational literature (such as *ta'amei ha-mitzvot*) counteracts the casualness of routine by investing it with ethical and moral significance. Other literature (such as the Kabbalistic variety) attempts to offset it by infusing (critics would say, confusing) the mundane with the sublime. Our examination of *chok* and *keri*, however, offers us another paradigm: the distinction of perspective.

Two people can walk the same road without following the same path. Outwardly alike in all respects, they can differ from one another in essence and purpose. What appears to one as a rut in which he is stuck, can strike the other as a groove, a comfortable niche in which he belongs. We must view them not by their actions alone, but by their motives – as regulated by their perspectives.

Rambam, in defining degrees of non-conformity with *Halakhah*, draws a similar distinction from which we may derive an important contemporary lesson in tolerance:

Those who are included in the category of Israel, we are obligated to love them and care for them and do everything God has commanded us concerning love and brotherhood. Even if a Jew committed a sin due to his lust and the overpowering nature of his evil inclination, he is punished according to the severity of his transgression, but still has a share [in the world to come], and he is deemed an "Israelite sinner" ("*mi-posh'ei Yisrael*"). (*Commentary on the Mishnah, Sanhedrin* 10:1)

Of all transgressions, however, the declaration of *keri* is the most reprehensible. According to Rambam, a Jew who rejects the direct providence of God – for better or for worse – preferring to see everything as casual happenstance, has committed a crime that is tantamount to heresy:

> Five are called heretics: He who says there is no God and the Universe has no Guide… (*Hilkhot Teshuvah* 3:7)

In other words, transgression of God's law due to nonfeasance is culpable, but however we would condemn it, it does not place the transgressor outside the pale of Jewish communal concern or redemption. Transgression of His law due to abhorrence, however, is both censurable and irremediable, and the treatment of providence as mere accident constitutes so thorough a rejection of the essence of Divinity as to constitute an irredeemable heresy.

HERGEL: A PRESCRIPTION FOR PEDAGOGY

How do the etymology and semantics of *chok* bear on *parah adumah* and what do they have to teach us about Jewish education?

Parah adumah ostensibly defies rational analysis and, as such, is the paradigmatic illustration of something we are asked to take entirely on faith. As Rashi (*Bemidbar* 19:2, ad loc.) puts it: "*gezeirah hi mi-lefanai ve-ain lekha reshut leharher achareha*" – "It is My decree; you may not question it." Paradoxically, however, the literature of *ta'amei ha-mitzvot*, to which we have referred, is replete with deliberation and speculation from *Chazal* through the modern period precisely on this particular statute. How do we account for this apparent inconsistency?

The resolution lies in an increased respect for our Sages as educators who were aware of the primacy of reason, on the one hand, and yet wary, on the other hand, of the prospective pitfalls of undermining faith by making *mitzvot* conditional on rationales that lacked conviction. Their solution was to advocate *hergel*, the automatic performance of *mitzvot* that was meant to coincide with their rational analysis. From the *lo lishmah* of the unthinking observance, they expected to emerge the *lishmah* of the reasoned performance. Far from denying the importance of reason, they encouraged it, but restricted its application. As Rambam writes:

> It is fitting for a person to comprehend the laws of the Holy Torah and to get to the bottom of their matters to the best of his ability. [However,] Anything for which he finds neither reason nor grounds, let him not treat it lightly; 'let him not presume to outdo God, lest He strike him'. Let him not contemplate such things the way he contemplates secular matters. (*Hilkhot Meʻilah* 8:8)

The transition from *hergel* to *chok* is clear. If we succeed in providing our students with the compelling incentive of reasoned argument, they will not only observe *mitzvot* but they will come to regard the *derekh ha-Torah* as a *groove*, a comfortable niche in which they feel they belong and into which they will continue to introduce their own students and children. If we fail, the automaticity of habit may insure their continued performance, but they will see it as a *rut* into which they have fallen and from which they will seek opportunity to escape. It is a difficult task and a precarious balance to maintain, but there is no realistic alternative.

Dr. Hillel Davis

בלק: Theater for the Ages

henever I read *Parashat Balak* I cannot help but think of the Broadway Theater. I imagine *Ha-Kadosh Barukh Hu* as the director of a play whose staging is quite complex. As the curtain rises or as the *parashah* begins, on the main part of the stage we see the encampment of the Jewish people, somehow depicted as row upon row of tents with the actors wandering around doing all the things one would expect them to do in the desert over the course of a 40-year journey. But with the transition from *Parashat Chukkat* to *Parashat Balak*, the lighting on stage has shifted and the tents and the people are only visible through the darkness, because the spotlight is now focused on the upper right hand corner of the stage where there, in an elevated alcove, we see two men talking. I have this vague recall of watching the Muppets with my children and seeing Statler and Waldorf sitting in the boxes and in their own curmudgeonly way commenting on the action below.

Once I have the staging set in my mind, then I think about the actors. I think how unique *Balak* is among all of the Torah portions. For here in this *parashah* we do not hear from the players who have occupied the stage and our attention for the past months. We actually hear nothing at all about any activity within the Jewish camp. In this scene the Jewish people are not the primary actors. We hear little directly from *Hashem*, not a word from Moshe. Rather, it is a dialogue between two men who in God's dramatic production are speaking about the very people who occupy the dimmed center stage. Fundamentally, *Balak* is a *parashah* of discussion between two non-Jews – Balak and Bil'am – who are engaged in trying to fix what they think is wrong in the world.

Until the last few verses of the *parashah* where the action shifts back to the Jewish camp and we read of the event with Zimri, and *Chazal* link the incident directly to Bil'am's advice, it is actually unclear as to how the conversations between Bil'am and Balak contribute to advancing any part of the overall story of the Jewish people. Ultimately, their grandiose plans seem to come to naught, and other than the *pasuk* of "Mah Tovu," which to this day serves as the introduction to our *shacharit* service, there seems to be no immediate or lasting impact on the Jewish people. We don't even know if the actors on the darkened stage – the Jewish encampment – ever have any idea that this conversation is taking place. The entire *parashah* seems to do nothing to move the desert narrative along. It almost seems to be one long dramatic aside as the Jewish encampment awaits its next move, a pause in the action if you will. It begs the question – other than a very entertaining story, the introduction of Bil'am's amazing donkey, and the opportunity for the Rabbis to discuss the place of Bil'am among the prophets, what purpose does the *parashah* serve?

Our appreciation for the value of each and every word of Torah compels us to suggest that if the spotlight has shifted to the dialogue between Balak and Bil'am, we must focus on these two individuals and understand the contribution they are making to and the role they play in the eternal story of the Jewish people.

The *parashah* begins by telling us that Balak saw all that the Jewish people had done to the Amorites (*Bemidbar* 22:2). It then continues on, saying, "Moab feared the Jewish people because they were so numerous and they were disgusted by them" (ibid., 3). The first and basic question is, was this fear justified? It's a critical question because we are led to believe that it is this fear that drives Balak to plot out his strategy.

At first glance the fear seems to be misplaced. We know that later the Torah will instruct the Jewish people, "And Hashem told me: do not distress Moab nor should you go to war with them for I will not give you from their land as an inheritance" (*Devarim* 2:9). The Jewish people seemingly posed no threat to Balak and his people, and yet Balak feels compelled to plot their destruction and initiate an attack.

So before moving on to the main protagonist, Bil'am, we should first consider Balak, who emerges as the prototype for one who possesses an irrational hatred of the Jewish people. It seems that even those who are not threatened and in some cases never even encounter a Jew, much less the Jewish people, even those who share no borders with the Jewish entity and have no need to interact with them, somehow they are among those who choose to lead the call for the Jews' destruction and marshal forces to actively plan their demise. And as has been true throughout history even to our own times, plotting against the Jewish people can serve as a rallying cry to bring together strange bedfellows, in our case, Balak and Bil'am, who can seemingly collaborate only on this topic. As the Talmud (*Sanhedrin* 105a) tells us in reference to the verse, "and the elders of Moav and Midian went:"

> Midian and Moav were never at peace. The *mashal* is of two dogs in the field who chose to be at odds until a wolf attacked. Only then did they collaborate and together they killed the wolf.

Rashi explains that we know they were never at peace based on the verse: "He who smites Midian in the field of Moav" (*Divrei Ha-Yamim* I 1:46).

Balak may be suffering from an irrational hatred, but he is not a fool and he has a creative bent. Balak chooses to take a unique approach to battling the Jewish people. Nowhere else in *Tanakh*, perhaps in history, do we find a foe of the Jewish people who chooses to do battle not with conventional warfare, but rather through the curses of a hired gun, Bil'am. So that begs another question – what led Balak to take on this highly unconventional strategy, an approach with which there seems to be no prior experience, much less a history of success?

While the Torah tells us that Balak was aware of Israel's previous military successes and implied is the notion that he feared the consequence of taking on the Jewish nation in conventional warfare, there appears to be more to his calculations. Balak recognized that in the realm of conventional warfare, the Jews had a secret weapon: *Ha-Kadosh Barukh Hu*. Certainly since leaving Egypt, *Hashem* had assumed responsibility for the defense of the people against their enemies; subsequently in Jewish history, He introduced the notions of *rabbim be-yad me'atim* (many in the hands of few) and *chazakim be-yad chalashim* (the strong in the hands of the weak) into our prayers, our vocabulary and our psyche. Military experts could never have predicted the victories the Jewish people have achieved on the battlefields through the years and all of that is due to God's intervention and His *chesed*: "God will fight for you and you shall be silent" (*Shemot* 14:14).

As a result of this concern, Balak chooses to eschew a conventional approach and instead engage in a battle of the spirit – a cultural battle in which the goal is to separate the Jews from their history, their tradition and their story. In this type of battle, it is not God who can save us; rather redemption and triumph lie in the hands of the people themselves. In order to emerge victorious, the children of Israel, of their own accord, must proclaim their allegiance to their traditional values and His Torah. Balak recognizes this well – he realizes that a physical confrontation with the Jewish people means a battle with God and that outcome is all too predictable and ultimately unwinnable. He views his chances as being much better if he were to challenge the Jewish people and their own commitment to tradition. He reckons that he has a much better chance trying to distance the Jews from Torah than trying to distance God from His people. And so he reaches out for Bil'am to do verbal and spiritual battle with the people Israel, to curse them in a way that would drive them away from their Protector. Balak serves as the prototype for those who are clever enough to try to do harm to the Jewish people by driving a wedge between them and *Hashem*, between them and their roots. Once again, history and experience suggest that Balak is an important model for so many of those who have plotted against our people over the years – attack the spirit; weaken the commitment; distance the people from their story and that can ultimately be far more damaging than any physical attacks that the people would sustain in conventional warfare.

If Balak is presented as a one-dimensional character, our Rabbis view Bil'am as far more complex. Classically referred to as *Bil'am Ha-*

Rasha (*Sanhedrin* 105b; *Avot* 5:9), in *Seder Eliyahu Rabbah* (Ch. 28, 14) it is said that so intense was his desire to curse the Jewish people that he could not even sleep the night before his encounter with them, and as a result *Hashem* had to appear to him, not in a dream as He had done with *Lavan*, but rather while Bil'am was awake.

On the one hand, his role as a *sonei Yisrael* is unquestioned in our tradition. As we are told, "Mar the son of Ravina told his son, 'for all those who we are told have no place in the world to come, you should not expound on the verses that refer to them; the exception is *Bil'am Ha-Rasha*. Whatever you find written about him, lecture on it to publicize his evil'" (*Sanhedrin* 106b). And yet there is a stream within *Chazal*, in which Bil'am is presented more as a buffoon than as a villain. On the verse, "and he knows the minds of the Almighty" (*Bemidbar* 24:16), the Talmud comments: "if he could not plumb to the depths of the mind of his own donkey, how could he know the thinking of the Almighty?" (*Berakhot* 7a). To which the Talmud responds that his strength was in that he could anticipate the moment at which *Hashem* would be angry and he learned to capitalize on that moment.

Or consider this in *Bemidbar Rabbah, Parashat Balak*, 20:

> Aram refers to an *"am ram,"* a lofty nation that was reduced by Balak and his actions. The *mashal* (metaphor) is someone who is walking with a king and he sees some common thieves. He leaves the side of the king to accompany the thieves. When he tries to return to the company of the king, the king refuses to allow it and says "go back to your prior company – the thieves that you left me for." So too, Bil'am, who abandons the company of *Hashem* to practice his magic tricks, *Hashem* will not allow him back into His company.

As a result, many of the traditional commentators tend to diminish the magnitude of his powers. In this light, for example, Ramban (*Bemidbar* 22:31, ad loc.) views Bil'am as a magician more than a prophet. For if he were a prophet, why would he need a special '*gilui einayim*' (revelation) to see the angel? Therefore, Ramban goes on, the verse in *Yehoshua* refers to him as the *"kosem,"* the magician (*Yehoshua* 13:22).

Ibn Ezra (*Bemidbar* 22:28, ad loc.) suggests that Bil'am had no power of his own and is nothing more than a tool of God, Who was using him for this specific purpose. "The truth is," Ibn Ezra writes, "his prophecy was granted only for the sake of the honor of Israel, for in fact he was nothing more than a magician."

Rabbenu Bechaye (*Bemidbar* 24:4, ad loc.) takes Bil'am down several pegs and also suggests that he did not have the stature of a prophet. As he writes, "The verse is alluding to the fact that he did not reach the level of the *Avot*, and certainly not the level of Moshe. For the prophecy of the *Avot* was '*be-Keil Shakkai*' and Bil'am's prophecy was '*be-machazeh Shakkai*.'"

But as Rabbenu Bechaye mentions, there are other statements of *Chazal* that are lavish in their praise for his capacity for prophecy. Not only is he listed among the seven who prophesied for the nations (*Bava Batra* 15b; *Bemidbar Rabbah* 57), but *midrashim* also go out of their way to compare him to Avraham and Yaakov. Most telling is the fact that the Rabbis go so far as to compare his prophetic powers to *Moshe Rabbenu* (*Midrash Tanchuma, Balak* 1; *Bemidbar Rabbah* 57) and in at least two almost incomprehensible midrashic sources it is suggested that *Bil'am's* powers in some ways even exceeded Moshe's (*Yalkut Shimoni* at the end of *Vezot Haberakhah* cited below; *Seder Eliyahu Rabbah* 28:14):

> When the verse says that no other prophet arose in Israel like Moshe, the implication is that within Israel there was no one comparable, but among the nations there was such a person, and who was he? Bil'am ben B'or. The difference was that Moshe did not know Who was speaking with him and Bil'am in fact did know. Moshe did not know when He would address him until He did, and Bil'am knew when to expect to hear from Him. Moshe could only address *Hashem* while standing and *Bil'am* could speak with Him while prostrated before Him."

What then are we to make of Bil'am? All-powerful or charlatan? A Jew-hater who is comparable to the *Avot*? Could it be that such deep venom should emerge from one who seems in so many ways to be designated by *Ha-Kadosh Barukh Hu* as a unique and distinct talent? Is it possible?

It appears that the answer is yes to all of these questions. Perhaps we might suggest that through this complex network of *midrashim*, we are presented with Bil'am as a paradigm for future *sonei Yisrael*, anti-Semites, who might at times be mistaken by us or others as buffoons and inept charlatans. In addition, it could well be, that at some future time, enemies of the Jewish people might come across as sounding or acting uncomfortably close to characters and personalities that we recognize and admire. The Bil'am we read of here is in fact a representative figure of generations of Jew-haters who will have great powers and capabilities, will be individuals who need to be reckoned with, and will appear in the guise of friends or charlatans, buffoons or true hatemongers. Bil'am, in this regard, is a foreshadowing of so many of the demons that the Jewish people would be forced to confront down through the ages.

There is one more comparison in *Chazal* that is worth mentioning. Bil'am is described as a descendant of or reincarnation of Lavan. The *midrash* tells us, for example, that *Hashem* spoke to both in the evening (*Bereishit Rabbah* 52:5) and He used similar language; both Lavan and Bil'am are known for their misuse of language – Lavan is famous for his lies and his deception, while Bil'am uses language to curse others (*Midrash Sekhel Tov, Bereishit*, Ch. 22). The suggestion is that both wished to uproot everything. By trying to prevent Yaakov and his family from returning to *Eretz Kena'an*, Lavan was attempting to uproot the very basis for the development of the Jewish people; Bil'am too is trying to keep Yaakov's descendants, the children of Israel, from returning from Egypt to *Eretz Kena'an*, and thereby prevent the development of this people into a nation. Conceptually, we should be much more comfortable in this realm – comparing true villains provides a *midrashic* comfort zone for us.

Bil'am is presented to us as the new and improved Lavan – he also wants to destroy the nation, but he is in a sense more sophisticated than Lavan for he comes armed not only with a plan but with a backup plan as well. Plan A is an attempt to physically eradicate the nation; Plan B is to destroy the nation through assimilation.

Bil'am is invited by Balak to take on a nation – a developing people forged in the slavery of Egypt that is just now growing to recognize the value of the individual as well as the meaning of community. It is a people rooted in dignity and on a mission – a people on its way to a collective rendezvous with destiny; this is a nation that was not bothering him or anyone else, and who only wanted to continue on their path to build lives of purpose and establish a community of morality and mission.

So one can only imagine the hired gun, Bil'am, or as *Chazal* refer to him, *"beli am,"* the man without a nation, justifying in his own twisted mind that individuals cannot be allowed to build or exist in this type of community. To his mind, community like this will drain resources from the elite who deserve them more, and he has no need for such a nation; such approaches only satisfy the weak. When he saw them from the mountaintop, he was overwhelmed and truly disturbed by what he saw. He recognized their sincere and intense desire for morality and decency, and he saw how as individuals they intended to live together in harmony and form a community of purpose without losing their sense of individuality and meaning. It was this intent that he hoped to curse, but which instead through God's intervention came out as *"Mah tovu ohalekha Yaakov"* – "How goodly are your tents, Jacob."

So he begins with Plan A, which is to eradicate and destroy the Jewish people. But *Hashem* does not allow that to happen. Unlike less devious foes, however, Bil'am has a Plan B: (i) motivate and create the opportunity for assimilation (ii) create the circumstances whereby the Jewish people will, of their own accord, destroy their most fundamental interrelationships, and (iii) erode the very moral fabric that is the basis of their society, thereby distancing themselves from *Ha-Kadosh Barukh Hu.* In addition to his brilliance and his cunning, Bil'am also serves as the paradigm of the relentless anti-Semite, the one who will not admit defeat.

This perhaps explains another level of the association between Bil'am and Lavan. Neither one was prepared to tolerate the continuing existence of *Am Yisrael.* Lavan tried to prevent the emergence of the nation, the children of Israel, through assimilation within his own household. After the failure of his initial plan, Bil'am too was willing to settle on assimilation as the final solution for the Jewish problem. And as we learn in the conclusion of *Parashat Balak,* thousands in fact did fall victim to his trap.

But ultimately the Jewish nation successfully survived all of Bil'am's machinations and they went on to enter the Land of Israel to build the society and community that Bil'am found so threatening. But the story remains with us because in too many ways we are not reading about an historical occurrence, but rather we are reading about current events. The Balak/Bil'am story is not a pause in the action of the *midbar* saga; rather it is both the precursor and prototype of the challenge of the Jewish experience through the millennia that followed. And one could in fact posit that some of our more recent experiences as a people suggest that the contemporary villains have learned well from Bil'am. Consider the 20th century when our parents and grandparents suffered a terrible decimation that, left unchecked, could God forbid have led to the achievement of Bil'am's goal of the extinction of the Jewish people, only to be followed by the impact of Plan B – falling prey to assimilation and the weakening of the communal fabric that has bound us a people. The story of the 20th century is perhaps even more tragic than the Bil'am story because as individuals and as a community we have suffered terrible losses from both plans: annihilation and assimilation.

Parashat Balak as an interlude in the *midbar* story? Hardly. For if the *midbar* represents the Jewish experience as we continue to aspire to the reality of *Am Yisrael im Torat Yisrael be-Eretz Yisrael*, then the conversation between Balak and Bil'am is all too representative of what we have experienced and continue to experience from so many of our foes and detractors. Is it a pause in the action? Hardly. We might even suggest that the story is especially crucial at this very moment in the saga of the Jews in the desert. They are still in the wandering stages; they are on the brink of entering the Land of Israel, but not quite there yet. These experiences, the Torah could be saying, threaten us as a nation – whether we reside within the land or outside the land. The encounters with our enemies will remain a challenge in *galut*, exile or in our Land of Israel. And certainly both elements of Bil'am's plan – annihilation and assimilation – remain as looming threats wherever we might reside. An aside? Hardly. Rather it is an all too stark reminder – an eternal reminder – of the continuing experiences of the Jewish people as we follow in the footsteps of our forefathers and travel the road back to our destiny as a people and to the Land of Israel.

And so we end as we began, with God as the Producer and Director, and the staging as suggested by *Parashat Balak* portraying a

בלק

picture of Balak and Bil'am – a sinister Statler and Waldorf – looming over the stage of Jewish history as eternal reminders of the challenges and obstacles we as a people will face, and with God's help and with our own resiliency and faith, will overcome.

Dr. Shawn Zelig Aster

פנחס: The Division of the Land of Israel: Archaeology, Anthropology, and *Halakhah*

"To These, the Land Shall be Divided"
(Bemidbar 26:53)

We are used to the idea that the Land of Israel was divided according to the tribes. Many Bible atlases contain detailed maps, showing the allotments of the twelve tribes, including that of Judah in the area south of Jerusalem, that of Efraim in the central portion of the country, and that of Asher along the northern coast. These maps are based on the division described in the Book of *Yehoshua* (Ch. 15–21).

But while the Torah mentions the allocation of land according to tribes (*Bemidbar* 26:55), this is in the context of a larger passage emphasizing individual allotments. The census in Ch. 26 of *Parashat Pinchas* seems to be connected to this more detailed allocation. After a census of the 601,730 male non-Levite Israelites between the ages of 20 and 60 (ibid., 51), the following paragraph of instructions appears:

> (53) To these, the land shall be divided in inheritance, according to the number of names.

> (54) For the many, you shall increase his inheritance, and for the few, you shall decrease his inheritance. Each one according to his counted men, shall the inheritance be given.

> (55) However, the land shall be given by lottery, to the names of their fathers' tribes they shall inherit.

> (56) According to the lottery, the inheritance shall be given, whether many or few.

The simplest, context-based reading of verses 53–54 would suggest that the words "many," "few," and "his" in these verses refer to the tribes. This is how Rashi interprets these verses: "To the tribe with many members, a larger portion was given" (Rashi, ad loc.).

The Ramban (ad loc.) however, points out that this is not how the verses are understood in *Sifre*. He implies that in *Sifre*, the words noted above refer not to the tribe, but to the *mishpachot*, the sub-tribal family divisions, each of which is named after a son (or grandson or great-grandson) of the 12 tribes. This interpretation also fits with the context, because *Bemidbar* (26:1–51) lists not only the names of the tribes, but also the names of the *mishpachot* (although not their numbers). Here is how *Sifre* understands this passage:

> "For the many, you shall increase his inheritance" (ibid., 54) – If ten men left Egypt, but only five (of these ten or their descendants) entered the land, to this I apply the principle 'For the many, you shall increase his inheritance.'

> "For the few, you shall decrease his inheritance" (ibid., 54) – If

five men left Egypt, but ten (of these five or their descendants) entered the land, to this I apply the principle 'For the few, you shall decrease his inheritance.' (*Sifre Pinchas* 132)

Two principles emerge from this *Sifre*:

1. The amount of land allocated to each Israelite who enters Israel depends on the entitlement of their ancestors, who left Egypt.
2. The basic grouping for allocating land in Israel is not the tribe but the sub-tribal family unit, known as the *mishpachah*.

The Ramban focuses on the second of these principles, and develops it further. The phrase "to these" (*Bemidbar* 26:53) means that the land allotments were given according to the *mishpachot*. Each *mishpachah*, named after a male ancestor, received an allotment. All members of a given *mishpachah* received land in close proximity to each other. It emerges from the Ramban's description that the *mishpachah* became an important element of the geographic arrangement of the Israelites in the land. Furthermore, the *mishpachah* was the most proximate and direct group with which each individual Israelite could personally identify.

But what was the *mishpachah*? How did it originate and develop? The Ramban discusses this in his commentary:

> "The custom in Israel was that [those who had descended into Egypt] became the heads of the father's houses, and all his descendants forever would define their ancestry according to that man, and would be called by his name, as a manner of honoring him, as the Arabs do still today, and as the Jews who live in their [the Arabs'] lands do (naming the family after an eponymous ancestor).... Each of those mentioned in Egypt became the head of their fathers' house, and the family would trace its genealogy to him." (Ramban, Commentary on *Bemidbar* 26:13)

The Ramban goes on to note that the list of *mishpachot* is not rigidly defined by those who came down to Egypt. In certain cases, the son or descendant of one of those who came down to Egypt might establish his own *mishpachah*. He notes that I'ezer and Chelek were great-grandsons of Menashe (*Bemidbar* 26:30) and yet established their own *mishpachot* "because these sons were great and honored, and they became leaders" (Ramban, *Bemidbar* 26:13). Furthermore, after the descent into Egypt, members of a particular tribe could choose to join an existing father's house or to establish their own.

"THE LAND WAS ALLOCATED TO THOSE WHO LEFT EGYPT"

The Ramban's explanation of *mishpachot* allows us to make sense of a highly counter-intuitive position presented in the Talmud's discussion of the allocation of the Land of Israel. In a tannaitic source cited in *Bava Batra* 117a, two possible positions are elaborated. R. Jonathan presents the apparently more logical position, "The Land of Israel was allocated to those who entered the land." R. Josiah presents what appears to be the more tortured position: "The land was allocated to those who left Egypt…this inheritance differed from all other inheritances in the world. For in all other cases, the living receive from the dead. But here, the dead received (their inheritance) from the living."

The Rashba elaborates on the apparently illogical position of R. Josiah. He gives the example of A, who left Egypt, along with his sons B and C who were below the age of 20 (and therefore did not receive their own allocation). In the desert, B had one son and C had two, and each of these three grandchildren was above 20 when the Israelites entered the land. Each of the three would receive a theoretical portion of the land. They theoretically hand these over to A, who then allocates half to the descendents of B and half to the descendents of C. The Rashba underlines that the right of heritage is possessed by "the old one, the great one of the house," i.e. the ancestor who left Egypt (*Chiddushei Ha-Rashba, Bava Batra* 117a).

This ancestor who left Egypt is (following Ramban) the eponymous founder of the *mishpachah*. R. Josiah is actually arguing that the right of heritage is that of the *mishpachot*, not of the individuals who entered the land.

By privileging the *mishpachah*, as R. Josiah argues, and by seeing it as the basic unit of land allocation, the Torah has forced those who entered the land to see the *mishpachah* as a basic unit of their identity.

HERITAGE RIGHTS AND THE *MISHPACHOT*

Why does the Torah privilege the *mishpachah*? The answer can be understood as part of the larger program of *Bemidbar,* Ch. 21–36, which begins the preparation of the Israelites to enter the Land of Israel. The Torah seeks to use the allocation of parcels of land within the country as a means of creating and reinforcing personal identity. The Torah is aware of the danger of the ideology which political scientist Daniel Philpott calls "territoriality."

> This is a principle that defines the set of people … by virtue of their location within borders. The people within these borders may not necessarily conceive of themselves as a "people" or a "nation" with a common identity… but their location within boundaries requires their allegiance to their sovereign.[1]

As the sovereign becomes stronger, the territorial identity becomes primary, and the people within the sovereign's borders develop a primary identity based on territory and its political organization. The Torah is aware that within the land, Israelites will live alongside non-Israelites (cf. *Shoftim* 1–3), and in some cases, that an Israelite sovereign will rule over Israelites and non-Israelites. If the individual's primary allegiance is to the land ruled by a given sovereign, his allegiance to the distinctive Israelite norms which we call Torah will cease to form the basic unit of his identity. In order to forestall the development of territoriality as the basic unit of the individual's identity, the Torah seeks to encourage an individual to identify with a *mishpachah.*

It is true that in theory, the Torah could have developed a system of identity based on identification with a nation or with a larger tribal unit. There are two reasons to prefer identifying an individual with the *mishpachah.* One reason is that noted by the Ramban. The natural tendency of some people is to identify with smaller sub-tribal units, *viz.,* with a clan or family (this being the tendency of nomadic peoples, their descendants, and those who live among them). In the way it allocates

---

1. Daniel Philpott, *Revolutions in Sovereignty: How Ideas Shaped Modern International Relations* (Princeton, NJ, 2001), p. 17.

land, the Torah seeks to promote this natural tendency among the Israelites who will settle in the land. It forces them to settle among their kin or those they regard as their kin and it emphasizes that heritage rights derive from the *mishpachot* and their eponymous ancestors. The Torah emphasizes this here in *Bemidbar* Ch. 26, and again in *Bemidbar* Ch.'s 27 and 36, in the story of *benot Tzelofchad*.

A second reason is to avoid creating a binary system of ethnic self-identification in which each individual is identified solely as Israelite or gentile. A binary system of this sort allows Israelites to identify themselves as "a non-gentile." Such a view seems to be reflected in some of Israelite-Philistine Biblical narratives, as in *Shemuel* I (14:6), and it is also present today. By identifying the individual with one of many *mishpachot*, the danger of defining one's ethnicity primarily as "non-gentile" is avoided. A more positive and nuanced self-identity emerges, one that necessarily connects the individual to an eponymous ancestor who left Egypt.

THE SAMARIA OSTRACA AND THE HISTORICAL RECORD

The most fascinating part of the story of the allocation of the land is the historical record. The sense of identification with the *mishpachah* continued among Israelites well into the eighth century BCE, at least 400 years after the initial settlement of the Israelites in the land.

This can be seen from the Samaria ostraca. These are a series of receipts or labels written in Hebrew on broken potshards (commonly used as a sort of "scrap paper" in antiquity), found in the fill of a building in the Biblical city of Samaria. Over 100 of these ostraca were found in archeological excavations in 1910, and are currently in the possession of Harvard University's Semitic Museum.[2] They record the delivery of olive oil and wine to Samaria, presumably to officials in the city who had land in various places in the surrounding countryside.

---

2. The most complete discussion of these ostraca is an unpublished PhD dissertation, by Ivan Tracy Kaufman, *The Samaria Ostraca: A Study in Ancient Hebrew Palaeography* (Harvard, 1966). A recent discussion can be located in S. Ahituv, *Echoes from the Past* (Jerusalem, 2008).

Many of these ostraca mention the "fifteenth year" of an Israelite king, presumably Yo'ash son of Yehu, who reigned in the first half of the 8th century. These ostraca identify the town or village from which the oil or wine was delivered, as well as the *mishpachah* to which that town or village belongs. The city of Samaria was in the tribal inheritance of Menashe, and the towns and villages are identified as belonging to one of the *mishpachot* of Menashe.

Two examples are:

Ostracon #23: "In the fifteenth year, from Chelek, belonging to Assa son of Ahimelekh. Rafu' ben Anamesh (perhaps the sender?). From Hazeroth (the name of a town, identified with Asirat al-Hatab near Samaria)."

Ostracon #45: "In the fifteenth year, from Choglah, belonging to Hanan son of Baara. Jonathan (perhaps the sender?). From Yatzith (the name of a town, identified with Yassid north of Shechem)."

In both of the examples cited, the name of the town from which the oil or wine was shipped is mentioned. But the name of the *mishpachah* also appears. In ostracon 23, the name Chelek appears, clearly identifiable with Chelek mentioned in *Bemidbar* 26:30. In other ostraca, the names Shemida (*Bemidbar* 26:32), Aseri'el (*Bemidbar* 26:31), and Avi'ezer (known from the story of Gid'on, perhaps to be identified with I'ezer in *Bemidbar* 26:30) appear. In ostracon 45, the name Choglah appears. Choglah was one of the *benot Tzelofchad*, each of whom received an allocation in the Land of Israel. It appears that at least on a popular level, the families of the *benot Tzelofchad* were considered *mishpachot*, and that towns settled by their descendants (such as Yatzith in ostracon 45) were said to be "in the region of Choglah," rather than in the region of Tzelofchad. Other ostraca mention the region of No'a, another of Tzelofchad's daughters.

Thus, the Torah's program of promoting identification of Israelites with their *mishpachot* succeeded. Perhaps the program succeeded even more than Torah called for: No'a and Choglah became *mishpachot*.

The division of the land of Menashe into regions named after the *mishpachot* can be seen from the Samaria ostraca, as well as from the study of ancient place-names. Aryeh Borenstein, an Israeli scholar, has devoted several articles to discussing the division of the land, and has published maps of the territory of Menashe, showing where each of the *mishpachot* was located.[3]

CONCLUSION

The basic program of the Torah's division of the land is to keep sub-tribal family units together. The logic of this position is explained by political and anthropological approaches to identity, and the historical development of this program is seen from archaeology.

Judaism, a wise man once said, is primarily about family and community. The Torah's system for allocating land in Israel, explained with reference to anthropology, and elaborated by archaeology, seems to underline this.

---

3. A. Borenstein, "The Administrative Division of the Land of Manasseh Based on the Samaria Ostraca," (Heb.), in *Mehkere Yehuda ve Shomron* 1 (1992), pp. 121–161; "How Was the Land Divided: The Archeological Element in the Talmudic Discussion of the Division of the Land," *Talpiyyot: Shenaton Ha-Mikhlala* 10 (1998), pp. 127–142. In the 1998 article, based on the numbers of times that *benot Tzelofchad* are mentioned in the Samaria ostraca, he concludes that Tzelopchad's daughters received a large portion of the land of Menashe and that the historical division of the Land of Israel was in accordance with the position of R. Josiah.

Rabbi Hershel Schachter

מטות: The Unique Prophecy of Moshe

The Torah introduces the *parashah* of *nedarim* with the phrase *"zeh ha-davar asher tzivvah Hashem"* – "this is exactly what *Hashem* has commanded" (*Bemidbar* 30:2). Rashi, in his commentary on that phrase, quotes from the *Tanna'im* that both *Moshe Rabbenu*, as well as the other prophets, will sometimes introduce their prophecies with the expression *"koh amar Hashem"* – "so does *Hashem* say," but only *Moshe Rabbenu*, who was on a higher level than the other *nevi'im*, was able to say *"zeh ha-davar"* – that this is precisely and exactly what *Hashem* is commanding. What are the *Tanna'im* driving at? What is the difference between *"zeh ha-davar"* and *"koh amar Hashem"*?

In *Kedushat Levi*, R. Levi Yitzchak of Berditchev explains this difference based on the *pesukim* in *Parashat Beha'alotekha*. The Torah distinguishes between the prophecy of *Moshe Rabbenu* as opposed to that of other *nevi'im*. *Moshe Rabbenu* was given direct dictation word for word and letter for letter. That is why only he can introduce his prophecy with the expression *"zeh ha-davar,"* this is exactly what *Hashem* commanded. All other prophets were shown a vision in a dream, and had to interpret the vision using their own language. That's why no other *navi* was able to proclaim *"zeh ha-davar,"* that this is precisely what *Hashem* said, but rather had to say *"koh amar Hashem,"* this is approximately what *Hashem* said, because it was their interpretation, and was using their own language to interpret a prophetic dream. This is what the Talmud was referring to when it pointed out that the prophecy of *Moshe Rabbenu* was crystal clear, as opposed to the prophecies of the other *nevi'im*; because only *Moshe Rabbenu* was given direct dictation.

But the question arises, how come *Moshe Rabbenu* every so often introduces his *nevu'ah* with the words *"koh amar Hashem"* if that expression implies that he is interpreting his vision using his own language?

At this point in his presentation, the *Kedushat Levi* explains that the differences between *Moshe Rabbenu* and the other *nevi'im* is not due to a difference between the personalities of the individuals involved, but rather due to a difference in the nature of their respective *nevu'ot*. *Moshe Rabbenu* was the only *navi* who was given *Torah u-mitzvot* that are binding throughout all the generations. The other *nevi'im* were only given *hora'at sha'ah* – prophecies only relevant for a short period of time. For Moshe, this direct dictation was only granted when he was given *Torah u-mitzvot*. Often, when *Moshe Rabbenu* was only given a prophecy that was merely a *hora'at sha'ah*, he too would receive *nevu'ah* in a vision, and would have to interpret that vision using his own language. In such instances, he too would introduce the presentation of his *nevu'ah* by saying *"ko amar Hashem."*

This is exactly what Rambam intended in the seventh of his Thirteen Principles of Faith, when he named *Moshe Rabbenu* the greatest *navi*. What this refers to is that only *Moshe Rabbenu* was given *nevu'ah* which is binding for all the future generations. That is what we refer to as *Torah u-mitzvot*. All the other prophets were only granted *nev'uah*, which by definition means *hora'at sha'ah*.

The ninth of the Rambam's Thirteen Principles of Faith states that the laws of the Torah are immutable. This is the key point of disagreement between Orthodoxy and the other Jewish denominations. Why such an obstinate insistence on no change? Every legal system has to update its laws to changing times.

The *Tanya* explains that we believe that the Torah is not merely a collection of laws and proper *hashkafot*. The entirety of the Torah is a description of God's essence, and therefore just as *Elokut* does not change, so too the laws of the Torah cannot change.

In *Parashat Beha'alotekha*, when the Torah contrasts the prophecy of *Moshe Rabbenu* with that of the other prophets, the expression used is *"u-temunat Hashem yabbit"* (*Bemidbar* 12:8) – that *Moshe Rabbenu* was the only individual who was allowed to "behold the image of God" (ibid.). What does that possibly mean? We all know that God has no body and no image! Apparently, the *Chumash* means to state that Moshe was the only *navi* to whom *Hashem* revealed his Torah, by way of direct dictation, word for word and letter for letter, and that Torah is *"temunat Hashem,"* a description of *Elokut*.

The difference between *"koh amar Hashem"* and *"zeh ha-davar"* conveys these *Ikkarei Ha-Emunah*.

Prof. Smadar Rosensweig

מַסְעֵי: Heritage and Legacy: Revisiting the Daughters of Tzelofchad

The *parashah* begins with a recapitulation of the journeys of *Benei Yisrael* in the desert. It is the last *parashah* of the Torah detailing the wanderings of *Benei Yisrael* en route to *Eretz Yisrael*. In contrast, *Sefer Devarim* was conveyed by Moshe to *Benei Yisrael* during the final five weeks of his life. It is Moshe's last will and testament to *Benei Yisrael* as the unique representative of *Hashem* on this earth. Ramban, in his introduction to *Sefer Devarim* describes the distinctive character of *Sefer Devarim*, as *Mishneh Torah*. The Vilna Gaon characterizes *Sefer Devarim* as Moshe's interpretation of *Hashem*'s word, and not a verbatim communication of the Divine message.

Consequently, *Parashat Masei* embodies the last direct Divine message to *Benei Yisrael*. It is one type of coda to the national experience in the desert, and a final transmission of the narrative that began with

Bereishit. The *parashah* begins with a retrospective summary (*Bemidbar* 33:1–12):

(א) אלה מסעי בני ישראל אשר יצאו מארץ מצרים לצבאתם ביד משה ואהרן: (ב) ויכתב משה את מוצאיהם למסעיהם על פי ה' ואלה מסעיהם למוצאיהם: (ג) ויסעו מרעמסס בחדש הראשון בחמשה עשר יום לחדש הראשון ממחרת הפסח יצאו בני ישראל ביד רמה לעיני כל מצרים: (ד) ומצרים מקברים את אשר הכה ה' בהם כל בכור ובאלהיהם עשה ה' שפטים: (ה) ויסעו בני ישראל מרעמסס ויחנו בסכת: (ו) ויסעו מסכת ויחנו באתם אשר בקצה המדבר: (ז) ויסעו מאתם וישב על פי החירת אשר על פני בעל צפון ויחנו לפני מגדל: (ח) ויסעו מפני החירת ויעברו בתוך הים המדברה וילכו דרך שלשת ימים במדבר אתם ויחנו במרה: (ט) ויסעו ממרה ויבאו אילמה ובאילם שתים עשרה עינת מים ושבעים תמרים ויחנו שם: (י) ויסעו מאילם ויחנו על ים סוף: (יא) ויסעו מים סוף ויחנו במדבר סין: (יב) ויסעו ממדבר סין ויחנו בדפקה:

1. These are the stages of the children of Israel, by which they went forth out of the land of Egypt by their hosts under the hand of Moses and Aaron. 2. And Moses wrote their goings forth, stage by stage, by the commandment of the Lord; and these are their stages at their goings forth. 3. And they journeyed from Rameses in the first month, on the fifteenth day of the first month; on the morrow after the Passover the children of Israel went out with a high hand in the sight of all the Egyptians, 4. while the Egyptians were burying them that the Lord had smitten among them, even all their first-born; upon their gods also the Lord executed judgments. 5. And the children of Israel journeyed from Rameses, and pitched in Succoth. 6. And they journeyed from Succoth, and pitched in Etham, which is in the edge of the wilderness. 7. And they journeyed from Etham, and turned back unto Pihahiroth, which is before Baal-zephon; and they pitched before Migdol. 8. And they journeyed from Penehahiroth, and passed through the midst of the sea into the wilderness; and they went three days' journey in the wilderness of Etham, and pitched in Marah. 9. And they journeyed from Marah, and came unto Elim; and in

Elim were twelve springs of water, and threescore and ten palm-trees; and they pitched there. 10. And they journeyed from Elim, and pitched by the Red Sea. 11. And they journeyed from the Red Sea, and pitched in the wilderness of Sin. 12. And they journeyed from the wilderness of Sin, and pitched in Dophkah.

Rashi (*Bemidbar* 33:1), quoting Rabbi *Moshe Ha-Darshan*, explains that all these encampments were mentioned in order to teach Divine mercy. Even though *Benei Yisrael* were punished to wander the desert for forty years, they were not constantly on the move without respite.

אלה מסעי - למה נכתבו המסעות הללו, להודיע חסדיו של מקום, שאעפ"י שגזר עליהם לטלטלם ולהניעם במדבר, לא תאמר שהיו נעים ומטולטלים ממסע למסע כל ארבעים שנה ולא היתה להם מנוחה, שהרי אין כאן אלא ארבעים ושתים מסעות. צא מהם י"ד, שכולם היו בשנה ראשונה, קודם גזירה, משנסעו מרעמסס עד שבאו לרתמה. שמשם נשתלחו המרגלים, שנאמר (במדבר יב, טז) ואחר נסעו העם מחצרות וגו' (שם יג, ב) שלח לך אנשים וגו'. וכאן הוא אומר ויסעו מחצרות ויחנו ברתמה, למדת שהיא במדבר פארן. ועוד הוצא משם שמונה מסעות שהיו לאחר מיתת אהרן מהר ההר עד ערבות מואב בשנת הארבעים, נמצא שכל שמנה ושלשים שנה לא נסעו אלא עשרים מסעות. זה מיסודו של רבי משה הדרשן.

Why were these journeys recorded? To inform us of the kind deeds of the Omnipresent, for although He issued a decree to move them around [from place to place] and make them wander in the desert, you should not say that they were moving about and wandering from station to station for all forty years, and they had no rest, because there are only forty-two stages. Deduct fourteen of them, for they all took place in the first year, before the decree, from when they journeyed from Rameses until they arrived in Rithmah, from where the spies were sent, as it says, "Then the people journeyed from Hazeroth [and camped in the desert of Paran]" (12:16); "Send out for yourself men…" (13:2), and here it says, "They journeyed from Hazeroth and camped at Rithmah," teaching us that it [Rithmah] was in the desert of Paran. Subtract a further eight stages which took place after Aaron's death-from

Mount Hor to the plains of Moab, during the fortieth year, and
you will find that throughout the thirty-eight years they made
only twenty journeys. I found this in the commentary of R. *Moshe
Ha-Darshan* [the preacher].[1]

Ramban (*Bemidbar* 33:1), adding to Rashi's commentary, quotes Rambam in *Moreh Nevukhim* to assert the importance of the historical con-
creteness of naming the places where great miracles took place. These
journeys and places are emphasized to bolster the belief of future generations by enabling the visualization of unfathomable miracles:

הוסיף הרב במורה הנבוכים (ג נ) תועלת בידיעתם, לומר הצורך להזכיר
המסעים גדול מאד, כי הנסים והאותות הנעשות היו אמיתיות לכל רואיהם,
אך בעתיד יהיו דברים בשמועה ויכזיבם השומע.

And the Rabbi [Moshe ben Maimon] added in the *Moreh
Nevukhim* another [explanation as to the] benefit [that we derive]
from knowledge [of these stages], saying: "There was a very great
necessity in mentioning the [stages of the] journeyings. For
[although] the miracles and wonders that were done were [rec-
ognized as] true ones by all who saw them, in later times these
events would be matters of hearsay, and those who hear about
them [then] might deny them altogether.[2]

Ibn Ezra (*Bemidbar* 33:1, 2, ad loc.), on the other hand, claims that recording these journeys was Moshe's initiative:

(א) אלה מסעי - כאשר חנו בני ישראל בערבות מואב וישבו שם חדשים
עד שבנו הערים הנזכרים, ולא זזו משם כי אם אחרי מות אהרן, כתב משה
כל המסעים: (ב) את מוצאיהם - איך יצאו ממקום למקום, על כן אחריו
למסעיהם. על פי ה' דבק עם למסעיהם:

---

1. *JPS translation.*
2. Translation taken from Charles B. Chavel, *Ramban: Commentary on the Torah,
   Bemidbar* (New York: Shilo, 1975).

"These are the journeys" – when *Benei Yisrael* encamped on the plains of Moav and they settled there for several months until the mentioned cities were built, and they didn't move from there until after the death of Aharon, during this time Moshe wrote of all their journeys.

Ramban (33:1) asserts that Moshe was merely responding to *Hashem's* will:

והנה מכתב המסעות מצות השם היא מן הטעמים הנזכרים, או מזולתן
ענין לא נתגלה לנו סודו, כי "על פי ה'" דבק עם "ויכתוב משה", לא כדברי
ר"א שאמר שהוא דבק עם "למסעיהם", שכבר הודיענו זה (לעיל ט כ) על
פי ה' יחנו ועל פי ה' יסעו.

Thus the writing down [the stages of] the journeyings was a commandment of God, either for the reasons mentioned above or for some other reasons, [for] a purpose the secret of which has not been revealed to us. For [the expression] 'by the commandment of the eternal' is connected with [the beginning of that verse], 'and Moses wrote,' unlike the opinion of Rabbi Abraham Ibn Ezra who wrote that it is connected with 'according to their journeys,' for Scripture has already informed us of this [fact, saying]: 'according to the commandment of the Eternal they remained encamped, and according to the commandment of the Eternal they journeyed.'[3]

According to both perspectives, the detailed report is significant. The construct of the wording and legacy is unusual and should not be perceived as a simple catalogue of places, borders and cities of refuge.

It is noteworthy that the *parashah* that presents the message of Divine mercy, and which anchors and concretizes religious belief for future generations, concludes with a second account of the story of the daughters of Tzelofchad as the final event in *Benei Yisrael's* odyssey in the desert.

3.   Translation taken from Chavel, *Ramban*.

Why is the narrative of the daughters of Tzelofchad given pride of place as the coda to the national exodus and desert experience? Perhaps it is a fitting thematic conclusion to the Exodus narrative which began with the efforts of Yocheved and Miriam to protect Moshe, thereby ensuring the Jewish future. The efforts of the Israelite women constitute bookends to the redemptive enterprise which began in *Shemot* and ends in *Bemidbar*.

Furthermore, the specific actions of the daughters of Tzelofchad were spiritually consequential, ensuring their literary immortality. It is instructive to examine this episode in greater detail.

The daughters of Tzelofchad are mentioned for the first time in the second census of *Benei Yisrael* in the desert in *Sefer Bemidbar* (26:33). This census helped determine the division of land in *Eretz Yisrael*. Tzelofchad had no male heirs and his five daughters were included under the tribe of Menashe. *Shevet Levi* was also counted within this census despite the fact that they were not eligible to inherit land in *Eretz Yisrael*. The passage that concludes the census declares that, "no man survived from the original census that took place when they entered the desert of Sinai. They were punished [as a result of the sin of the spies] and only Kalev ben Yefuneh and Yehoshua Bin Nun survived" (*Bemidbar* 26:63–65).

(סג) אלה פקודי משה ואלעזר הכהן אשר פקדו את בני ישראל בערבת מואב על ירדן ירחו: (סד) ובאלה לא היה איש מפקודי משה ואהרן הכהן אשר פקדו את בני ישראל במדבר סיני: (סה) כי אמר ה' להם מות ימתו במדבר ולא נותר מהם איש כי אם כלב בן יפנה ויהושע בן נון:

63. These are the persons enrolled by Moshe and Eleazar the priest who registered the Israelites on the steppes of Moav, at the Jordan near Jericho. 64. Among these there was not one of those enrolled by Moshe and Aharon the priest when they recorded the Israelites in the wilderness of Sinai. 65. For the Lord had said of them, "They shall die in the wilderness." Not one of them survived, except Kalev son of Yephunneh and Yehoshua son of Nun.

Following this census, the Torah records that the daughters of Tzelofchad inquired about their eligibility to assume their father's legacy in

Eretz Yisrael. The juxtaposition of the story is informative. The language used in the retelling is instructive and the response of Moshe is unusual. The consequences of this episode to the conclusion of *Sefer Bamidbar* are also significant.

The main narrative and subsequent halakhic ruling are related in only eleven verses (*Bemidbar* 27:1–11):

(א) ותקרבנה בנות צלפחד בן חפר בן גלעד בן מכיר בן מנשה למשפחת מנשה בן יוסף ואלה שמות בנתיו מחלה נעה וחגלה ומלכה ותרצה: (ב) ותעמדנה לפני משה ולפני אלעזר הכהן ולפני הנשיאם וכל העדה פתח אהל מועד לאמר: (ג) אבינו מת במדבר והוא לא היה בתוך העדה הנועדים על ה' בעדת קרח כי בחטאו מת ובנים לא היו לו: (ד) למה יגרע שם אבינו מתוך משפחתו כי אין לו בן תנה לנו אחזה בתוך אחי אבינו: (ה) ויקרב משה את משפטן לפני ה': (ו) ויאמר ה' אל משה לאמר: (ז) כן בנות צלפחד דברת נתן תתן להם אחזת נחלה בתוך אחי אביהם והעברת את נחלת אביהן להן: (ח) ואל בני ישראל תדבר לאמר איש כי ימות ובן אין לו והעברתם את נחלתו לבתו: (ט) ואם אין לו בת ונתתם את נחלתו לאחיו: (י) ואם אין לו אחים ונתתם את נחלתו לאחי אביו: (יא) ואם אין אחים לאביו ונתתם את נחלתו לשארו הקרב אליו ממשפחתו וירש אתה והיתה לבני ישראל לחקת משפט כאשר צוה ה' את משה:

1. The daughters of Tzelofchad, of the Manassite family – son of Hepher son of Gilead son of Machir son of Manasseh son of Joseph – came forward. The names of the daughters were Machlah, No'a, Choglah, Milkah, and Tirzah. 2. They stood before Moshe, Eleazar the priest, the chieftains, and the whole assembly, at the entrance of the Tent of Meeting, and they said, 3. "Our father died in the wilderness. He was not one of the faction, Korach's faction, which banded together against the Lord, but died for his own sin; and he has left no sons. 4. Let not our father's name be lost to his clan just because he had no son! Give us a holding among our father's kinsmen!" 5. Moshe brought their case before the Lord. 6. And the Lord said to Moshe, 7. "The plea of Tzelofchad's daughters is just: you should give them a hereditary holding among their father's kinsmen; transfer their father's share

to them. 8. Further, speak to the Israelite people as follows: 'If a man dies without leaving a son, you shall transfer his property to his daughter. 9. If he has no daughter, you shall assign his property to his brothers. 10. If he has no brothers, you shall assign his property to his father's brothers. 11. If his father had no brothers, you shall assign his property to his nearest relative in his own clan, and he shall inherit it.' This shall be the law of procedure for the Israelites, in accordance with the Lord's command to Moshe."

Rashi (*Bemidbar* 26:64) quotes the *Midrash Tanchuma* to explain why the death of the entire wilderness generation is juxtaposed with the request of the daughters of Tzelofchad to inherit land in *Eretz Yisrael*.

סד) ובאלה לא היה איש וגו' - אבל על הנשים לא נגזרה גזרת המרגלים, לפי שהן היו מחבבות את הארץ. האנשים אומרים (במדבר יד ד) נתנה ראש ונשובה מצרימה, והנשים אומרות (במדבר כז, ד) תנה לנו אחוזה. לכך נסמכה פרשת בנות צלפחד לכאן.

"And of these there was no man" – But on the women the decree of the spies did not fall, because they loved the land. The men say 'Let us appoint a leader and let us return to Egypt,' and the women say 'give us a possession.' Therefore, the section of *benot Tzelofchad* is next to this.

The women did not participate in the sin of the spies because of their love for Israel. The women's lineage is related all the way back to Yosef because of his acute love for *Eretz Yisrael*, as expressed by his insistence in his final request of his brothers that he be ultimately buried there (*Bereishit* 50:25). Until the incident of *benot Tzelofchad*, Yosef's legacy was transmitted and actualized exclusively by Yehoshua who was descended from the tribe of Efraim, the son of Yosef. It was, after all, Efraim who received the right hand of Yaakov's blessing. (*Bereishit* 48:14). The *benot Tzelofchad* are the first descendants of Menashe to claim the love of Israel as their family legacy. This is particularly striking since they are women, and the daughters of one who died as a result of sin. They requested his inheritance to perpetuate their father's name.

Moshe did not answer them immediately and related their question to *Hashem*. The response that followed established that "the daughters of Tzelofchad speak properly" and that they will "be given a possession of inheritance among the brothers of their father, and the inheritance of their father will pass unto them" (*Bemidbar* 27:7).

What were their merits? Usually, when *Benei Yisrael* complained, their approach to Moshe is formulated in hostile language. The episode of the spies is introduced with "and they murmured" (*Bemidbar* 14:2). Leaving Mount Sinai, the nation is described as *"mit'onenim"* – "evil complainers" (*Bemidbar* 11:1). In sharp contrast, *benot Tzelofchad*'s approach is described as conciliatory, as "drawing near" (*"va-tikravnah"*). In their appeal to the religious hierarchy of their generation, they employ language that is similar to the requests of the impure who were excluded from the paschal lamb in the desert and who were given a second opportunity to observe the Divine imperative (*Bemidbar* 9:6).

The Talmud (*Bava Batra* 119a) notes that the Torah generally relates *halakhot* as dicta absent historical background. Here as well, the Torah could have easily relayed the laws of inheritance without the story of the daughters of Tzelofchad's request. The Talmud therefore concludes that the *benot Tzelofchad* narrative was chosen with the intention of "crediting them for their approach."

Yet here, as in only a minority of circumstances, Moshe first confers with *Hashem* before responding. What is so unusual about these women that they deserve such honorable mention? The Talmud (ibid. 119b) suggests that their method of inquiry reflected the embodiment of three significant attributes:

תנא: בנות צלפחד חכמניות הן, דרשניות הן, צדקניות הן. חכמניות הן -
שלפי שעה דברו, דא"ר שמואל בר רב יצחק: מלמד שהיה משה רבינו יושב
ודורש בפרשת יבמין, שנאמר: [דברים כ"ה] כי ישבו אחים יחדו, אמרו לו:
אם כבן אנו חשובין - תנה לנו נחלה כבן, אם לאו - תתיבם אמנו! מיד:
ויקרב משה את משפטן לפני ה'. דרשניות הן - שהיו אומרות: אילו היה
[לו] בן לא דברנו. והתניא: בת! אמר ר' ירמיה: סמי מכאן בת. אביי אמר:
אפילו היה בת לבן לא דברנו. צדקניות הן - שלא נישאו אלא להגון להן.

A *Baraitha* taught: The daughters of Tzelofchad were wise. They were expounders of the Torah and they were righteous. 'They were wise,' for they spoke in a timely fashion. For R. Shemuel bar B. Yitzchak said: this teaches us that Moshe, our teacher, was sitting and expounding the passage in the Torah which details the laws of *yibbum*. It stated in the passage, 'when brothers dwell together.' [The daughters of Tzelofchad] thereupon said to Moshe: if we are considered equal to a son inasmuch as we exempt our mother from *yibbum*, give us our inheritance as you would a son; and if we are not considered equal to a son in regard to inheritance, let our mother be required to undergo *yibbum*. Immediately 'Moshe brought their case before *Hashem*.' 'They were expounders of the Torah,' for they said to Moshe, 'If our father would have had a son, we would not have spoken' [thus they knew the law]. But it was taught in a *Baraitha* [that they said, 'if our Father would have had] a daughter.' How can that *Baraitha* be explained? R. Yirmiah said: delete from here the word daughter [for the text is incorrect]. Abaye said: [it means] even if there would have been a daughter of a son left behind by our father, we would not have spoken. 'They were righteous,' for they only married men who were fitting for them.[4]

They displayed wisdom (*"chakhmaniot"*) by the impeccable timing of their query, as it was based upon the legal implications of Moshe's exposition of the rules of *yibbum*, which unequivocally establish that all children qualify as legacy regardless of gender. They also exhibited halakhic intelligence and reverence (*"darshaniyot"*), by focusing on what was halakhically viable. Furthermore, they demonstrated righteousness (*"tzidkaniot"*), by delaying their marriages until after the resolution of this issue. Their approach conveyed their self-image as part of the spiritual halakhic continuum of *Benei Yisrael*.

Their spiritual posture particularly stands out in the context of broader national developments. While *Benei Yisrael* were floundering in

---

4. Translation, with minor modifications, taken from Schottenstein edition of *Tractate Bava Batra*, (Mesorah Publications, Brooklyn, NY).

an identity crisis regarding their relationship to *Hashem, Halakhah* and Israel, these women retained and nurtured their inner religious compass. The *Bemidbar Rabbah* (Vilna, *Parashah* 21) states that throughout the desert experience, the women did not participate in the two major sins of the generation. They did not participate in the sin of the golden calf nor in the sins associated with the spies. They did not donate their jewelry to construct the calf and instead of clamoring to return to Egypt they wanted to advance to *Eretz Yisrael*. These values were further epitomized in the actions and language of the daughters of Tzelofchad.

These attributes highlight the importance of the daughters of Tzelofchad and explain why *Sefer Bemidbar* concludes with a repetition of their story.

In the final chapters of *Sefer Bemidbar*, the tribal leaders of Menashe approached Moshe after assessing the ramifications of the Divine edict to pass on a father's inheritance to the female heirs if there are no sons. They apprised Moshe of the prospect that if the daughters marry outside the tribe of Menashe "their inheritance will be subtracted from the inheritance of our fathers and be added to the inheritance of the tribe into which they will marry" (*Bemidbar* 36:3). This change will be permanent because the land will not revert back to Menashe, even during the Jubilee year (Rashi, *Bemidbar* 36:4).

What is most striking and important about this grievance is the way it was presented to Moshe. While, as we stated earlier, most complaints against *Hashem* and Moshe were formulated in a hostile manner bearing a pugilistic linguistic signature, the language utilized by the leaders of Menashe reflect the positive hallmarks of the language spoken and the actions taken by the daughters of Tzelofchad. The leaders of Menashe "come close" – "*va-yikrevu*" (*Bemidbar* 36:1). They approach the general leadership of *Benei Yisrael* including Moshe (*Bemidbar* 36:1). They speak reverently to Moshe and refer to him as "master" (*Bemidbar* 36:2). Moshe's response also invokes the language initially addressed to the *benot Tzelofchad*: "Correctly does the tribe of the children of Yosef speak" (*Bemidbar* 27:7; 36:5).

Moshe's proposed solution (36:6–9) addresses the complexity of the various concerns:

(ו) זה הדבר אשר צוה ה' לבנות צלפחד לאמר לטוב בעיניהם תהיינה
לנשים אך למשפחת מטה אביהם תהיינה לנשים: (ז) ולא תסב נחלה לבני
ישראל ממטה אל מטה כי איש בנחלת מטה אבתיו ידבקו בני ישראל:
(ח) וכל בת ירשת נחלה ממטות בני ישראל לאחד ממשפחת מטה אביה
תהיה לאשה למען יירשו בני ישראל איש נחלת אבתיו: (ט) ולא תסב נחלה
ממטה למטה אחר כי איש בנחלתו ידבקו מטות בני ישראל:

6. This is what the Lord has commanded concerning the daughters of Tzelofchad: They may marry anyone they wish, provided
they marry into a clan of their father's tribe. 7. No inheritance of
the Israelites may pass over from one tribe to another, but the
Israelites must remain bound each to the ancestral portion of his
tribe. 8. Every daughter among the Israelite tribes who inherits
a share must marry someone from a clan of her father's tribe, in
order that every Israelite may keep his ancestral share. 9. Thus
no inheritance shall pass over from one tribe to another, but the
Israelite tribes shall remain bound each to its portion.

The suggestion seems to be a contradiction. They can "be wives to
whomever is good in their eyes, but only to the family of their father's
tribe shall they become wives" (*Bemidbar* 36:6). Can they marry anyone
or just a member of Menashe? The Talmud (*Bava Batra* 120a) explains:

אמר רב יהודה אמר שמואל: בנות צלפחד הותרו להנשא לכל השבטים,
שנאמר [במדבר ל"ו], לטוב בעיניהם תהיינה לנשים, אלא מה אני מקיים
[במדבר ל"ו] אך למשפחת מטה אביהם תהיינה לנשים? עצה טובה השיאן
הכתוב, שלא ינשאו אלא להגון להן.

R. Yehudah said in the name of Shemuel: The daughters of Tzelofchad were permitted to marry into any of the tribes, for it is stated
'to those who are favorable in their eyes shall they become wives.'
But how can I explain 'but only to the family of the tribe of their
father shall they become wives?' Scripture offered them sound
advice, that they should marry only men that were fitting for them.

While the women retained the freedom to marry into any tribe, they were strongly encouraged to wed within Menashe in order to secure Menashe's portion in the land of Israel. Although initially they were awarded inheritance without qualification, *benot Tzelofchad* responded with equanimity to Moshe's more restrictive proposal (36:10–13):

(י) כאשר צוה ה' את משה כן עשו בנות צלפחד: (יא) ותהיינה מחלה תרצה וחגלה ומלכה ונעה בנות צלפחד לבני דדיהן לנשים: (יב) ממשפחת בני מנשה בן יוסף היו לנשים ותהי נחלתן על מטה משפחת אביהן: (יג) אלה המצות והמשפטים אשר צוה ה' ביד משה אל בני ישראל בערבת מואב על ירדן ירחו:

As *Hashem* commanded, so did the daughters of Tzelofchad do. The daughters of Tzelofchad, Machlah, Tirtzah, Choglah, Milkah and No'a married the sons of their uncles. To the tribes of the sons of Menashe, son of Yosef, they became wives and thus the heritage was preserved. These are the commandments and laws that God commanded Moshe for *Benei Yisrael* in the plains of Moav by the Jordan at Jericho (*Bemidbar* 36:10–13).

In light of these developments, we can better appreciate the previous depiction of *benot Tzelofchad* as righteous ("*tzidkaniot*"). It is noteworthy that the Torah's language regarding the proposal to marry within their tribe is ambiguous. The Talmud clearly interprets the language as suggestive in nature and not legally binding. Yet *benot Tzelofchad* chose to follow the proposal as a commandment! The verse clearly states: "As *Hashem* commanded so do the daughters of Tzelofchad do."

The daughters of Tzelofchad realized that the prime objective of inheritance was the perpetuation of name and legacy. This is what they state in their original claim (*Bemidbar* 27:4). Consequently, they did not just accept the letter of the law, but the spirit of the law as well. They were sensitive to the fact that marrying outside the tribe of Menashe would defeat the whole purpose of their original request.

Sefer Bemidbar concludes as *Benei Yisrael* were poised to enter *Eretz Yisrael*, ushering in a new era. The duty and responsibility to perpetuate the law both in spirit and letter would be the charge of this new generation as they undertook the challenge of integrating the love and enthusiasm for Israel with reverence for the Divine word. What better way to exemplify these principles than with the narrative of the daughters of Tzelofchad, a fitting coda to the Exodus and wilderness experience.

ספר דברים

Rabbi Josh Joseph

דברים: The Question to Everyone's Answer: An Introduction to *Devarim*[1]

In his introduction to *Sefer Devarim*,[2] the Netziv shares with us a theme that continues throughout the book, and sheds light on the importance of the *sefer* as the culmination of our sacred *Chumash*. As with his famous introduction to *Sefer Bereishit*, where he focuses on the book's alternate name, "*Sefer Ha-Yashar*," the Netziv analyzes another appellation for *Devarim*, namely "*Mishneh Torah*." Eschewing the classic

---

1. A word of thanks is due to my father, Rabbi Howard Joseph, shlit"a, who has been teaching me about the Netziv for decades, and whose *parashah* blog www.theprofoundword.com, continues to inspire my every *Shabbat*. If the reader finds value in this essay it is most likely due to his influence. One extra note: the title is borrowed from a song by the Steve Miller Band, with the full lyric reading: "The question to everyone's answer is usually asked from within" (*Book of Dreams*, 1977).
2. *Ha'amek Davar*, volume 5, *Petichah Le-Sefer Devarim*. All references to the "Netziv's introduction" refer here; all translations are mine.

understanding of this alias as "a repetition of the Torah,"[3] he sees the *sefer* as a "*shinun shel Torah*," an instrument for study of the Torah that will explicate and clarify the intricacies of the Torah – "*le-faresh dikdukei ha-Torah.*"[4] In this – the ultimate Mosaic presentation – we, the students of Torah, would expect nothing less than a final crescendo through which life's questions will be answered and a mode for continuing our relationship with the *Ribbono Shel Olam* will be proffered. As we will see, the teachings and messages of the *Mishneh Torah* do, in fact, provide us with the guidance and direction we seek today as individual members of the Jewish people, just as its teachings provided guidance and direction for Benei Yisrael as they prepared to enter the next phase of their relationship with *Hashem* in the Land of Israel.[5]

To demonstrate the significance of this *sefer*, the Netziv cites two examples of its role in our collective story. First, *Parashat Shoftim* clearly and literally points to the *Mishneh Torah* as being a crucial component of what a king must write, learn and carry with him at all times:

> It will be when he sits on the throne of his kingdom, he will write this *Mishneh Torah*... And it will be with him and he will read from it every day of his life so that he will learn awe of *Hashem*; to keep all the words of the Torah and its laws in order to act upon them; so that his heart will not be haughty over his brothers; and so that he will not turn from the commandment[s]...[6]

Even though the *mitzvah* of writing refers to the whole Torah, nevertheless the Netziv insists that the king's priority remains the *Mishneh Torah*

3. *Chazal* refer to *Sefer Devarim* as "*Mishneh Torah*" in several places, for example *Berakhot* 21a. The Netziv cites *Tosafot* (*Gittin* 2a), who use the name to explain that a *get* has twelve lines corresponding to the blank lines between the various *sefarim* of the Torah. However, they explain that the break between *Bemidbar* and *Devarim* is different since "*Mishneh Torah*" means that it is merely a repetition of the rest of the Torah. Thus, clearly, according to *Tosafot, Mishneh Torah* means "repetition."
4. See also Targum Onkelos, *Devarim* 17:18, "*patshegen Oraita*" (the explanation and clarification of Torah).
5. The Netziv is the ideal tour guide for our journey with his poetic formulations and visionary insights, and his introduction is well worth reading in the original.
6. *Devarim* 17:14–20.

as a first among equals with the other parts of the *Chumash* in guiding and teaching the king in the ways of *Hashem.*

His second example, though,[7] takes the reader a step further on the path to understanding the specific message the Torah has for each of us. The Netziv quotes the *midrash* from *Bemidbar Rabbah*[8] which refers to the *Mishneh Torah* as the "*signon*" (insignia) for Yehoshua, the next generational leader of *Benei Yisrael.* When *Hashem* sought out Yehoshua, according to the *midrash*, He discovered him in the midst of learning, holding in his hands the *Mishneh Torah.* The Netziv explains that Yehoshua, *Rabban Shel Yisrael,* leader of Israel, always examined and reviewed this *sefer.*

Why? What secrets does it contain? Why does the Netziv insist that one can learn from it "every kind of teaching"?[9] The telling story of *Hashem*'s encounter with Yehoshua, as well as the commandment for the king of Israel to write and carry the *Mishneh Torah* with him at all times, demonstrate for the Netziv the following vital lesson:

> One should understand, based on all of this, that one who examines carefully the words and teachings in this book that came from Moshe our Teacher through Divine inspiration, [will see that] *every person will find their own value [as] honey and milk... and from this each person will understand his own strength and will find his own straight path to walk upon – according to his own wanderings through the world; and the light of this book will be the candle for his steps.*

Thus, the Netziv suggests that every member of *Benei Yisrael* can realize his or her own strengths, and find his or her own path, from the teachings in *Sefer Devarim*, through in-depth study of the *Mishneh Torah.* Following the paradigm of Yehoshua, and as *Hashem* prescribed for future kings, our study of this *sefer* will provide us with the answers to life's questions.

---

7. In actuality, the Netziv refers to the *midrash* of Yehoshua before discussing the commandment for a king to write a *Mishneh Torah.*
8. Ch. 6.
9. Netziv, *Petichah Le-Sefer Devarim.*

As he concludes his introduction, the Netziv gives us a clue as to our next steps on this path of self-understanding and self-actualization. In a parenthetical note, he sends the reader to *Parashat Eikev*[10] for further elaboration on this theme of finding one's own direction. The *pasuk* states:

> *Ve-attah Yisrael mah Hashem Elokekha sho'el me-immakh ki im le-yir'ah et Hashem Elokekha?...*[11]

The *pasuk* as normally read – with a question mark following the second instance of the word "*Elokekha*" – translates as "what does *Hashem* want from you"? It then continues to answer the question, stating that *Hashem*'s sole request is "*yir'at Shamayim*," fear, or awe, of Heaven. Based on this classic reading of the *pasuk*, Rashi points out that *Chazal*[12] learn from here the famous line of "*ha-kol be-yedei Shamayim chutz me-yir'at Shamayim*,"[13] that everything in our lives is in the hands of *Hashem*, except for our awe of *Hashem*.

However, the Netziv is satisfied neither with this reading, nor with this understanding – neither from a literal standpoint nor for its philosophical and communal implications. The Netziv points out[14] that in actuality much more is being asked of *Benei Yisrael* than just *yir'at Shamayim*; indeed, he believes that *everything* is being asked of us. A closer look at the *pasuk* reveals that our initial reading does not include the entire verse, and that even the subsequent verse continues the theme:

> *... lalekhet be-khol derakhav u-le-ahavah oto, ve-la'avod et Hashem Elokekha be-khol levavekha u-ve-khol nafshekha; lishmor et mizvot Hashem ve-et chukotav asher Anokhi metzavkha ha-yom, le-tov lakh.*

> ...to walk only in His paths, to love Him, and to serve the Lord

---

10. *Devarim* 10:12–13.
11. Ibid.
12. *Berakhot* 33b.
13. Rashi, *Devarim* 10:12.
14. *Ha'amek Davar* 10:12.

your God with all your heart and with all your soul, to keep the
Lord's commandments and laws which I command you this day,
so that it shall be good for you (*Devarim* 10:12–13).

Apparently, not only is *yir'at Shamayim* in our hands, but we must follow in *Hashem*'s ways, love Him, worship Him with all of our heart and
soul and keep His commandments. Quite a tall order! Indeed, insofar
as religious requirements are concerned, there is not much more to be
wanted of us. How, then, can we each be expected to fulfill all that is
being required of us? Further, the Netziv wonders how a single question
can be asked of every person, as each person has different talents, abilities and understanding. Could it be that the person who spends all day
studying Torah is being asked the same question as one who does not?

In order to solve this difficulty, the Netziv punctuates the *pasuk*
as follows:

Ve-attah Yisrael mah Hashem Elokecha sho'el me-immakh?...

This slight change in punctuation gives a completely original meaning
to the *pasuk*, changing the translation from "what does *Hashem* want
from you..." to "what is *Hashem* asking of you?" Indeed, to demonstrate
the plausibility of this alternative reading, the Netziv comments on the
grammar of the *pasuk*, noting that there are several spots where a *vav*
is missing, thus rendering strange stops in the list. To wit, why is there
no *vav* before *lalekhet* or *lishmor*? "Rather," he explains "it is clear that
each one of these is like the beginning of a statement."[15]

With this in mind, he notes that in fact, *Hashem* is making *four distinct requests of four distinct groups.*[16] Of the first group, *Hashem* requires

---

15. *Ha'amek Davar* 10:12.
16. In two places within this comment (ibid.), the Netziv suggests different sources for
the four-group division. The reference that is most clear is *Nitzavim* (*Devarim* 29:9)
where *Benei Yisrael* are divided into the following four groups: 1) *rasheikhem shivteikhem*; 2) *zikneikhem ve-shotreikhem*; 3) *kol ish Yisrael*; and 4) *tapekhem, nesheikhem
ve-gerkha*. Here, the Netziv actually suggests expanding the groupings from four
to 48 as he notes that the word *"shivteikhem"* in the first grouping, *"rasheikhem
shivteikhem,"* connotes that within each of the four groups, each *shevet* is judged

yir'at Shamayim; of the second, *ahavah* and *avodah*; the third group must keep the *mitzvot*; and the fourth group must act for the sake of what is good, *"le-tov."*[17] No group is comparable to another; each has its own question to answer – no more, no less:

> Each group has its own covenant (*berit*), and what *Hashem* asks of one, He does not ask of the other; and it is almost forbidden for the second group [to answer the first's question] ... [18]

In his commentary on *Parashat Nitzavim* (29:9), the Netziv continues this theme, and notes:

> ...not every person's judgment and equations (*din ve-cheshbon*)

differently (i.e. 12 × 4 = 48). Earlier in the piece, he points to another possible way to divide *Benei Yisrael* into four, based on the famous *pasuk* in *Parashat Balak*, which we recite every day as we enter a place of worship: *"mah tovu ohalekha Yaakov, mishkenotekha Yisrael"* – which, since the nouns are in plural, can be understood to refer to two *ohalim* plus two *mishkenot*. See there (*Bemidbar* 24:5–6), particularly for his understanding of women in this context.

17. *Pesukim* 12 and 13 would then read as follows:
    "Ve-attah Yisrael mah Hashem Elokeikha sho'el me-imkha"?
    Group 1: *"ki im le-yir'ah et Hashem Elokeikha."* [The leaders of *Benei Yisrael* should be focused on *yir'ah* (awe of *Hashem*), lest they grow haughty in their positions and sin against God and/or people.]
    Group 2: *"lalekhet be-khol derakhav u-le-ahavah oto, ve-la'avod et Hashem Elokekha be-khol levavekha u-ve-khol nafshekha."* [Our spiritual leadership must be as concerned with the elements of *ahavah*, i.e. prayer and Torah study, as these are what the Netziv refers to as the *"lechem Hashem,"* or 'God-sandwich.']
    Group 3: *"lishmor et mitzvot Hashem ve-et chukotav asher Anokhi metzavvekha ha-yom."* [The path of the typical *Ba'al ha-bayit* is one of adhering to *Hashem's* commandments; more specifically, the Netziv implores each individual to find one *mitzvah* with which he or she can find a special relationship.]
    Group 4: *"le-tov lakh."* [At the core of the Jewish experience lies a deep desire and even skill for bringing good into the world, which provides direction for this last group.]
18. *Ha'amek Davar* 10:12.

are equal... [Rather, in fact] each person is judged based on *the question that Hashem is asking him...*[19]

A person is only judged based on the question that is asked of him or her. We cannot look at another person and try to answer his or her question, or judge where they stand in answering what is being asked of them. Rather, it behooves us to spend some time trying to understand what it is that *Hashem* is asking of us, as individual members of *Kelal Yisrael*, who belong to one of these groups.[20]

Often, we are so busy figuring out our answers that we don't stop to think about what the questions are. In several places, *Chazal* note that a *bat kol*, a Heavenly voice, cries out from *Har Sinai* every day, unbeknownst to most of *Benei Yisrael*.[21] Are we listening for *Hashem's* voice? If we were to listen, would we be better able to hear the specific question that *Hashem* is asking us?

Dear Reader, what question is *Hashem* asking you?

Several years ago, President George W. Bush invited Bono, lead singer of rock band U2 to the National Prayer Breakfast in Washington, DC where he told the following story:

A number of years ago, I met a wise man who changed my life. In countless ways, large and small, I was always seeking the Lord's blessing. I was saying, "Look, I have a new song, would you look out for it. I have a family, I'm going away on tour, please look after them. I have this crazy idea, could I have a blessing on it?" And this wise man asked me to stop. He said, "Stop asking God to bless what you're doing. Get involved in what God is doing – because it's already blessed."[22]

19. Ibid., 29:9. As noted above, in note 14, the Netziv expounds upon this theme in some fascinating ways.
20. The specifics of the groups these pages do not allow. However, the commentary of the Netziv cited in note 15 begins to outline one of the possible groupings that the Netziv suggests.
21. Note for example, *Pirkei Avot* 6:2.
22. USA Today, Feb. 2, 2006 has a full transcript of his remarks.

We must focus on what *Hashem* is asking us to do and not on what answers we want or feel the need to have.

This concept should not be a foreign one to us. After all, in *Pirkei Avot*,[23] Rabban Gamliel states:

> Do His will as if it were yours, so that He may do your will as if it were His...

The Netziv explains that the theme of *Sefer Devarim* – the book of *Mishneh Torah* – is "*shinun shel Torah*," learning how to learn Torah. This learning can help lead us to a fuller understanding of our own goals, both as members of a group as well as individually. Through the medium of our listening, we will not only continue to foster our relationship with *Hashem*, but we will also be better able to truly understand ourselves. If we can only stop and listen to the question that *Hashem* is asking of us, the answers of self-actualization and a closer relationship with *Hashem* will be within our grasp.

---

23. 2:4. Translation follows Rabbi Jonathan Sacks, *Koren Siddur*, p. 640.

Rabbi Allen Schwartz

ואתחנן: Informed Love

After Moshe's initial plea to enter the Land of Israel, from which our *parashah* receives its name, the bulk of *Parashat Vaetchanan* is dedicated to recreating the scenario of the revelation at Sinai. The repetition of the Decalogue itself appears in our *parashah*, and is surrounded by a series of verses that exhort the Israelites to heed, learn, observe and listen to God, all as pre-requisites to the performance of His will. Consider this list from our *parashah*: *shema... la'asot* 4:1; *limadeti... la'asot* 4:5; *u-shemartem... la'asot* 4:6; *lelamed... la'asotkhem otam* 4:14; *shema... u-shemartem la'asotam* 5:1; *ve-shama'nu... ve-asinu* 5:24; *u-shemartem la'asot* 5:29; *Ve-shama'ta... ve-shamarta la'asot* 6:3; *Shema...* 6:4–9; *nishmor la'asot* 6:25; *Ve-shamarta... la'asotam* 7:11

What clearly emerges from this list is the sensible idea that in order to properly perform God's will, we must be learned, informed and knowledgeable. The rush to performance without proper training can lead to chaos, confusion, or worse. And it did.

Our Sages teach us that the Israelites were coerced into receiving the Torah at Sinai. God held the Torah above their heads, the Talmud relates,[1] until they accepted His word. This stands in stark contrast to the eager willingness of those gathered at Sinai to accept the Torah, as is evident from their famous assertion of *"na'aseh ve-nishmah."*[2] Why would God have to coerce those who declare such a willing assertion?[3]

Rav Joseph Soloveitchik *zt"l* explained the coercion as a function of the miracles Benei Yisrael had recently seen. Their rush to accept the Torah was simply the natural result of their redemption. This is actually *consistent* with their assertion of the *"na'aseh"* before *"nishmah."* Their phrasing indicates that they didn't give it much thought, and this precedence of performing before the necessary introductory intellectual connection to God, is precisely what led to the golden calf. The Israelites connected emotionally to God through His miracles in the Exodus story, but without the anchor of an intellectual relationship, the emotional component of that relationship was quickly undermined.[4]

The Rambam seems to make the same point in his *Mishneh Torah*, by first codifying the laws subsumed under the category of *Madda (knowledge)*, followed by those subsumed under the catergory of *Ahavah (love)*. He, too, would want the foundation of our relationship with God to be moored in the intellect.

The Rav also explained, in a number of different contexts, that the parallel forms of *Mussar Av* and *Torat Em* in *Sefer Mishlei* make the same point. The concept of *Mussar Av* refers to the intellectual component of Judaism, while the concept of *Torat Em* refers to the emotional component. A child attains *sheleimut* (completeness) through exposure to both of these components, with the *Mussar Av*, which always appears first in the verse (see *Mishlei* 1:8, 6:20), laying the groundwork for the *Torat Em*.

Additionally, the Rav found the expression of these two aspects of our relationship with God in the *mitzvot* that fall under a mathematical model of observance, and those that fall under an aesthetic model. The aesthetic *mitzvot* touch our artistic and emotional sensitivities. These

---

1. *Shabbat* 86a.
2. *Shemot* 24:7.
3. *Tosafot, Shabbat* 88a s.v. *kapah*; *Tosefta Bava Kamma* 7:3; *Rashi, Devarim* 32:20 s.v. *lo amun bam*.
4. See *Tosefta Bava Kama* 7:3

are the *mitzvot* that make us feel good by appealing to our senses. The concept of *hiddur mitzvah* (beautifying the *mitzvah*) fits this category, and is for us an essential religious expression. Then there is the mathematical model of religious expression. This model is expressed with less emotion, but not with less zeal. The mathematical model of *mitzvot* is the one in which we measure the *matzah* and *maror* at the Seder and scrupulously weigh every *ke-zayit* or *ke-beitzah* in the performance of God's will.

The Rav considered the blowing of the *shofar* to be a quintessentially aesthetic *mitzvah*. We are all ready to be profoundly touched by the shrill sound of the ram's horn, invoking the memories of *Akeidat Yitzchak* and reminding us of the tears of our own mother beckoning us to repent. What could be a more emotional moment for the Jew? Yet we all forgo this *mitzvah* when *Rosh Ha-Shanah* falls out on *Shabbat*, lest one dolt forget that it is *Shabbat* and traverse four *amot* in a public domain with a *shofar* in hand. Once again, the Rav showed us how the intellectual model takes preference over the emotional model.

It would seem that the golden calf was not the first misplacement of the order of intellectual and emotional connection. Consider the following: When Moshe heard from God at the burning bush that Pharaoh would refuse his initial demand for freedom, Moshe objected that this would lead the people to lose faith in him.[5] God then instructed Moshe to show miracles to the people to assure them that he was really sent by God, and that there is a purpose to Pharaoh's refusal. It is clear from this order, that Moshe was to first appeal to the Israelites *without* the use of miracles, and that the miracles should only be used *to bolster Benei Yisrael's faith*, should they refuse to heed Moshe's initial words. The problem is that Moshe showed *Benei Yisrael* the miracles at the outset.[6] Here too, the foundation of *Benei Yisrael's* faith was predicated upon miracles. It is no wonder then, that the emotional connection drawn from the miracles swiftly dissipated, and the Israelites quickly soured on Moshe after Pharaoh's refusal to let them go.[7]

---

5.   This is Ramban's rendition of *"ve-hen lo ya'aminu li,"* (Ramban, *Shemot* 4:1).
6.   *Shemot* 4:29–31.
7.   *Shemot* 5:20–21.

ואתחנן

The relationship between God and his people in the first four books of the Torah is like that of a parent and a child. We were rather passive in the initial stages of the relationship – being guided, being redeemed, and being led through the desert. In *Sefer Devarim*, however, an attempt is made to make the relationship more reciprocal, like that of a spouse. This seems counter-intuitive to this presentation – surely a spousal relationship is first and foremost emotional. Perhaps so. However, for a spousal relationship to thrive, it must be suffused with knowledge of one another. Love is not blind. Infatuation is blind. Love needs to be informed. For love to work, a couple needs to know as much as possible about each other. This is why the first expression of "love" in the Torah is *"ve-ha-Adam yada et Chavah ishto,"*[8] the Man *knew* Chava his wife.

There is a powerful lesson of love from the very first arranged marriage in the Torah. Avraham's servant stipulated that the first girl who would respond to his request by offering water to both him and his camels would be worthy of marrying Yitzchak. The Torah tells us that the servant directed his request to one specific girl and that he actually ran directly to Rivkah with his request.[9] Rashi wonders why the servant ran specifically to her, and not towards any of the other maidens around the well. As an answer, Rashi cites the *midrash*[10] that says that the water rose out of the well and into Rivkah's jug. The servant was so taken by this spectacle that he ran straight towards her to offer her the "test."[11] This only begs the question, why if Rivkah was accustomed to such miraculous occurrences happening on her behalf, did the servant feel the need to test her? He should have disposed of the test then and there! Surely such a miracle worker would be a good match for Yitzchak!

We can explain this test in light of the above delineation between intellect and emotion. Avraham's servant was so emotionally touched by the spectacle of the miracle that he ran to Rivkah, and came close to choosing her on emotion alone. He quickly grasped the situation, how-

8. *Bereishit* 4:1.
9. *Bereishit* 24:17.
10. *Bereishit Rabbah* 60:5.
11. Ramban (*Bereishit* 24:17, ad loc.) explains that the absence of the root *sh'b* in this verse teaches that she had no need to lower her jug into the water, for it rose on its own.

426

ever, and included the intellectual component in the form of the test. Her disposition to the miraculous, in our contemporary terms, may refer to her looks, statuesque figure, her father's wealth, her gregarious personality, her intelligence or bright wit. Yet none of this, on an intellectual level, means a thing in a relationship, if she is not a *Ba'alat chesed*. That is why the test was necessary. Relationships based solely on an emotional component are on a weak foundation, and they are in grave danger of failing if they are not bolstered by the intellect.

This is why our sages indicate that we are bound to the Torah not from saying *"na'aseh ve-nishmah,"* but from our acceptance of God in the Purim story. Unlike at Sinai, the Purim story did not have a miraculous component. The Jewish people were not overcome with the miracles of old. Yet they accepted there and then what God had already revealed.[12]

One question remains, however. How can we possibly be critical of *"na'aseh ve-nishmah"* when we consider the positive nature in which *Chazal* interpret it? In fact, the Talmud glowingly reports that when *Benei Yisrael* so readily preceded *"nishmah"* with *"na'aseh,"* the angels crowned each one who said so. Perhaps the angels did so in light of the following Biblical verse: *"Barkhu Hashem melakhav giburei koach osei devaro lishmo'a be-kol devaro"* – "Bless the Lord, His angels, mighty creatures who do His bidding, ever obedient to His bidding" (*Tehillim* 103:20). In other words, the angels crowned us because we preceded *"nishmah"* with *"na'aseh,"* which is what *they* usually do. So, returning to our question, how can we be critical of *"na'aseh ve-nishmah"*?

The answer lies in the fact that while there is no room for an emotional or intellectual component for angels, there is for us. The order of *"na'aseh ve-nishmah" is* indeed praiseworthy if it does not subsequently crumble at its first test. However, the key to making and keeping everlasting commitments that can withstand any trial or test, is to combine *madda* (the intellectual component) and *ahavah* (the emotional component), in *that* order.

12. See *Shabbat* 86a. *Yerushalmi Berakhot* 60b.

Rabbi Dr. Moshe Dovid Tendler

עֵקֶב: How to Transmit Faith

> *What does* Hashem *ask of you? Only to be in awe of Him, to love and worship Him with all your heart and with all your soul.* (Devarim 10:12)

Three of the 613 commandments are referred to in this exhortation of *Moshe Rabbenu*: to be in awe of *Hashem*, to love Him, and to worship Him in prayer.

The Talmud (*Berakhot* 33b) notes the deprecating tone set by the word "only": "Is it an insignificant achievement to reach the heights of love, awe, worship of *Hashem*?" The Talmud answers this rhetorical question by noting: "Indeed for Moshe it was but a minor achievement" (ibid.).

Not only for Moshe, but for his generation as well. Moshe was exhorting a nation freed from bondage by the mighty hand of *Hashem*. They all saw the sea split, the air filled with locusts, and animals called forth from the waters and forests of Egypt in obedience to *Hashem's* directives. They did not only believe in *Hashem* because He was the God of their ancestors, they "saw" *Hashem*! They "knew" *Hashem*! They had empirical proof of His existence and of His control of the natural forces that are the Divine laws of nature. This achievement of knowledge, knowing in lieu of believing, was the educational goal of the lengthy protocol *Hashem* went by in order to free the nation of Israel. Surely He could have freed them without delay. Why the slow pace of their deliverance from enslavement? The reason is stated in *Sefer Shemot*, "So that you will "know" (not just "believe") that I am God" (*Shemot* 10:2).

But what of later generations? Moshe warns, "Your children did not know *Hashem*; they did not see His mighty hand" (*Devarim* 11:2). Transmitting your faith to future generations will not be an easy task. The generation of Moshe knew *Hashem*; future generations must believe in *Hashem*. How do you teach belief? How do you transmit faith?

In the *Kuzari*, Yehudah Ha-Levi has the rabbi respond to the king's question of "who is your God?" by identifying Him as "the God who led the descendents of Abraham, Isaac and Jacob out of Egypt with signs and miracles, who split the sea and the Jordan River in a miraculous way." The rabbi did not respond "the God of Creation," rather, he cited empirical evidence for His dominion over the laws of nature; describing Him not only a God of faith but as a God Who revealed Himself to the millions by His miracles so that they could point with their finger and exult "This is my God" (*Shemot* 15:2).

The Rambam instructs us in the fulfillment of the *mitzvah* "to love *Hashem*." How is this love attained? "When one observes the wonders and wisdom of nature – all being the works of His hands…one strives to know *Hashem*. This striving leads to the emotion of loving *Hashem*" (Rambam, *Hilkhot Yesodei Torah* 2:2). *Yir'at Hashem* – to be in awe of the God of nature, leads to "*ahavat Hashem*." Awe is the prelude to love. To see God in nature is the pathway to love God and to reinforce faith with knowledge; to substitute certitude in place of vacillating doubt.

Many years, the Torah portion that is read on the *Shabbat* after *Tu Be-Av* is *Parashat Eikev*. The Talmud records an enigmatic statement of R. Shimon ben Gamliel: "The days Yom Kippur and *Tu Be-Av* have no equal among the Holy Days of the nation of Israel" (*Ta'anit* 30b–31a). Why is this so? Understandably Yom Kippur is a "special" day. It is a day when our sins are forgiven. However, what is the significance of *Tu Be-Av* that equates it with Yom Kippur?

Several answers are recorded in the text. One of them seems to be at first glance most inadequate. It is the answer given by Rabbah and Rav Yosef. *Tu Be-Av* is the day the populace ceased cutting wood for the *Mizbeach* (the Altar). Why would this fact give such great significance to the day of *Tu Be-Av* so as to equate it with Yom Kippur? Careful analysis of the comment of R. Eliezer recorded there provides an explanation: "After *Tu Be-Av*, the heat from the sun begins to diminish so that the wood does not dry as quickly, and becomes subject to infestation by insects and worms. Wood so infested is forbidden to be used on the Altar" (ibid.).

Thus, *Tu Be-Av* directs the mind to ponder the workings of the Divine laws of nature. On *Tu Be-Av*, God commands the sun to cool down. The wood-infesting insects are now permitted to feast on the wood. On *Tu Be-Av*, we recognize the control God exercises over the natural world. Yom Kippur focuses on God who controls the destiny of mankind, who shall live and who shall die. *Tu Be-Av* directs our attention to the God who controls natural law, who reveals Himself to us as *Elokim*, the Law Giver who ordained the laws of nature.

Therefore, the Talmud equates the two days. *Tu Be-Av* is tantamount to Yom Kippur. On both days we pay homage to our God and recognize Him as the one who controls the destiny of mankind as well as the laws of nature.

How should we transmit our faith, our knowledge, to future generations? Make them aware from earliest youth of the omnipresence of our God. When experiencing the clap of thunder, recite a blessing to *Hashem* whose "power fills the world." When seeing the ocean waves, recite a blessing to the One, "Who called the oceans into existence."

In the same vein, on *Pesach* night, the Seder rituals are designed to reaffirm annually that our forbearers "saw" and "knew" *Hashem* as they experienced the majesty of His mighty hand. On the night of the Seder we are to envision ourselves as if we are the generation freed from Egyptian bondage. In doing so, we attain the emotions of awe and love of *Hashem* as required in fulfilling the *mitzvot* of *yir'at Hashem, ahavat Hashem* and *avodat Hashem*.

Prof. Shoshana Schechter

ראה: *Berakhah, Mikdash* and Social Justice

ontext is everything. Before delving into an analysis of the specifics of *Parashat Re'eh*, we need to understand the backdrop of *Sefer Devarim* as a whole. This *sefer* is a mirrored reflection of the previous *sefer, Bemidbar*. In *Devarim*, as in *Bemidbar, Benei Yisrael* are on the threshold of entering *Eretz Kena'an*, but it is now 39 years later and we have before us the second generation of *Benei Yisrael*, since the first generation from *Sefer Bemidbar* was derailed as a result of *chet ha-meraggelim*. Moshe, who had been leading the Jews for the past 40 years, and who had seen the previous generation die out and the new generation take the helm, knew he was not going with them into the land. *Sefer Devarim* was his final message to his beloved people, his "Last Lecture," if you will. His goal was to ensure that this next generation would not fail as the previous one did. He was desperate to guarantee not only the Jews' success in entering and conquering the land, but also their success in living in the land while maintaining a relationship to God and a strict adherence to the Torah. He also understood the tremendous challenges all this entailed. This generation faced different challenges than the previous

one. The previous generation and their ancestors had been enslaved for
210 years, and as a result lacked the self-confidence needed to go and
conquer the land. Moshe, as their leader, understood the need to build
them up and strengthen their collective self-esteem in order to enable
them to successfully enter the land. Unfortunately, they were not able
to muster up the self-confidence needed for the mission to succeed,
and as a result they were unable to go through with it. The next generation, however, did not lack self-esteem. On the contrary, they were
born into a nation that was feared by other nations. If anything, their
self-confidence posed a threat to their relationship with God. Moshe
understood this new challenge and therefore throughout *Devarim* (but
especially at the beginning) he reminds *Benei Yisrael* that they could not
have gotten this far without the help of *Hashem*. His message is that they
should never think that *"kochi vi-otzem yadi asah li et ha-chayil ha-zeh"* –
"my own power and the might of my own hand have won this wealth
for me" (*Devarim* 8:17).

And there we have the context of *Devarim*. *Benei Yisrael*, after
40 years of wandering in the desert, are used to travelling and camping
together. With their arrival at their destination imminent, everything is
about to change. They will have to acclimate to the transition between
their previous supernatural relationship with God and their newfound
natural relationship with God (see the Netziv's Introduction to *Bemidbar*). They will be scattered throughout *Eretz Kena'an*, living off their own
means and not from the Heavenly *man* that sustained them in the desert.
Social classes will begin to emerge. Moshe exhorts them throughout the
sefer to maintain their relationship with God despite all these changes.

Parashat Re'eh, like all of *Devarim*, is about transition. Throughout the *parashiyyot* of *Devarim*, *Vaetchanan* and *Eikev*, Moshe has been
reminding *Benei Yisrael* about their history with God in the desert. He
recounts the giving of the Torah, the sin of the spies, the giving of the
man, and stresses the idea of reward and punishment – all for the sake
of urging this new generation of *Benei Yisrael* to follow God and adhere
to His Torah. The basic principles of faith have been re-established and
the people are continuously reminded that the *berit* that was enacted
between *Benei Yisrael* and God was not just with the previous generation
in the past, but it applies to every generation, now, today. *"Et ha-berakhah*

asher tishme'u el mitzvot Hashem Elokeikhem... asher Anokhi metzavveh etkhem ha-yom" – "the blessing, if you obey the commandments of the Lord your God that I command you this day" (*Devarim* 11:27). Once the basic tenets of faith have been reestablished and emphasized, Moshe must turn the focus toward the new changes in lifestyle. A major theme in this particular *parashah* is how to deal with this new upcoming society, both physically and spiritually. *Benei Yisrael* are on the verge of creating a new society, one that is no longer cohesively surrounding the *Mishkan*, as they were when they camped in the desert. A hierarchy of classes will develop with the newfound accumulation of property. *Benei Yisrael* will need to understand how to deal with their upcoming wealth and property.

The fundamental philosophy of the Torah on wealth, ownership and social status is clearly presented here. While the Torah recognizes the right of man to accumulate wealth and property, the essential condition is the recognition that it is all *"birkat Hashem"* (a blessing from God) – it is therefore not completely ours because God retains rights to it. Our right to own property and wealth is limited, in that God dictates what we do with that wealth. On a simple level, we are commanded to give *tzedakah* (*Devarim* 14:28) in the form of *ma'aser ani*, defined as giving poor people one tenth of our produce every three years. In the construction of this *mitzvah*, we see a more profound articulation, in that we are told that it's not merely a discharge of an obligation to give the *ma'aser*, but rather, our obligation is that the *levi, ger, yatom, ve-ha-almanah* (Levite, stranger, orphan, and widow) must eat and be satisfied (ibid., 29). As Rashi points out, one must *give* them enough to satisfy them (Rashi, *Devarim* 14:29, s.v. *ve-akhlu ve-save'u*). Upon fulfillment of this obligation, we are told, *"lema'an yevarekhekha Hashem"* (ibid., 29), then we will be the recipients of the *berakhah* of *Hashem* and be successful in all our endeavors. At the completion of the *ma'aser* process, the Torah uses a parallel construction to describe the *viddui ma'aser* (*Devarim* 26:14). The culmination of this *viddui* is *"asiti ke-khol asher tzivvitani,"* which Rashi explains as meaning, *"samachti ve-simachti bo"* – "I've enjoyed it and I've caused others to enjoy it as well." Enjoying and having others enjoy it with you is the essential fulfillment of the *mitzvah*. This leads to the final statement requesting God to see the action from up high and bless *Benei Yisrael, "hashkifah mi-me'on kodshekha"* (ibid., 15), with the *"barekh"* (bless) as an imperative to complete the cycle that is described here in our *parashah*.

This recognition of the limitations of our wealth and the obligations contained therein are not restricted to acts of charity. They are rooted in the very fabric of the soon-to-be-established economic system. Immediately following the acts of charity of *ma'aser ani*, the basic laws of *shemittat kesafim* are described (*Devarim* 15:1–2). At the end of the seventh year, all loans are nullified. Beyond the land and its produce not being ours for a year, our money in the form of loans is also not ours anymore. This annulment of debt is also repeatedly described as a source of *berakhah* (ibid., 4–6).

A subtle though significant outgrowth of the Torah's description of this *mitzvah* is a message of equality in social status. Annulling a loan removes one's power over someone else, as the Talmud quotes from *Mishlei* (22:7), *"ashir be-rashim yimshol ve-eved loveh le-ish malveh,"* meaning that the rich rule over the poor and the borrower is beholden to the lender. The Torah hints at this point with the use of the words, *"achikha"* and *"re'eihu,"* implying fellowship (*Devarim* 15:2). This idea is further highlighted by the text's distinction between a *nakhri* who is outside the community and a Jew who is within (ibid., 3).

Following the completion of the description of this *mitzvah*, the Torah continues with a new topic, telling us that to passively have our loans annulled is not sufficient. Rather, we must proactively provide loans – *"patoach tiftach"* (ibid., 11) – with disregard for an imminent *shemittah* year. The very thought of considering not to offer a loan because of *shemittah* is defined as a *"davar bliya'al,"* tantamount to *avodah zarah* (ibid., 9).[1] Here too, parallel to the obligation of *ma'aser ani*, we are commanded to provide people in need with *"dei machsoro"* (ibid., 8), that which they need to provide for that which they are lacking. We are explicitly urged to give to the poor person because it is on account

---

1. The term *"bliya'al"* is used in the context of an *ir-nidachat*, a city which has to be destroyed because of *"bliya'al"* – defined there as *avodah zarah*. *Ketuvot* 68a further states, *"kol ha-ma'alim einav min ha-tzedakah ke-ilu oved avodah zarah."* So too here the meaning is the same.

of this thing (providing loans for those in need) that *Hashem* will bless us (ibid., 10).

The Torah is presenting a radical model of ownership and wealth. A person's contribution to the welfare of the individuals and the community becomes the source of his blessings and abundance. People often think that they give to others because they are affluent. The Torah asserts here that this should not be our approach, but on the contrary, we are affluent because we give to others. Poverty and wealth are up to us. We must not be the cause of too much poverty.[2] The choice is ours, and if we choose the *berakhah* by recognizing that our wealth is from God and we are therefore using it appropriately to help others, we'll be blessed with more *berakhah*, more wealth.

This concept continues to be emphasized in the *parashah*, immediately following the imperative to give *tzedakah*, in the context of having an *eved*. We are told in *Devarim* (15:12–15) that we must set a slave free after six years. The slave to whom the Torah is referring was in a desperate state, which is why he sold himself into slavery initially. He was destitute, on the lowest level of society. When we set him free, we are forbidden to send him off empty handed, but rather he should be given *ha'anakah*, gifts of livestock, grain and wine, that the Torah clearly emphasizes are gifts from *Hashem* (ibid., 14). Even with our wealth, we are reminded of our vulnerability, that we ourselves were slaves in Egypt, and would not have been freed without God's intervention. This is God's way of reminding us, again, that despite having achieved wealth and power we are still not so powerful. We are not better than those in the lower classes because we have wealth. Rather, we only have wealth because God has given it to us. It is our responsibility to do good things

---

2.   R. Hirsch elaborates on this idea in the *parashah*, explaining that God is asserting that poverty will not cease to exist *"mi-kerev ha-aretz"* – "from the world," but that this condition of need that naturally arises in the world, you are commanded to prevent from recurring *"be-artzekha"* – "in your land," meaning, in the land of God's Torah. In this land, he asserts, "Every poor brother is to find in his richer relations his 'brother' and every poor and needy person belongs to 'you,' the community. Under the regime of a dutiful Torah nation, penury and need would only temporarily affect any individual and with God's assistance, be changed to a happy existence on earth commensurate with the dignity of a human being" (R. Hirsch, *Devarim*, ibid., 11).

with the *berakhah* that God has bestowed upon us. This section ends with the identical message of *"u-verakhekha Hashem,"* that if you follow these instructions, God will bless you in all that you do (ibid., 18).

This attitude exists not only in economics and social justice – in its intuitive place of *bein adam la-chavero* – but extends further to the manner in which the ritual, *bein adam la-Makom,* takes place as well. The refrain of *"ba-makom asher yivchar,"* in the place that God chooses to establish His Sanctuary, is repeated throughout this *parashah* an astounding 18 times. Through this emphasis, Moshe is establishing a ritual center of gravity for the new land. The *Mikdash,* *"ha-makom asher yivchar Hashem,"* is the place where everyone gathers to rejoice and give thanks to God and from where the values of Torah radiate. It is in this context specifically that, in order to fulfill *"ve-samachta lifnei Hashem"* in its entirety, one must share with those in need. Indeed, the full experience of *"ha-makom asher yivchar Hashem"* can only occur with the sharing of blessing with others. Thus, ritual fulfillment of *Mikdash* is inextricably linked to the *chesed* shown to those on the fringe of society.

The *simchah* that the Torah commands in celebration of the *Shalosh Regalim* is equal between "your sons and daughters" as well as "the orphans and widows in your midst." *"Ve-samachta lifnei Hashem… attah u-vinkha u-vitekha"* is together with *"ve-ha-levi asher bi-sh'arekha ve-ha-ger ve-ha-yatom ve-ha-almanah asher be-kirbekha"* (*Devarim* 16:11, 14) in the context of the holidays of both *Shavu'ot* and *Sukkot,* the two *chagim* that have *simchah* as an imperative in their celebrations. The two groups have equal weight when it comes to the celebration of these *chagim.* From here, Rashi explains beautifully, *"arba'ah sheli kneged arba'ah shelkha"* – that God promises that if we take care of His four (*levi, ger, yatom, almanah* – Levite, stranger, orphan, and widow), then He will take care of our four (*vinkha, vitekha, avdekha, amatekha* – son, daughter, male servant, and female servant). The next *pasuk* states again *"ve-zakharta ki-eved hayitah"* – "and you should remember that you were slaves" (ibid., 12), a reminder of our vulnerability and the similarity between us and those on the fringe. The *parashah* ends with the same theme that has been repeated throughout the description of the *Shalosh Regalim,* *"ish ke-matnat yado"* (ibid., 17), that we give according to that which we have, in accordance with the blessing that God has given us.

The *Keli Yakar* points out that *"ke-matnat yado"* should be *yadkha*, but *"yado"* implies that it's referring to *yad Hashem*, reminding us not to feel bad about giving away our possessions, since our possessions come from God and we give based on what He has given us.

The place God chooses to dwell within, besides being a ritu-alistic venue, is also a center of Torah study. We are commanded to spend time *"ba-makom asher yivchar,"* aside from the times of the *Sha-losh Regalim*. *Ma'aser sheni*, for example, must be eaten in *Yerushalayim*, *"lema'an tilmad le-yir'ah et Hashem"* – "so that you shall learn to fear God" (*Devarim* 14:23). From this, the *Sifre* learns- *"lo nitan ma'aser sheni ela bishvil talmud ve-yir'ah"* – *"Ma'aser sheni* was solely commanded in order for you to learn Torah and in order for you to fear God." This means that we spend time in *Yerushalayim* aside from the *chagim* for the express purpose of learning Torah. In this educational mode, the Torah again highlights the notion of enjoying *Hashem's berakhah "ba-makom asher yivchar,"* (ibid., 24, 26) without abandoning those in need. In this case it means not abandoning the *levi* who is in your midst because he does not have his own portion (ibid., 27).

The theme of the place that God chooses being a place of justice and equality goes beyond *Parashat Re'eh* – it is the consistent motif of *Yerushalayim* throughout history. According to *Chazal*, one of the names of *Yerushalayim* is *Tzedek*. For this reason the kings of *Yerushalayim* are referred to as Malki-Tzedek and Adoni-Tzedek. The Rashbam and Ibn Ezra (*Bereishit* 14:18, ad loc.) both explain that just like the king of Egypt is called Pharaoh and the *Pelishti* king is called Avimelech, the king of *Yerushalayim* is called Malki-Tzedek, or Adoni-Tzedek in the time of Yehoshua. He is called this since he is king of the place of *tzedek*.

Yerushalayim is therefore destroyed when it loses its claim to its honorable name. The *navi* Yeshayahu consistently echoes this idea, asserting that the entire point of *Yerushalayim* is to take care of those on the fringe of society, the *yatom* and *almanah* (*Yeshayahu* 1:10–17). Yeshayahu relays that God is rejecting the sacrifices of *Benei Yisrael* because *"eikhah hayetah le-zonah"* (ibid., 21). *Yerushalayim* has lost its way, because those people who are essential to our rejoicing before God are now the victims of our cruelty. Yeshayahu is essentially urging us to go back to *Parashat Re'eh* and remember how we must celebrate before

God in *Yerushalayim* and with whom. Yeshayahu concludes his admonishment stating *"acharei khen yikare lakh ir ha-tzedek kiryah ne'emanah. Tziyon be-mishpat tipadeh ve-shaveha bi-tzedakah"* – "afterwards you shall be called the City of Righteousness, the Faithful City. Zion will be redeemed with justice, and those that return to her, with righteousness" (ibid., 26–27). Only by re-establishing justice and *tzedakah* in *Yerushalayim*, and returning to the model laid out in *Parashat Re'eh*, can *Yerushalayim* be redeemed and recapture its name of *"ir ha-tzedek, kiryah ne'emanah"* – "the City of Justice, the Faithful City."

The outcome remains our choice. Establishing care for the vulnerable as part of our basic economic structure, our rituals, our educational system, and our celebrations before God, guarantees that we will receive the *berakhah* of *Hashem*. Seen from this perspective, the very first sentence of *Parashat Re'eh* – "*Re'eh Anokhi noten lifneikhem ha-yom berakhah u-klalah. Et ha-berakhah asher tishme'u*" – "See this day I set before you a blessing and curse: The blessing, if you obey..." – is an apt introduction for all the *mitzvot* contained therein. The message here is both that it is our initial choice to receive the *berakhah*, and that the *berakhah* is only brought to fruition (in the last *pasuk* of the *parashah*) by returning to *Hashem* what He has given us in appreciation, according to "*virkat Hashem Elokekha asher natan-lakh*." We give based on what we receive, but we receive based on what we give.

Prof. Suzanne Last Stone

שופטים: *Parashat Shoftim* and Constitutionalism

*P*arashat Shoftim, which deals with the institutions of government, deserves a central place in the history of constitutional thought. *Devarim* (16:18 through 18:22) describes the four bodies that provide governance and guidance of the polity: magistrates and officials (ibid., 16:18ff), king (ibid., 17:4ff), levitical priests (ibid., 18:1ff), and the prophet (ibid., 18:15ff). The questions of interpretation generated by the description of these bodies will be startlingly familiar to any student of Article III of the United States Constitution. But, more importantly, the overall structure of government hinted at here – four branches, each with its own jurisdiction, yet each subordinated to Torah law – anticipates the core idea of modern constitutionalism: the rule of law over all governmental bodies. The rule of law is the most important political ideal in contemporary Western civilization. Its origin is often traced to Plato and Aristotle. Yet long before the rise of classical Greek thought, this ideal is concretized in our *parashah.*

The rule of law most clearly emerges from *Parashat Shoftim*'s description of the king. This is a king enjoying strikingly limited powers.

Indeed, the only positive duty of the king is to keep a Torah scroll by his side so that he will not deviate from the law to the right or to the left. The king is hedged with restrictions aimed at curbing arrogance and reminding him that he is no more than a first among equals, and must not raise himself above his brothers. This is a king who is constituted by the law and ideally answerable to it. The verses leave open, however, how the rule of law will be sustained in practice. Both the *Mishnah* and the *Yerushalmi* imply that the king enjoys sovereign immunity. "The king neither judges nor is he subject to judgment" (*Sanhedrin* 2:3). As first among equals, the king is subordinate to God's rule and God calls the king to account (see *Yerushalmi Sanhedrin* 20a). The Babylonian Talmud, however, ascribes this early *takanah* to a historical incident: the Sanhedrin's failure of nerve when confronted with King Yannai's intransigence (*Sanhedrin* 19a–b). In theory, the king is subject to judicial judgment but, in practice, enforcing the law against the ruler requires extraordinary moral fortitude. Shimon ben Shetach's heroic confrontation with Yannai thus takes its place alongside later contests between judges and kings, such as that of Sir Edward Coke and King James I, in the great legal narratives about defense of the rule of law.[1]

If the central dilemma of kingship is how to guard against despotism, the central dilemma of prophecy is how to guard against deception. A prophet may "presume" to speak in God's name a word that God "did not command him to utter" or speak "in the name of other gods" (*Devarim* 18:20). A prophet who incites idolatry or speaks in the name of other gods is, by definition, false. As for all other prophets, Scripture declares: "And should you ask yourselves, 'How can we know that the word was not spoken by the Lord?' – if the prophet speaks in the name of the Lord and the word does not come true, that word was not spoken by the Lord; the prophet has uttered it presumptuously; do not stand in dread of him" (ibid., 22). The falsification of prophecy is thus remitted to the judgment of history.

The possibility of true and false prophecy raises fascinating epistemological and evidentiary issues bearing on the critical question, who

---

1. See Robert M. Cover, *The Folktales of Justice: The Tales of Jurisdiction*, 14 Cap. U.L. Rev. 179 (185).

deserves our trust in public life?[2] But an equally critical question, which bears on modern understandings of the rule of law, is conceptual: what is the basis of the prophet's authority? *Parashat Shoftim* hints at two potential bases of authority. In verse 15, the prophet himself seems to be endowed with institutional authority: "God will raise up a prophet like me [Moshe]; him you shall heed" (*Devarim* 18:15). Later, however, there is no reference to the authority of the prophet himself; rather, what is authoritative is the word of God that the prophet conveys. There is no obligation to heed the prophet but, rather, to heed "the words the prophet speaks in My [God's] name" (ibid., 20). What is authoritative is not the prophet but rather, the appearance of the will and word of God through the medium of the prophet.

These two conceptions of authority have radically different political and legal implications. In verse 20 above, authority is lodged in a factual event that precedes and is outside the system that the event generates. The factual event of revelation is the source of authority of its content, the words of God. Similarly, in modern political thought, the factual event of the consent of the people or of revolution is the source of authority of government or law that the event precedes and generates. This factual event can be replicated at any time and cannot be temporally confined. Logically, each time revelation occurs or the people consent, new content, new political structures, and new law may be generated. Prophecy, from this perspective, is a dangerous challenge to order.

Alternatively, authority may be conceived as constitutive, constituted by and internal to the system initially generated. The comprehensive character of modern understandings of the rule of law is an expression of this form of authority. In Marbury v. Madison, for example, the United States Constitution is presented as "fundamental and paramount law." This law becomes the authority for and source of the whole political order and all later political action is referred back to and judged by this law. The original, external act of constitution-making subsumes all later external political acts under its rule, even though these later external acts may be based on the same factual activity that authorized the initial

2. See generally Suzanne Last Stone, "Between Truth and Trust: Prophecy and Self-Deception," *Hebraic Political Studies* (Dec. 2009).

Constitution. Thus, authority no longer derives from and has its source in a factual event outside the system that can appear again at any time. Instead, authority is now lodged in the object that the initial founding event generated, the Constitution.[3]

Famously, Maimonides adopts this second conception of prophetic authority, which is implied by verse 15 above. Thus, in his discussion of prophetic authority in his Code he cites verse 15 ("To him [the prophet] you shall heed") and never mentions verse 20. We believe post-Mosaic prophets, Maimonides writes, not because they convey the word of God – for even signs and wonders are inconclusive proof that the prophet was sent by God. Rather, we accept the testimony of credible prophets because Moshe commanded that we must "heed" them (Maimonides, *Mishneh Torah, Hilkhot Yesodei Ha-Torah* 8:2). Maimonides is thus claiming that the obligation to listen to a true prophet arises only because Mosaic law so requires. The authority of post-Mosaic prophets is not the word of God; rather, prophetic authority is now constituted by and internal to the system generated by the initial revelation to Moshe, in which authority is now lodged. All later prophecy must come under the rule of law created by the initial authorizing revelation and will have to be coordinated with and subject to the authority of the system of governance generated by the initial revelation to Moshe. As Maimonides writes, since we listen to prophets solely because Moshe so commanded, "how could we possibly accept, on the basis of a sign, someone who comes to deny the Mosaic prophecy?" (ibid., 8:3). Conformity to the rule of Mosaic law, rather than performance of miracles, is the mark of the authentic prophet.

In conceiving of the prophet's authority in dramatically modern constitutional terms, Maimonides is not simply following one option bequeathed by scripture in verse 15, he is also pursuing the basic logic of *Parashat Shoftim* in its entirety: to clarify the fundamental and paramount nature of the rule of Torah law.

---

3. On the phenomenology of Marbury and the rule of law, see Paul W. Kahn, *The Reign of Law* (Yale University Press, 1997).

Dr. Barry L. Eichler

כי תצא: Enhancing Our Appreciation of Torah: The Law of the Wayward and Defiant Son

T he advent of archaeology as a full-fledged discipline has resulted in the discovery and decipherment of ancient languages such as Sumerian, Akkadian, Egyptian, Elbaite, Amurrite, Ugaritic and Hittite. These languages have provided us with new insights into Hebrew grammar and lexicography that help elucidate the Biblical text. Our recovery of the primary source materials written in these languages has given us direct access to the civilizations of the ancient Near East. These civilizations provide us with the rich historical, religious, literary and cultural backdrop against which the Torah was given. We are thus privileged to gain a deeper appreciation of the books of *Tanakh* by studying them in their ancient Near Eastern context.

At the very onset, we should bear in mind that the use of such disciplines as comparative Semitics, the study of ancient cultures, and even archaeology, for the study of the Bible, is neither foreign nor really new to traditional Jewish scholarship. Throughout the long history of Jewish Biblical exegesis, many of our *Rishonim* utilized these disciplines in their attempt to fathom the plain sense of the Biblical texts and to interpret the message of Scripture. We need pause only to mention a few examples:

R. Saadia Gaon of the early 10th century is considered by many to be the father and founder of the field of Hebrew philology. His treatises in the field of Hebrew grammar and lexicography make use of his knowledge of other Semitic languages, chiefly Arabic. To R. Saadia, Hebrew philology was the necessary scientific apparatus for interpreting Scripture. Subsequent Spanish Jewish grammarians and medieval Jewish exegetes further refined this discipline.

Maimonides, in the 12th century, was one of the first to advocate the study of ancient cultures for a deeper appreciation of Biblical truths. In his discussion of the Divine commandments in Part III of his *Moreh Nevukhim*, the Rambam utilized the ancient chronicles (extant in Arabic translations) of the idolatrous tribes known as the Sabaeans, in order to gain insights into Biblical precepts. Maimonides believed that many of the laws of the Torah were given to cure mankind of idolatrous practices. For example, the Rambam sought to comprehend the Torah's injunction against the eating of blood (*Vayikra* 17:10) by referring to the Sabaean practice of eating blood in order to commune with the spirits of the dead. This practice was based on the Sabaean belief that blood was the food of the spirits. The Rambam went so far as to lament that his knowledge of Sabaean doctrines was incomplete since they had been extinct for almost 2,000 years (Rambam, *Guide to the Perplexed* III:49). The Rambam then went on to assert that if the rules of the Sabaeans and the events of those days were known to us, we should be able to see plainly the reason for most of the practices mentioned in the Torah.

Nachmanides of the 13th century gives testimony to the use of archaeological survey, albeit primitive, as a means of ascertaining the correct interpretation of Biblical texts. *Bereishit* (35:16) states that Binyamin's birth and Rachel's tragic death took place while Yaakov and his family were still *"kivrat ha-aretz"* from Efrat. Does this expression denote that the tragedy occurred at a great distance from Efrat and hence Yaa-kov could not bring Rachel into the city for burial; or does the expression denote a short distance from Efrat and nevertheless Yaakov chose not to bury Rachel within the city? In his commentary, the Ramban addresses this problem, cites the opinions of Menachem ben Saruk, the *Midrash*, Rashi and Radak, and accedes to the opinion of Radak. But subsequently he adds the following remarks: "This I originally wrote while still in Spain, but now that I was worthy and came to Jerusalem... I saw with my eyes that there is not even a mile between Rachel's grave and Bethlehem. This explanation [of Radak] has thus been refuted, as have the words of Menachem" (Ramban, ad loc.). The Ramban also realized that while archaeological data could answer certain queries it could at the same time give rise to other problems. He therefore goes on to state, "I have also seen that Rachel's grave is not in Ramah nor near to it [as the plain meaning of the verse in *Yirmiyahu* (31:14) would seem to indicate: 'A voice is heard in Ramah...Rachel is weeping for her children']. Instead, Ramah which is in Benjamin is about four Persian miles distant from it, and Ramah of the hill-country of Efraim is more than two days travel from it. Therefore, I say that the verse stating 'A voice is heard in Ramah' is a metaphor, in the manner of rhetorical expression, meaning to say that Rachel wept so bitterly that her voice was heard from afar in Ramah, which was on top of the mountain of [the territory of] Benjamin."[1]

To my mind, the above references clearly place the study of Torah in light of our knowledge of the ancient Near East within the spirit of traditional Jewish exegesis. If so, the imperative to such study should not be limited to the category of *"da mah she-tashiv,"* but rather includes the positive aspect of providing new opportunities to appreciate the Biblical text and its message.[2]

As religious Jews, we believe in the eternity of Torah. On the

1. These examples have been culled from my article, "Study of the Bible in Light of Our Knowledge of the Ancient Near East" in *Modern Scholarship in the Study of Torah: Contributions and Limitations,* ed. Shalom Carmy (Northvale, NJ, 1996), pp. 81–100.
2. For an attempt to give tangible expression to the positive results which can be achieved through the application of new data gleaned from the world of the ancient

other hand, we realize that it was given to us in a particular historical moment and its eternal message was cloaked in the contextual garb of a particular time period so that its recipients would be capable of understanding its message. When interpreting the Torah, therefore, we must be cognizant of the fact that it is also, in a sense, contexted in time. It is the Oral Law which guarantees that the eternal message of Torah be preserved and transmitted across the generations. To help us explore these concepts more deeply, let us examine the law of *"ben sorer u-moreh"* (*Devarim* 21:18–21) in its ancient Near Eastern context.

The Biblical law deals with parental authority and filial disobedience. To better appreciate the Biblical message of this law, it would be helpful to place the law in its ancient Near Eastern context. In ancient Near Eastern tribal societies, which were governed by heads of clans, patriarchal authority in family matters seems to have been paramount. Even in urbanized settings in Mesopotamia, where loyalty to the clan was attenuated and replaced by loyalty to the polity and its king, patriarchal authority in family matters remained dominant.[3] From ancient Mesopotamian law collections it is evident that there was an attempt by the king to deal with societal issues involving patriarchal authority over one's wife and minor children. In formulating the laws of adultery, Laws of Hammurabi 129 states:

Near East to the Biblical text, brief examples are cited from the areas of grammar, lexicography, history and culture in my article, "Study of the Bible in Light of Our Knowledge of the Ancient Near East," see note 1.

3. Raymond Westbrook states in his introductory chapter on the character of ancient Near Eastern law that he does not believe that there is evidence of a "right of life and death" over one's children, see Raymond Westbrook (ed.), *A History of Ancient Near Eastern Law* 1, (Leiden, Netherlands, 2003) p. 50. All of the extant evidence is derived from urbanized societies which under closer scrutiny do reflect tensions between the authority of the polity and patriarchal authority, rooted in tribal societies. The fact that "honor killings" of children who have disgraced their family by their shameful acts are still carried out under patriarchal authority to this very day is evidence of the tenacity of the "right of life and death" associated with absolute patriarchal authority. Cf. Joseph Ginat, *Blood Revenge: Family Honor, Mediation and Outcasting* (Brighton, UK, 1997). I would like to thank my colleague, Dr. Aaron Koller, for directing me to this reference.

> If a man's wife is seized lying with another man, they shall bind them and throw them into the water. If the woman's husband wishes to spare his wife, the king shall spare his subject.

In a similar vein, Middle Assyrian Laws A15 states:

> If a man has caught another man upon his wife and the charges are substantiated against them, they may both be killed with no liability attaching to the husband. If upon catching them, he has brought him before the king or the judges, and they have found him guilty – if the husband puts his wife to death, the man shall also be put to death; if the husband cuts off his wife's nose, he shall turn the man into a eunuch; but if he lets his wife go free, he shall let the man go free.

In both laws, the king acknowledges the absolute authority of the husband to punish his adulterous wife as he so chooses. The laws can only demand that the paramour, who is the king's subject, be treated in a manner which is consistent with the punishment that the husband metes out to his wife. There is no attenuation of patriarchal authority, merely the demand for equal treatment of wife and royal subject.

A similar conclusion may be drawn from the Mesopotamian law dealing with incestuous relations between a father and his daughter. Laws of Hammurabi 154 states:

> If a man has carnal relations with his daughter, they shall banish that man from the city.

Although the king clearly disapproves of the father's actions, the law chooses to banish the man (and his household) rather than limit his patriarchal authority over his daughter.

It is also clear from Mesopotamian laws which evoke the principle of vicarious punishment that within Mesopotamian society minor children were considered the property of the father. For example, Laws of Hammurabi 229–230 state:

If a builder constructs a house for a man but does not make his work sound so that the house collapses and causes the death of the householder, that builder shall be killed. If it causes the death of the son of the householder, they shall kill the son of that builder.

From the above laws it is clear that patriarchal authority over one's wife and minor children was a potent force in ancient Near Eastern societies. Against this backdrop, let us re-read the law of the wayward and defiant son:

[יח] כי יהיה לאיש בן סורר ומורה איננו שמע בקול אביו ובקול אמו ויסרו אותו ולא ישמע אליהם [יט] ותפשו בו אביו ואמו, והוציאו אתו אל זקני עירו ואל שער מקמו. [כ] ואמרו אל זקני עירו בננו זה סורר ומרה, איננו שמע בקלנו, זולל וסבא [כא] ורגמהו כל אנשי עירו באבנים ומת, ובערת הרע מקרבך, וכל ישראל ישמעו ויראו.

If a man has a wayward and defiant son, who does not heed his father or his mother and does not obey them even after they discipline him, his father and mother shall take hold of him and bring him out to the elders of his town at the public place of his community. They shall say to the elders of the town, "This son of ours is wayward and defiant; he does not heed us. He is a wastrel and a drunkard." Thereupon the men of his city shall stone him to death. Thus you will sweep out evil from your midst; all Israel will hear and be afraid. (*Devarim 21:18–21*)

When the Israelites heard this law, they were aware of the absolute nature of patriarchal authority in their own times. Taken in its ancient Near Eastern context to which we too are now privy, certain aspects of the law now stand out with greater clarity. The issue of filial disobedience is no longer a private family matter in which the father wields absolute authority. The concurrence of the mother comes clearly into play as well as does the public role of the elders of the community which limit the absolute authority of the father. Only the men of the community have the right to execute the son after the deliberations of the elders. In this light, the essential purport of the Torah is to protect the child from the absolute and capricious authority of the father even as it seeks to strengthen parental authority by deterring filial insubordination, which undermines the stability of its society and the transmission of its values.[4]

This essential message of the law of the wayward and defiant son, namely, the protection of the child from absolute patriarchal authority,[5] was also clearly understood by the Oral Law and reflected in its teachings. This is the reason that the *mishnah* in *Sanhedrin* severely restricts the application of this law, limiting it only to a son during the three month period in which he attains puberty. The halakhic-midrashic reading of the verses further narrows its application:

[משנה מסכת סנהדרין פרק ח משנה ד] היה אביו רוצה ואמו אינה רוצה אביו אינו רוצה ואמו רוצה אינו נעשה בן סורר ומורה עד שיהו שניהם רוצים רבי יהודה אומר אם לא היתה אמו ראויה לאביו אינו נעשה בן סורר ומורה היה אחד מהם גידם או חגר או אלם או סומא או חרש אינו נעשה בן סורר ומורה שנאמר (דברים כ"א) ותפשו בו אביו ואמו ולא גדמין

---

4. The centrality of the theme of limiting patriarchal authority within this law is underscored by its contextual relationship to the previous law (*Devarim* 21:15–17), which limits patriarchal authority by nullifying the father's right to give preferential treatment to the son of his beloved wife to the detriment of the firstborn son of his rejected wife in matters of inheritance.

5. Mesopotamian legal texts also deal with matters of filial insubordination, such as failure to respect the parents, failure to provide for them in their old age, and failure to mourn and bury them upon their death. Punishments meted out to such wayward sons include bodily mutilation of the offending organ (e.g., hand or tongue), disinheritance and enslavement, cf. Joseph Fleischman, *Parent and Child in Ancient Near East and the Bible* [Hebrew], (Jerusalem, Israel, 1999). It should be noted that many of these texts deal with adult children who obligate themselves to care for their adopting parents in old age in return for an inheritance portion. Unlike Mesopotamian law, Biblical law does not recognize adoption, so such comparisons are not valid. Furthermore, in Mesopotamian texts, most cases involve adult children, who upon reaching adulthood are considered to be subjects of the crown. For this reason, the death penalty in urbanized Mesopotamia may not have been invoked for adult filial insubordination.

וְהוֹצִיאוּ אוֹתוֹ וְלֹא חִגְּרִין וְאָמְרוּ וְלֹא אִלְּמִין בְּנֵנוּ זֶה וְלֹא סוּמִין אֵינֶנּוּ שׁוֹמֵעַ
בְּקוֹלֵנוּ וְלֹא חֵרְשִׁין

If his father was willing [to accuse him] but his mother was not
willing, or if his father was not willing but his mother was willing, he cannot be condemned as a wayward and defiant son; but
only if both were willing. R. Judah says: If his mother was not fit
for his father he cannot be condemned as a wayward and defiant
son. If either of them was maimed in the hand or lame or dumb
or blind or deaf, he cannot be condemned as a wayward and defiant son, for it is written: "his father and mother shall take hold
of him" – so they were not maimed in the hand; "and bring him
out" – so they were not lame; "they shall say" – so they were not
dumb; "this son of ours" – so they were not blind; "he does not
obey our voice" – so they are not deaf. (*Sanhedrin* 8:4)

The limitations of applications (*mi'utim*) of the law of the wayward and
defiant son stipulated in the *mishnah* are more than simply *gezerot ha-
katuv*. These limitations introduce social aspects of the child's home
environment which may have led to his filial defiance and lack of parental
reverence. Discord between parents as well as severe physical or mental
deficiencies are viewed by the Oral Law as extenuating circumstances
which may have caused him to assume a wayward and defiant posture
not based solely on his own inclinations. In such cases, the wayward son
is not held legally liable for his insubordination.

The restrictions placed by the Oral Law on the prosecution of a
wayward and defiant son reflect the Baraitha, quoted in *Sanhedrin* 71a:

דְּתַנְיָא: בֵּן סוֹרֵר וּמוֹרֶה לֹא הָיָה וְלֹא עָתִיד לִהְיוֹת

The Baraitha states: There never has been an adjudicated case of
a wayward and defiant son, and never will be.

At first reading, it seems puzzling that the Oral Law should actively minimize the application of a Biblical law to such an extent that the law could
never be carried out. However, knowing the contextual background of

the Biblical law allows us to appreciate the law as an injunction to protect children from abusive patriarchal authority. The Oral Law was clearly cognizant of the Torah's primary consideration to protect the child from parental abuse. Thus the law of the wayward and defiant son is a reminder to us in our day as in past days, that it is a Divine command to be diligent in preventing children from being abused.

Rabbi Zvi Sobolofsky

כי תבוא: *Bikkurim* and the Seder: A Fresh Start

here are two components to the *mitzvah* of *bikkurim*, which is the annual bringing of one's first fruit to the *Beit Ha-Mikdash*. The actual bringing of the fruit and the reading of the *pesukim* mentioned in *Parashat Ki Tavo* comprise this *mitzvah* in its entirety.

Mikra bikkurim – the reading of these *pesukim* – is clearly linked to the celebration of *Pesach*. These *pesukim* encapsulate the story of the *Yetziat Mitzrayim*, beginning with Yaakov's descent to *Mitzrayim* and culminating with the entry of the Jewish People into *Eretz Yisrael*. *Chazal* emphasize this connection, as is evident from the manner that they formulated the text of the *Hagaddah*. The *mishnah* in *Pesachim* teaches us that we fulfill our obligation of retelling the story of *Yetziat Mitzrayim* at the Seder by elaborating specifically on these *pesukim*. Our Seder does not revolve around the narrative in *Sefer Shemot* which tells directly of the events of *Yetziat Mitzrayim*. Rather, *mikra bikkurim* is the vehicle to relate the story at our Seder tables, just as the farmer did annually upon offering his new fruit.

Why did *Chazal* choose *mikra bikkurim* as the most appropriate method to express our gratitude to *Hashem* during our celebration of *Pesach*? What is the real message of *bikkurim* that singles it out as the ultimate celebration of *Yetziat Mitzrayim*?

When a farmer brings his *bikkurim*, he recites a *pasuk* before actually beginning *mikra bikkurim*. "I declare today that I have arrived in *Eretz Yisrael*." The word "today" is difficult to understand. If it refers to the fact that the farmer is bringing the *bikkurim* "today," that is obvious. If the farmer is declaring that he has arrived in *Eretz Yisrael* "today" that is not true. One offers *bikkurim* even after having lived in *Eretz Yisrael* for many years. *Chazal* interpreted the word "today" to refer not to the actuality of bringing *bikkurim* for the first time, but to the mindset that should accompany this *mitzvah*. Although one may have brought *bikkurim* for many years, every year must be viewed as a new experience. Having just completed a new harvest, the farmer is filled with excitement. This excitement must transform how he views the gift of *Eretz Yisrael* that brought forth this harvest. It is not sufficient to thank *Hashem* for a gift given thousands of years ago. Rather, one is obligated to view the precious gift of *Eretz Yisrael* as just being received. Thus, *Chazal* interpret the word "today" to teach us that the *Halakhah* requires the farmer to view his entering into *Eretz Yisrael* to be occurring "today."

This obligation to relate to kindnesses performed for us by *Hashem* as not mere events of the past but as current events unfolding before us is the central theme of the Seder: *"Be-khol dor va-dor chayav adam lir'ot et atzmo ke-ilu hu yatza mi-Mitzrayim"* – "In every generation one is obligated to view oneself as if he himself left *Mitzrayim*" (*Hagadah*). One who merely reads the *Hagaddah* as events of the past has not properly experienced the Seder. The Rambam notes that the two *mitzvot* that *Chazal* instituted to demonstrate our status as free men – drinking four cups and leaning – are rooted in this Torah requirement of reaching a mindset that the events surrounding *Yetziat Mitzrayim* are occurring in the present. Although according to the Torah one need not perform specific acts to demonstrate this reality, *Chazal* ordained these two *mitzvot* as vehicles to achieve the state of mind of viewing our freedom as a gift just received. The most appropriate text to use to express our gratitude at the Seder is the one used annually by the farmer offering *bikkurim*. We, on *Pesach*, like the farmer holding his new crops, express our appreciation to *Hashem* "today."

There is an additional *mitzvah* that accompanies both the bringing of *bikkurim* and the re-telling of *Yetziat Mitzrayim* on *Pesach*. Both of these *mitzvot* are accompanied by *shirah* – song. The *Mishnah* teaches us that *bikkurim* must be brought accompanied by song, and that the culmination of *Maggid* at the Seder is the recitation of *Hallel*. It is these songs that express the very nature of these two *mitzvot*. The *Rishonim* discuss why a *berakhah* is not recited before the saying of *Hallel* at the Seder. R. Hai Gaon suggests that the nature of *Hallel* on *Pesach* night is different than on other occasions. *Hallel* is usually a form of "*keri'ah*" (recitation), whereas at the Seder it is a form of "*shirah*" (song). Rabbi Joseph B. Soloveitchik explained that usually *Hallel* is recited as a response to events of the past. Thus, *Hallel* on *Chanukkah* is a planned event. It is the same *Hallel* we recited the previous year, as there is no obligation to view the miracles of *Chanukkah* as unfolding in the present. A *berakhah* is part of the preparation for a *mitzvah* we know we are about to perform. However, the *Hallel* at the Seder is a spontaneous reaction to miraculous events occurring right now. Reciting a *berakhah* would indicate that the *Hallel* is planned, thus detracting from the spontaneity the *Halakhah* is trying to create. A song of *Hallel* is the sudden outburst triggered by the excitement of the moment. It is this *shirah* that also captures the emotion of the one bringing *bikkurim*. The realization that he is entering *Eretz Yisrael* for the first time creates such emotions that his response is a sudden outburst of a joyous song.

As we read the *mikra bikkurim* both in *Parashat Ki Tavo* and at our Seder, let us focus on the gifts that *Hashem* bestows upon us. Let us approach these gifts with a feeling of excitement and freshness, and let us express that excitement with an outburst of song.

Rabbi Daniel Stein

נצבים: "It is Not in Heaven:" The Relationship Between *Teshuvah* and *Talmud Torah*

> *For this* mitzvah *which I command you this day, it is not hidden from you, nor is it far off. It is not in heaven that you should say, 'Who shall go up for us to heaven, and bring it to us, that we may hear it and do it?' Nor is it beyond the sea, that you should say, 'Who shall go over the sea for us, and bring it to us, that we may hear it and do it.' For the matter is very near to you, in your mouth and in your heart to do it.* (Devarim 30:11–14)

In these *pesukim* the Torah describes the uniquely accessible nature of an unidentified directive, known to us only by its cryptic pseudonym "this *mitzvah*." Since *Devarim* Ch. 30 begins with a description of repentance, the Ramban (ad loc.) assumes that the commandment

459

being described here is also *teshuvah*, repentance. However, the Talmud (*Eruvin* 55a) ascribes parts of the aforementioned verses, namely the phrases "It is not in heaven" and "nor is it beyond the sea," to the *mitzvah* of *Talmud Torah*. Similarly, the Talmud (*Bava Metzia* 59b) pronounces that a heavenly voice is immaterial when resolving matters of Jewish law because "it is not in heaven." Therefore, the Netziv, R. Naftali Tzvi Yehudah Berlin, *Ha'amek Davar* (*Devarim*, ad loc.), questions the Ramban's analysis, which seems to run counter to the Talmud's overt statements.

Presumably, there is in fact no contradiction here at all, and the Ramban and the Talmud address two different planes of interpretation. The Ramban's interpretation is the *peshat*, a face value contextual explanation, while the Talmud's version is the *derash*, or a second layer of deeper meaning. Nevertheless I believe there is a common theme that connects these two *mitzvot* which allows them to be interchangeable in this context. Moreover, this shared facet not only links these two otherwise unrelated *mitzvot*, it also underscores a more nuanced perspective of our obligation vis-à-vis *Talmud Torah* specifically.

THE INSTINCTIVE NATURE OF *TESHUVAH*

The twelfth of the Rambam's Thirteen Principles of Faith is the belief in the coming of the Messiah, who according to the Rambam, will precipitate the final redemption of the Jewish people (Rambam, *Hilkhot Melakhim* 11:1). The Rambam's fervent position on this issue is curious in light of another ruling of the Rambam on a related point. The Talmud (*Sanhedrin* 97b) records a dispute between R. Eliezer and R. Yehoshua regarding the nature of the final redemption. R. Yehoshua believes that the advent of the final redemption of the Jewish people is unconditional, while R. Eliezer argues that the final redemption will only materialize if the Jewish people do *teshuvah*. Since the Rambam elsewhere (Rambam, *Hilkhot Teshuvah* 7:5) sides with R. Eliezer, his mandate of unequivocal faith in the coming of the Messiah is problematic. In other words, since the Jews may never do *teshuvah*, perhaps the final redemption will never occur. The Rambam (ad loc.) addresses this issue himself, saying: "and the Torah has already guaranteed that the Jewish people will do *teshuvah* at the end of their exile, after which they will be redeemed immediately as it states, 'And it shall come to pass, when all these things have come

upon you…and you shall return to *Hashem* your God.'" The Rambam justifies his unqualified belief in the arrival of the Messiah and the final redemption by arguing that the *teshuvah* of the Jewish people is inevitable.

The inescapable nature of the *teshuvah* described by the Rambam gives rise to a more fundamental question regarding the Jewish people's ability to express their free will. Doesn't the certainty of *teshuvah* under any circumstances deny the unpredictable nature of free will? R. Joseph B. Soloveitchik, *z"l*, cited by Pinchas Peli in *Al Ha-Teshuvah* (Jerusalem, 1975) pp. 190–254, explains that the *teshuvah* of the Jewish people is indeed unavoidable, for the intrinsic nature of the Jewish people is to do *teshuvah*. Therefore, in the same way that one's free will has not been violated by one who forecasts that he will eventually eat food or sleep, so too, the free will of the Jewish people has not been circumvented by predictions of *teshuvah*. Furthermore, while it is undeniable that the individual Jew, or even the entirety of the Jewish people, may be able to corrupt their innate tendency towards *teshuvah* for a limited period of time, in the end the model will emerge intact, just as the acrobat who temporarily walks on his hands will ultimately walk upright. R. Soloveitchik added that this natural propensity towards *teshuvah* justifies the *mishnah*'s claim that, "all members of Israel have a portion in the world to come" (*Sanhedrin* 10:1).

This notion regarding the Jewish people's natural inclination towards *teshuvah* is evident in other aspects of *teshuvah* as well. The Rambam writes, "All of the *mitzvot* in the Torah, whether positive commandments or negative, if one has violated one of them, either intentionally or unintentionally, when he does *teshuvah* and returns from his sin, he is obligated to confess before God" (*Hilkhot Teshuvah* 1:1). R. Joseph Babad, *Minchat Chinuch*, Sec. 364, wonders why the Rambam assumes the sinner will repent without mentioning any specific *mitzvah* to do so. R. Menachem Krakovski, *Avodat Ha-Melekh* (Jerusalem, 2002), *Hilkhot Teshuvah* ad loc., resolves the matter by noting that since the desire to do *teshuvah* is intrinsic and the Torah has already assured that the Jewish people will ultimately do *teshuvah*, a specific command to do *teshuvah* is unnecessary and perhaps inappropriate.

Moreover, R. Isaiah Horowitz, *Shenei Luchot Ha-Berit* (Haifa, 1991), Chapter *Torah Ohr*, identifies the root of the word *teshuvah* as "*shav*" – "return," depicting one who was lost from his path and is now returning. While this explanation would sufficiently describe the *teshuvah* performed by the Jew who was once on the correct path, it does not seem to relate to the Jew who is discovering the path of Torah and *mitzvot* for the first time. However, perhaps the "return" of *teshuvah* is not necessarily to a previously occupied state, but to the normal state. Since the desire to do *teshuvah* is instinctive to every Jew, a refusal to do *teshuvah* can be viewed as a departure from the destined path, and the process of *teshuvah* is the prescribed means of returning to that path.

LEARNING TORAH *IN UTERO*

Just as repentance is the Jewish visceral reaction to sin, it seems that learning Torah as well is not merely a laudable act and endeavor, but the innate quest of the Jew. The Talmud (*Niddah* 29b) states that while a Jewish fetus is *in utero*, an angel teaches the entire Torah to the fetus. Subsequently, when the fetus is on the verge of being born, the angel returns and taps the baby on the upper lip causing him to forget all that he has learned. Many commentaries question the purpose of the angel's exercise to teach the Torah, only to later cause it to be forgotten.

R. Hershel Schachter, *Nefesh Ha-Rav* (Jerusalem, 1994) p. 72, explains in the name of the Rav *z"l*, that the purpose of teaching the fetus Torah even though it will ultimately be forgotten is to instill in every Jewish person a natural love of the Torah. Since the Torah was part of the Jew's native environment, the Torah remains familiar and elicits a feeling of nostalgia for one's original surroundings. Hence this experience *in utero* serves to create the instinctive longing to regain the Torah knowledge once had but since lost, thereby rendering Torah knowledge and study as indelible landmarks in the landscape of the Jewish psyche.

Therefore, it seems that the destiny of the Jewish people includes not only the proclivity to perform *teshuvah*, but to engage in intense Torah study as well. Due to this commonality between these two *mitzvot* both have been correctly identified as the subject of the aforementioned verses, "For this *mitzvah* which I command you this day, it is not hidden from you, nor is it far off… For the matter is very near to you, in your mouth and in your heart to do it."

REDEFINING THE *MITZVAH* OF *TALMUD TORAH*

This experience *in utero* serves not only to engender a basic affinity with Torah study, it also defines and sets the stage for the obligation of Torah study as a whole. The *Yerushalmi* (*Shekalim* 6:1) indicates that while we have become accustomed to recognizing two distinct sections of the Torah – the *Torah She-Bikhtav*, the "written" parts of the Torah, and the *Torah She-Be-Al Peh*, the "oral" parts of the Torah – the original plan was to have only one cohesive unit of Torah with one form of transmission. The *Yerushalmi* states that inscribed on the first set of *luchot* was not only the *Torah She-Bikhtav* but the entire *Torah She-Be-Al Peh* as well. Apparently God had initially intended to have the complete Torah written on the *luchot*, but once the Jewish people sinned with the golden calf and the first set of *luchot* were broken, the plan changed. The second set of *luchot* contained only the *Torah She-Bikhtav* because the *Torah She-Be-Al Peh* had now been designated as a strictly oral tradition. The *Beit Ha-Levi*, R. Joseph Dov Soloveitchik of Brisk, *She'elot U-Teshuvot Beit Ha-Levi* (Jerusalem, 1995) vol. 3 *Derush* 18, contends that what precipitated this modification was a result of the impending retribution which would later be visited upon the Jewish people in the wake of the sin of the golden calf, and that transition changed the nature of the *mitzvah* of *Talmud Torah* forever.

The Talmud in *Eruvin* (54a) proclaims that had the Jews not sinned with the golden calf there would never have been a Diaspora, a *galut*. All exiles and persecutions which later befell the Jewish people were in some part a function of the sin of the golden calf, even though it occurred many years prior. The *Beit Ha-Levi* claims that this development prompted the change in the content of the *luchot* as well. In order for the Jewish people to maintain their unique relationship with God throughout the trials of *galut*, it was necessary for them to have their own reserved section of the Torah. Indeed, the *Torah She-Bikhtav* has been translated into every language known to man, and can be found in every motel room across the world. Only the study of the *Torah She-Be-Al Peh* preserves the unique bond between God and the Jewish people. It is for this reason that the Talmud in *Gittin* (60b) affirms that the covenant between God and the Jewish people has been primarily established, and maintained, through the study of the *Torah She-Be-Al Peh* specifically.

This notion that the *Torah She-Be-Al Peh* was targeted at the Jewish *galut* experience is echoed by the Netziv (Netziv, *Ha'amak Davar, Shemot* 19:19), who notes that the *Torah She-Be-Al Peh* only developed and flourished once the Jews were exiled into *galut*. Not only were the *Mishnah* and the Talmud composed and compiled in the aftermath of the destruction of the Second Temple, but the entire enterprise of *Torah She-Be-Al Peh* has only been intensified the deeper the Jewish people have sunk into the mire of *galut*. The Netziv claims that this phenomenon is hinted at by the sounding of the *shofar* at Mount Sinai, which unusually "grew louder and louder" (*Shemot*, ad loc.). The growing intensity of the *shofar* call which cut through the smoke of Mount Sinai represents the mounting force of the *Torah She-Be-Al Peh* which will only progress in the fog of *galut*.

The *Beit Ha-Levi* continues to say that the creation of the *Torah She-Be-al Peh*, spawned by the sin of the golden calf, has redefined the nature of the *mitzvah* of *Talmud Torah*. While prior to the sin of the golden calf the Jew was separate from the text he studied, in this new reality, the *mitzvah* of *Talmud Torah* demands that the Jew and the text become one. In other words, while previously, Torah study only required the ability to adhere to an existing text, studying the *Torah She-Be-Al Peh* presently also demands that those engaged in its study embody the text through fully assimilating and integrating its content. This is borne out by the verse "write them on the tablets of your heart" (*Mishlei* 3:3), which the *Beit Ha-Levi* reasons refers to the study of *Torah She-Be-Al Peh* which must be "written" on the "tablets" of one's personality.

This grand form of *Talmud Torah* is highlighted by R. Chaim of Volozhin's hagiographical comment regarding the difference between the Torah knowledge of his brother, R. Zelmele, and that of R. Chaim's teacher, the Gaon of Vilna. R. Chaim prefaced by observing that while most Jews can recite the prayer "*Ashrei*" by heart, they cannot recite "*Ashrei*" backwards by heart. This distinction, explained R. Chaim, separated R. Zelmele from the Gaon of Vilna as well. R. Zelmele was fluent in the Torah as most Jews are fluent with "*Ashrei*," but the Gaon had an even deeper grasp of the Torah, for he knew it backwards and forwards. The Brisker Rav, R. Yitzchak Zev Soloveitchik, once asked that if one is proficient in the entire Torah, what is gained by knowing it backwards and forwards? He explained that R. Chaim meant to describe the difference between one who recites something from memory, which only flows in one direction, versus one who is reading from a text, which permits multidirectional analysis. R. Zelmele remembered the entire Torah, and that enabled him to recite the entire Torah "forwards," but the Gaon of Vilna had become fully united with the Torah to the extent that it was "written on his heart," which allowed him to recite it "forwards and backwards" as one who analyzes a written text.

However, in essence, this definition of the *mitzvah* of *Talmud Torah* is troubling. Since the Torah is foreign to the body, how can the two converge? Isn't the body trained to expel alien objects? The Rav *zt"l* has suggested that it is perhaps for this very reason that the angel teaches the fetus Torah even though it will be forgotten. The angel is setting the tone for the future by fashioning man, in his original form, together with Torah. Since the Torah was originally part of the inception of man, it is possible and even expected of man, to reunite with the Torah. A similar concept exists regarding marriage as well. Since the expectation of marriage is that a husband and a wife become unified, as the *pasuk* states "and they will become one flesh" (*Bereishit* 2:24), it was necessary to form Eve from the body of Adam. If Adam and Eve had not been formed from the same flesh, they could not subsequently be expected to become truly joined as one flesh. This argument, as well, demanded that man be created together with the Torah in order to facilitate his noble and ambitious mission to become reunited with the Torah.

Rabbi Mark Dratch

וילך: What "Now"?

ויאמר ה' אל משה הנך שכב עם אבתיך וקם העם הזה וזנה אחרי אלהי
נכר הארץ אשר הוא בא שמה בקרבו ועזבני והפר את בריתי אשר כרתי
אתו: וחרה אפי בו ביום ההוא ועזבתים והסתרתי פני מהם והיה לאכל
ומצאהו רעות רבות וצרות ואמר ביום ההוא הלא על כי אין אלקי בקרבי
מצאוני הרעות האלה: ואנכי הסתר אסתיר פני ביום ההוא על כל הרעה
אשר עשה כי פנה אל אלהים אחרים: ועתה כתבו לכם את השירה הזאת
ולמדה את בני ישראל שימה בפיהם למען תהיה לי השירה הזאת לעד
בבני ישראל: כי אביאנו אל האדמה אשר נשבעתי לאבתיו זבת חלב ודבש
ואכל ושבע ודשן ופנה אל אלהים אחרים ועבדום ונאצוני והפר את בריתי:
והיה כי תמצאן אתו רעות רבות וצרות וענתה השירה הזאת לפניו לעד כי
לא תשכח מפי זרעו כי ידעתי את יצרו אשר הוא עשה היום בטרם אביאנו
אל הארץ אשר נשבעתי: ויכתב משה את השירה הזאת ביום ההוא וילמדה
את בני ישראל: (דברים ל"א:ט"ז-כ"ב)

And the Lord said unto Moshe, "Behold, thou shalt sleep with thy
fathers; and this people will rise up, and go a whoring after the
gods of the strangers of the land, whither they go to be among
them, and will forsake Me, and break My covenant which I have
made with them. Then My anger shall be kindled against them

in that day, and I will forsake them, and I will hide My face from them, and they shall be devoured, and many evils and troubles shall befall them; so that they will say in that day, 'Are not these evils come upon us, because our God is not among us?' And I will surely hide My face in that day for all the evils which they shall have wrought, in that they are turned unto other gods. And now write this song for yourselves, and teach it the children of Israel; put it in their mouths, that this song may be a witness for Me among the Children of Israel. For when I shall have brought them into the land which I swore unto their fathers, that floweth with milk and honey, and they shall have eaten and filled themselves, and waxen fat; then will they turn unto other gods, and serve them, and provoke Me, and break My covenant. And it shall come to pass, when many evils and troubles are befallen them, that this song shall testify against them as a witness; for it shall not be forgotten out of the mouths of their seed: for I know their imagination which they go about, even now, before I have brought them into the land which I swore." Moshe therefore wrote this song the same day, and taught it the Children of Israel. (*Devarim* 31:16–22)

Write this song, copy these verses of rebuke, these words of Torah, this ode of hope. God commands Moshe to write a song – the words of *Ha'azinu* (*Devarim* 32) – and with it to transcribe the entire Torah. This verse also serves as the 613th Biblical commandment, the obligation for us in every age to write our own scrolls. By doing so, each of us makes a contribution to the perpetuation of Torah, its values and laws, and strengthens the link between ourselves and God forged at Sinai as an eternal covenant.

Why does the Torah refer to itself as a song? Why is this *mitzvah* of writing a Torah scroll given in the context of rebuke, where the Torah predicts an era of *hester panim* (Divine hiddenness and punishment)? What does this juxtaposition add to the underlying themes of this, the last of God's commandments? And why is the *mitzvah* introduced with the word "*ve-attah*" (and now)? Why "now"? What "now"?

Let us suggest four answers.

PREPARATION FOR THE DARK NIGHT OF *HESTER PANIM*

Hester panim is an episode of Divine abandonment, a time when God goes into hiding and the human world is a dark and dangerous place.

> No moment was more difficult for the world than the moment the Holy One, blessed be He, said to Moshe, "I will surely hide My face." (*Yerushalmi Sanhedrin* 10:2)

During *hester panim*, our fates are subjects of chance as we live exposed, uncertain, vulnerable and weak. Our prayers echo back to us from the hollow chambers of Heaven and the search for God seems endless and futile. It is in preparation for such an era that God tells *Moshe Rabbenu* to write a song that will be a testament to God's presence, to Divine revelation, and to God's love, care, and compassion: "this song will be a witness for Me among the children of Israel." Moshe is to write about a time of Divine immanence, when God was very present in the world and when He was very real in the lives of His people. The words of this song are intended to serve as a reminder of what once was, and as the seeds of a vision of what could be yet again. The strains of the verses are meant to stir hope in us during these dark nights of exile and to offer reassurance to us when we are discomfited. This is what the Psalmist means when he writes, "the Lord will command His loving-kindness in the daytime, and in the night His song shall be with me" (*Tehillim* 42:9). Reish Lakish teaches,

> All who occupy themselves with Torah at night, the Holy One, blessed be He, spreads over them a thread of kindness in the daytime, as it says, "the Lord will command His loving-kindness in the daytime." And what is the reason that the Lord will command His loving-kindness in the daytime? So that "in the night His song will be with me." (*Chagigah* 12b)

And this is why the verse begins with the word *"ve-attah."* Write that song *now* when your faith is strong, *now* when your situation is assured, *now* when God's presence is manifest. Write it *now* – and then it will be an *"eid,"* a testimony that you can read, study, and cherish later.

COMFORT DURING *HESTER PANIM*

It is no accident that the Torah refers to itself here as a *"shirah,"* a song or a poem. This is because it is specifically at a time of *hester panim*, when the Divine seems so remote and we are living lives that are often spiritually void, that we need the comfort and inspiration of song. In fact, throughout the Bible, it is song that arouses a connection to the holy. In *Shemuel* (*Shemuel* I 9:5) we meet the *benei nevi'im*, a company of prophets, who used music as a way to initiate prophecy. Similarly, in *Melakhim* II (3:15), the Lord comes upon Elisha only after the minstrel played. David is awakened at night by music (*Tehillim* 57:9) and, at times, discovers inspiration through the very act of writing the Psalms:

לדוד מזמור - מלמד ששרתה עליו שכינה ואחר כך אמר שירה. מזמור
לדוד - מלמד שאמר שירה ואחר כך שרתה עליו שכינה. ללמדך שאין
השכינה שורה לא מתוך עצלות, ולא מתוך עצבות, ולא מתוך שחוק, ולא
מתוך קלות ראש, ולא מתוך דברים בטלים, אלא מתוך דבר שמחה של
מצוה. שנאמר, "ועתה קחו לי מנגן והיה כנגן המנגן ותהי עליו יד ה'." אמר
רב יהודה אמר רב: וכן לדבר הלכה. (פסחים קי"ז ע"א)

"Le-David Mizmor" – "To David, a Psalm," suggests that the *Shekhinah* rested upon him [first] and then he wrote [that] song; *"Mizmor Le-David"* – "A Psalm of David," suggests that he [first] wrote [that particular] psalm and then the *Shekhinah* rested upon him. This teaches you that the *Shekhinah* rests [upon a person] neither in indolence nor in gloom, nor in frivolity nor in levity, nor in vain pursuits, but only through a state of rejoicing connected with a religious act, for it is said, "'But now bring me a minstrel.' And it came to pass, when the minstrel played, that the hand of the Lord came upon him.'" R. Yehudah said in Rav's name: "And it is likewise so in a matter of *halakhah*." (*Pesachim* 117a)

The song of Torah and the poetry of its verses can elevate us beyond the prosaic nature of our existence in order to reconnect us with God and reintroduce the *Shekhinah*, the Divine presence, in our lives. And it is never too late! *"Ve-attah"*! Now! Despite it all and because of it all, write the poem, sing the song.

RESPONSE TO THE DARK NIGHT OF *HESTER PANIM*

When our bodies ache, our hearts agonize, and our souls writhe due to misfortune or pain or evil or suffering, we grope for explanations: Why this? Why me? What now? For many of us, the question of God's justice and our attempts at theodicies consume us and exhaust us. Although we are trapped in a Jobian whirlwind, God does not appear to us; we do not hear His voice. Our teacher, Rabbi Joseph Soloveitchik, *zt"l*, offered his approach to this problem. In his *Kol Dodi Dofek*, as well as in his essay, "A Halakhic Approach to Suffering," he teaches that the ideal response to suffering is not the question "why," but, rather, the question "what now?" What do we do now? How do we learn and grow from our experiences? How do we transform our suffering into opportunities for goodness and achievement?

The Torah tells us *"ve-attah,"* and *now*, write for yourselves this song. By inscribing the song of Torah in our own handwriting, we use Torah values to transform the world in which we live and to readjust the paradigms of our lives; we look to write a new chapter of godliness and ethics in our lives and in the lives of our families and communities; and we add our own unique voices and ideas to the chorus of Jews who sang the songs of Torah, throughout the generations, in hosannas of exaltation and in elegies of lamentation.

Indeed, Rambam codifies this as a *halakhah*:

אַף עַל פִּי שמצוה ללמוד ביום ובלילה אין אדם למד רוב חכמתו אלא בלילה, לפיכך מי שרצה לזכות בכתר התורה יזהר בכל לילותיו ולא יאבד אפילו אחד מהן בשינה ואכילה ושתיה ושיחה וכיוצא בהן אלא בתלמוד תורה ודברי חכמה, אמרו חכמים אין רנה של תורה אלא בלילה שנאמר קומי רוני בלילה, וכל העוסק בתורה בלילה חוט של חסד נמשך עליו ביום שנאמר יומם יצוה ה' חסדו ובלילה שירה עמי תפלה לאל חיי, וכל בית שאין נשמעים בו דברי תורה בלילה אש אוכלתו שנאמר כל חשך טמון לצפוניו תאכלהו אש לא נופח...אמרו חכמים כל המבטל את התורה מעושר סופו לבטלה מעוני וכל המקיים את התורה מעוני סופו לקיימה מעושר, וענין זה מפורש הוא בתורה הרי הוא אומר תחת אשר לא עבדת את ה' אלהיך בשמחה ובטוב לבב מרוב כל ועבדת את אויביך, ואומר למען ענותך להטיבך באחריתך.

Even though it is a commandment to learn Torah day and night, most of one's wisdom is acquired only at night. Therefore, one who wants to attain the crown of Torah should be careful not to waste even a single night sleeping, eating, drinking, chatting, etc., but should engage in the study of Torah and worldly wisdom. The Sages said that the song of Torah is only at night, as it is written, "Arise, sing out in the night." Anyone who learns Torah at night will have a thread of kindness during the day, as it is written, "The Lord will command His steadfast love in the daytime, and in the night His song shall be with me, a prayer to the God of my life"...The Sages said that anyone who neglects Torah study for riches will eventually become poor, and that anyone who learns Torah despite being poor will eventually become rich. This idea is mentioned in the Torah: "Because you did not serve the Lord your God with joyfulness and with gladness of heart for the abundance of all things, you shall therefore serve your enemies...in hunger, and in thirst, and in nakedness, and in want of all things." The Torah has also said, "...that He might afflict you, and that He might test you, to do you good at your latter end." (*Hilkhot Talmud Torah*, 3:13)

Rambam teaches that the Torah we learn during the challenging nights of our lives is the Torah that is ultimately the most meaningful, the most creative, and the most impactful. Without a doubt, this is the Torah that pulls us out of our despair and back into life after we retreat to the refuge of our beds. This is the Torah that heals our demoralized spirits crushed by pain and suffering. This is the song of Torah that cries out: "Arise, sing out in the night." It is the writing of this Torah that ultimately rewards us when we commit to it and persist in it out of *oni* (*ayin-nun-yud*), not poverty, but because of and despite our *innui* (*ayin-nun-vav-yud*), periods of affliction. Writing our Torah in response to affliction has the potential to transform suffering into joy, darkness into light, and oppression into liberation.

THE *MITZVAH* TO WRITE TORAH

"And now, write this song for yourselves" is the commandment to write a *Sefer Torah* (Rambam, *Hilkhot Sefer Torah*, 7:1), a scroll from which we are expected to learn and be inspired. However, the *Tur* expands the parameters of this *mitzvah*. He writes:

מצוות עשה על כל ישראל אשר ידו משגת לכתוב חומשי התורה ומשנה
וגמרא ופירושיהם...וכתב א"א הרא"ש ז"ל שזה [לכתוב ספר תורה] לא
נאמר אלא לדורות הראשונים שהיו כותבין ספר תורה ולומדים בה, אבל
האידנא שכותבין ספר תורה ומניחים אותו בבית הכנסת לקרות בהם
ברבים - מצוות עשה על כל ישראל אשר ידו משגת לכתוב חומשי התורה
ומשנה וגמרא ופירושיהם להגות בהן הוא ובניו. (*Tur, Yoreh De'ah* 270)

Citing his father, Rabbeinu Asher (the Rosh), the *Tur* posits that the obligation to write a scroll applied only in ancient times, when that scroll was the text from which people studied their religious tradition. Already in his days, Torah scrolls were not used by individuals; they were designated only for ritualized public Torah readings in the synagogues. Individuals learned from books – Bibles, Talmuds, commentaries and codes. Therefore, according to the Rosh, the obligation is fulfilled by acquiring a library of religious texts and not by writing a scroll. His opinion is codified in the *Shulchan Arukh*.

Many commentators (for example, the *Perishah* and the *Taz*) challenged the proposed evolution of this obligation. How is it possible, they wondered, for later rabbinic authorities to adopt the spirit of the law and dismiss the letter of law? How could they transform the very essence of the Biblical obligation? How could the Rosh and the *Shulchan Arukh* say, "*ha-idna mitzvah likhtov Chumashei Torah u-Mishneh ve-Gemara u-peirusheihem*"?

The answer to this challenge may be found in the Biblical verse itself: "*ve-attah*" – "and now write for yourselves this song." The Torah is telling us that "now," when the contemporary mode of study is with Torah scrolls, write for yourself a Torah scroll. But when circumstances change, and "*ha-idna*," now that people learn through books – or

וילך

computers or audio files – the demands of the *mitzvah* have changed. The essence is the same: "Write for yourselves this song," create and acquire resources to learn Torah. The practical fulfillment, however, is "*ve-attah*," always sensitive to ever changing resources and technologies.

CODA

> Great is song for it incorporates the present and the past and the future, and it incorporates the World to Come. (*Sifre, Parashat Ha'azinu*, 28)

The song of Torah is great.

Song links us to our glorious past: the Psalms sung by the Levites in the Jerusalem Temple; the Lord's song sang in the foreign lands of our diasporas; the prayers of millennia of Jews sung in praise, in long-ing, and in lamentation; the words of Torah sung at wooden *shtenders* in *yeshivot* by great luminaries and simple laymen; and the song of hope sung as we dreamed of returning to our Promised Land.

Song binds us together in the present: the haunting melodies shared by a community at a *seudah shelishit*; the spontaneous *siman tov u-mazal tov* sung by friends, neighbors, and family celebrating shared joy, pride, and achievement; the varied words of Torah emanating from more *yeshivot* and *kollelim* and *midrashot* and day schools than at any other time in our history; and the previously unheard voices of women scholars who enhance the harmonies of Torah and Jewish life in ways both traditional and uniquely their own.

Song draws us to dare to dream about our future: of the "*shir chadash*," the new melody that will mark the messianic redemption; of the "*az yashir Moshe*," the song of Moshe that will once again be sung by those who sang it long ago; and of our laugh-filled mouths and the song-laden lips when God and our people will return to Zion.

And all of this is the *shirah* of the World to Come! Each time we sing the song of Torah we give expression to the *chayei olam nata be-tokheinu*, to the eternal and eschatological reality that exists *attah*, right now, in the pages of our holy books and that resonates *attah*, right now, in our souls and our imaginations. Each time we write our own *shirah*, we link past, present and future and, no matter the challenges and difficulties and fears, that song is our little piece of *Olam Ha-Ba*, right now, in our own lives.

Rabbi Dr. Jacob J. Schacter

האזינו: *Teshuvah,* Punishment and the Leadership of Moshe

And the Lord spoke to Moshe that selfsame day, saying: "Go up to this mountain of Avarim, Mount Nevo, which is in the land of Moav, that is facing Yericho, and behold Eretz Kena'an that I give unto the Children of Israel as an inheritance. And die on the mountain which you will ascend and be gathered unto your people, as Aaron your brother died on Mount Hor, and was gathered unto his people. Because you both trespassed against Me in the midst of the Children of Israel at the waters of Merivat-Kadesh, in the Wilderness of Zin; because you both did not sanctify Me in the midst of the Children of Israel. For you shall see the land from afar, but you will not enter there, into the land that I am giving to the Children of Israel." (Devarim 32:48–52)

With this powerful, sad and tragic communication between God and Moshe, our Torah portion ends. After a lifetime of service to the Jewish people, Moshe is informed that he will not accompany the Jewish people into the Land of Israel.

The episode of "the waters of Merivat-Kadesh" responsible for this tragic decree raises a number of important questions, and has occupied the attention of Biblical exegetes and scholars from ancient times to the present day. For Maimonides, it represented "one of the most difficult problems in the Torah, concerning which many things have been said, and which has been asked many times" – "*safek mi-sfeikei ha-Torah she-ne'emru bo devarim rabbim ve-nishal p'amim rabbim*."[1] First of all, what, exactly, was the sin of Moshe, described for the first time in *Bemidbar* Ch. 20? Remarkably, the Torah does not explicitly describe this most fundamental event in Moshe's life, and many different suggestions have been made to explain what happened. They range from his having hit the rock instead of speaking to it, hitting the rock twice instead of once, expressing anger at the Children of Israel ("*shim'u na ha-morim;*" *Bemidbar* 20:10), giving the impression that he and Aharon were responsible for the water coming forth from the rock instead of God, his apparent cowardice in retreating to the sanctuary when confronted by the Jewish people, and more. Abarbanel cited ten suggestions in his commentary to *Bemidbar* Ch. 20 and rejected most of them as being "far from the truth" – "*rechokim min ha-emet*" (Abarbanel, ad loc.). S.D. Luzzatto wrote, "Moshe our Teacher committed one sin but the exegetes have loaded upon him thirteen sins and more, for each of them invented a new sin."[2] R. Isaac Arama noted that the matter is particularly complex because behavior considered by some (R. Chananel, for example) as rebellious, was considered by others (R. Yosef Albo, for example) as laudable, and he wrote that after all the suggestions, "we have no commentary that will assuage the ear with regard to the sin" – "*ve-ain lanu peirush yishakhech*

---

1.   Maimonides, "Eight Chapters," introduction to *Commentary on the Mishnah, Avot,* Ch. 4, end. This formulation of his is also cited in Nachmanides, *Commentary on the Torah, Bemidbar* 20:1.

2.   S.D. Luzzato, *Perush Shada"l Al Ha-Torah* (Tel Aviv, 1965), 472.

et ha-ozen be-chet.[3] At the end of the day, this matter is not conclusive and we can only hope to share the optimism expressed by Maimonides who wrote, after surveying all the existing suggestions, *"u-re'eh mah she-ne'emar bo u-mah she-amarnu bo anachnu, ve-ha-emet ya'aseh darkho"* – "Let what others have said be compared with our opinion and the truth will surely prevail."[4]

Second, whatever the sin may have been, why did it result in Moshe being denied his most fervent life's wish? After all, by this time in his life, what had Moshe *not* done on behalf of the Jewish people? In the words of the *Yalkut Shimoni*, even after only a short time as leader of the Jews, Moshe "took them out of Egypt, split for them the sea, brought down for them the manna, raised up for them the well, prepared for them the quail, surrounded them with clouds of glory, [and] fashioned the Tabernacle."[5] Add to that his leading the Jewish people in the wilderness for four decades, surely, as the Torah repeatedly makes clear, no simple matter and no easy achievement. No one – ever – had greater merits than Moshe; no one – ever – was closer to God than Moshe. Even if his sin was a grievous one, did it warrant the apparently harsh punishment he received?

Third, it would appear to be the height of irony that this Torah passage, read every year on a *Shabbat* close to Yom Kippur, seems to deny or challenge the very efficacy of the act of repentance or *teshuvah* that is absolutely central to this time of year. Surely Moshe must have been embarrassed by what he did, whatever it may have been; surely

---

3. R. Isaac Arama, *Akeidat Yitzchak, Parashat Chukkat, Sha'ar* 80.
4. Maimonides, ad loc. For a summary of the sins that were suggested by medieval and modern commentators, see Shmuel Cohen, "Parashat Mei Merivah Ve-Shitat Rabbenu Chananel," *Megadim* 20 (1993), pp. 43–44, n. 1.

    There is a large secondary literature on this episode. Among the presentations I found most interesting are Nehama Leibowitz, *Studies in Bamidbar* (Jerusalem, 1980), pp. 236–47; Jeffrey M. Cohen, "The Striking of the Rock and the Sin of Moshe and Aaron Reconsidered," *Niv Hamidrashia* 15 (1980), pp. 100–14; John A. Beck, "Why Did Moses Strike Out?: The Narrative-Geographical Shaping of Moses' Disqualification in Numbers 20:1–13," *Westminster Theological Journal* 65 (2003), pp. 135–41; Yaakov Blidstein, *Ezev Nevo: Mitat Moshe Be-Midreshei Hazal* (Alon Shevut, 2008), in passim; below, n. 8.
5. *Yalkut Shimoni, Vayikra* 1:427.

he must have regretted what he did, whatever it may have been; surely he must have resolved never to do it again, whatever that "it" may have been. What happened to the power of *teshuvah*? Were the gates of *teshuvah* closed to this greatest of all Jews? Here we are, deeply impacted by the drama of *Rosh Ha-Shanah* and the intensity of Yom Kippur, in the midst of attempting to engage in a genuine sincere introspective quest for personal salvation and atonement, and it would appear that we are being told that *teshuvah*, in fact, is impossible and makes no real difference. And, for all people, it seems to have made no real difference for the greatest of the great, for none other than Moshe our Teacher himself!

These problems are compounded by the fact that this was not the first time Moshe was commanded to draw water from a well. Many years before, one generation and close to forty years earlier, shortly after the Jewish people left Egypt, God told him to take his rod and *smite* the rock in order that water come out from it (*Shemot* 17:6). Assuming, as many commentators including Rashi do,[6] that his sin this later time was hitting the rock instead of speaking to it, should not the fact that Moshe was explicitly commanded to *hit* the rock the first time such an event occurred significantly mitigate the nature of his sin here close to forty years later?

Perhaps the answer to these questions lies in the difference of the nature and character of these two generations, the one for whom God told Moshe to *hit* the rock and the one for whom God told Moshe to *speak* to the rock. The first was a generation that personally and directly experienced the awesomeness, might and power of God through the many explicit and dramatic miracles He performed for them, first in Egypt and then during and after the Exodus from that country. Those miracles were awesome and powerful, and when *that* generation needed water, God's miracle needed to be of the same order of magnitude. And, as a result, God told Moshe to *hit* the rock. This was the kind of act they could understand; this was the kind of God to whom they were accustomed.

Contrast this generation to the next one for whom God performed miracles of an entirely different order. This time there was no thunder and lightening, no striking choreography and no dramatic

---

6. Rashi, *Bemidbar* 20:12, s.v. *le-hakdisheni*.

pyrotechnics, but rather manna falling gently from Heaven, a well quietly offering water and clouds of glory softly providing protection. This generation was accustomed to more subdued, subtle and quiet miracles and a more subdued, subtle and quiet God. And so, when *this* generation needed water, it was absolutely essential that Moshe *speak* to the rock. This was a generation that would not understand a rock-hitting God; it could respond only to a rock-speaking God.

From this perspective, God's denial of Moshe's fervent wish to lead the Jewish people into the Promised Land should not be understood as a punishment, and Moshe's inability to change the decree should not be understood as reflecting the lack of the power of *teshuvah*. Rather, when Moshe hit the rock this time as well, God realized, perhaps, that Moshe was viewing the second generation through the same lens through which he viewed the first, that he was communicating with the second generation the same way he communicated with the first, and therefore concluded that he would be an inappropriate leader for them. Of course, Moshe could be forgiven for whatever sin he committed. Moshe the individual could certainly be reconciled with the God whose teachings he so carefully transmitted, the God whom he so faithfully served, and the God whose people he so selflessly led for decades. The problem lay not in Moshe the individual; it lay in Moshe the leader. When Moshe hit the rock instead of speaking to it, God perhaps realized that he would no longer be suited to serve as the leader of the next generation of Jews. Someone else would now be needed who could better lead them at this most crucial juncture in their developing national identity and early national history.

This point is sharpened by the striking rabbinic tradition which teaches that Moshe the private citizen was, indeed, given the opportunity to enter the Promised Land. Had he wanted to enter as a student of Yehoshua's, that option would have been available to him, but it was something he could not bring himself to do. It was only Moshe in his capacity as Jewish leader who was prohibited from entering "the land that I am giving to the Children of Israel."[7]

---

7. See *Midrash Rabbah, Devarim* 9:9; *Sifre, Pinchas* #135. For the problematics surrounding this story, see Yaakov Blidstein, *Ezev Nevo*, pp. 123–33.

The essence, the substance, of the teachings of Judaism, needs to be constant from one generation to the next. But the idiom, style, manner, approach and mode of communication of that essence or that substance, may, and for some, must, change from one generation to the next. What was effective in the Middle Ages is not necessarily effective in the twenty-first century; what worked well in Eastern Europe will not necessarily work well in America. The message is the same; the medium changes from time to time and from place to place.[8]

8. For other suggestions more or less analogous to mine, see Steven D. Fraade, "Moses at Meribah: Speech, Scepter and Sanctification," *Orim* 2:1 (1986) pp. 43–67; Yitzchak Shaveh, "Chet'o shel Mosheh," *Megadim* 20 (1993), pp. 35–42; Nathaniel Helfgot, "'And Moshe Struck the Rock': Numbers 20 and the Leadership of Moses," *Tradition* 27:3 (1993), pp. 51–58; and Mosheh Lichtenstein, "Moshe's Leadership and the Transition of Generations," www.vbm-torah.org/parsha.62/35chukat.htm. The Netziv also highlights Moshe's failure to differentiate between the generation that left Egypt and the one he was addressing here, although he describes the difference differently. See *Ha'amek Davar, Bemidbar* 20:1–12, in passim. See too R. Elchanan Samet, *Iyyunim Be-Parashot Ha-Shavua*, vol. 2 (Jerusalem, 2002), pp. 225–26, idem., *Iyyunim Be-Parashot Ha-Shavua: Sidrah Sheniyah*, vol. 2 (Tel Aviv, 2009), p. 253.

Rabbi Yosef Blau

וזאת הברכה: The Greatness of Moshe

Thaskell

The last verses of the Torah describe the greatness of Moshe. First, the Bible posits that there will never be a future prophet comparable to Moshe, who had a unique relationship with *Hashem*. Next mentioned are the miracles Moshe performed in Egypt. Lastly, the concluding verse of the Torah hints at the splitting of the sea and the receiving of the Ten Commandments at Sinai. Rashi, however, is puzzled by the last three words, *"le-einei kol Yisrael"* – "in the sight of all of Israel" (*Devarim* 34:12). Rashi's question emerges from the fact that the people did not see Moshe receive the tablets, since the people remained at the bottom of the mountain when Moshe was given the Torah. Rashi, therefore, deduces that this final phrase, the ultimate compliment to Moshe, refers to his publicly breaking the tablets and not to the giving of the Torah (Rashi, ad loc.).

On the surface, it is difficult to imagine that this response to the sin of the golden calf is remotely comparable to leading the Jews out of the slavery of Egypt, teaching them the Torah, and nurturing them for forty years in the wilderness, to the extent that it should be the last thing referred to in the Torah. In fact, the other classical commentaries all interpret *"le-einei kol Yisrael"* as referring to Moshe's leadership role in the Jewish people's acceptance the Torah at Sinai.

Moshe is described at his death as an *"eved Hashem"* – "a servant of *Hashem"* (*Devarim* 34:5), a term which implies a loyal follower who obeys his master. The Talmud (*Shabbat* 87a) includes the breaking of the tablets as one of three instances where Moshe acted independently and *Hashem* approved of Moshe's decision after the fact. It is this tension between being the loyal servant and acting independently that explains the critical nature of the breaking of the tablets.

After the people sinned with the golden calf (even according to the explanation of the Ramban reducing its severity), *Hashem* offered Moshe the opportunity to replace the Jews with his own descendants. Moshe refused the offer, and prayed that the Jewish people not be wiped out. When *Benei Yisrael* were given a reprieve, Moshe was not told how to rectify the situation. He faced the ultimate test of leadership. What was he prepared to risk in purifying the Jewish people, teaching them about the consequences of their sins, and preserving their relationship with *Hashem, all at the same time?* Dramatically, he demonstrated that accepting the Torah, even proclaiming *"na'aseh ve-nishma"* – "we will follow the laws before we understand them," does not guarantee the permanence of the relationship between Hashem and the Jewish people, and he broke the tablets. The tablets containing the Ten Commandments would need to be earned again, through an internal struggle that would yield casualties.

Beyond loyalty and full commitment to observing *Hashem'*s commands is the challenge of internalizing values, so that one will choose wisely when there are no instructions as to how to act. Moshe was the servant who intuitively knew how to respond when his Master trusted him to take the initiative. Thus, Moshe successfully saved his people and preserved their bond with *Hashem* by breaking the tablets, and eventually, carving out a second set of tablets at God's command.

This insight into personal growth and responsibility helps explain difficulties in the early part of the *parashah* dealing with the blessing Moshe gives to the twelve tribes. In contrast to Yaakov's blessings, in which Yaakov lumped Shimon and Levi together and criticized the anger that they had demonstrated in wiping out the city of Shechem, Moshe, in his blessings, lauds Levi and does not mention Shimon. Why does Moshe praise Levi while leaving out Shimon?

Levi's descendants apparently took Yaakov's rebuke of their forefather to heart, learned to control their emotions, and dedicated themselves to defending the Torah. As part of Moshe's response to the sin of the golden calf, after he had broken the tablets, the tribe of Levi joined Moshe in punishing the sinners, even though it meant fighting against their relatives. This commitment on the part of *Shevet Levi* was made despite it being unclear how the broken tablets would be replaced and what would happen to *Benei Yisrael* after the punishment for the sin of the golden calf had been meted out.

In contrast to Levi's descendants, though, the descendants of Shimon had not yet learned how to modify their behavior. The only mention in the Torah of their leadership after the incident in Shechem, was in their worshiping the cult of Pe'or and in one of their tribal princes having relations with a princess of Moav. Strikingly, it is Pinchas, a descendant of Levi, who killed the prince of Shimon and ended the plague that the indiscretion had caused.

Thus, Yaakov had warned against negative traits, yet did not reject any of his sons.

Moshe, in contrast, reacted to the lessons that were and were not learned in the years that followed Shimon and Levi's actions in Shechem.

Moshe's primary characteristic was humility. He is described as the most modest person who ever lived, and he was a reluctant leader, even from the beginning (initially declining *Hashem*'s command that he return to Egypt to lead the Jews out of slavery). Yet when necessary, with the entire future of the Jewish people and its relationship with *Hashem* at risk, Moshe expressed the righteous indignation of his ancestor Levi, and broke the tablets.

Proper use of one's character traits, and being able to act decisively when there is no clear Divine directive, are the true keys to greatness. Moshe's breaking of the tablets preserved the Jewish people, and therefore this action merits being the last act referred to in the Torah. The breaking of the tablets led to the carving of a second set of tablets that permanently bound the Jewish people to the Torah, and these second tablets allowed us to remain forevermore *banim la-Makom*, the children of *Hashem*.

Rabbi Menachem Leibtag

Concluding Essay: A Conclusion or the Beginning?

Moshe Rabbenu, our greatest prophet (as the final lines of *Chumash* testify), concludes his career by blessing each of the tribes. Were his blessings a type of prophecy that would pre-determine the fate of Jewish history?

As a conclusion to this volume, we examine the nature of these blessings, in order to determine if their purpose, like prophecy itself, was to predict the future, or to shape it.

On *Simchat Torah*, we hear the Torah reading of *Vezot Haberakhah* so many times, that we can recite those blessings by heart. Nonetheless, most of us have little understanding in regard to what they are about. Furthermore, there is no apparent logic in the order of the tribes in these blessings. As highlighted by the table below, they do not follow the order of their birth, nor do they group according to the matriarchs.

THE ORDER OF THE TRIBES

Order of Birth	Matriarch	*Shevet*	Order Appearing
1	Leah	Reuven	1
4	Leah	Yehudah	2
3	Leah	Levi	3
12	Rachel	Binyamin	4
11	Rachel	Yosef [Efraim & Menasheh]	5
6	Leah	Zevulun	6
5	Leah	Yissachar	7
9	Zilpah	Gad	8
7	Bilhah	Dan	9
8	Bilhah	Naftali	10
10	Zilpah	Asher	11

As you study this list, note how on the one hand, the order is certainly not random, as the children of the maidservants (Bilhah and Zilpah) are grouped at the end, while the children of Rachel are 'sandwiched' together between Leah's elder and younger children. On the other hand, there doesn't appear to be an apparent reason for Rachel's children to be inserted in this manner. And of course, as you noticed, Shimon is missing!

Furthermore, although it's pretty clear why Reuven is first, as he is the oldest, why does Moshe skip from Reuven to Yehudah? Likewise, why does Binyamin precede his older brother Yosef, and why do the children of Rachel 'interrupt' Moshe's blessings to the children of Leah? Finally, why does Zevulun precede Yissachar, why does Gad precede Dan, and why do the children of Bilhah 'interrupt' the children of Zilpah?

Even in *Parashat Bemidbar*, where we find the tribes listed in various orders as they prepare to organize the camp around the *Mishkan*, we find no list that even slightly resembles this order of the blessings in *Vezot Haberakhah*.

To understand the rationale behind this order, we must first consider the nature and purpose of these blessings.

FROM YAAKOV TO MOSHE

Vezot Haberakhah is not the first time in *Chumash* where we find that each tribe receives a blessing. Recall from back in *Parashat Vayechi*, how *Yaakov Avinu* blesses each tribe before his death. Unlike Moshe, Yaakov addresses the tribes in a very logical order, according to the matriarchs, and according to their ages: Reuven, Shimon, Levi, Yehudah, Zevulun & Yissachar (note slight deviation), Dan (first-born of Bilhah), Gad (first born of Zilpah), Asher, and Naftali. As those blessings relate to the personal destiny of each son, it makes sense that they would follow in the order of oldest to youngest.

Moshe, by contrast, is not the dying father of twelve sons. Rather, he is the departing leader of twelve tribes to whom he has given the Torah and who are about to inherit the Land of Israel. As we would expect, his blessings accurately reflect this setting and these circumstances.

In the first part of our analysis, we will show how each of Moshe's blessings relates in one form or another to either the tribe's forthcoming military conquest of the land, to their leadership potential, or to the quality of the specific *nachalah* (territory) that they are destined to inherit.

Afterward, we will show how these observations will enable us to answer our original questions concerning the strange order of the tribes in these blessings.

THE GIST OF THE BLESSINGS

Let's quickly review the gist of each blessing, one tribe at a time, noting how each blessing relates to either the defining characteristic of that tribe's inheritance (*nachalah*), or to the tribe's role in the imminent conquest of the land.

Reuven

At first glance, *Moshe Rabbenu's* opening remarks to the tribe of Reuven appear to be simply a blessing of 'life:' "Let Reuven live and not die, and let his numbers be counted" (*Devarim* 33:6).

Nonetheless, both Rashi and Seforno explain how these remarks actually relate to the forthcoming conquest of the land. Rashi explains how this blessing addresses Moshe's concern that Reuven would not receive a *nachalah* at all – as he may have lost that right when Yaakov cursed him (on account of his sin with Bilhah; see *Bereishit* 49:3–4), just as he forfeited his claim to the *bekhorah* (birthright). [See also Targum Onkelos, ad loc.]

Furthermore, the fact that Reuven had already set up camp *outside* the Biblical borders of *Eretz Kena'an* (in Transjordan) provided yet another reason to doubt whether Reuven would truly become an 'official' tribe of Israel. Hence, Rashi explains that the purpose of Moshe's blessing was to counter these fears, thus reassuring Reuven that he will remain 'alive,' i.e. a full-fledged member of the tribes of Israel.

In contrast, Chizkuni offers a 'military' explanation for this blessing. Considering that the tribe of Reuven had recently promised to take the front line in the forthcoming battles to conquer *Eretz Kena'an* [i.e. to be the "*chalutz*" – see *Bemidbar* 32:20–32], Moshe bestows upon them a blessing of 'life' to help them survive this most dangerous task, praying on their behalf that their "number" (*mispar*) – population – should remain the same after battle as it was beforehand. Note how both commentators make every effort to relate this blessing (and all the others) to the forthcoming events, as the twelve tribes now prepare to conquer the land.

Yehudah

> Hear *Hashem* the [battle] cry of Yehudah and help him lead his people. Make his hands strong for him, and help him against his enemies. (*Devarim* 33:7; also see Rashi and Ibn Ezra, ad loc.)

Clearly, the *berakhah* to Yehudah relates to his military leadership, as Moshe foresees that the soldiers of Yehudah will be particularly enthusiastic and diligent in the conquest of their portion in the Land (see *Yehoshua* 14:6–12 and *Shoftim* 1:1–15).

Levi
After a short reference to Aharon, the tribal leader of the tribe of Levi, Moshe addresses Levi as follows:

> They shall teach Your laws to Yaakov and Your instructions to Israel; they shall offer incense offerings (*ketoret*)...and whole-offerings (*olot*) on the altar. God should bless his 'resources' (*cheilo*) and favor his undertakings. Help him smite the loins of those who rise against him, and don't allow his enemies to succeed. (33:8–11)

This blessing to Levi focuses on this tribe's responsibility to provide spiritual leadership, i.e. to teach God's laws and officiate in His Temple. Interestingly, however, even this faculty is presented in military jargon (e.g. the words *"cheilo"* and *"machatz"* in *Devarim* 33:11).

Whereas all other tribes earned their *nachalah*, a specific, designated portion of land, *shevet Levi* was scattered among the various tribes in order to serve as teachers throughout the country (note *Devarim* 18:1–2, "God is their inheritance"). Understandably, then, their blessing relates to that leadership responsibility, rather than to their allocated portion in the land.

Binyamin

> Beloved to God, He shall allow His *Shekhinah* to dwell securely within him. He constantly protects him, as He rests between his shoulders. (33:12)

This blessing focuses on the special quality of Binyamin's inheritance, as his tribe is designated to house the *Beit Ha-Mikdash*.

Yosef [Efraim and Menasheh]

> God's blessing is given to his land, with the bounty of dew from heaven ... with the bounty of the earth in its fullness ... His horns are like those of a wild ox, with them he gores other nations ... these are the tens of thousands of Efraim and these are the thousands of Menasheh. (33:13–17)

The precise translation of this blessing is somewhat elusive, but it clearly speaks of the bountiful nature of their inheritance. It appears that Yosef will bear the responsibility of forming the backbone of Israel's agrarian economy (as was Yosef's job in Egypt; see *Or Ha-Chayyim* here).

The final verse alludes to Yosef's military competence that will grant him victory over enemy nations. Specifically, Rashi understands the final *pasuk* as a reference to the leadership of Yehoshua – a descendant of Efraim – who led *Am Yisrael* in their conquest of *Eretz Kena'an*.

Zevulun and Yissachar

> Rejoice Zevulun as you go out [to war; compare with *Bemidbar* 27:17] and Yissachar in your tents. [Their prosperity will catalyze] a call to other nations to ascend God's mountain (see Ibn Ezra & Seforno) where they will offer proper sacrifices, for they draw from the riches of the sea and from the hidden hoards of the sand. (33:18)

The opening sentence may refer to Zevulun's military prowess (see Ibn

Ezra's interpretation, in contrast to Rashi's, and see *Shoftim* 5:18), but the conclusion of the *pasuk* clearly relates to the location of their *nachalah* along the Mediterranean, thus forming Israel's gateway to foreign trade and, consequently, economic relations with other nations. Moshe anticipates that these business alliances will lead to their ultimate recognition of the God of Israel.

The *nachalah* of Yissachar, too, facilitates international trade (and influence), as it lies in Emek Yizrael – the Jezreel Valley, at the heart of the Via Maris – the ancient trade route connecting Egypt with Mesopotamia. [See Seforno 33:19, who alludes to Yissachar's role in international trade.]

Furthermore, Rashbam (*Bereishit* 49:14, ad loc.) understands the "tents" of Yissachar as a reference to this tribe's involvement in agriculture, while Rabbenu Yosef Bekhor Shor (ibid., ad loc.) associates Yissachar's tents with the cattle industry (compare with *Bereishit* 4:20). All this, too, relates directly to Yissachar's portion: the fertile soil of Emek Yizreel renders it an ideal location for both agriculture and livestock breeding.

Gad

> Blessed be He who enlarges [the *nachalah* of] Gad. He is poised like a lion to tear off arm and scalp [i.e. military strength]. He chose for himself the best [*nachalah*] .... (20–21)[1]

Once again, Moshe's blessing focuses on the unique nature of the given tribe's *nachalah*, Gad's initiative to widen his inheritance in Transjordan, as well as their military capabilities.

Dan

> Dan is like a lion's whelp that leaps from the Bashan. (22)

Dan's blessing obviously relates to their military might and the location of their *nachalah* – at the western slopes of the Golan Heights ("Bashan"

---

1. The rest of the *pasuk* is very difficult, but most likely refers to his *nachalah* as the chosen spot for Moshe's burial site – see Rashi.

is the Biblical name for the Golan – see *Devarim* 3:8–10), today the area of Tel Dan and Kiryat Shemona in the Hula Valley of the Upper Galille. Similarly, Rashi explains the lion metaphor as a reference to Dan's location on the border, standing guard against enemy intrusion.

Naftali

> Naftali should be satiated [for his *nachalah* is] full of God's blessing, to the west and south (of his brother Dan) he shall/must conquer his land. (23)[2]

Again, Moshe's *berakhah* relates to the agricultural potential of this *nachalah* and the conquest of that portion. This correlates with the location of Naftali's *nachalah* in the fertile region of the Upper Gallilee, to the west and south of Tel Dan (including Zefat & Har Meron).

Asher

> May Asher be the most blessed of sons, may he be the favorite of his brothers and may he dip his foot in oil. Iron and copper are your door-bolts, and your security should last for all your days (24–25)

This blessing relates to the two unique characteristics of Asher's *nachalah*: its abundance of olive trees (and hence olive oil) and its location on Israel's northern border. Ramban explains that Asher's portion guards the country's northern border (and thus serves as an 'iron lock,' securing the country).

SUMMARY

As we have shown, all of these blessings focus on the agricultural nature of each *nachalah* and the forthcoming conquest of the land. In fact,

---

2. See Ibn Ezra's comments regarding the word *"yerashah."* See also Ramban – note why he quotes the *Midrash*.

almost all the commentators, especially Ibn Ezra, Chizkuni, and Seforno (in addition to Rashi and Ramban), relate to these aspects throughout their interpretations of these *pesukim*.

These observations can help us understand the underlying intention of the blessings that *Moshe Rabbenu* bestows at this time. Aware of the military capabilities of each tribe and the anticipated geographic division of the land (note *Devarim* 34:1–4), Moshe blesses each tribe – encouraging them to achieve their fullest potential in the forthcoming conquest of *Eretz Kena'an*.

In essence, that may be what blessings are all about – the fulfillment of personal potential!

Based on this understanding, we can return to our original question and make some sense out of the seemingly random order of their presentation.

'ORDER' OF INHERITANCE

As these blessings relate to the *nachalot* – the upcoming inheritance of each tribe, we posit that their order progresses in a manner that corresponds to their geographical location.

Reuven is first, not just because he is the oldest, but rather because Reuven was the first tribe to conquer his portion, as recorded in *Bemidbar* Ch. 32 (as well as *Devarim* 3:16–19).

If this theory was correct, we would now expect Gad to receive the next blessing (who joined *shevet Reuven* in their conquest of Transjordan). Instead, we find that the next blessing goes to Yehudah (*Devarim* 33:6–7). However, there appears to be an overriding rule that governs the order of these blessing – that Moshe first blesses the tribes from Yaakov's wives (i.e. the children of Leah and Rachel) – and only afterward blesses the tribes from the maidservants (Bilhah & Zilpah).

This principle neatly explains the order when Moshe blesses these four tribes (from the maidservants) towards the end of the *parashah*. Note how he begins by blessing Gad (see *Devarim* 33:20), because they conquered their *nachalah* first (in Transjordan) – even though Dan is the older brother.

These observations can also help clarify the meaning of Reuven's blessing. Moshe must emphasize that *even though* Reuven's *nachalah* lies outside the borders of *Eretz Kena'an*, they retain their status as an 'official' *shevet* (as we explained earlier).

Yehudah First

Once we skip Gad, Reuven is followed by Yehudah – the first of the tribes to successfully conquer their portion of land (as detailed both in *Yehoshua* Ch. 14–15 and *Shoftim* 1:1–15). This also explains why Yehudah's blessing focuses on their military power.

Next, *Moshe Rabbenu* works his way from south to north, from Yehudah (in the south) through Binyamin to Efraim and Menasheh, and later to Zevulun and Yissachar. This principle (of geographical order) explains why Binyamin precedes Yosef, for his *nachalah* is located north of Yehudah, but south of Efraim. But what happened to Shimon and Levi?

A 'Solution' for Shimon

Our approach thus far can also provide us with a clue as to why Shimon does not receive a blessing in *Vezot Haberakhah*. Considering that Shimon's *nachalah* is later included (or 'swallowed up') within the borders of Yehudah (see *Yehoshua* 19:1 & 19:9), one could conclude that Shimon basically never received their own *nachalah* (a fulfillment of Yaakov's 'blessing' to Shimon in *Bereishit* 48:5–7). Furthermore, in the aftermath of *chet benot Mo'av* (the sin with the daughters of Moab) their numbers were severely reduced (see *Bemidbar* 26:14; compare with *Bemidbar* 1:23).[3]

Why Levi and Binyamin Come First

Now, we must explain why Levi follows immediately after Yehudah, before all the other tribes.

To do so, we must first explain why according to our theory (that

---

3. Note Rashi on *Devarim* 33:7, where he quotes a *Midrash Tehillim* that the *berakhah* to Shimon is actually included within the *berakhah* to Yehudah: "*Shema* Hashem" contains the first letters of Shimon's name, *shin.mem.ayin*. In fact, the same wording is used when Shimon is first named by his mother: "*ki shama Hashem ki senu'ah anokhi*" (see *Bereishit* 29:33).

the blessings relate specifically to the *nachalot*) – Levi should not have received any blessing, for they were not destined to receive any portion in the land – as Moshe himself has stated earlier:

> The *kohanim-levi'im* – the entire tribe of Levi – shall not receive a *nachalah* with the rest of Israel…God is his *nachalah*, as He spoke to him. (*Devarim* 18:1–2)

However, a closer analysis of this *pasuk* can provide us with a very meaningful reason for not only the nature of Moshe's blessing to Levi, but also its position! Note how the tribe of Levi did, indeed, receive a *nachalah* – not a tract of land, but rather "*nachalat* Hashem" – i.e. as a tribe, they are destined to serve the people as God's representatives.

Towards that purpose, God separated the entire *shevet* of Levi to serve in the *Beit Ha-Mikdash* and to teach Torah to *Benei Yisrael*. Hence, this responsibility is considered their *nachalah*.

Even though this special *nachalah* does not carry a distinct geographical border, nonetheless the *Beit Ha-Mikdash* ("*makom asher yivchar Hashem*;" see *Devarim* Ch. 12) was to become the central location for the fulfillment of these responsibilities. Considering that the permanent *Beit Ha-Mikdash* was destined to be built in Jerusalem (i.e., *Har Ha-Moriah*, see *Divrei Ha-Yamim* II 3:1), *Moshe Rabbenu* treats the tribe of Levi as though its *nachalah* will be that city.

As we all know, the city of Jerusalem is located precisely between the borders of the tribes of Yehudah (to the south) and Binyamin (to the north; see *Yehoshua* 15:8 and 18:16) – therefore his blessing follows that of Yehudah (and precedes the blessing to Binyamin) – and deals with their tribal responsibilities to teach Torah to Israel, and officiate in the Temple:

> …They shall teach Your laws to Yaakov and Your Torah to Israel – they shall put incense and whole burnt-offering upon Your Altar. God should bless his substance, and accept the work of his hands… (*Devarim* 33:10–11)

Even though the cities wherein the Levites will live are scattered among the tribes, Jerusalem will remain their center; and hence Levi follows Yehuda.

Binyamin

As the order proceeds from south to north, Binyamin receives the next blessing, i.e. following Levi. This juxtaposition to Levi also explains why Moshe's blessing to Binyamin focuses first and foremost on this tribe's role as the territory wherein God will allow His *Shekhinah* to dwell (*Devarim* 33:12). Recall how Jerusalem is located on its southern border, while the *Mishkan* was located in other cities within Binyamin, such as Gilgal, Nov, and Givon. Accordingly, Binyamin's blessing deals exclusively with God's promise that His *Shekhinah* will dwell within this tribe's borders ("shoulders").

Yosef and the Shomron

As we proceed northward from the territory of Binyamin, we enter the region settled by the children of Yosef, first Efraim and then Menasheh (located farther to the north). Once again, our theory also explains why Moshe's blessing to Yosef focuses primarily on the land's vast agricultural potential and the tribe's military strength.

Yissachar and Zevulun

To explain why Yissachar and Zevulun follow Menasheh, we must consider once again the geography of the land.

Thus far, we have seen how the blessings proceed from North to South. However, as the borders of Efraim and Menasheh extend from the Mediterranean Sea to the Jordan River, we have not yet found an example of whether an eastern territory should precede a western one (or vice versa). We do encounter this problem with regard to Yissachar and Zevulun, as both occupy the area of the Jezreel Valley, just to the north of Yosef's northern border, with Zevulun to the west and Yissachar to the east.

As we explained earlier, this territory serves as the gateway to foreign trade, convoys and shipping, as reflected in Moshe's blessings to Yissachar and Zevulun.

Although no geographical reason seems to warrant Zevulun's

precedence over his older brother, Yissachar, *Moshe Rabbenu* follows the pattern set by *Yaakov Avinu*, who also blessed Zevulun before Yissachar (see *Bereishit* 49:13–14). It should also be noted that Zevulun precedes Yissachar in *Sefer Yehoshua* (Ch. 19), in the context of the apportionment of the land among the tribes. (Rashi also provides an answer relating to the famous Yissachar/Zevulun 'work/study Torah' arrangement.)

Benei Ha-Shefachot

As we explained above, Moshe blesses the children of Yaakov's maidservants only after he completes the blessings to Leah and Rachel's children. However, consistent with his pattern heretofore, he presents his blessings in the order of their *nachalot*, rather than the order of their births.

Moshe opens his blessings to this group by addressing *Shevet Gad*, who, together with Reuven, took their *nachalah* first, in Transjordan (*Bemidbar* 32:1–4). As the area of Tel Dan (in the Hula Valley) was originally destined to be the site for Dan's inheritance (see *Devarim* 34:1–2), and this area is located closest to the *nachalah* of Gad, Dan's blessing follows Gad.

As Naftali's portion is located in the upper Eastern Galilee, just to the west of Dan's portion – Naftali follows Dan.

Finally, Moshe blesses Asher, whose *nachalah* is located in the upper Western Galilee – to the west of Naftali. Asher's borders also form the most northern border of Israel – and hence a fitting tribe to conclude this series of blessings.

These geographic considerations explain not only the logic behind the progression of Moshe's blessing, but also provides us with a better appreciation of the content of these final four blessings, as they focus on the beauty of the land, each tribe's need for expansion, and how they protect Israel's northern and eastern borders. Moshe's blessings thus encourage these tribes, who reside far away from the center of the country to rise to the challenges that their inheritances present.

The Opener and the Finale

Now that we have explained the individual *berakhot* and their sequence, we conclude by taking a quick look at *Moshe Rabbenu's* opening and concluding comments, to see how they relate to our discussion thus far.

Moshe introduces these blessings with a four-*pasuk* 'opener' (see *Devarim* 33:2–5) and a corresponding four-*pasuk* 'closer' (ibid., 26–29). The introductory *pesukim* – the precise translation of which requires further discussion – clearly point to *Ma'amad Har Sinai* and Moshe's role as the transmitter of the laws commanded at *Har Sinai*.

Moshe's closing remarks focus on God as the Protector of Israel, who provides close supervision (ibid., 26), assistance in battle (ibid., 26, 27, 29), and agricultural and economic prosperity (ibid., 26 and 28).

Not only do these opening and closing remarks form the appropriate framework for the individual blessings, they also directly relate to the primary theme of *Sefer Devarim*, and for that matter, *Chumash* as a whole. God has chosen the Jewish nation to represent Him as His model nation to guide mankind in the proper direction. To that end, He gave them the Torah (ibid., 2–5), which contains the specific laws whose observance in the Promised Land leads to the realization of that goal.

A CONCLUSION AND A BEGINNING

Now, before his death, Moshe blesses *Benei Yisrael* to fulfill that potential – that God assist them in their achievement of these goals, in the *nachalot* they are about to conquer and occupy. But these blessing do not determine what *will* happen, rather they serve as a guide for each tribe to recognize their own potential – so they know what *can* happen. That knowledge should inspire each tribe to rise to these challenges, as they now recognize what they can achieve.

In that sense, *Moshe Rabbenu*'s blessings at the end of *Chumash* serve as guide for the tribes of Israel that can help shape their future, as they undertake a new beginning as they prepare to conquer the land and establish a nation representing God.

Certainly, a most appropriate way for *Moshe Rabbenu* to finish the Torah, and thus conclude his life's mission!

Not only does *Chumash* conclude with a blessing, it also began with a blessing, when God blessed the Sabbath Day at the conclusion of Creation. God also began His relationship with *Avraham Avinu* with a blessing – that Avraham "be a blessing" (see *Bereishit* 12:1–2 "*ve-heye berakhah*"). That blessing, just like those of *Moshe Rabbenu*, can also be understood as a challenge, more than a promise – for the greatest blessing that man can receive is to be a blessing to others, to be the 'giver,' not the 'taker.'

May our study of Torah help guide us, so that we can fulfill our potential as well – to become the "great nation" that God envisioned, in the Land that He promised to our forefathers.

Contributors

RABBI ELCHANAN ADLER serves as a Rosh Yeshiva at RIETS and occupies the Eva, Morris and Jack Rubin Chair in Rabbinics. Rabbi Adler studied previously at Yeshivas Beis Yosef, Mirrer Yeshiva and Mesivta Tiferes Yerushalayim (MTJ), where he received *semikhah*. Rabbi Adler holds a BA Summa Cum Laude in Psychology from CUNY and an MS in Secondary Jewish Education from Yeshiva University's Azrieli Graduate School. Rabbi Adler is the author of *Mitzvat HaShabbat*, a Hebrew *sefer* which deals with the evolution of the *mitzvah* of *Shabbat*. He has published numerous Torah articles in both Hebrew and English, and has served as co-editor of the Torah Journal, *Or HaMizrach*. He resides in Passaic, NJ, along with his wife and five children.

RABBI HAYYIM ANGEL is the Rabbi of the historic Congregation Shearith Israel of New York (the Spanish & Portuguese Synagogue, founded in 1654). He also teaches advanced undergraduate Bible courses at Yeshiva University. He has published over 60 scholarly articles, primarily in Bible. Forty of them are collected in two books, *Through an Opaque Lens* (Sephardic Publication Foundation, 2006), and *Revealed Texts, Hidden Meanings* (KTAV-Sephardic Publication Foundation, 2009).

DR. SHAWN ZELIG ASTER serves as Assistant Professor of Bible in Yeshiva College and as an associate faculty member in the Bernard Revel Graduate School of Jewish Studies. He holds a PhD in Bible and Assyriology from the University of Pennsylvania. His areas of interest include Biblical history and geography, and the relationship of history to *Nevi'im Acharonim*.

RABBI ASSAF BEDNARSH received his *semikhah* from RIETS, and holds a BA from Princeton University and an MA in Jewish History from Yeshiva University's Bernard Revel Graduate School of Jewish Studies. After completing his *semikhah* and studying in the RIETS Kollel Elyon, he taught in Yeshiva University High School for Boys and in Stern College for Women. He subsequently made *aliyah* and now teaches in the RIETS Israel Kollel in Jerusalem, where he occupies the Ruth Buchbinder Mitzner Chair in Talmud and Jewish Law. He lives in Alon Shevut with his wife Leora and their six children.

RABBI YOSEF BLAU is the *Mashgiach Ruchani*, Director of Religious Guidance, at Yeshiva University. He is the President of the Religious Zionists of America, and is on the boards of the Orthodox Forum and several groups working for Jewish teenagers, the environment, and the protection of the vulnerable members of society. He edited *Lomdus: The Conceptual Approach to Jewish Learning.*

RABBI BENJAMIN BLECH is a Professor of Talmud at Yeshiva University and an internationally recognized educator, religious leader, author, and lecturer. A recipient of the American Educator of the Year award and the author of twelve highly acclaimed best-selling books, he writes regularly for major newspapers and journals and was recently ranked #16 in a listing of the 50 most influential Jews in America.

RABBI KENNETH BRANDER is the inaugural Dean of Yeshiva University Center for the Jewish Future (CJF). Rabbi Brander is also the Rabbi Emeritus of the Boca Raton Synagogue, founding dean of the Boca Raton Community Kollel, and founder of the Weinbaum Yeshiva High School of Broward and Palm Beach Counties. During his 14 years of service to that community, he oversaw its explosive growth from 60 families to some 600 families. He is currently a PhD candidate in general philosophy at Florida Atlantic University (FAU). Rabbi Brander has authored many articles in various scholarly journals and also co-edited *The Yeshiva University Haggadah*.

RABBI SHALOM CARMY teaches Jewish studies and philosophy at YU. He is editor of *Tradition*. He received his BA and MS from Yeshiva University, and received his rabbinic ordination from its affiliated Rabbi Isaac Elchanan Theological Seminary, studying under Rabbis Aharon Lichtenstein and Joseph Soloveitchik. He has edited some of R. Soloveitchik's work for publication, *Modern Scholarship in the Study of Torah: Contributions and Limitations, Jewish Perspectives on the Experience of Suffering*, as well as several other works. He writes a regular personal column in *Tradition*, and contributes regularly on Jewish and general subjects to *First Things* and other journals.

RABBI ZEVULUN CHARLOP is the Dean Emeritus of RIETS, and has authored numerous scholarly essays, including "The Making of Orthodox Rabbis," "God in History and Halakha from the Perspective of American History," and contributions in the *Encyclopedia Judaica*. He has served as president of the American Committee for the United Charities in Israel, the General Israel Orphans Home for Girls in Jerusalem, and the National Council of Young Israel Rabbis. Rabbi Charlop is the editor of three novellae on Torah and Talmud by his late father, the noted Rabbi Jechiel Michael Charlop, and is the spiritual leader of the Young Israel of Mosholu Parkway (Bronx, NY).

RABBI YITZCHOK COHEN is a Rosh Yeshiva at YU, and gives *shiurim* in Talmud as well as *sichot mussar.*

RABBI DR. HILLEL DAVIS graduated YC, received his Masters from Bernard Revel in Modern Jewish History and then *semikhah* from RIETS. He then received a Masters and PhD in Organizational Psychology at NYU, after which he worked as a Human Resources professional for close to 25 years. He returned to Yeshiva as the Vice President for University

Life in 2003. He is married to Rachayl Eckstein Davis and they live in Oceanside, NY, where they raised four more YU grads.

RABBI MARK DRATCH is an instructor of Jewish Studies and philosophy at the Isaac Breuer College of Yeshiva University. After serving as a pulpit rabbi for 22 years in congregations including Toronto, ON, and Stamford, CT, he founded JSafe (The Jewish Institute Supporting an Abuse-Free Environment). Active in the area of abuse in the Jewish community, he also serves in leadership and advisory capacities at FaithTrust Institute and Jewish Women International. He served as a member of the Executive Board and as Vice President of the Rabbinical Council of America and served as chairman of its Task Force on Rabbinic Improprieties, formulating its policy guidelines for responding to abuse allegations against member rabbis. A graduate of Yeshiva University (Yeshiva College, 1979; RIETS (rabbinic ordination), 1982; Ferkauf Graduate School (Jewish Education), 1982), he is also Camp Rabbi of Camp Morasha.

DR. BARRY L. EICHLER, Dean of Yeshiva College, is Professor of Bible and Cuneiform Studies at Yeshiva University's Bernard Revel Graduate School of Jewish Studies and Yeshiva College. Prior to his appointment at YU, he served as a professor of Assyriology at the University of Pennsylvania for 40 years in the Department of Near Eastern Languages & Civilizations and as a curator of the Babylonian Tablet Collection of University's Museum of Archaeology and Anthropology. Eichler founded Penn's Jewish Studies Program and served as its chair for over a decade (1982–1995). His major research and teaching interests focus on cultural inter-relationships between Biblical and ancient Near Eastern civilizations, with primary interest in the field of ancient law. He has taught Mesopotamian, Biblical and Jewish law at the Penn Law School. His other major area of interest is Sumerian literature and lexicography, which related directly to the NEH funded Pennsylvania Sumerian Dictionary Project.

DR. YAAKOV ELMAN is Professor of Judaic studies at Yeshiva University, and an associate of Harvard's Center for Jewish Studies. He has authored, edited or translated eight books, and dozens of articles on Talmud, Jewish Biblical Exegesis, and rabbinic intellectual history.

RABBI DANIEL Z. FELDMAN is an instructor of Talmud and Jewish Studies at the Stone Beit Midrash Program of Yeshiva University, and serves as the Director of Rabbinic Research at YU's Center for the Jewish Future. He is an alumnus of Yeshivat Kerem B'Yavneh and received his ordination (*Yoreh Yoreh* and *Yadin Yadin*) from the Rabbi Isaac Elchanan Theological Seminary, where he was a fellow of the Bella and Harry Wexner Kollel Elyon. Rabbi Feldman is the co-editor of six volumes of talmudic essays, and the author of *The Right and The Good: Halakhah and Human Relations* (Jason Aronson, 1999; expanded edition, Yashar Books, 2005) and *Divine Footsteps: Chesed and the Jewish Soul* (Yeshiva University Press, 2009), as well as three volumes of talmudic essays entitled *Binah BaSefarim*. Rabbi Feldman is the spiritual leader of Etz Chaim of Teaneck, NJ, where he resides with his wife, Leah, and their children.

RABBI DAVID FOHRMAN directs the Hoffberger Institute for Text Study, and his talks are available on the web at *www.rabbifohrman.com*. He teaches themes in *Tanakh* as adjunct faculty at Yeshiva University, and delivers *shiurim* periodically through videoconference to the Gruss Kollel in Jerusalem. He delivers special lectures to teachers and high school students throughout the tri-state area, and nationally, through the sponsorship of Project Chazon. He is author of *The Beast that Crouches at the Door: Adam and Eve, Cain and Abel, and Beyond*, and a forthcoming book on the *Megillah* entitled *The Queen You Thought You Knew*.

RABBI MENACHEM GENACK is a RIETS Rosh Yeshiva, CEO of the Orthodox Union Kashrus Division, General Editor of OU Press, and Rabbi of Congregation Shomrei Emunah, Englewood, New Jersey. He is the editor of *The Seder Night: An Exalted Evening* and *Rabbi Joseph B. Soloveitchik: Man of Halacha, Man of Faith*, and is co-editor of the journal *Mesorah*.

RABBI OZER GLICKMAN is a Rosh Yeshiva in the Rabbi Isaac Elchanan Theological Seminary where he has taught Talmud and *Halakhah* to *semikhah* students for the past decade. He also serves as the Senior Resident Rabbinic Scholar at the YU Center for Jewish Law and Contemporary Civilization at the Benjamin N. Cardozo School of Law where he is also Adjunct Professor of Law. Rabbi Glickman holds a BA (in philosophy) from Columbia University and has pursued graduate studies in philosophy and religion at Columbia and the University of Toronto. An expert in financial markets and risk management, he also holds an MBA (Finance) from the Stern School of New York University where he was a University Fellow.

RABBI SHMUEL GOLDIN has served as spiritual leader of Congregation Ahavath Torah in Englewood, New Jersey, since 1984. He has been an instructor of Bible, Talmud and philosophy at the James Striar School and the Isaac Breuer College of Yeshiva University for over twenty years. He is also the founding director of and lecturer at The Eve Flechner Torah Institute. Rabbi Goldin is the author of three popular volumes on the Torah: *Unlocking the Torah Text: Bereishit, Shmot* and *Vayikra*, all of which have been published by Gefen Publishing Company and OU Publishers. Rabbi Goldin currently serves as First Vice President of the Rabbinical Council of America. Additionally, he is founding chairman and current rabbinic advisor to Jewish Education for Future Generations, a standing committee developed to respond to the rising cost of day school tuition in the Bergen County area. The innovative approaches developed by JEFG have served as models for other communities throughout the United States.

RABBI MEIR GOLDWICHT is the Joel and Maria Finkle Visiting Israeli Rosh Yeshiva. He joined YU as a Rosh Yeshiva at Rabbi Isaac Elchanan Theological Seminary (RIETS) and the Mazer Yeshiva Program. He received *semikhah* from the renowned rabbinic authorities Rabbi Zalman Nehemia Goldberg in 1980, and HaRav HaGaon Betzallel Zolti *zt"l* chief Rabbi of Jerusalem, and Rabbi Ovadyah Yosef, HaRav Rashi of Israel. Rabbi Goldwicht has been a *Ram* at Yeshiva Kerem B'Yavneh, and has given *shiurim* extensively at Stern College, all over the metropolitan area, and in Israel.

RABBI MARK GOTTLIEB is Head of School at Yeshiva University High School for Boys in New York. He also serves as the Dean of the Tikvah High School Scholars program, an interdisciplinary leadership institute promoting Jewish Thought and the enduring human questions. Previously, Rabbi Gottlieb was Principal of the Middle & Upper School at the Maimonides School in Brookline, MA, and has taught at The Frisch School, Ida Crown Jewish Academy, Loyola University in Chicago, Hebrew Theological College (Skokie, IL) and the University of Chicago. After graduating YUHSB/MTA, Rabbi Gottlieb received his BA at Yeshiva College, his rabbinical ordination at the Rabbi Isaac Elchanan Theological Seminary of Yeshiva University and his MA in Philosophy at the University of Chicago. He is currently completing his dissertation in philosophy at the University of Chicago on the problem of translation and the tasks of education in a cosmopolitan culture. He is a member of the advisory board of *Tradition: A Journal of Orthodox Jewish Thought* and the Orthodox Forum's Steering Committee. He lives with his wife and five children in Teaneck, New Jersey.

DR. NAOMI GRUNHAUS is Assistant Professor in the Rebecca Ivry Department of Jewish Studies at Stern College. She holds a PhD in Judaic Studies from New York University. Dr. Grunhaus is author of several articles on Biblical interpretation and is nearing completion of a book on the interplay between *peshat* and *derash* in Radak's Biblical commentaries. She has been teaching *Tanakh* and *parshanut* in Jewish schools for more than twenty-five years.

RABBI SHMUEL HAIN has served as Rosh Beit Midrash (academic head) of the Graduate Program for Women in Advanced Talmudic and Biblical Studies (GPATS) at Yeshiva University since 2005, where he has overseen the placement of 25 graduates in full-time Jewish communal service positions (educational, synagogue and Jewish non-profit) while teaching Talmud and mentoring the students. He is also the Founder and Director of RIETS' Iyun program and the Rosh Kollel of Camp Morasha's Beit Midrash Program. Rabbi Hain also serves as Rabbi of Young Israel Ohab Zedek, a growing, vibrant community synagogue in North Riverdale/Yonkers. Rabbi Hain chaired and edited the 2010 Orthodox Forum, entitled *The Next Generation of Modern Orthodoxy*. He was editor of *Kol Zvi*, the Torah Journal published by Yeshiva University's Kollel Elyon, and is currently completing a *sefer* on *Seder Nashim*.

RABBI JOSH JOSEPH is Chief of Staff and a Vice President to Yeshiva University President Richard M. Joel. In addition to managing the Office of the President and working with administration, academic and lay leadership, he runs the Presidential Fellowship in University and Communal Leadership, and several project teams and task forces. Rabbi Joseph had previously been Director of Special Projects for YU's Center for the Jewish Future, served as Executive Director of the Orthodox Caucus, worked on Wall Street and served as a pulpit rabbi. Rabbi Joseph completed his undergraduate degree with honors at the University of Pennsylvania and received both rabbinic ordination and a Master's in Jewish philosophy from YU's Rabbi Isaac Elchanan Theological Seminary and Bernard Revel Graduate School.

DR. AARON KOLLER is Assistant Professor of Bible at Yeshiva College. He received his doctorate from the Revel Graduate School, and is interested especially in Iron Age history and culture of the Levant, as well as later Jewish cultural and intellectual history. He has written papers on Aramaic dialectology and drinking practices.

RABBI DR. NORMAN LAMM was elected President of Yeshiva University and Rosh Ha-Yeshiva of RIETS in August 1976, succeeding Dr. Samuel Belkin and Dr. Bernard Revel. He now serves as Chancellor of Yeshiva University. He was ordained as a rabbi by Rabbi Isaac Elchanan Theological Seminary in 1951, and earned a PhD in Jewish philosophy from Yeshiva University's Bernard Revel Graduate School in 1966. A pulpit rabbi for twenty-five years, he served as spiritual leader of The Jewish Center in Manhattan, Congregation Kodimoh in Springfield, MA, and as assistant rabbi of New York City's Congregation Kehilath Jeshurun. Rabbi Lamm has edited or co-edited over twenty volumes, including *The Library of Jewish Law and Ethics*. He was the founder and first editor of *Tradition* and associate editor of *Hadarom*, a journal of Jewish law, founder of the *Torah U-Madda Journal*, and founder of the *Orthodox Forum*.

PROFESSOR YAEL LEIBOWITZ serves on the Judaic Studies Faculty at Stern College for Women. She has an MA from Columbia University in Judaic Studies, and is a frequent lecturer around the tri-state area.

RABBI MENACHEM LEIBTAG, founder of the Tanach Study Center (www.tanach.org), is one of the pioneers of Torah Education via the internet. His weekly essays on *parashat ha-shavua*, read by literally thousands of subscribers world wide, introduce a vibrant analytical approach to thematic study of the Bible and reflect over twenty-five years of experience as a teacher at Yeshivat Har Etzion in Israel. Rabbi Leibtag teaches as well at Yeshiva Shaalvim and Midreshet Lindenbaum.

RABBI DR. AARON LEVINE is the Samson and Halina Bitensky Professor of Economics at Yeshiva University. His research field is the interface between economics and Jewish Law, particularly as it relates to ethical issues of the marketplace and the role of government in economic public policy. The author of five books and numerous papers on these topics, Dr. Levine's latest book project is *Judaism and Economics*, to be published by Oxford University Press.

DR. MICHELLE LEVINE is Associate Professor of Bible at Stern College for Women. She has recently published a book with Brown University Press, *Nahmanides on Genesis: The Art of Biblical Portraiture*. Dr. Levine has written articles and delivered papers on medieval Biblical exegesis, and she lectures extensively on various topics on the Bible and Biblical commentaries.

RABBI DOVID MILLER has served as the Associate Director of the RIETS Israel (Gruss) Kollel since its inception in 1977. He also occupies the Gottesfield Heller Chair in Talmud and Rabbinics at RIETS. He is simultaneously the Rabbi of Kehillat Ateret Nof in Har Nof, Jerusalem. Rabbi Miller made *aliyah* in 1971, served for over 20 years as a lecturer in the IDF chaplaincy, taught in various educational frameworks in Jerusalem and Be'er Sheva, and was Rosh Ha-Yeshiva of BMT (Beit Medrash Le-Torah).

RABBI YAAKOV NEUBURGER is a Rosh Yeshiva in the Mazer Yeshiva Program, and is the spiritual leader of Congregation Beth Abraham in Bergenfield, NJ. From 1986–1990, he was spiritual leader of the Jewish community at the Yeshiva University's Albert Einstein College of

Medicine and the Jack D. Weiler Hospital. A Toronto native, Rabbi Neuburger received *semikhah* from Yeshiva University's affiliated Rabbi Isaac Elchanan Theological Seminary in 1979. He was one of the first to receive *Yadin Yadin* ordination from RIETS. Rabbi Neuburger is a 1977 graduate of Yeshiva College. He also holds a master's degree in psychology from Columbia University.

PROFESSOR NECHAMA PRICE has been on faculty at Stern College in the Bible and Judaic Studies departments for the past six years. Prior to that, she graduated *magna cum laude* from Stern College majoring in Judaic Studies. After college, she completed the Stern College Graduate Program for Advanced Talmud Studies, received an MS in Jewish Education from Azrieli Graduate School, and an MA in Bible from Bernard Revel Graduate School. For the 2008–2009 academic year, Mrs. Price was elected as "Professor of the Year" at Stern College and received the senior class Judaic Studies Professor Award. She lives in Bergenfield, New Jersey with her husband and three children.

PROFESSOR DEENA RABINOVICH is the director of the Legacy Heritage Foundation program at Yeshiva University's Stern College for women, where she has also taught *Tanakh* since 2004. Deena taught *Chumash* at Yeshiva University High School for Girls from 2004 through 2009. Prior to that, she taught *Tanakh, Torah She-Be-Al-Peh* and English Literature at the North Shore Hebrew Academy Middle School in Great Neck where she also served as Assistant Principal. A doctoral candidate at the Azrieli Graduate School of Jewish Education, she is a winner of the Gruss Award for Excellence in Teaching and the Grinspoon-Steinhardt Award for Excellence in Jewish Education. During the 1997–98 academic year, she participated in the Lead Educators Education program at the Melton Center of the Hebrew University in Jerusalem.

RABBI DR. EDWARD REICHMAN is an Associate Professor of Emergency Medicine and Associate Professor in the Division of Education and Bioethics at the Albert Einstein College of Medicine of Yeshiva University, where he teaches Jewish medical ethics. He received his rabbinic ordination from the Rabbi Isaac Elchanan Theological Seminary of Yeshiva University and writes and lectures internationally in the field of Jewish medical ethics. He is the recipient of a Kornfeld Foundation Fellowship, and has been a member of the advisory boards of the Institute for Genetics and Public Policy, the New York Organ Donor Network, the Halakhic Organ Donor Society, and the Rabbinical Council of America. His research is devoted to the interface of medical history and Jewish law.

RABBI HERSHEL REICHMAN, a Rosh Yeshiva of the Yeshiva Program, has authored 5 volumes of *Reshimot Shiurim* of Rav Yosef Dov Soloveitchik, which include *Massekhtot Sukkah, Shavuot, Nedarim* and *Bava Kamma*. Rabbi Reichman has a PhD in Operations Research from NYU.

RABBI YONA REISS is the Max and Marion Grill Dean of Rabbi Isaac Elchanan Theological Seminary. Rabbi Reiss is a graduate of Yeshiva College, and went on to receive his law degree from Yale Law School, where he was a senior editor of the Law Journal. He received his rabbinic ordination from RIETS, where he also earned the distinction of *Yadin Yadin*. Rabbi Reiss served as director of the Beth Din of America from 1998 to 2008. From 1992 to 1998, Rabbi Reiss worked as an associate at the international law firm of Cleary Gottlieb Steen & Hamilton in New York City. Rabbi Reiss serves on the editorial board of *Tradition* magazine. A frequent writer on a variety of topics relating to both Jewish and secular law, he has published widely in Jewish publications, as well as in the Wall Street Journal and New York Law Journal. Rabbi Reiss and his wife Mindy have six children and live in Riverdale, NY.

RABBI DR. MICHAEL ROSENSWEIG occupies the Nathan and Perel Schupf Chair in Talmud at RIETS. He is a 1980 graduate of Yeshiva College, and earned an MA and a PhD from the Bernard Revel Graduate School while studying under Professor Haym Soloveitchik. After receiving *semikhah* from RIETS, Rabbi Rosensweig was among the first group to complete intensive post-graduate studies in RIETS' Caroline and Joseph S. Gruss Kollel Elyon. In 1997, Rabbi Rosensweig was appointed Rosh Kollel (Dean) of the prestigious Israel Henry Beren

Institute for Higher Talmudic Studies (*Ha-Machon Ha-Gavohah Le-Talmud*) at RIETS.

PROFESSOR SMADAR ROSENSWEIG is a Professor of Bible at Stern College for Women, Yeshiva University. She received her BA from Barnard College and her MA and M. Phil. from Columbia University in Jewish History.

RABBI YONASON SACKS, the Henry H. Guterman Professor of Talmud at the Yeshiva Program/Mazer School of Talmudic Studies of Yeshiva University, has been a Rosh Yeshiva since 1994. Rabbi Sacks graduated from Yeshiva College in 1981. He was ordained by RIETS in 1984, and two years later was awarded *Semikhah Yadin Yadin*. Rabbi Sacks has written many sefarim, including *Hagadat Chazon L'Yamim*, *Chemdat Yamim*, and three volumes of *Chazon L'Yamim*, and is the spiritual leader of Congregation Agudas Israel of Passaic, New Jersey.

RABBI HERSHEL SCHACHTER earned his BA from Yeshiva College, an MA in Hebrew Literature from the Bernard Revel Graduate School in 1967, and was ordained that same year. Since 1971, Rabbi Schachter has been Rosh Kollel in RIETS' Marcos and Adina Katz Kollel (Institute for Advanced Research in Rabbinics) and also holds the institution's Nathan and Vivian Fink Distinguished Professorial Chair in Talmud. In addition to his teaching duties, Rabbi Schachter lectures, writes, and serves as a decisor of Jewish Law. A prolific author, he has written more than 100 articles, in Hebrew and English, for such scholarly publications as *HaPardes, Hadarom, Beit Yitzchak,* and *Or Hamizrach*. He has written a number of *sefarim,* including *Ginat Egoz, Eretz Ha-Tzvi, B'ikvei Ha-Tzon, Nefesh Ha-Rav* and *Mi-Peninei Ha-Rav.*

RABBI DR. JACOB J. SCHACTER is University Professor of Jewish History and Jewish Thought and Senior Scholar at the Center of the Jewish Future, Yeshiva University. He is the Founding Editor of *The Torah U-Madda Journal* and author and editor of several books and dozens of articles.

PROFESSOR SHOSHANA SCHECHTER is assistant professor of Bible at Yeshiva University's Stern College for Women and director of the Basic Jewish Studies Program. She also teaches Bible and English at Ateres Bais Yaakov High School in Rockland County, New York. A graduate of Stern College, Mrs. Schechter holds a master's degree in Jewish history from Yeshiva University's Bernard Revel Graduate School of Jewish Studies, as well as a master's degree from the Columbia School of Journalism. She lectures widely on topics in the Bible and has been involved in Jewish outreach programs on four continents. She is the proud mother of five children and lives with her husband, Yitzchak, in New Hempstead, New York.

DR. YITZCHAK SCHECHTER is a clinical psychologist and director of the Center for Applied Psychology (CAPs) at Bikur Cholim in Monsey, NY. CAPs is a behavioral health center serving the needs of the Orthodox, Ultra-Orthodox and Chassidic Jewish Community in Rockland County. He has developed a wide array of programs addressing communal and clinical challenges and has supervised many clinicians in working with issues of psychology and religion. He has previously taught at Stern College for Women, where he started the Psychology and Religion course. He is also a clinical research fellow at the Institute for University-School Partnership at Azrieli Graduate School of Jewish Education developing a research and training program for school administrators on the topic of child abuse. He maintains a private practice in Rockland County focusing on the intersection of psychological and religious issues.

RABBI ALLEN SCHWARTZ is the Raymond J. Greenwald chair of Jewish Studies at Yeshiva University, and the Rabbi of Congregation Ohab Zedek, New York.

RABBI EZRA SCHWARTZ has recently begun serving as the Rabbi of Mt. Sinai Jewish Center. In addition to his responsibilities at the *shul* he continues to be deeply involved in Yeshiva University, from which he holds five advanced degrees, including *Yadin Yadin*. He serves as the *Bochen* of the RIETS/Mazer Yeshiva Program. He is also a Rebbe in YU's

Stone Bet Midrash Program and coordinates RIETS' program in Contemporary *Halakhah*. For the past six years he has been on the staff of President Richard Joel where he remains Assistant to the President for Research and Communications.

DR. DAVID SHATZ is Professor of Philosophy at Stern College for Women, Editor of *The Torah U-Madda Journal*, and Editor of the series *Me-Otzar Ho-Rav: Selected Writings of Rabbi Joseph B. Soloveitchik*. Dr. Shatz has edited, co-edited, or authored thirteen books (including a volume of his collected essays) and has published over sixty articles and reviews, dealing with both general and Jewish philosophy. After graduating as valedictorian of his Yeshiva College class, he earned *semikhah* from RIETS and a PhD with distinction in general philosophy from Columbia University. In recognition of his achievements as a scholar and teacher, Dr. Shatz was awarded the Presidential Medallion at Yeshiva University.

RABBI ZVI SOBOLOFSKY is a Rosh Yeshiva at Yeshiva University. Rabbi Sobolofsky studied at Yeshivat Kerem B'Yavneh and Yeshiva University. He attended RIETS, finishing in 1990, and proceeded to the Azrieli Graduate School of Jewish Education and Administration where he obtained a master's in 1996. He was appointed Rosh Yeshiva in the spring of 2002 and began teaching Talmud at Yeshiva University and its affiliated RIETS in the fall of that year. In addition to his role as Rosh Yeshiva in RIETS, Rabbi Sobolofsky also serves as the spiritual leader of Congregation Ohr HaTorah in Bergenfield, New Jersey. Rabbi Sobolofsky also lectures at the Bergen County Beis Medrash Program (BCBM) housed at Congregation Bnai Yeshurun in Teaneck, New Jersey. Rabbi Sobolofsky is the author of a *sefer*, *Reishit Koach*, on *Massekhet Bekhorot*.

DR. MOSHE SOKOLOW is the Fanya Gottesfeld-Heller Professor of Jewish Education and Associate Dean of the Azrieli Graduate School of Jewish Education.

RABBI DANIEL STEIN is a *Maggid Shiur* in the Mazer Yeshiva Program as well as the director of the Fourth Year Halacha L'Ma'aseh Program within RIETS. Rabbi Stein earned his bachelor's degree in Judaic studies from Yeshiva College, where he graduated as the valedictorian of the Mazer Yeshiva Program. He received *semikhah* from RIETS while he was a distinguished fellow of its Wexner Semichah Honors Program as well as its post-*semikhah* institute, the Wexner Kollel Elyon. Prior to teaching in the Yeshiva Program, Rabbi Stein was a *Sho'el U-Meishiv* in the Yeshiva Program and the director of its Presidential Bekius Program.

PROFESSOR SUZANNE LAST STONE is University Professor of Jewish Law and Contemporary Civilization, Professor of Law, and Director of the Center for Jewish Law and Contemporary Civilization, Benjamin N. Cardozo School of Law, Yeshiva University. She is a graduate of Princeton University and Columbia University Law School and was a Danforth Fellow in 1974 in Jewish History and Classical Religions at Yale University. Before joining the Cardozo faculty, Stone clerked for Judge John Minor Wisdom of the Fifth Circuit Court of Appeals and then practiced litigation at Paul, Weiss, Rifkind, Wharton and Garrison. In addition to teaching courses in Jewish Law and Political Thought and Jewish Law and American Legal Theory, she currently teaches Federal Courts and Law, Religion and the State. Professor Stone is the co-editor-in-chief of *Diné Israel*, a peer review journal of Jewish law, co-edited with Tel Aviv Law School. She is also on the editorial boards of the *Jewish Quarterly Review* and of *Hebraic Political Studies*. Her publications include: "In Pursuit of the Counter-text: The Turn to the Jewish Legal Model in Contemporary American Legal Theory," (*Harvard Law Review*); "The Jewish Conception of Civil Society," in *Alternative Conceptions of Civil Society* (Princeton University Press); "Feminism and the Rabbinic Conception of Justice" in *Women and Gender in Jewish Philosophy* (Indiana University); and "Rabbinic Legal Magic" (*Yale Journal of Law & Humanities*).

RABBI MICHAEL TAUBES is presently a Rebbe at the Yeshiva University High School as well as at the Yeshiva University Mechinah Program. He is also the Rav of Congregation Zichron Mordechai of Teaneck, New Jersey and has served as a writer and editor for ArtScroll/Mesorah Publications, working on the translation of the *Yerushalmi*. He is the author of *The Practical Torah*, a collection of presentations of *Halakhah* based on the *parashat ha-shavuah*, and has edited several works based on the teachings of Maran HaRav Yosef Dov Soloveitchik published by the Orthodox Union.

RABBI DR. MOSHE DOVID TENDLER serves as a Rosh Yeshiva in RIETS, a professor of biology at Yeshiva College, and a professor of Jewish medical ethics at Yeshiva University. He is also Rav of the Community Synagogue of Monsey.

DR. SHIRA WEISS teaches Jewish philosophy at Stern College and *Tanakh* at The Frisch School, where she is also Assistant Principal. Dr. Weiss is completing her Doctorate at Bernard Revel Graduate School in Medieval Jewish Philosophy and also holds an EdD in Jewish Education and Administration from Azrieli Graduate School.

RABBI NETANEL WIEDERBLANK earned BA in economics at Yeshiva University, an MA in Jewish Philosophy from the Bernard revel Graduate School of Jewish Studies, and *semikhah* from RIETS. Subsequently, he was a fellow at the Bella and Harry Wexner Kollel Elyon at Yeshiva University. Rabbi Wiederblank currently teaches *Tanakh*, *Halakhah*, and Jewish Philosophy at the Isaac Breuer College and Mechinah Program at Yeshiva University.

RABBI MORDECHAI WILLIG is the Rabbi Dr. Sol Roth Professor of Talmud and Contemporary Halachah at RIETS. He has been a Rosh Yeshiva at the Mazer School of Talmudic Studies since 1973 and a Rosh Kollel at RIETS. Rabbi Willig received a BA in mathematics from Yeshiva College in 1968 and an MS in Jewish History in 1971 from the Bernard Revel Graduate School. He received *semikhah* that same year. He has served as spiritual leader of Young Israel of Riverdale in the Bronx, NY, since 1974, and has written three volumes of *Am Mordechai*, and many articles in Torah scholarship journals.

The fonts used in this book are from the Arno family

The Michael Scharf Publication Trust
of Yeshiva University Press

Maggid Books
The best of contemporary Jewish thought from
Koren Publishers Jerusalem Ltd.